Justice and Faith

THE FRANK MURPHY STORY

GREG ZIPES

University of Michigan Press
Ann Arbor

Errors

p 10
53
116

ISBN-13: 978-0-472-03853-4 (print)
ISBN-13: 978-0-472-12894-5 (ebook)

2024   2023   2022   2021   4   3   2   1

I dissent, therefore, from this legalization of racism . . . All
residents of this nation are kin in some way by blood or culture
to a foreign land. Yet they are primarily and necessarily a
part of the new and distinct civilization of the United States.
They must, accordingly, be treated at all times as the heirs of
the American experiment, and as entitled to all the rights and
freedoms guaranteed by the Constitution.

—Supreme Court Justice Frank Murphy in his World War II–
era dissent in *Korematsu v. United States*, criticizing President
Franklin Delano Roosevelt's decision to send 120,000
Japanese Americans to internment camps. (*Korematsu v.
United States*, 323 U.S. 214, 242, 1944)

But he shall judge the poor with justice . . . . And justice shall
be the girdle of his loins, and faith the girdle of his reins.

—Passages in Isaiah 11:4–5, marked in Frank Murphy's Bible.
(Clifford A. Prevost, "Murphy Takes Post in Cabinet," DFP, Jan.
3, 1939)

Preface

Frank Murphy was a mayor of Detroit, a governor of Michigan, an attorney general of the United States, and a Supreme Court justice. As a trial lawyer, he projected with a "bell-clear" voice in packed courtrooms, where he was known to speak for up to seven hours.[1] He was adored by women's groups, the African-American community, and union card holders. When he died in 1949, an estimated 20,000 people viewed his body in Detroit's City Hall in a five-hour period, many coming straight from their factory jobs in "shirt sleeves and with dinner pails."[2]

Throughout his career, Murphy influenced the country's values in tangible ways, cementing its focus on individual dignity and liberties at a time when this country could have moved in a far more authoritarian direction.[3] He supported the use of the federal government to solve problems in ways never seen before. He was present at one inflection point after another in the country's development during the early twentieth century. Through his words and deeds, he played a part in inoculating the political and judicial system from darker forces that are always present in the United States, benefiting us to this day.

I will give just a few examples. In 1925, he was a young Detroit criminal court judge assigned to the murder trial of Ossian Sweet. Based in part on the way Murphy ran the trial, an all-white jury twice refused to convict Sweet and the other Black defendants in the killing of a white man. Because of this positive result, Black leaders decided they could place some faith in the court system in pursuing a civil rights agenda, thus helping to start the slow march to *Brown v. Board of Education* in 1954.

Then, as an incorruptible Detroit mayor, Murphy provided crucial cover for Franklin Delano Roosevelt (FDR) during his first presidential run. With the charismatic Murphy as his prime example, Roosevelt could demonstrate to the heartland that he was not beholden to the crass ethnic city bosses associated with the Democratic Party. Murphy energetically crisscrossed the country, giving rousing speeches on behalf of FDR. From that point forward, the two men were close, with Roosevelt supporting Murphy's meteoric political rise, to the jealous bewilderment of others in his administration.

In 1935, Murphy was FDR's man in the Philippines as that United States possession moved to independence. The Philippines had a potentially volatile brew of ethnic and religious minorities. Although he had no template to follow—much of the colonial decoupling happened after World War II and not before—Murphy ensured that the process was largely peaceful. And his innovations to the Philippine Constitution reflected his conception of an ideal democratic system. He predictably insisted that the Philippines adopt a constitution with an executive and legislative branch fashioned after the United States model but with some surprisingly significant modifications. Under his guidance, the Philippine president could only serve for one six-year term, and that president would be elected by a straight vote of the people. The legislature was unicameral and had nothing like the United States Senate.

As the governor of Michigan, Murphy mediated a peaceful resolution to the great sit-down auto strikes in 1937 and cemented the role of unions in the American workplace. Here too he was in close contact with FDR, who remained safely in the background while Murphy took the heat from business leaders and conservatives.

Murphy loudly sounded the alarm about the Nazis in the late 1930s, pointing out their treatment of Jews at a time when few in this country were focused on the disturbing events taking place abroad. During World War II, he used his bully pulpit as a Supreme Court justice to voice his concerns over the loss of civil liberties in this country, culminating with three significant opinions in December of 1944, including his dissent in *Korematsu v. United States*.

Given Murphy's involvement in many of the defining moments that created modern America, why have those who should know better ignored or marginalized his accomplishments? Why is he largely unknown by the American public? These are questions I seek to answer in this book. Much of the conventional wisdom about Murphy is negative: He was strange. He lacked intellectual heft. He was lazy. I hope to debunk many of the falsehoods that have latched onto Murphy and so hurt his historical standing. I will unearth the origins of these misperceptions and reintroduce a man I have grown to admire greatly.

Murphy is rightly known for his dissent as a Supreme Court justice in 1944. Executive Order 9066 was President Roosevelt's World War II–era directive that placed more than 120,000 Americans of Japanese origin in internment camps for much of the war. Most were American citizens, effectively jailed without any semblance of due process. The internments could not compare to the atrocities in Europe, but as many recognized even at the time, these actions against a vulnerable minority directly contradicted a set of ideals (democracy, civil rights, liberty, opportunity, and equality) that most Americans held with pride.

The Supreme Court meekly blessed the constitutionality of the internments when the issue finally made its way to the High Court in 1944, a full two years after the Japanese Americans had been shipped to the interior of the country. Murphy was now a justice on the Supreme Court, and he filed a scathing dissent. He was never one to mince words. In the first paragraph of his *Korematsu* dissent, he called the policy of internal displacement a descent "into the ugly abyss of racism."[4]

He continued by mocking the logic of the executive order. Murphy highlighted the fact that, between the time of the attack on Pearl Harbor in 1941 and the issuance of *Korematsu* in 1944, Japanese Americans had not engaged in even a single act of treasonous behavior. Germany and Italy were also at war with the United States, and no such general order was issued against the American descendants from these countries. He pointed out that the government had ample resources to deal with individual acts of disloyalty.

How brave was Murphy in standing up to the establishment? Significantly, Murphy was a firm and devoted ally of Roosevelt, and a New Dealer to his core. Murphy owed his position on the Supreme Court to FDR and regularly competed with others in FDR's orbit for the president's approval. Justice Felix Frankfurter and others told him that a strongly worded dissent would be used as propaganda to criticize the president and the country. Yet as a matter of conscience, he moved forward.

Other great men, with full knowledge of the facts behind the internments, fell short of their ideals. Earl Warren was the future chief justice who heroically arm-twisted the other justices to sign on to a unanimous decision in *Brown v. Board of Education,* thereby ending "separate but equal" in public schools. But during World War II, as the attorney general and then as the governor of California, Warren was an enthusiastic supporter of Roosevelt's executive order. He wanted to rid his state of its Japanese-American inhabitants, whom many there regarded as an economic threat. At the time, California was a state with seven million people, of which a grand total of 90,000 or so were of Japanese descent. In Warren's view, this small population had to go, and he deployed language we recognize today as shocking and vile to espouse his views.

Justice William O. Douglas was lauded by *Time* magazine upon his retirement in the 1970s as the greatest civil libertarian to serve on the Supreme Court.[5] Justice Felix Frankfurter, another of Murphy's colleagues on the Supreme Court, was a founder of the American Civil Liberties Union (ACLU).[6] Yet Justices Douglas and Frankfurter voted in *Korematsu* to uphold the eviction of the Japanese Americans from the West Coast. Frankfurter, Douglas, and Warren have all been the subject of laudatory books and articles as befitting important Supreme Court justices and their decisions in the World War II–era cases have been ignored or downplayed.[7]

As a justice on the Supreme Court, Murphy used the word *racism*—or some variation thereof—in three different cases on the same day in December 1944. Certainly, *Korematsu* remains the best known of the three. But the fact that he used that word in two other cases shows that his word choice was not a fluke. The second case decided that day also related to the Japanese-American internment. Mitsuye Endo was a United States citizen who had lost her California state job due to her national origin and was transported to Utah with her family under FDR's expulsion order. In *Ex parte Endo,* Murphy wrote a separate opinion, calling out

Endo's confinement as "another example of the unconstitutional resort to racism inherent in the entire evacuation program."[8]

The third case that came down that day had nothing to do with the Japanese-American internments. In *Steele v. Louisville & N.R. Co.*,[9] a union local bargained away the rights of Black employees, placing them first in line if there was a need for staff reductions and lower salaries. Murphy agreed with his brethren that the local's actions were wrong. But Murphy was the only one to brand the union action as *racist*, and indeed he was the only Supreme Court justice to employ that word during his time on the court, or for many years thereafter.[10] In *Steele*, Murphy risked alienating his great political allies in organized labor, but he plunged ahead.

As I will argue, Murphy was doing on that day in 1944 what he had done his entire life. He believed it was his duty to protest whenever American values—individual due process, assumption of innocence, a welcoming attitude toward the "other"—were trampled. This country was a grand experiment. People from all corners of the globe had to live together and thrive. He was determined to ensure its success. And he had faith that his allies, whether Roosevelt or the unions, would respect him on those occasions they needed to be called out.

Murphy had an impressive, diverse political resume and also an interesting personal life. He always found excuses not to marry and remained a bachelor his entire life. Even FDR tried to play the matchmaker. After Germany had invaded Poland in 1939, Roosevelt took time out of his schedule to introduce Murphy to a Tennessee widow, with FDR writing, "Is there anything I can do to help? . . . I am, as you know, highly discreet and my fees are reasonable!"[11] But nothing came of this or any other attempts to pin Murphy down.

Much has been made of his relationship with Edward Kemp, and specifically whether they were romantically linked. Both were lifetime bachelors. They were companions from their college years until Murphy's death. They went on long trips together, including a six-week cruise to Europe when both were young men. The existing evidence on whether they were romantic partners remains inconclusive. But if we are to speculate on Murphy's romantic inclinations and sexual preferences, we must also

consider that he had serious girlfriends. Joan Cuddihy was prominent in the last four years of Murphy's life. Murphy affectionately
referred to her as his "lamb" and wrote poetry for her. These relationships were covered by the press, but their letters also reflected
intimate moments they shared. Perhaps most intriguingly, Beulah
Young, a groundbreaking publisher of Black newspapers and a
close political ally of Murphy, wrote Murphy at least one passionate love letter, which she asked him to destroy. That letter, however, survives in the Murphy papers at the Bentley Library.

What is clear is that Murphy easily connected to people, on an
intellectual and physical level. In this regard, he was particularly
effective in communicating with the common laborer and the
vulnerable ethnic groups crowding the cities. A key to his popularity was his ability to speak the truth during dark times and,
simultaneously, to provide hope. During the depths of the Great
Depression, he was known as the "Dew and Sunshine" mayoral candidate in Detroit. But his charisma was such that those
in the top echelons of society also wanted his friendship and
approval.

Murphy had a peripatetic career. Unlike other towering figures, he did not spend 30 years in one job, clawing his way to the
top. This is no doubt another reason he is largely forgotten today.
Although he had a large impact on America, his achievements were
spread in different areas as the United States was entering the modern era. His life did not follow a clean narrative arc. And it was
unfortunate that he died relatively young, right before the Supreme
Court started to really focus on the inequalities in United States
society. He would have been a fiery presence on the Warren Court
in the 1950s and 1960s.

Every American, whether arriving by first class or shackled in
the galley of a slave ship, fell under Murphy's definition of those
entitled to the full benefits of the American dream. He adhered to
the notion that everyone had a right to keep, and take pride in,
their hyphenated past, their Irish traditions, their Catholicism or
Jewish faith, their heritages—whatever they might be. He was a
proud Catholic and enjoyed attending mass at his local Harbor
Beach church during his frequent visits throughout his life. But
this allegiance to religion or country of origin was not a blind

one. Murphy regularly supported politicians outside his "clan" that articulated his conception of American liberty, tolerance, and individual autonomy, as when he backed FDR over the Catholic and half-Irish Al Smith in the 1932 Democratic Party primary.

Murphy engaged in a tricky balancing act. The issues he grappled with, the contours and limitations of constitutional freedoms, are the subject of bitter fights in the twenty-first century. From a distance, we can see that the landscape has shifted from Murphy's time. For all the current disagreements, the country has become more inclusive and the government more active in solving economic and social problems, which is not to suggest that the country has solved its problems of racial and economic inequality. In his own small way, Murphy contributed to those significant changes in how the United States views itself.

Acknowledgments

I am a New York–based lawyer. To be successful with this project, I needed access to Murphy's personal papers, which are located at the University of Michigan. Here, I benefited from a farsighted project funded in part by the National Endowment for the Humanities. Back in the early 1990s, a great effort was made to place many of Murphy's collected papers on microfilm. I obtained special permission from the Bentley Library to ship sections of this microfilm collection to the New York Public Library. I am grateful to the University of Michigan Library staff for all their help and innumerable courtesies.

Back in New York, I reviewed the microfilm in the Milstein Microform Reading Room at New York Public Library's main building on 42nd Street, spending many fruitful weekends over the course of a year.

Barbara McGowan, a youthful spirit, runs the Frank Murphy House and Museum in Harbor Beach. She was always willing to speak to me and speculate about all matters relating to Murphy. She knew why I asked questions before I had to explain myself. She let me bring in Matthew Leppek, a talented photographer from nearby Bad Axe, who photographed almost every inch of the big house and law office. From these photos, I was able to scour artifacts, memorabilia, letters, and newspaper clippings from that amazing collection as though I were there.

Then there is the indefatigable Holly Yasui, the daughter of Minoru "Min" Yasui. Her dad was the named plaintiff in Japanese-American internment cases during World War II. She was generous with her time and in sharing anecdotes about her father. We spent an enlightening and emotional evening with students at the New York University Law School. There, at an Asian-Pacific American Law Students Association event, I had the privilege to introduce Holly (via Zoom, before Zoom was the way to communicate) and Professor Karen Shimakawa, also the daughter of internment camp survivors.

I pulled in favors from friends around the country to complete this project. Sean Murphy and his children Kyle and Keely (no known relation to Frank) were kind enough to visit the Wilson Library at the University of North Carolina close to where they now live. There, they reviewed the papers of Eugene Gressman, Murphy's favorite Supreme Court clerk and later a significant scholar in his own right.

By luck of geography, I grew up in the beautiful Hudson Valley, about 10 miles from Franklin Roosevelt's home. His estate is also a quick train ride from New York City. My parents and various teachers took me there on many occasions. Revisiting the archives for this project, I found the librarians and archivists there to be supremely helpful, and they were also forthright in explaining the gaps in their collections, mostly caused by FDR himself. Roosevelt was not someone who kept diaries or allowed his staff to take notes during meetings. Luckily, the library in Hyde Park contains extensive papers of people associated with FDR, including original letters from Frank Murphy.

Many people were generous with their time after receiving a random email from a lawyer in New York (me). To cite just a few examples, I communicated with Scott O'Brien, the biographer for Ann Harding, one of Murphy's girlfriends. Scott confirmed her handwriting on a note to Frank Murphy dated 1933, well after her move to Hollywood and marriage to an actor. And Michael Goldfield, a labor historian at Wayne State University, described his views on whether unions would have survived if the Supreme

Court had overturned the National Labor Relations Act (NLRA) of 1935 (also known as the Wagner Act), as was expected by many at the time. He and graduate student Cody Melcher shared with me a draft article on the subject, which has since been published.

Detroit lawyer Lillian Diallo provided some context for the grand jury proceedings of the kind conducted by Frank Murphy. Bruce J. Schulman of Boston University and Richard Gamble of Hillsdale College answered questions on the topic of "civic nationalism." Tim Retzloff, professor of history and LGBTQ studies at Michigan State, gave me guideposts for describing Frank's personal life. Bruce Travis Fisher confirmed certain facts about his mother Ada Sipuel Fisher, who desegregated the law school at the University of Oklahoma, where Professor Melissa Mortazavi connected me to Mr. Fisher.

Leslie Woodcock Tentler, professor emerita of history at Catholic University and an expert on Catholic American history, was generous with her time. And I was doubly fortunate to learn that her mother knew Josephine Gomon, who passed stories of Frank Murphy down to her. Professor John T. McGreevy at Notre Dame also took time to email me; his book, *Catholicism and American Freedom: A History*, published in 2003, is a wonderful resource. And I enjoyed speaking to Professor Catherine O'Donnell, another expert on Catholicism in colonial and early American history.

On Philippine affairs, University of Michigan professor emerita Adelwisa Agas Weller and her working group catalogued Filipino items now found in the Frank Murphy Museum in Harbor Beach. They reviewed a draft chapter in my book on Murphy's tenure in the Philippines.

I benefited greatly from the research of Timothy Parker at the Walter P. Reuther Library of Wayne State University, who came highly recommended, and, as I discovered, whose reputation was well warranted. He catalogued and sent me files and papers from the labor collection where Frank Murphy was well represented. Lisbeth Rubin, a University of Michigan student, reviewed documents in Ann Arbor.

Then there are the many libraries that have put their priceless collections online, allowing me to scoop up articles and memoranda that would have been unavailable to biographers even 20 years ago. These online resources include the Library of Congress Prints and Photographs Division, the Smithsonian Institution, the National Parks website, the Columbia University Libraries, the Detroit Public Library, the Harry S Truman Presidential Library, the Princeton University Libraries, the Kent State Libraries, the University of Massachusetts at Amherst, the Henry Ford Museum, the United States Holocaust Museum, the Charles and Margaret Hall Cushwa Center for the Study of American Catholicism, the Catholic News Archive, the Jewish Telegraphic Agency, the UC Irvine Libraries, the Detroit Historical Society website, *Automotive News*, the *Philippines Free Press Online*, the American Presidency Project at UC Santa Barbara, the George C. Marshall Foundation, and Professor Douglas O. Linder's Famous Trial website. Jstor.org and ibiblio are online collections of importance. And, Wikipedia is a resource of extraordinary reach. Newspapers.com, with its diverse library of newspapers from around the country, helped immensely to take me back to the time Frank Murphy visited this or that small town.

I am sorry that I took on this project too late to meet J. Woodward Howard and Sidney Fine, both biographers of Frank Murphy whose names appear often in my book, and Eugene Gressman, his law clerk who defended Murphy against his critics for a half-century after his death. I wish they had the opportunity to read my manuscript and fill in gaps and correct my errors. The book would have been much better with their input.

Finally, a special thanks goes to my editors, including Scott Ham and Danielle Coty-Fattal at the University of Michigan Press. My wonderful and brilliant Aunt Anita Weiner was insightful in her close review of the manuscript. She has been a positive presence for my entire life, and I am grateful that this project has allowed me to reconnect with her in a meaningful way. My nephews Sam and Alex Zipes ably helped me on certain research questions I had. And Nils Kuehn, a first-rate proofreader, scrubbed my final draft. The people listed in this section do not necessarily endorse my viewpoints and all errors remain my own.

A Note on Labels and Names

I faced a fundamental problem in quoting from newspapers and documents from Murphy's era. These sources often used words and terms that we recognize today as shocking, hurtful, patronizing, or improperly euphemistic. When I felt that I could not avoid terms as Murphy and his contemporaries used them, I put these terms in quotes and tried to provide context.

More generally, in this book, I frequently refer to race, religion, gender, and sexual orientation. These subjects justifiably evoke strong feelings. At all times, I have tried to be sensitive in my word choice and to humanize those who have been marginalized or persecuted for simply living their lives. This is obviously hard to do, regardless of best intentions. Complicating matters further, the very concepts of what it means to be a member of a certain group shifts over time. A person reading this book 20 years hence (I should be so lucky!) might have significant problems with my word choices or my antiquated scientific assumptions.

The important women and local Detroit Black leaders, among others, in Murphy's life do not receive their due in a biography such as this one, because often times their words were not saved for posterity. Their side of the story must be created in other ways, and like a reflection of a reflection, their viewpoints get blurred. This is a horrible injustice, and one that I struggled with as I wrote this book. I hope the reader can understand that my intentions were good.

Endnotes

1. "Character of Michigan's 'Labor Governor' Analyzed," *TTH*, June 2, 1937 (describing his voice).

2. James S. Pooler, "'The Forgotten Man' Remembers Murphy," *DFP*, July 22, 1949, 1.

3. "Late Justice Murphy Honored in Capital," *NYT*, Mar. 7, 1951. (As Supreme Court Chief Justice Fred Vinson stated in a eulogy to Murphy, through Murphy's own character, "The democracy that we loved gained compassion and vigor.")

4. *Korematsu*, 323 U.S. at 233.

5. William O. Douglas became the longest-serving Supreme Court justice. He was appointed in 1939 and served into the 1970s. "The Law: The Court's Uncompromising Libertarian," *Time.com*, Nov. 24, 1975, accessed Apr. 19, 2020, http://content.time.com/time/magazine/article/0,9171,913732,00.html.

6. Roger Baldwin to Felix Frankfurter, Feb. 28, 1920, Princeton University Libraries, American Civil Liberties Union Collection: Roger Baldwin Years (1920–1950), accessed Apr. 19, 2020, https://i2.wp.com/blogs.princeton.edu/mudd/wp-content/uploads/sites/41/2012/07/MC001.01.120.30.jpg?ssl=1.

7. Upon Justice Douglas' death in 1980, President Jimmy Carter said, "William O. Douglas was a lion-like defender of individual liberty. He was fiercely certain that the simple words of the Bill of Rights were meant to protect the humblest citizen from an exercise of arbitrary power, and he never deviated from that passionate conviction." Spencer Rich, "William O. Douglas Dies at 81," *Washington Post*, Jan. 20, 1980. Justice Black's *Korematsu* decision was dismissed by his admirers as "aberrational." "Justice Black, Champion of Civil Liberties for 34 Years on Court, Dies at 85," *NYT*, Sept. 26, 1971. The Harvard Law School established a chair in Frankfurter's honor for his role as "the foremost spokesman for the judicial conservative wing, famous for his sharp dissents to 'activist' Court decisions, such as in the Tennessee reappointment case." School Plans Frankfurter Chair of Law, The Harvard Crimson, Apr. 29, 1963, accessed May 30, 2020, https://www.thecrimson.com/article/1963/4/29/school-plans-frankfurter-chair-of-law/#:~:text=The%20Law%20School%20has%20announced,School%20faculty%20for%2025%20years. As will be discussed, Frankfurter's philosophy was on full display when he filed a concurrence in *Korematsu*, supporting the Japanese-American internments.

8. *Ex Parte Endo*, 323 U.S. 283, 307-308 (1944).

9. *Steele v. Louisville & N.R. Co.*, 323 U.S. 192 (1944).

10. Murphy used the word for the last time in *Duncan v. Kahanamoku*, 327 U.S. 304, 334 (1946), in connection with his criticism of the use of military trials in Hawaii during World War II. Hawaii was placed under martial law during World War II. In his concurrence, Murphy expressed his views that martial law was imposed on Hawaii solely because of its large Japanese-American population: "Racism has no place whatever in our civilization. The Constitution as well as the conscience of mankind disclaims its use for any purpose, military or otherwise. It can only result, as it does in this instance, in striking down individual rights and in aggravating rather than solving the problems toward which it is directed. It renders impotent the ideal of the dignity of the human personality, destroying something of what is noble in our way of life. We must therefore reject it completely whenever it arises in the course of a legal proceeding."

11. FDR to Frank Murphy, Mar. 15, 1940, FDRL, PSF, Supreme Court, 1938–1944, Box 166.

Contents

CHAPTER 1 — Childhood on the Shores of Lake Huron   1

CHAPTER 2 — Murphy's Formal Education and His Exposure   10
to Progressive Ideas

CHAPTER 3 — World War I: A Leap over the Top   16

CHAPTER 4 — United States Attorney's Office: Enforcing Laws   26
as a Patriotic Duty

CHAPTER 5 — Private Practice as a Path to Politics   36

CHAPTER 6 — Reformer on the Criminal Court Bench   45

CHAPTER 7 — The Ossian Sweet Trial: A Black Defendant   62
and a White Jury

CHAPTER 8 — Murphy as Mayor: Calling a Depression   75
a Depression

CHAPTER 9 — Mayor Murphy's Direct Appeal to Washington   96
for Aid

CHAPTER 10 — The New Deal and Murphy   107

CHAPTER 11 — Murphy to the Philippines   124

CHAPTER 12 — The Campaign for Governor   139

CHAPTER 13 — A Governorship Dominated by Labor Strife   148

CHAPTER 14 — Murphy's Ineffective Reelection Campaign   167

CHAPTER 15 — Murphy as Attorney General of the United States   181

CHAPTER 16 — The Supreme Court: Murphy's Initial Years   200

CHAPTER 17 — The Japanese-American Internments and the   231
Supreme Court Curfew Cases

CHAPTER 18 — Murphy's Supreme Court Confronts the Expulsions   **249**

CHAPTER 19 — Last Years   **271**

CHAPTER 20 — Conclusions   **290**

Bibliography   **306**

Index   **312**

Illustrations follow page 138

CHAPTER 1

Childhood on the Shores of Lake Huron

⚖️

William Francis "Frank" Murphy was born in 1890 in the small town of Sand Beach on the shores of Lake Huron,[1] about 120 miles north of Detroit. His family was one of about 50 Catholic families in this hamlet of about 1,100.

John Murphy, Frank's father, was a successful lawyer. Working from the family home, John developed a thriving legal practice and was known as a skilled trial attorney, one of the most prominent in the Thumb region (so named because the Lower Peninsula of Michigan looks like a mitten). Among his clients were a railway company and a bank, and he was involved in litigation involving lumber interests in the area.[2] He was also a heavy drinker, but this did not seem to inhibit his professional career.[3]

Murphy's father had a colorful past he kept hidden. As a 16-year-old, John participated in an anti-British uprising in Canada that followed the American Civil War. His group consisted of Canadians and some United States citizens of Irish extraction known as the Fenians. Ireland was under the military control of Great Britain at the time, and the Fenians wanted to free the Irish Republic by force of arms. Their ill-defined goals included fostering an uprising in Canada, at the time a British Colony.

The British authorities quickly crushed the rebellion in Canada.[4] Murphy's father had to flee Ontario to avoid imprisonment

1

and, therefore, crossed the border to Michigan. With his intelligence and ambition, he attended law school at the University of Michigan, leaving his past completely behind.

Frank's father was known to be a bit eccentric. He kept his hair longer than other men in town and wore a bolo tie. Frank's childhood friend Frank Potts recalled that his father kissed neighborhood children, publicly and affectionately—and sometimes to their discomfort.[5]

Frank Murphy himself may indeed have been born in a one-room cabin, but if so, he moved out within the first year of his birth.[6] In reality, Murphy grew up in a prosperous household in Sand Beach because of his father's success as a lawyer. Frank's childhood house, a few blocks from Lake Huron, was and remains a handsome one-and-a-half-story frame building with clapboard siding and a steep gable roof to allow the ample winter snows to slide off.[7]

Frank's mother Mary was born in upstate New York and came to Sand Beach at an early age. There, she worked in her brother's music store and sang in the choir of the Catholic and Baptist churches.[8] Frank developed an especially close relationship to his mother. Much has been written about his sexually charged letters to her later in his life. When he was 28-year-old Army officer stationed in Europe, he penned these plaintive lines to his mother: "Tonight if I could sit near you or brush your hair or stroke your forehead or just feel your presence I would be in paradise." He also wrote: "What a honeymoon that would be . . . You are my girl and whenever I wander down a lover's lane I want to be with you."[9]

His mother was the more religious of his two parents, and Murphy followed her lead. At seven, Frank became an altar boy at the local Catholic church. Upon confirmation at age 12, at the insistence of his mother, he made a pledge to abstain from alcohol until the age of majority, and then went further, vowing not to drink alcohol throughout his life.

Murphy's bedroom was accessible by walking through his parents' bedroom, which meant his mother could keep close track of his comings and goings. In this way, his living arrangement mirrored that of his later political ally Franklin Delano Roosevelt

(FDR), whose mother's bedroom remained next to his marital bedroom in Hyde Park, New York, until her death in 1941.

Despite owning one of the biggest houses in town, his family blended in. His parents sent him to the town's public schools, and they worshipped at the local Catholic church, a simple wood frame structure until it was upgraded in 1917. Murphy later encountered some discrimination as a Catholic. But as a child, in his small town, any exposure to bigotry was minimal.

Murphy was undoubtedly born with certain advantages, most notably that he could, and did, spend a lot of time in his father's law office. Early essays by Frank were written on his father's legal stationary seemingly because those were the closest pieces of paper available to him. Frank would have seen his father meeting with clients and drafting briefs, but also conducting the business of the local Democratic Party. John was active in party politics and held various patronage positions in Huron County. He even ran for Congress but lost in a then-heavily Republican state.[10] Frank followed his father's lead in certain respects, most notably by going into the practice of law. In other ways, he rejected his father's way of doing business, as when he later spurned "machine" politics and patronage as a means of staying in power.

Frank had two brothers and a sister who remained close throughout their entire lives. As a family friend described them, the brothers "would often walk down the street, two abreast, three abreast . . . and all locked arms. It was sincere affection . . . but it made for conversation."[11] This unbreakable bond was a key to Frank's later success, as the family members supported each other personally and professionally.

His younger brother George had a career that most closely tracked Frank's. They both became lawyers and served as criminal court judges in Detroit. They collaborated and supported each other throughout their lives. While Frank was the governor of Michigan, he camped in George's judicial chambers as the brothers worked to defuse the great sit-down strikes that engulfed the auto industry in the late 1930s, avoiding a violent outcome that seemed inevitable. And George also remained a bachelor for much of his life, marrying only a few years before Frank died.[12]

Their sister Marguerite was enamored with Frank. "What's a husband compared to a darling brother," she wrote him when she was approaching 30.[13] She eventually married and adopted a daughter but remained close to her brother. When Murphy became a national figure, pictures of him with Marguerite and her daughter at notable events circulated in newspapers. When Murphy enrolled in the Army later in his life, in a quixotic effort to serve in a combat role during World War II, he listed his sister as the contact person in case of an emergency. Marguerite chided him in one letter while he was a justice on the Supreme Court to immediately take care of a cough.[14]

Frank's older brother, Harold, was born two years before him.[15] Harold was the first brother to assume a political role. With Woodrow Wilson's election as president, the local machine leaders wanted to reward John Murphy, their father, for sticking it out as a Democrat in a heavily Republican state. They gave Harold a job in a local post office. Harold remained in various government positions his entire life, although he had less of a direct role in Frank's political rise than his brother George. Harold was the first sibling to die, in 1946, and Frank's major health issues started soon after.[16]

The siblings were undeniably close. Three of the four Murphy siblings married late in life. Frank Murphy did not marry at all. Could there have been some shared childhood trauma, perhaps caused by their father's drinking, that kept the siblings tightly bound to their mother and each other? No evidence exists that Frank's father was abusive to him or any other member of the family, but such a matter might not have been recorded in letters or diaries.

Or perhaps the explanation for their allergies to marriage is less sinister. The siblings grew up in a time when it was beginning to become socially acceptable to marry later in life, particularly for families that faced separation and dislocation as they made their way in a new land.[17]

Murphy's place of birth had a varied and vibrant economy. The immediate area was originally settled as a lumber processing center to exploit the vast stretches of virgin pine in Huron County.[18]

By the late 1800s, most of the surrounding forests had already been stripped and turned into farmland.

The enclave's defining feature during Murphy's childhood was its excellent port. During storms, Lake Huron sometimes throws up ocean-sized waves of 30 feet or more.[19] The federal government recognized the need to build a safe harbor for ships filled with ore, grain, and other raw materials as they travelled from the Upper Peninsula to feed the already heaving industrial areas to the south in and around Detroit. Murphy's hometown of Sand Beach had changed its name to Harbor Beach in 1900 to reflect the recent completion of its massive man-made anchorage, by some measurements still the largest fresh-water harbor in the world.[20] By walking a few hundred feet from his house to the shoreline, a young Murphy would have seen a lighthouse perched dramatically offshore and a kaleidoscope of boats.[21] Murphy later adopted the view that the federal government could be a force for good; it is possible he remembered the massive benefits that this federal building project brought to his hometown.

Large factories were located to the south in the Detroit area, but at the time it was still possible for smaller facilities in rural Huron County to thrive. In addition to its port, Harbor Beach had agricultural-processing facilities. During his high school summers, Murphy was employed in the town's starch factory[22] at the insistence of his father, who wanted to instill a strong work ethic in him and keep him grounded.[23] His experiences at the factory, and his close contacts with the workers, were to have a significant effect on him. At least according to his later telling, Frank worked the hours of a typical worker, from 7:00 AM to 6:00 PM. His jobs included ladling liquid starch into troughs, piling heavy crates onto trucks, and toiling in rooms where the temperature reached 140 degrees Fahrenheit.

Right before going to college, Murphy became a foreman at a local factory, where he supervised 300 "Polanders." An average high schooler such as Murphy could not aspire to a supervisory position at a factory without connections. In a college essay on the subject, Murphy freely acknowledged that his father had secured the job. At the same time, his father required him to work at the factory under dangerous, uncomfortable conditions, thus show-ing that Frank was not particularly spoiled or pampered.

Frank was the quarterback of his high school's football team and centerfielder of the baseball team. This would have been impressive in a large school, but Frank's class only had 10 stu-dents. Nevertheless, the Murphy boys were indeed athletically gifted. For several years, his brother George held the world record in the two-mile indoor relay along with his teammates at the University of Michigan.[24] Frank boxed; he was said to be one of the best amateur boxers in the state of Michigan even at the age of 41.[25] Frank once bragged to a girlfriend that he stayed fit by walk-ing on his hands. He learned to ride horses and played polo.[26] His horse-riding jaunts gained him some notoriety later in his life, when he was often seen in the company of young women on the bridal paths in the Washington, DC area when he should have been attending to official duties as the country's attorney general.

In high school, Frank did well academically but not spectacu-larly so.[27] The *Harbor Beach Times* later described him as "one of the brightest students the school has ever had and his oratory is of the highest order."[28] In fact, the class valedictorian was Mary Brennan, Murphy's cousin from his mother's side. Yet it was Frank and not Mary who was chosen to give the commencement speech at his high school graduation. Murphy later strongly sup-ported the right of women to vote and participate as full citizens in the United States (and the Philippines), but at least at that point, he simply accepted his role and delivered a barnstorming speech. Murphy struck an optimistic tone, stating, "There is no royal road to honor in this country." He went on, "We all have a chance; and with a staunch character we cannot fail to have success."[29]

Murphy grew up in an environment where his opinions were encouraged and respected.[30] He had a voice, and he spoke his mind. Harbor Beach gave him these gifts. The values of this small town were his reference point when he entered the bigger stage and met other Americans who had far different conceptions of an ideal America. As the United States Attorney General in 1939, on the brink of the United States' involvement in World War II, Murphy described the "hallmark" of civilization as "the idea that every man, no matter how meek and humble and inconspicuous, shall have his place in the sun."[31]

Murphy also absorbed Catholic values and traditions during his youth, carrying them with him his entire life.[32] He went on to become one of the most prominent Catholic figures in the country and was chosen by FDR to fill "Catholic" political seats. By 1946, Pope Pius VII referred to Murphy as the "ranking American Catholic," concluding that "[Murphy's] great heart and mind are always inspired by true Christian love for the cause of human solidarity, regardless of race, creed or political considerations."[33] And whenever Murphy returned to Harbor Beach, he attended Sunday Mass in the local church like anyone else. By all accounts he was sincere and humble, mingling with other congregants and chatting with the local priest about the sermon.

One aspect of Murphy's character is surprising, given the place in which he grew up. With a busy port outside his front door, he should have taken some interest in nautical matters. Murphy would have encountered wizened seamen in his town, some with harrowing tales of rescue by the active local Coast Guard.[34] He would have heard the stories of those ships that did not make it, including some that came tantalizingly close to the port before sinking with all hands onboard.

Yet, Murphy never expressed romantic interest in the sea. He did not wax in private letters to friends about the constantly changing hues of the water and sky that presaged a storm about to sweep in from the lake. This failure to focus on the dramatic natural surroundings around him, like his vow to never drink alcohol, reflects a priest-like asceticism and seriousness that also defined Murphy's personality—and which manifested itself throughout his life.

Endnotes

1. Frank Murphy's application to serve in the Army during World War II contains the date and place of his birth, recites the birthplace of his mother and father, and lists his sister as his next of kin. FMP, reel 92.
2. Fine, *Detroit Years*, 3.

3.   Frank Potts, Jan. 8, 1965, transcript of interview conducted by Sidney Fine, Frank Murphy Oral History Project, FMP, p. 3 (describing the father's drinking).

4.   The Fenians were a transatlantic association consisting of the Irish Republican Brotherhood, founded in both Dublin and the United States in about 1858. The United States government may have looked the other way as this group organized, as a kind of retribution for Great Britain's support of the Confederacy.

5.   Frank Potts, Jan. 8, 1965, transcript of interview conducted by Sidney Fine, Frank Murphy Oral History Project, FMP, pp. 1, 2 (describing the father's kissing).

6.   "Time Stands Still at Frank Murphy Home," *DFP*, Aug. 2, 1994, 10D.

7.   Evelyn J. Lutz, "Museum Depicts the Life and Times of Former Governor," *Tri-county Times* (covering Fenton, Linden, and Holly, Michigan), Aug. 5, 2002, www.tctimes.com/museum-depicts-life-and-times-of-of-former-governor/article_6e492e39-9c6f-51f4-ad2f-93024e144490.html.

8.   Fine, *Detroit Years*, 4.

9.   Ibid, 7.

10.   Fine, *The New Deal Years*, 204.

11.   Frank Potts, Jan. 8, 1965, transcript of interview conducted by Sidney Fine, Frank Murphy Oral History Project, FMP, p. 2.

12.   "Recorder's Judge George Murphy, 64, Dies," *DFP*, July 12, 1961, 1 (providing details about George Murphy's life).

13.   Fine, *Detroit Years*, 6.

14.   Marguerite Murphy to Frank Murphy, FMP, reel 98.

15.   Upon the death in 1946 of Harold, Frank's brother, newspapers reported Harold's age as 50. "Murphy Flies to Detroit for Brother's Rites," *DFP*, October 22, 1946, 7. The reference to Harold's age was incorrect as Harold was older than Frank.

16.   "Frank Murphy's Kin Sued on Non-Support Charge for Divorce," *TTH*, May 12, 1936, 10.

17.   The high rates of lifelong bachelorhood among the Irish provoked periodic discussions in the Irish and Catholic press of the danger of "Irish race suicide." Chauncey, *Gay New York*, 77, n. 24 (citing articles in *America*).

18.   Florence McKinnon Gwinn, *Pioneer History of Huron County* (Bad Axe: Huron County Pioneer and Historical Society, 1922), 3.

19.   Melville, *Moby-Dick*, Ch. 54—The Town-Ho's Story. ("For in their interflowing aggregate, those grand fresh-water seas of ours,—Erie, and Ontario, and Huron, and Superior, and Michigan—possess an ocean-like expansiveness, with many of the ocean's noblest traits . . . they are swept by Borean and dismasting blasts as direful as any that lash the salted wave; they know what shipwrecks are, for out of sight of land, however inland, they have drowned full many a midnight ship with all its shrieking crew.") However, Melville may have gone overboard when he stated the Great Lakes "contain round archipelagoes of romantic isles, even as the Polynesian waters do."

20.   Untitled article, *DFP*, Nov. 17, 1900, 8 (discussing the village's name change, and the "insane" opposition to the change by the sailors familiar with the village).

21. "From Humble Home to Supreme Court, Success Story of Frank Murphy," *TTH*, Jan. 4, 1940, 1.

22. Plaque located in Harbor Beach, Michigan, entitled *History of Industry in Harbor Beach*, the Harbor Beach Lions Club.

23. Fine, *Detroit Years*, 2.

24. Photograph, "UM Track, 1915, 2-mile Relay Team, Donnelly, Murphy, Carroll, Ufer; tied world indoor record," Bentley Historical Library, Bentley Image Bank, accessed Apr. 18, 2020, http://quod.lib.umich.edu/b/bhl/x-bl019827/b, l019827.

25. "Before Death Took Toll of Murphy Family," from "Murphy Souvenir Section" of newspaper, probably from *DFP*, Apr. 23, 1933, FMM; "Political Glamor Boys Dewey and Murphy Compete for Crime-Busting Honors," *Life Magazine*, July 31, 1939, 18 (reference to Murphy's boxing).

26. See, *The Filipino Primitive*, 73–74. (Murphy was presented with a silver horseshoe for scoring his first goal and captaining his team to victory while in the Philippines.)

27. The small town of Harbor Beach produced two people, Murphy and James Lincoln, whose names adorn municipal buildings in Detroit. Murphy's high school teacher was Esther Lincoln. Esther's son James later became an assistant to Murphy when Murphy was the Attorney General of the United States. James became a prominent judge in his own right and made a mark in the area of juvenile criminal reform. James was honored when the Probate Court in Detroit was named after him. My summary of James Lincoln's life is taken from the Bentley Library's description of the James H. Lincoln papers, which it holds.

28. "The High School Graduates of Class of '08, Do Themselves Great Credit," *The Harbor Beach Times*, June 26, 1908, FMP, reel 91.

29. Fine, *Detroit Years*, 16.

30. Howard, *Mr. Justice Murphy*, 4–5.

31. Frank Murphy, "Civil Liberties and the Cities," an Address Before the Joint Meeting of the United States Conference of Mayors and the National Institute of Municipal Law Officers, the Waldorf-Astoria, New York City, May 15, 1939, United States Attorney General website, "Murphy speeches."

32. "Justice Frank Murphy Accepts Honorary Chairmanship," *NYT*, Apr. 17, 1944, 25. (Murphy accepted the appointment as chair of the Committee of Catholics for Human Rights, composed of "300 outstanding Catholics throughout the United States.")

33. Proclamation dated Aug. 23, 1946, FMM. F.C. Gowen drafted the proclamation as "the Personal Representative of the President of the United States of America to the Pope." Contemporaneous newspapers described F.C. Gowen as a foreign service officer who was able to arrange meetings with the Pope. "Commander Rome Describes His Audience with Pope Pius," *Baltimore Sun*, Mar. 25, 1946, 26.

34. "No Bodies Recovered," *DFP*, Aug. 22, 1899, 3. ("Today's search by the tug Frank W. and steamer Sand Beach, with the life-saving crews from Pointe Aux Barques and Harbor Beach, have failed to locate the wreck of the schooner Hunter-Savidge, which capsized off Pointe Aux Barques yesterday afternoon, with the loss of five lives.")

CHAPTER 2

Murphy's Formal Education and His Exposure to Progressive Ideas

In 1908, Murphy departed for the University of Michigan. His father was delighted; he had earlier taken Frank on a tour of the campus and hoped that his son would attend his alma mater. At a time when most children growing up in a small town would not have endeavored for a higher degree, Murphy's parents expected their children to attend college.

Until this time, Murphy had never been more than "a four-hour walk" from his home.[1] Yet the 16-year-old transitioned easily to his bustling new surroundings.

His gregariousness and speaking skills soon got him noticed.[2] At one event during his first year at Michigan, he addressed a throng that had jammed Hill Auditorium, the largest performance venue on campus. He complained that Michigan's "spirit, sentiment and tradition" had suffered at the hands of the current students. He pleaded for his classmates "to rejuvenate the old spirit, the old red blood, the old devotion to this institution." He pontificated, "A student without sentiment, without love for his college as far as college life is concerned is like a man without a country."[3]

This would be a Murphy trait throughout his life. He was protean in how he appeared, fully formed, in whatever new environment he was in. He proved to be fearless when speaking before large crowds and acting at home in new and sometimes hostile environments. Here, he rose from his small-town background to become a student leader. And after law school, he moved to the dynamic city of Detroit without displaying any anxiousness and almost instantly established himself as a top trial attorney.

One secret, perhaps, was that he was game for the types of activities that endeared him to friends and acquaintances. One letter home to his brother Harold describing his college exploits constituted local news. The Harbor Beach newspaper breathlessly reported that Murphy gave "a splendid outline of the experience recently enjoyed at that college as a freshman." For one, he was compelled to eat several garlics. He was "then ordered to climb a tree and remained there all night."[4]

He displayed an earnest and serious side as well, worrying about the state of the country and the world. His high school experiences at the factory were fermenting in his mind. In a sociology paper—his one surviving academic paper from college—Murphy expressed concern about the lives of the workers, some of whom were significantly older than him. He complained that they were made to wake at 5:30 in the morning, "go to work at 7, work until 6:00 in the evening . . . go to bed at 9:00 o'clock. I would like to know how they are going to advance under such conditions." He had already concluded that a shorter workday was appropriate, to allow the workers to "come in contact with more of the world, broaden them, raise their moral standards, and teach them to think."[5] At the time, there were no legal restrictions on work hours.[6]

In a speech he gave as the governor of Michigan in 1937, one can see that he remained focused on the issues he had first identified in his sociology paper from college, when he decried the "large industrial establishments where thousands of workers are subject to control by one directing head, and where they have scant opportunity to express individual initiative in their work. For the masses of workers, creative craftsmanship has been replaced by machine precision, uniformity, and monotony—a

dreary triumvirate of forces which combine to make of the individual a sort of infinite nothing."[7] To Murphy, the modern factory
worker deserved a fulfilling life. His attitude explained why he
was later to become a champion for common laborers.

In 1910, at the age of about 20, Murphy dove into his first
political campaign when he became chairman of the Publicity
Committee for the Osborn Club at his university.[8] Chase Osborn
was a Republican, successfully running as a candidate to be the
Michigan governor. Osborn had a homespun appeal, was born
in a log cabin in 1849, and was named "Chase" by his parents in
honor of the abolitionist who became Lincoln's secretary of the
Treasury.

One can see Murphy's attraction to this governor. Osborn was
a progressive and favored workers' compensation. He was a
visionary who supported women's suffrage, then just a distant
dream and not incorporated as the law of the state in Michigan
until 1918.

Murphy backed a winner. Michigan was a Republican state
and Osborn prevailed in his reelection campaign. The Osborn
interlude was important not only because it introduced Murphy
to politics but also for another reason. During the campaign,
Murphy met two other Michigan students, Edward Kemp[9] and
Norman Hill,[10] who were also working on the Osborn campaign
and who would stay with him through thick and thin, relocating
with him whenever he moved, whether to Lansing, Detroit, or the
Philippines. Hill eventually married and named one of his four
children "Frank."[11]

Murphy's dalliance with the Republican Party seemed to end
with his support of Osborn. By 1912, two years later, Murphy was
a firm supporter of Woodrow Wilson, the Democratic candidate
for president. As for Osborn's political career, he fell victim of
a growing schism within the Republican Party, one that would
ultimately transform the American political system and shift
the energy of the two-party system from the Republicans to the
Democrats, culminating in FDR's New Deal.

The dilemma Osborn and other Republicans faced during the
reelection campaign in 1912 was that the Republicans' progressive hero, Theodore Roosevelt, had bolted the Republican Party,

forming the Progressive Party (more popularly known as the Bull Moose Party) after losing the Republican primary to his hand-picked successor, William Taft. Roosevelt's decision to challenge the Republican candidate in 1912 split the Republican vote and threw the election to Woodrow Wilson and the Democrats.

But Roosevelt also forced the Republican Party to the right politically to distinguish itself from the Bull Moose party. During his campaign, Roosevelt proposed a strict limitation on all campaign contributions, legislation to minimize industrial accidents through federal regulation, and suffrage for women.[12] With Roosevelt now claiming these positions, the Republican Party jettisoned its enthusiasm for these planks. This internecine fight created a significant opportunity for the Democratic Party to recruit progressives to the Democratic side after the Bull Moose Party folded with Roosevelt's defeat. The shift of energy from the Republican Party to the Democratic Party was gradual but culminated with the election of FDR in 1932.

Osborn resolved his immediate dilemma by not running for governor again, so that he would not have to declare his loyalty to a Republican presidential candidate running against Roosevelt. But Governor Osborn never forgot Murphy. He remained a lifetime Republican but crossed party lines to support Murphy's unsuccessful bid for reelection as Michigan governor in 1938.[13]

As an undergraduate, Murphy enrolled in the "combined literary and law course." He was a mediocre student. He contracted diphtheria during his junior year and did not complete his work those semesters.[14] Even the well-educated and well-fed fell sick and died from diseases that are rarely known today. In one picture from his University of Michigan days, Murphy is seen in a hospital bed that had been wheeled outside, his father by his side. The hospital stay was the first of many ailments at different points in Murphy's life.

Murphy appears to have never completed his undergraduate degree. Nevertheless, he successfully enrolled in law school at the University of Michigan. His grades again were not good. He managed to receive his law degree on time in 1914 only because the day before graduation a professor retroactively granted his petition for two additional credit hours (with a D grade) in a first-year property course.[15]

His poor grades in college and law school were surprising, as he later exhibited many of the skills that should have made him a good student. As mayor and governor, he was meticulous in his preparation of his policy positions, seeking input from experts both on and outside his staff. Later, as a member of the Supreme Court, he displayed mastery of the law when he wanted to, arguing with the other justices about obscure areas of constitutional theory and scribbling his positions in the margins of draft opinions. He also sprinkled his political speeches and writings with classical and religious allusions, making use of the most modern trends in criminology and sociology. Unlike his college paper on the Harbor Beach starch factory, Murphy's letters to professional colleagues later in life were polished, with only a rare grammatical or typographical mistake that could be expected in the age of the typewriter—when people sometimes decided that an entire rewrite of a page with one or two mistakes was not worth it. By the time of his death, he had accumulated a library of about 1,500 books.

It was not just that Murphy was erudite. He also had a gift for communicating in a manner that people could understand. His jury instructions as a criminal court judge in a particularly famous case, the Ossian Sweet trial, were scholarly but, at the same time, accessible to the lay-person jury. He put much thought into how he expressed his ideas.

Why then was he such a bad student? The answer is not obvious. Given Murphy's ambitions, he should have showed more concern about his studies. Nevertheless, during his early life, he had been exposed to many different cultures and creeds, and the swirling ideas of social justice from his church and prominent politicians of the time. He had developed an empathy for the less fortunate and a sense that America was a special place where people could thrive regardless of their backgrounds. This was a powerful foundation, but one that left him restless and longing for a job where he could fulfill his ambitions.

Endnotes

1. "Character of Michigan's 'Labor Governor' Analyzed," *TTH*, June 2, 1937, 5.
2. He had a wide group of friends on campus. "Frank Murphy (age 18) with a group of friends," Bentley Historical Library, Bentley Image Bank, accessed Apr. 18, 2020, https://quod.lib.umich.edu/b/bhl/x-hs11995/HS11995?lasttype=boolean;last view=thumbnail;med=1;resnum=4;size=20;sort=relevance;start=1;subview=detail;vi ew=entry;rgn1=ic_all;select1=all;q1=frank+murphy.
3. Fine, *Detroit Years*, 27.
4. FMP, reel 91 (a press release or a draft of a Harbor Beach newspaper story).
5. College Sociology Paper, FMP, reel 91.
6. Ibid. His professor branded the observations he made about the workers in the starch factory as interesting but not particularly professionally researched and gave him a B+ for this college paper.
7. Frank Murphy, Address delivered before the National Conference of Social Work, Indianapolis, Indiana, May 1937, *Murphy Collected Speeches, 1937–1938.*
8. Fine, *Detroit Years*, 21.
9. "Death Takes E.G. Kemp," *TTH*, Nov. 23, 1962, 2.
10. "Murphy Aide Lands in City, Prepares for Return of Governor Elect," *DFP*, Dec. 2, 1936, 2 (describing the return of Norman Hill to Detroit from the Philippines).
11. "Obituary, Zoe Hill," *DFP*, Apr. 5, 1962, 35 (listing children, including Frank).
12. "Progressive Battle Hymns; Songs of Peace and Prosperity; Progress and Patriotism," (1912), 10 (outlining the 33 propositions of the Progressive [Bull Moose] Platform, including suffrage to men and women alike, limitations on campaign contributions, court reform, minimum wages for working women, and fixing of minimum safety and health standards for various occupations).
13. "Vote Taxes Detroit Equipment," *DFP*, Nov. 9, 1938, 1 (describing Chase Osborn's support of Murphy in 1938).
14. Fine, *Detroit Years*, 23; Howard, *Mr. Justice Murphy*, 10.
15. FMP, reel 91 (Frank Murphy law school transcript).

CHAPTER 3

World War I:
A Leap over the Top

After he graduated from law school in 1914, Frank opened an office in Harbor Beach, before quickly moving to Detroit to practice law.[1] He also started his involvement in Democratic Party politics, benefiting from his father's connections. In 1916, Murphy served as assistant secretary at the state convention of the Democratic Party. There, he befriended important Democratic leaders in Michigan.[2] He left a strong enough impression that local party leaders were to soon nominate Murphy for a congressional seat, albeit one in which the Democrats did not stand a chance of winning.

Murphy volunteered for the Army Reserves within a week after the United States declared war against Germany in June 1917.[3] Knowing his reputation for piety, one reporter recounting his life gleefully reported that he had "cheated" his way into the Army. Murphy had bad eyesight, a possible disqualification for military service. But at an Army post in Fort Wayne, Indiana, Murphy appeared before a sergeant "blessed" with the name of Shea. "Fighting Irish," Shea said with a smile. "Well son, we'll take care of the eye business." When Murphy took the eye test, he could not see the little letters, but Shea whispered them to him, or so the story went. "That's how young Frank Murphy got into the Army," his sergeant later recalled to this reporter.[4]

Murphy's belief in the war aims of the United States was not universally held in the United States. Despite the rousing words of Wilson about a "war to end all wars" and "to make the world safe for democracy," Americans did not rush to enlist. A million men were needed, but in the first six weeks after the Declaration of War only 73,000 volunteered. In response, the United States passed conscription laws to fill its military ranks.

Murphy for his part had no qualms about joining the fight. After volunteering, he expressed a romantic vision about a "leap over the top" of the trenches.[5] At this time, at least, he had a waifish confidence that this great country was inevitably heading down the right path and that the decisions by its leaders were made for the right reasons.

Murphy's biographer Sidney Fine raised the specter that his tough talk about wanting to fight during the World Wars may have arisen partly because he was anxious about his masculinity.[6] In this regard, Theodore Roosevelt's war exploits were a model for young Frank. When Murphy learned of Theodore's death in January 1919, he wrote to his mother that Roosevelt was "strong, virile physically and mentally and always ready to fight even when the odds are against him. I know of no man living who can do as many things so superbly as Mr. Roosevelt could. America has lost her greatest champion."[7]

Theodore Roosevelt quit his post as the assistant secretary of the Navy at the outbreak of war between Spain and the United States in 1898, eager to form his own regiment—quickly termed the Rough Riders.[8] In similar fashion, Murphy had quit his law practice to join the Army. And, as will be seen, Murphy tried to join a combat unit in World War II, even though he was a Supreme Court justice at the time.

Murphy attended the Reserve Officers' Training Camp at Fort Sheridan in Illinois shortly after the United States entered World War I. He was commissioned as a first lieutenant in the infantry and was sent to Cambridge, Massachusetts, for some specialized infantry training under the direction of French officers.[9]

Murphy was treated better than an average soldier, often living in private houses with time to spend at country clubs. While stationed in the United States and later abroad, Murphy made it a practice to attend society events at fine hotels and the homes of the affluent.[10] He developed a taste and enjoyment of the entertainment scene of the "upper crust" of society, something that he would retain throughout his lifetime.

While in the Midwest, it appears that Murphy was a cog in the vast propaganda effort to build up support for the war. President Woodrow Wilson established the Committee on Public Information (CPI) on April 13, 1917, a week after he signed Congress's Declaration of War. George Creel, a veteran newspaperman, was put in charge of the CPI. Creel urged Wilson to create a government agency to coordinate "not propaganda as the Germans defined it, but propaganda in the true sense of the word, meaning the 'propagation of faith.'"[11] Creel launched a league of speakers to roust the citizens of the United States out of their torpor and create excitement for American participation in the Great War on the side of the British and their allies.

Murphy may have been one of Creel's speakers, or he was assigned that role on an ad hoc basis.[12] He gave many speeches, sometimes to large crowds.[13] His overtly political speeches probably would be impermissible today for someone in the armed services. When he spoke in Ann Arbor, Michigan, at a meeting to raise money for the Student Friendship War Fund of the YMCA, Murphy described the Germans as being "like devils who wanted to rule the world" and lambasted German intrigue and deceit.[14]

But he also focused on the uniqueness of America, words that were to echo in speeches and writings throughout his life. In that speech at the YMCA, he described the building as the "place where everyone rubs elbows, . . . where creeds and race differences are leveled, and the seeds of democracy sown," and he predicted that "a new race of men" would return to America from the war.

Yet Murphy was not the perfect war promoter. He wrote a thoughtful essay on his father's legal stationary, seemingly to himself, describing the pros and cons of conscription even as he fully supported the war.[15] The recent conscriptions into the United States Army were modeled on the German way, and Germany itself was "opposed to reason, and contrary to the established custom of this government, a government built on democracy and individualism."

He went on in this letter, "Never in our history have we resorted to conscription to uphold our honor or protect our interests[;] and we stand today the most respected and strongest nation in existence."[16] He ended the essay on a weak note, supporting conscription because, regardless of the conceptual problems, the president of the United States supported conscription.

At Fort Sheridan, Murphy was given an opportunity to exercise his legal talents as an Army lawyer but was eventually removed from his duties because of his tactics. In his last case before his removal, he defended a soldier in a court martial by arguing that "this case is brought to trial only as the result of gross and wanton negligence on the part of those who investigated the case."[17] Here, he cleverly made the trial about the motivations of the leadership. And Murphy prevailed after he established that the trial against his client had been ordered by the division commander.

The brass was not happy. Murphy's comments about the military leadership were found to be "both untrue and highly insubordinate," and he was unceremoniously removed from the military attorney ranks.[18] But he seemed to suffer no other recriminations and remained an officer in the Army.

Many years later, Supreme Court Justice Murphy expressed dismay at the general lack of oversight over military tribunals by civilian courts. He believed military courts lacked due process protections. In *Duncan v. Kahanamoku* in 1946, Murphy filed a concurrence (meaning he agreed with the results of the majority opinion but had his own reasons) stating his view that "abhorrence of military rule is ingrained in our form of government. Those who founded this nation knew full well that the arbitrary power of conviction and punishment for pretended offenses is the hallmark of despotism . . . The Bill of Rights translated that belief into reality by guaranteeing the observance of jury trials and other basic procedural rights foreign to military proceedings."[19]

These skeptical views of military tribunals he expressed as a Supreme Court justice were probably influenced by his experiences as a military lawyer. Although the Supreme Court refused to review military court martials during World War II, Murphy made clear he would have done so.[20] He wanted military justice, with its less rigorous protections for defendants, to be subject to the High Court's review.

On June 26, 1917, the first 14,000 U.S. infantry troops landed in France to begin training for combat. After four years of bloody stalemate along the western front, the entrance of America's well-supplied forces into the conflict marked a major turning point in the war and helped the Allies to victory.

Murphy was one of the two million American soldiers ultimately called to the battlefields of Western Europe. He crossed the Atlantic on the *Vestris*, a passenger steamship that was repurposed for the war. The trip was perilous, with German U-boats lurking.[21] The *Vestris* was subject to at least one torpedo attack during Murphy's voyage. This vessel survived numerous crossings during World War I and returned to service as a passenger steamship, but then sank in 1928, killing more than 100 men, women, and children.

On August 9, 1918, while in France, Murphy learned that he had been nominated by the state Democratic Party to be the candidate for Michigan's Seventh Congressional District. However, he stood no chance of winning in a heavily Republican district and soon withdrew himself from consideration.[22] His father likely had a hand in his nomination. Nevertheless, the fact that he was singled out in this way was a positive sign for his political future.

As an officer, Murphy was initially assigned to coordinate logistics in a non-combat role and expressed impatience at the lack of action. Murphy eventually transferred to a fighting unit, again as an officer. He arrived on the front just hours before the Armistice officially ended the war on November 11 and was not presented with his new command until the next day.[23] So Murphy missed fighting in the war. "Fate" had "dealt" him an "uppercut and called off the war." He added, "Fate must repay me for this."[24]

He might have regretted any "leap over the top" of the trenches if he had known the realities of the war. During World War I, Americans such as Murphy wanting to go overseas lacked knowledge of the misery on the western front, partly because of the successful propaganda campaign of Creel and others. By the time of the American entry into the war, the western front was static, extending through eastern France and up through Belgium to the coast. Those in defensive positions had an almost absurd advantage over the attackers. Well-placed machine gun nests manned by a few men each killed thousands, starting from the moment the soldiers lifted their heads above the trenches to begin their advance.[25]

As it was, 116,708 American military personnel died during World War I from all causes (influenza, combat, and wounds), with 50,000 of them dying during active service.[26] The vast majority of the combat deaths occurred during an eight-month period in 1918.

Following the Armistice, Murphy's division was sent to occupy portions of Germany. There, he finally saw some of the devastation of the war. As recounted by Sidney Fine, in Lorraine, where the American troops were hailed as liberators, Murphy observed men and women rummaging for crusts in the garbage.[27] He would "never forget the scenes of war's devastation." He "passed through Villages [sic], forests, churches even hillsides blown to atoms. Crosses, crosses, crosses everywhere marking graves . . . Horses dead with their four legs pointed straight up mark all the fields where the battles raged."[28]

When traveling through Belgium, Murphy was impressed by the way President Wilson, then at the height of his world influence, was viewed by the common people in Europe. "The reverence the masses of people have for him," Murphy stated, "measures up to adoration . . . The only harsh things we hear about our President comes from our own people."[29] Murphy came away from the experience overseas with the sense that his country was both powerful and necessary to keeping peace in the world.

World War I provided insular Americans from the heartland a chance to escape and demonstrate leadership on an international platform. Harry S Truman was probably the most notable example, entering the armed services as a failed haberdasher and leaving with important connections and a reputation for leader-ship. Murphy's military experience similarly opened doors, lead-ing to his appointment as a federal attorney and the beginning of his political career. His status as a veteran helped give him cred-ibility with the voting public.[30] Veterans' groups lined up behind him in each of his subsequent electoral races.

After the war, Murphy spent significant time with Edward Kemp, whom Murphy met at the University of Michigan. Kemp had been attending Oxford University, and like Murphy, enlisted immediately when the United States entered the war. He became a lieutenant and then a captain in a heavy artillery unit and saw action in the battle of Saint-Mihiel and the Meuse Argonne Sector.[31]

They met up again in England after the fighting ceased. In one letter to his "darling mother" from Europe after World War I, Murphy described seeing a parade attended by the king and queen in front of Buckingham Palace.[32] The soldiers of the Guard's Division, "crack fighters" all, were walking by, and Murphy described being able to peer over the crowd. Murphy wrote that he had hoisted his shorter friend Kemp onto his shoulders so that he would have a similar opportunity to view the pagentry.[33] As described in Murphy's letters to his mother, "Eddie" was not just Murphy's companion but his "pardner."[34]

Their close contact was a recurring pattern in their lives. But for every example of an unusually close interlude, there is usually a counterexample. Here, the two men did not stay together for long. Murphy left Kemp when Murphy decided to attend Trinity College in Ireland. These two men, who had an opportunity to spend time together free from the glare of conservative rural Michigan, chose to part ways.

But at the same time, Murphy seemed in no hurry to meet a woman and settle down. When describing his joy at attending dinners and parties, he complained to his mother about one thing. He said, "Too many women smoke cigarettes in England," and "I don't like it."[35] This can be read as an excuse to not consider a significant population of eligible women, or it could just be a non-smoker expressing his views. In this regard, he did not complain when men smoked. And as will be seen, he continued to enjoy the nightlife and parties his entire life, where smoking would have been commonplace.

Murphy did not second guess the United States' involvement in World War I, but he became reflective of war's moral toll. In a speech he wrote in the 1920s, he asked: "What reaction must the average non-Christian have had to the great war? We need [not] be partisans of either side in order to sense that the amazement which must have stirred the two-thirds of the earth's peoples which are non-Christians, at the sign of Christians lashing Christian with torrents of deadly hate, praying to the same God for slaughtering each other . . . and worst of all, an aftermath of rancor and intolerance fastened on the human race."[36] His speech had echoes of Lincoln's famous words about the North and South during the Civil War during his Second Inaugural Address: "Both read the same Bible and pray to the same God; and each invokes His aid against the other."

Murphy was perceptive in identifying the long-term effects of the Great War, the bitterness it engendered on all sides, the calls for vengeance against foes, real and imagined. While at Trinity College, Murphy criticized British shows of force. The English soldiers paraded down a main street with "bayonets fixed and glistening in the sun. These things were done purely to menace the inhabitants and to give them [a] hint of mastery."[37] This statement likely reflected a certain bias. He was, after all, of Irish Catholic descent. He contrasted this with the policies of the United States after the war: "As victors in Germany. . . we Americans refrained from such unnecessary humiliation . . . Yet Ireland still suffers under it as she has suffered for 3 centuries."[38]

As will be seen, Murphy felt that the United States derived its strength exactly because it exercised compassion toward the vanquished and the weak. And he took it personally when the United States fell short of its ideals. Throughout his life, Murphy combined an obvious political ambition with a kind of an idealism and self-reflection that potentially could have hurt him at the polls. In 1938, his instincts completely failed him, stopping his political rise in its tracks.

Endnotes

1. Murphy's certificate showing his admission to the bar on June 23, 1914, located in the Frank Murphy Museum.
2. Fine, *Detroit Years*, 34.
3. Article fragment, probably from *DFP*, Apr. 23, 1933, FMM.
4. Ibid.
5. Fine, *Detroit Years*, 47.
6. Ibid, 35.
7. Frank Murphy to Mary Murphy, undated letter fragment, FMM.
8. Clay Risen, *The Crowded Hour, Theodore Roosevelt, the Rough Riders, and the Dawn of the American Century* (New York: Scribner, 2019).
9. Howard, *Mr. Justice Murphy*, 14.
10. Fine, *Detroit Years*, 40.
11. George Creel, *Rebel at Large: Recollections of Fifty Crowded Years* (New York: G. P. Putnam's Sons, 1947), 158.
12. *Rebel at Large* was in Murphy's book collection when he died, and it can be found today in Murphy's house in Harbor Beach.
13. Article fragment, *TTH*, June 14, 1918, 6. ("Lieut. Frank Murphy of Camp Custard has been secured to deliver the address of the graduating class at the commencement exercises. Murphy is one of the most fluent speakers in the state and his many friends are pleased to have the opportunity of hearing him before he leaves for France.")
14. Fine, *Detroit Years*, 41.
15. Memorandum or letter on the merits of conscription in Murphy's hand, FMP, reel 91.
16. Ibid. The United States imposed a form of conscription during the Civil War.
17. Fine, *Detroit Years*, 39, 46.
18. Fine, *Detroit Years*, 46.
19. *Duncan v. Kahanamoku*, 327 U.S. 304, 324 (1946) (citing *The Federalist*, no. 83).
20. Joshua E. Kastenberg and Eric Merriam, *In a Time of Total War: The Federal Judiciary and the National Defense* (New York: Routledge, 2016). ("Between 1941 and 1946 the [Supreme] Court never once granted *certiorari* to a Navy or Army court-martial, and only Murphy, Rutledge, and Black ever voted for a grant of review.")
21. World War II–era statement of Murphy's military service, including the ship he crossed the Atlantic on. FMP, reel 92.
22. Fine, *Detroit Years*, 44.
23. Ibid, 48.
24. Ibid.
25. Dan Carlin's podcast, *Blueprint for Armageddon*, contains graphic details of life for a soldier on the western front. Many soldiers were blown to bits, and tens of thousands of bodies were never recovered. The United States, a late-comer to the war, has never recovered the remains of thousands of soldiers. The Tomb of the Unknown Soldier in Arlington, Virginia, was inspired by this galling fact.

26. "American War and Military Operations Casualties: Lists and Statistics," *Congressional Research Service*, Version 24, accessed Apr. 19, 2020, https://fas.org/sgp/crs/natsec/RL32492.pdf.

27. Fine, *Detroit Years*, 48.

28. Ibid.

29. Ibid, 51.

30. Ibid, 57.

31. "Death Takes Edward Kemp," *TTH*, Nov. 23, 1962, 2.

32. Frank Murphy to Mary Murphy, Mar. 22, 1919, FMM.

33. Ibid.

34. Frank Murphy to Mary Murphy, Mar. 12, 1919, FMM.

35. Frank Murphy to Mary Murphy, probably 1919, on American Red Cross paper, FMM.

36. Speech of Frank Murphy, Armory, Detroit, Mar. 29, 1923, FMP, reel 141.

37. Frank Murphy to Mary Murphy, Mar. 22, 1919, FMM.

38. Ibid.

CHAPTER 4

United States Attorney's Office: Enforcing Laws as a Patriotic Duty

In 1919, Murphy was at an inflection point. He had faithfully served his country overseas. Prior to his deployment in Europe, he had gained experience speaking in country club settings throughout the upper Midwest on the merits of the Great War, meeting the rich and powerful. He had proven himself to be an able litigator in military court. Now that the war was over, he had his pick of jobs in the private sector, and he had a rich list of contacts. Detroit was a boomtown. Between 1900 and 1925, Detroit grew from 285,000 to 1.5 million, making it the fourth largest city in the country.[1]

On the political front, the Republicans dominated in Michigan, and Murphy should have joined the party out of expedience, if for no other reason. In many areas, Murphy could have found common cause with those Republicans and felt comfortable inside the Republican big tent. Detroit was a center of scientific management in business and government. Many Republicans were highly educated, lived in cities, and believed that the government could be useful in promoting a better educational system and workplace safety.

Murphy instead chose his own path, both on the job front and politically. From 1919 until 1922, he served as an assistant United

States attorney, a job in the United States Department of Justice.[2] Murphy joined a small office of four attorneys in Detroit, supervised by the United States attorney for the Eastern District of Michigan. At the time, prosecutors were installed at least partly based on their politics, in the tradition of the patronage system. The president was a Democrat and Murphy knew he might be replaced if a Republican were elected as president.[3]

Murphy was successful in his craft, winning all but one of the cases he tried during his stint in the United States attorney's office. His lone defeat came as the result of a hung jury, and in a letter to a friend, he characterized the facts in the case as weak, with none of the witnesses willing to state that the defendant was at the location of the crime. He spoke for four hours in his summation to the jury and modestly noted in a letter to his family that a large crowd had gathered to hear him speak. Under the circumstances, the hung jury outcome was impressive, even if his choice to prosecute this case seemed wrongheaded.

Murphy's oratorical skills were becoming well-known. Described by a federal examiner who was investigating his office as "a young man of considerable ability," Murphy was so effective in addressing a jury that employees in the federal building typically flocked to the courtroom to hear him perform. In describing his performance, one reporter wrote, "The bad man is quickly shorn of his wings and halo, and painted ebony black with horns, cloven feet, and fork-pointed tail thrown in for good measure."[4]

Later, one observer noted a particular trait about Murphy's speaking style: "His voice is so low, even in ordinary conversation, that if it were not exceptionally well placed at times it would be difficult to hear him. In the midst of the most strained arguments between counsel he scarcely raised it. Yet every word he spoke carried to the farthest corner of the crowded courtroom."[5]

Murphy immediately displayed a soft side toward the defendants he prosecuted. In his first appearance as a prosecutor, he recommended clemency for two 19-year-old first offenders, who were to be sentenced for auto theft. "I am glad," Frank wrote home, "that my first performance as prosecutor was to recommend leniency." When a counterfeiter he prosecuted was sentenced to three years in jail, Murphy discovered that his family was destitute and bought them dinner, and then arranged for a charity to look after them.[6]

One focus of his office was on the prosecution of industrialists who had gouged the government during World War I. The subject was especially fraught because the government had enforced wage controls during the war. While low-paid workers were told to sacrifice with artificially low pay, the corporate heads in many instances were getting rich. In his campaign to become a judge in 1922, Murphy summed up his work in the United States attorney's office as a time when he "prosecuted successfully the biggest cases against war profiteers in America."[7] And he was probably correct in his assessment. In perhaps the largest case brought by the federal government anywhere, Assistant United States Attorney Murphy prosecuted a $30 million fraud committed by politically powerful industrialists. He flipped one to testify against the other two, who were convicted and sent to Leavenworth Penitentiary. The third, who turned state's evidence, got off with a fine.[8]

Murphy, as usual, displayed great stamina. For the summation in this case, Murphy spoke for seven hours straight.[9] Two of the defense attorneys died soon after, said to come from the strain of this trial. Following the convictions, Murphy received commendations from Attorney General A. Mitchell Palmer and General John Pershing, the former commander of the United States Expeditionary Forces on the western front during World War I.[10]

Frank later developed a reputation as a fighter against profiteering and graft. As FDR's Attorney General, he attacked with zeal the Democratic city bosses and their manipulation of city budgets and contracts. And then finally, as a Supreme Court justice, in the middle of World War II, he found reason to take one last swipe at the profiteering that took place during World War I (sometimes cases take time to make it to the Supreme Court). In the case of *Bethlehem Steel* in 1942, he stated:

> I do not wish to be understood as expressing approval
> of an arrangement like the one now under review,
> by which a company engaged in doing work for the
> Government in time of grave national peril—or any

other time—is entitled to a profit of 22 percent under contracts involving little or no risk and grossing many millions of dollars. Such an arrangement not only is incompatible with sound principles of public management, but is injurious to public confidence and public morale. The fact that such cases were common during the last war, as evidenced by the circumstances recited in the opinion of the Court, provides no justification to my mind for such a practice then or now. No man or set of men should want to make excessive profits out of the travail of the nation at war, and government officials entrusted with contracting authority, and the Congress bestowing such authority, should be alert to prevent it.[11]

Murphy joined in the majority opinion in *Bethlehem Steel*. But he filed his own concurrence, believing that his brethren did not go far enough in condemning corporate greed during times of national crisis. Such polemical attacks, while arising from his heart, garnered him a reputation as difficult to work with on the High Court. Other justices may have felt the same as he did, but they typically limited their written opinions to foster a consensus. We will return to this point about how Murphy's writing style while a Supreme Court justice hurt his standing and legacy, but for now it is worth noting that he first started down this path in the U.S. attorney's office.

Murphy's largest caseload as an assistant U.S. attorney came because of the passage of the Eighteenth Amendment in 1920, prohibiting the sale and use of alcohol. In the first years of Prohibition, 195 of the 585 criminal cases initiated by his local office out of Detroit were the result of Prohibition violations. Likewise, of the 162 civil cases brought by his office, 60 were initiated under the Prohibition Act.[12]

Murphy enforced the alcohol laws but not with a religious zeal one might expect from a teetotaler fulfilling a promise he made to his mother. A court or jury, looking for an excuse not to convict under the Prohibition laws, could be swayed by a doctor's testimony that the alcohol checked the spread of influenza and pneumonia. In at least one instance, Murphy cooperated with the judge to distribute contraband rum to local doctors.[13]

Alcohol was readily available at the high-society functions that Murphy was now attending.[14] He was pragmatic, hoisting a beer with others during his political campaigns, well-aware that his voters had different opinions than did he about alcohol's merits. But Murphy also knew from his experiences at the starch factory in Harbor Beach about alcohol's ill effects on the working man. For Murphy, alcohol was cynically distributed to these workers to buy their votes and keep them from engaging in constructive endeavors.

Prohibition laws were proving difficult for Murphy's small office to enforce. The ban on liquor led to a rise in organized crime, as the bootlegging of alcohol became more lucrative. Detroit was a nerve center for illegal smuggling. The Detroit River is a natural border with Canada, but it is 70 miles long and only a half a mile wide, providing ample ways to avoid customs control. Murphy would have known the bootleggers' techniques after prosecuting many cases. Small boats with single outboard motors could easily make the crossing. In the winter, members of the Purple Gang based in Detroit crossed the frozen Detroit River to Canada in a lightweight automobile to make the deal.

The executive office for U.S. attorneys in Washington, DC, by now controlled by a Republican president, attempted to get Murphy's Detroit office to do more to enforce Prohibition. At the end of 1921, the Washington office issued a memorandum that the Detroit Attorney General had been neglectful in the institution and prosecution of ongoing cases.[15] Among other things, the study noted that the prosecutor's office had lost the confidence of important federal overseers, including the prohibition director for Michigan and the collector of the internal revenue in Detroit.[16]

This criticism rankled Murphy. Once in elected office, and then as a justice on the Supreme Court, Murphy complained about political pressures for prosecutors to bring convictions at all costs. In 1948, one year before his death, he tried to convince his Supreme Court brethren (unsuccessfully) to exclude evidence obtained by the police in an illegal search. In support, he stated, "Under our legal system the way of the prosecutor is hard, and the need of 'getting results' puts pressure upon prosecutors to indulge in that lawless enforcement of law which produces a vicious circle of disrespect for law."[17]

Murphy was a model of probity as a teetotaler and was duty bound to prosecute crimes in connection with Prohibition. But as stated, he genuinely enjoyed the nightlife and would have known friends and family members who routinely violated the liquor laws. As would become clear, with lifestyle decisions, he had a "live and let live" mentality that was part of his personality. He was never a scold. In fact, he was the best of company in a party where the boys "had a few," without touching anything stronger than ginger ale himself.[18] Later, when Murphy was a judge, he was involved in a particularly tense trial; people were waiting for the jury to conclude its deliberations. In that instance, he allowed his clerk "to unlock an adjoining courtroom so that [Clarence Darrow, one of the attorneys] might have a private space for entertaining; someone purloined a few bottles of scotch." Although Prohibition was theoretically in full swing, the parties then "passed the evening in conversations made exciting by a deepening alcoholic haze."[19]

In this regard, one category of drinkers did not garner his compassion. When drunk drivers were brought before him as a criminal court judge, he tended to throw the book at them. It was not uncommon for him to impose prison time of 30 to 60 days for those caught drinking and driving.[20] These impaired drivers posed a threat to others, and Murphy had little difficulty in dealing harshly with them.

As in other areas of his life, Murphy was able to justify seemingly inconsistent positions. It is one thing to look the other way at some recreational alcohol use. But attending nightclubs during Prohibition represented a clear and present danger to Murphy's reputation. The historian George Chauncey observed that "the proliferation of illegal speakeasies and nightclubs after Prohibition led to the wholesale corruptions of policing agencies, the systematic use of payoffs, and the development of crime syndicates that offered protection from these police."[21] Murphy must have known that his nights out could have exposed him to charges of corruption. Like other powerful figures, he had a supreme confidence that he could not be "bought" and probably was correct with that assessment.

As to speculation that Murphy was gay, one question is why he was never caught by the active Detroit vice squad. As a public figure, how did he avoid a scandal or exposure by political opponents? One possible answer is that he learned the value of discretion during this time of Prohibition, along with other law-abiding citizens who enjoyed the nightlife. As Chauncey said, "All speakeasies—and not just gay speakeasies—had to bribe the authorities and warn their customers to be prepared to hide what they were doing on a moment's notice."[22] What happened in the nightclubs stayed in the nightclubs.

Murphy's other great focus as a prosecutor—besides Prohibition violations—was in connection with the First Red Scare. Attorney General A. Mitchell Palmer was President Wilson's attorney general from 1919 to 1921. Palmer underwent a startling transformation from pacifist to hawk. He was the subject of an unsuccessful assassination attempt and was said to have changed his viewpoint in the area of law and order. In Palmer's attempt to suppress alleged homegrown communists and anarchists, this Quaker was eventually to employ exaggerated rhetoric, illegal search and seizures, unwarranted arrests and detentions, and the deportation of several hundred suspected radicals.

As a federal prosecutor in the Detroit area, Murphy had no qualms about carrying out his duties in connection with the Palmer Raids. "I sympathize deeply with the downtrodden people and people of the lower classes," he wrote to his parents. "I am with them in all of their struggles for social and industrial uplift." At the same time, his basic trust in his government remained. If the attorney general ordered the raids, he assumed a good reason existed. "I have no sympathy for the foreigner who comes to this country and conspires to overthrow the government,"[23] Murphy continued.

He witnessed the consequences of the raids. In Detroit, 800 men were imprisoned for three to six days in "a dark, windowless, narrow corridor running around the big central areaway of the city's antiquated Federal Building; they slept on the bare stone floor at night. . . they were compelled to stand in long lines for access to the solitary drinking fountain and the one toilet."[24] As further described in the *Nation* at the time, "All this time there was a state approaching chaos in the offices of the Department of Justice. . . . Frantic wives and children haunted the lower halls in the Federal Building, hoping to catch a glimpse of their men through the narrow apertures of the top-floor corridor railings." The crime of these 800 men was that they were affiliated with the House of the Masses, the headquarters of the Communist Party in Detroit. None of the men were served with a warrant. Some were arrested only because they were in a café on the first floor of building.

Murphy said nothing, publicly at least, to protest these appalling conditions. Here the Republicans were the ones who spoke up. The mayor of Detroit in 1920 was the Republican James Couzens, later to be a United States senator for the state of Michigan. In contrast to the Democratic administration, Couzens complained bitterly about the condition of these imprisoned men.[25]

Murphy was asked to run for Congress again in 1920 by the party bosses. This time he agreed, while maintaining his full caseload as an assistant United States attorney. But the Democratic Party's candidates were generally trounced in 1920. This was the election when a young FDR was part of the losing Democratic Party ticket for the presidency. As for Murphy, he received fewer than one-fourth the votes of his Republican adversary.[26] The country had enough of foreign intervention and Wilson's idealism. Many believed that the League of Nations, championed by the Democrats, would compromise United States sovereignty. People also wanted a return to the certainty that many believed the Republicans brought in running the country's economy.

Murphy was not that broken up by his loss. About a week later, he gave a "snappy" speech at a huge Michigan football rally in Ann Arbor.[27] He had developed a deep connection to this institution and was a favorite pep rally speaker at Michigan's Hill Auditorium. The *Michiganensian* labeled him the "verbal tornado" of Michigan.[28] He was also a desired speaker at political events in Detroit.[29] The *Detroit Times* described him as "young, fiery, upstanding" and the "class of the younger Democrats."[30]

He had a gift for taking over a room when he spoke. But with the new Republican president and Murphy's strong association with Democratic politics, Murphy's time as a federal prosecutor was drawing to a close.

Endnotes

1. Howard, *Mr. Justice Murphy*, 17.
2. Murphy referred in a speech in 1939 to being in the "district attorney's office" in Detroit "working with the representatives of the United States Government and the FBI in its early days." The district attorney's office is a state (and not a federal) agency. He may have mislabeled the office he worked for.
3. This system has changed. Line attorneys at the Department of Justice are apolitical and discharge their duties without regard to which president is in office. In modern times, only the United States attorneys are expected to tender their resignations when a new president comes in.
4. Fine, *Detroit Years*, 59; "Two Men, Very Much Alike Are Alfred J. Murphy and Frank Murphy," *Detroit Justice*, 8, FMP, reel 141 ("Bad men feared Frank Murphy the District Attorney, and well they might"); FMP, reel 95 (*Detroit Justice* article is located here).
5. Haldeman-Julius, *Clarence Darrow's Two Greatest Trials*, 53.
6. Fine, *Detroit Years*, 60.
7. Ibid, 64.
8. "Character of Michigan's 'Labor Governor' Analyzed," *TTH*, June 2, 1937, 5.
9. "Before Death Took Toll of Murphy Family," from "Murphy Souvenir Section" of newspaper, probably from *DFP*, Apr. 23, 1933, FMM.
10. Ibid. ("Colonel Felder, chief counsel for the defense, publicly congratulated the young prosecutor on his masterly argument . . . A. Mitchell Palmer, then United States Attorney General, and General Pershing both extended official commendations to Murphy.")
11. *United States v. Bethlehem Steel Corp.*, 315 U.S. 289, 310 (1942).
12. Fine, *Detroit Years*, 59.
13. "U.S. to Supply Liquor Monday," *DFP*, Jan. 21, 1920. ("The decision to release the whisky [to influenza and pneumonia patients], several thousand quarters of which is entrusted in the care of the marshal, was reached Friday afternoon at a conference between Robert Grogan, Chief Deputy United States Marshal, Judge Arthur J. Tuttle of the federal court, Frank Murphy, Assistant United States Attorney, and Dr. George McKean, president of the Wayne County Medical association, following a telegram from United States Attorney General A. Mitchell Palmer.")
14. "Before Death Took Toll of Murphy Family," from "Murphy Souvenir Section" of newspaper, probably from *DFP*, Apr. 23, 1933, FMM (explaining that although he did not drink, he did not complain when others did so).
15. Fine, *Detroit Years*, 69.

16.   Ibid, 69. The Anti-Saloon League was a private organization. That advocacy group had spearheaded the Prohibition drive. The report stated that the Detroit Attorney General's office was neglectful in not including this organization in its updates.

17.   *Wolf v. Colorado*, 338 U.S. 25 (1949). The Supreme Court eventually did shut the door to the admission of this kind of evidence. *Mapp v. Ohio*, 367 U.S. 643 (1961), was a landmark case in criminal procedure that overruled *Wolf*. In *Mapp*, the United States Supreme Court decided that evidence obtained in violation of the Fourth Amendment, which protects against "unreasonable searches and seizures," could not be used in state court proceedings. Previously, the amendment was held to apply only in federal proceedings.

18.   "Before Death Took Toll of Murphy Family," from "Murphy Souvenir Section" of newspaper, probably from *DFP*, Apr. 23, 1933, FMM.

19.   Boyle, *Arc of Justice*, 298.

20.   "Murphy Fines Three Drunken Motorists," *DFP*, Mar. 15, 1925, 13.

21.   Chauncey, *Gay New York*, 306.

22.   Ibid.

23.   Fine, *Detroit Years*, 66.

24.   Frederick R. Barkley, "Jailing Radicals in Detroit," *The Nation* 110, no. 2848 (1920): 16.

25.   Robert W. Dunn, ed., *The Palmer Raids* (New York: Labor Research Association, 1948), 33, accessed on May 30 2020, https://archive.org/details/ThePalmerRaids/page/n21/mode/2up?q=murphy; Fine, *Detroit Years*, 68–69.

26.   The vote tallies were provided in the *Lansing State Journal*, Dec. 6, 1920, 10.

27.   "[University of] Michigan Must Win," *DFP*, Nov. 13, 1920, 19.

28.   The 1917 *Michiganensian*, 53.

29.   "Detroit Man to Speak," *BCE*, Mar. 16, 1920, 1.

30.   Article fragment, *IDG*, Aug. 31, 1920, 1 (listing Frank Murphy as a candidate).

CHAPTER 5

Private Practice as a Path to Politics

For a brief time after his stint in the United States attorney's office, Murphy entered private legal practice. He almost immediately had more clients than he could handle. And he also now had a girlfriend, Hester Everard. Murphy had met her when, as a soldier in the United States Army, he was sent to Detroit in 1918 to speak at a Liberty Loan drive.[1] As previously noted, Murphy gave speeches to try to build enthusiasm for the war, and the purchase of war bonds was touted as a patriotic duty. As he toured, he mingled with the elite and their eligible daughters.

Hester was the daughter of a president of a pulp and paper company in Detroit. For the next 10 years, they maintained a relationship of mismatched expectations. His letters to her during that period ran hot and cold but filled her with hope that he might choose her as a wife. At one point after having known her for five years, he said that he had "never known any girl so good, so unselfish, and so lovely and gracious about all things."[2]

But at times his letters seemed to be designed to drive her away. In one, he stated, "Cleverness in business and [the] professions [are] almost completely without virtue. There are many men in Detroit who are financial successes who are total losses in character, intellect and lofty purpose. We contribute nothing by the silly effort that the crowds recognize as success. It is all rot."[3]

Hester must have wondered how to react to the comments of a young man whom she assumed was poised to enter together with her the upper crust of Detroit business circles. When she had finally waited enough for the never-to-come marriage offer and informed him she was now moving on, he expressed his regret, stating that his remedy was returning to "home and mother."[4] This response may have provided her with some comfort that she had made the right choice in abandoning him.

As Murphy sailed to the Philippines in June 1933 to assume a political position, well after Hester had married, he wrote to her that he would trade everything "if once more I could go back on the slope of a gentle hill at Gull Lake [in southwestern Michigan], there in the perfume of June with you reading verses."[5] This letter was presumptuous, and a bit preposterous, given her long wait for him to commit and her subsequent marriage.

His letters to his romantic partners often referred to his mother, as above, and to other older women. In 1934, he was corresponding with Ann Parker (Murphy wrote extensively to at least three women with the first name of Ann: Ann Harding, Ann Parker, and Ann Walker). Parker was the daughter of one of his aides while he was the governor general in the Philippines and one of many young women in Murphy's orbit throughout the years.

After first inquiring of her father's health, Murphy wrote, "Only one girl writes to me letters sweet as yours—that is your mother. Her letters are near enough in composition, spirit and tone to my own mother's."[6] Later, he described to his young admirer a boring dinner he would have to attend: "You know who I will be thinking of and longing for." Presumably, he meant young Ann. But given his comments about her mother in that same letter, he might have been more specific about the subject of his desire. He signed off with "Love," but probably not in the way Ann hoped, such as when he wrote, "God keep and love you my beloved Ann."

In her book *Mom: The Transformation of Motherhood in Modern America*, Professor Rebecca Jo Plant described how attitudes about mother-child relationships changed from the beginning of the twentieth century. She noted that during World War I, *Stars and Stripes* newspaper published poems by soldiers about mothers that read like odes to lovers. She called this a kind of "pre-Freudian sensibility, in which the expression of passionate and romantic desires had a purview beyond the heterosexual couple." But "romanticized depictions of mother-son relationships that earlier seemed innocuous or laudable would be regarded as disturbing and unnatural by the mid-twentieth century."[7]

Murphy's letters romanticizing women of his mother's generation must be seen at least partly in the context of its time. Dwight Eisenhower, during his West Point years prior to World War I, wrote a letter to a girlfriend asking her "to believe in me and trust me as you would your dad."[8] Murphy and Eisenhower were, in part, seeking to convey deference and respect to the women's parents.

The politically ambitious Murphy now involved himself in high-profile legal matters that seemed designed to gain the favor of important constituencies. In one case, he represented Sarah Elizabeth Lewen, the owner of the exclusive Madame LaGrande millinery shop in Detroit. Lewen had been found guilty in 1921 of the murder of a six-year-old boy.[9]

The trial took place before the Detroit Recorder's Office Judge William Heston, a burly former All-America football player in college. During the trial, Heston had allowed testimony about Lewen's overall character, generating great anger among women's groups. Socially prominent clubwomen in Detroit believed Lewen had been framed and bullied. They secured the aid of Murphy in appealing Judge Heston's decision to the Michigan Supreme Court.[10]

Murphy expertly handled the appeal, focusing on the innuendo regarding Lewen. Since Lewen had not produced a witness to vouch for her character, as the state prosecutors had argued, she had no character. Murphy astutely argued that the statements were irrelevant as to whether she committed the murder.[11]

The appeals court agreed with Murphy and rebuked Judge Heston for allowing the statements about Lewen's character to be considered by the jury. The *Lewen* case established Murphy as a crusader and won him the trust of women's groups, which were becoming increasingly active in social and political causes. His unmistakable charm no doubt helped. He would have their support in future runs for office.

His reputation as an evangelical helping the dispossessed and despised grew with time. In 1923, also while he was in private practice, Murphy helped secure the readmission to the Detroit Bar of an attorney who had refused to register for the draft during World War I. Murphy, a war veteran, nevertheless respected the attorney's position, stating, "We punish those who[m] frequently we should reward for courage and honesty . . . In my opinion, the profession needs men who are willing to suffer for their conscience. Also, 10 years hence we may say he was right about the war."[12]

The attorney Murphy helped in this instance was Maurice Sugar, a fellow Michigan law graduate. As Sugar told it, "I was walking down Woodward Avenue when I ran into an old legal adversary, Frank Murphy."[13] The two had clashed as opposing counsel when Murphy, for a brief time, represented the Employers Association.[14]

Murphy took Sugar's case on the spot. He was tenacious as always in trying to reinstate Sugar, as a licensed attorney, first convincing a judge to order the executive committee of the Detroit Bar—"the very body, little changed, that had disbarred him in the first place"—to reconsider the case.[15] Then Murphy cajoled the bar to reinstate Sugar. As a Sugar biographer stated approvingly, "Frank Murphy let his thirst for justice outweigh his political fears and got away with it. It would not be the last time."[16] Murphy refused any payment from Sugar. The two men's lives would later intersect when Murphy was governor of Michigan and Sugar was legal counsel for workers engaging in sit-down strikes in 1937. Sugar's respect for Murphy helped push him toward compromise during this great confrontation between management and unions that many predicted would end in violence. These types of long-term relationships, hidden from the historical narrative, sometimes were decisive in altering behavior.

One more point about Murphy's representation of Sugar should be emphasized. Murphy was running for a criminal judge position at the time, and his open and public representation of a "draft dodger" and suspected communist did not seem to enter into his calculations in taking on the case. Nor did the fact that he personally disagreed with Sugar's stance regarding World War I.

Murphy continued throughout his life to support those unwilling to serve in the military for religious or ethical reasons. During World War II, at the same time he was badgering the top Army brass to allow him to join a combat unit, he wrote opinions as a Supreme Court justice supporting the right of the Jehovah's Witnesses to avoid military service on religious grounds. In *Falbo v. United States*, his High Court colleagues upheld a conviction and prison sentence for a Jehovah's Witness minister who refused to report for civilian service, an alternative for those who did not wish to serve in the Army.[17] Murphy was the only justice to dissent on the nine-member court. He declared, "The law knows no finer hour than when it cuts through formal concepts and transitory emotions to protect unpopular citizens against discrimination and persecution."[18]

At about this time, Murphy met two men crucial to his later political successes. The first was Father Charles Coughlin, who was building a Catholic parish in Royal Oak about 12 miles outside of Detroit. Coughlin might have remained an unremarkable and isolated priest, and a private friend of Murphy, if not for the new medium of radio. Commercial radio was less than six years old when Coughlin began broadcasting in 1926. He gained early popularity when he denounced the Ku Klux Klan (KKK), which had been growing in strength in reaction to the rush of largely Catholic and Jewish immigrants to America. The KKK was also capitalizing on the release of D.W. Griffith's film *The Birth of a Nation*.

Coughlin created a vast national radio following in the 1930s. He was initially supportive of FDR's economic policies, coining the popular phrase "Roosevelt or Ruin." As will be seen, Coughlin pushed FDR to appoint Catholics, and Murphy was a direct beneficiary of Coughlin's success.

Coughlin, however, soon turned harshly critical of the New Deal and adopted an ugly anti-Semitic tone with his speeches. After meeting with FDR in 1935, Coughlin stated that Roosevelt "either willingly or unwillingly determined that the nation shall be a country of, by and for bankers." Republicans were in on the plot, as well as "the Tugwells, the Frankfurters and the rest of the Jews who surround him."[19] Vehemently anti-communist (as were many in the Catholic Church), in the late 1930s, Coughlin expressed support for some of the fascist policies of Adolf Hitler, Benito Mussolini, and Emperor Hirohito of Japan.

As will be seen, Murphy's loyalty to President Roosevelt was sacrosanct and well-known. When push came to shove, Murphy chose the president over Father Coughlin. Further, Michigan Jews were generally strong supporters of Murphy, as reflected in election returns, and Murphy later led several organizations focused on saving European Jews during World War II. Yet even in spite of their vast differences, Murphy and Coughlin maintained their friendship—so much so that Murphy's family asked Coughlin to give a eulogy at Murphy's funeral in 1949. Joseph Kennedy, another strong Catholic supporter of FDR, and the father of the future president, also remarked that he kept his friendship with Coughlin even after they split politically. For his part, FDR tried to use their friendship to his advantage. On one occasion, he told Joseph Kennedy to consult with Murphy about Coughlin and decide on a strategy for dealing with him. They both took at least one trip together to speak to Coughlin.

The second important connection developed by Murphy during this formative post–World War I period was with Walter Chrysler. Murphy met the family through a roommate, Bryon Foy. The two men lived together in Detroit before Foy married Chrysler's daughter. Murphy was the best man at Foy's wedding to Walter Chrysler's daughter Thelma and was later the godfather of their daughter Joan Foy.[20] In 1928, Chrysler offered Murphy the opportunity to join the Chrysler Corporation as legal counsel. Although Murphy refused, he received a sizable retainer fee from Chrysler at the beginning of 1929.[21] Murphy was serving as a criminal court judge by the time he received his retainer from Chrysler. A Michigan state statute did not allow a judge to engage in private practice or to "be in any way connected with any attorney or firm of attorneys engaged in such practice."[22] According to Fine, "Murphy was clearly violating the law in accepting a retainer from the Chrysler firm."[23] This was not just a theoretical conflict. As a criminal court judge, Murphy decided disputes between unions and car companies while holding stakes in those companies.

Notwithstanding his public persona of a man of great integrity, Murphy violated the public trust on this and other occasions. During the General Motors (GM) strike of 1937, Murphy as governor of Michigan held stock in GM.[24] The car company and the United Auto Workers (UAW) union negotiators likely did not know about his financial position (the funds were in a stock broker's account).[25] Then as a Supreme Court justice, Murphy employed a publicist and accepted money and gifts in exchange for speeches to various groups.[26]

By receiving money from the Detroit elite and moneyed interests (and as previously noted, by attending their parties with illegal alcohol), Murphy was being quite conventional—a politician who liked fancy, shiny objects and who believed his personal habits would not affect his ability to work for the less privileged. And, whatever the merits of this cavalier attitude, it does appear that Murphy never sold out the working man. As for Chrysler, their personal relationship would play a key role in resolving the great sit-down strikes in 1937, which included Chrysler factories.

But there is little question that Murphy could have made a fortune in private legal practice if that had been the life he had chosen for himself. In addition to his connections to Walter Chrysler and the Midwest country-club set, he had the good fortune of being in the epicenter of United States industrial might from his perch in Detroit. In this way, at least, he was sincere in devoting his life to public service.

Murphy wasn't to prove to be particularly careful with his money. He was generous with his family, and this led to a lack of savings later in his life. Although it is not clear why he felt this was important to do, he sent money home to his parents when he was serving in the Army in Europe. In a letter to his mother, he asked if his father had received the money he sent: "Was he glad to get the $500 I sent the other day? I want you two to spend every cent of it."[27] Murphy later provided support to his brother George and sister Marguerite as well as their families. Although Murphy earned significant income throughout his lifetime, he died with a minimal estate because of his profligate spending on those close to him and on himself.

Murphy was accustomed to a lavish lifestyle, even within the limitations he set. He enjoyed attending extravagant parties as a young man and later allowed the society women of Palm Beach and Washington, DC, to throw large fetes in his honor. While on assignment for FDR in the Philippines, he lived in a palace, even while presenting himself in the press as a "Lawrence of Arabia"–type figure, utterly uninterested in material objects.[28] He was able to hide his inclinations to live well from the public.

Endnotes

1. Fine, *The Detroit Years*, 86–89.
2. Ibid, 87.
3. Ibid, 89.
4. Ibid, 87.
5. Ibid, 88–89.
6. Frank Murphy to Ann Parker, July 30, 1934, from Manila, FMP, reel 148.
7. Plant, *Mom*, 91.
8. Newton, *Eisenhower*, 16.
9. "Asked to Review Case of Alleged Son Killer," *BCE*, Mar. 3, 1922, 2.
10. Sara Elizabeth Lewen was tried again and found guilty. "Mrs. Lewen Found Guilty for 2nd Time," *DFP*, July 8, 1924, 1. By now, Murphy was a criminal court judge and was no longer involved with the case.
11. Fine, *The Detroit Years*, 78.
12. Ibid.
13. Johnson, *Maurice Sugar*, 98.
14. Ibid, 55.
15. Ibid, 98.
16. Ibid, 99.
17. *Falbo v. United States*, 320 U.S. 549 (1944).
18. Ibid at 560–561.

19. Fine, *New Deal Years*, 222. Father Coughlin supported the Christian Front, an anti-Semitic and pro-Nazi organization active from about 1938 until the United States entered World War II. Under the banner of anti-communism, it encouraged boycotts of Jewish merchants, used the slogan "Buy Christian," and published the Christian Index, a directory of non-Jewish merchants in part of New York City.

20. Fine, *Detroit Years*, 84.

21. Ibid, 193–194.

22. Ibid, 194.

23. Ibid.

24. James M. Rubenstein, *Making and Selling Cars: Innovation and Change in the U.S. Automotive Industry* (Baltimore: Johns Hopkins University Press, 2001), 145. (Professor Rubenstein has stated that Murphy "owned GM stock worth more than $100,000, which he sold on Jan. 18, a week after intervening in the strike.") This amount seems exaggerated. *See* Fine, *Washington Years*, 10. ("A few days after his nomination [as Attorney General], Murphy sold 2,500 shares of GM stock he had purchased in 1938 and realized a capital gain of more than $23,000.")

25. Fine, *New Deal Years*, 301.

26. Thomas Brady to Eleanor Bumgardner, FMP, reel 87. (Brady reported that "the Justice was so well received in Philadelphia . . . Attached please find two checks re: the Philadelphia engagement, one made payable to Justice Murphy, and the other made to your order for the expenses.")

27. Frank Murphy to Mary Murphy, about 1919, FMM.

28. "Character of Michigan's 'Labor Governor' Analyzed," *TTH*, June 2, 1937.

CHAPTER 6

Reformer on the Criminal Court Bench

In 1922, Murphy announced his run for the Recorder's Office, the official name for Detroit's criminal court. Judges elected to the Recorder's Office were officially non-partisan, but the candidates often advertised their political affiliations. The criminal court was at the time dominated by pro-business judges who consistently ruled in favor of corporations in labor disputes, often jailing striking workers under criminal trespassing statutes. Today, the idea that workers can stand outside a factory and picket is well established, but in the 1920s, these types of activities were prosecuted as violations of the property rights of the factory owners.

Republican progressives had restructured the criminal court in conjunction with a new Detroit City Charter in 1918, adding more judges. The reformers' intentions were good. They believed that more judges would lead to more time for individualized justice. Progressives generally wanted the trial-level courts to rehabilitate, "to make productive citizens of juvenile delinquents, to administer new state programs of aid to mother-headed families, to institutionalize hereditary mental defectives, and, not least, to compel errant husbands to support their families."[1]

The law of unintended consequences applied. In practice, this increase in the number of judges did not mean rehabilitation. The Detroit business interests brought their resources to the fore, and their slates of candidates tended to win. In practice, more judges meant that they had more time to consider punishments for petty crimes. They also had time to decide workplace-related cases. The fortified bench of "law and order" judges imposed strict penalties for petty offenses and treated worker protests at work as criminal or civil trespass and not as legitimate forms of free speech.

In the 1920s, the national Democratic and Republican Parties were in flux. The Republicans were transitioning from their "big tent" philosophy to a more limited focus, concentrating on the vote of businessmen and Americans who feared the immigrant tide. But they still had certain institutional advantages over the Democrats. Most notably, the rural farmers voted for the Republican Party, grateful for assistance during prior economic downturns. And it was still the party of Abraham Lincoln. "The Republican Party is the ship and all else is the sea around us," Frederick Douglass said after the Civil War. The Grand Old Party was still the party for Black people, even after major betrayals, the abandonment of Reconstruction, and the failure to strongly oppose Jim Crow in the South.[2]

The Democratic Party consisted of urban ethnic bosses and Southern segregationists. But encouragingly, this party was increasingly attracting upper-class progressives who would have been Republicans a generation before. To these educated technocrats, public officials should actively work in the public's interest.[3] The modern state, with its ability to concentrate and control resources, was starting to emerge at the expense of local institutions, towns, religious communities, and customs. The government was seen as an equalizer against companies seeking to profit from technologies that advanced the public good, and municipalities began supplying fresh water and electricity at regulated prices.

Within the progressive movement, fissures existed. Some were more focused on improving the morals of the lower class. Prohibition was the prime example of this paternalistic approach. These crusaders believed that banning alcohol would allow working people to pursue more meaningful lives.

Other progressives had more faith in the teeming masses and believed that with proper education and guidance, they could become citizens in the fullest sense, participating in voting and enjoying upward mobility. As would become clear, Murphy was in this latter category.

On the campaign trail for the job of criminal court judge, Murphy focused on winning the support of factory workers and ethnic immigrant groups. He proved to be creative and insightful in attracting their loyalty by identifying issues of common concern. For example, he argued that the sheer number of arrests in Detroit was inherently unfair to the poor. The destitute and workers agitating for better working conditions were being arrested as a harassment technique, borne out by the fact that the actual conviction rate was much lower than the arrest rate. He argued that the poor needed a criminal court judge who understood their plight. Since he favored "evenness" in the application of the law, he urged the enactment of a law providing a public defender for those defendants unable to afford a lawyer, an idea he would support for the rest of his political career.[4]

Murphy, with his Catholic and Irish background, was an attractive candidate for the various ethnic groups, but he took no chances. He made sure that the Polish, Greek, Swiss, and other ethnic organizations knew about him. In Murphy's personal papers stored at the University of Michigan are his campaign pamphlets from this first electoral race in the various languages of the immigrants of Detroit.[5]

He was assisted in his election bid by the ham-handed approach of the Detroit Republicans, who in the end ceded the immigrant vote to the Democrats. In this respect, a backlash against the nation's new arrivals was sweeping the country, which culminated just two years later in national legislation that banned almost all new immigration.[6] But as is the case today, a divide existed between rural and urban areas on the efficacy of immigration. Detroit had about 465,000 inhabitants as of 1910; 150,000 were of foreign birth. More than 20 percent of those over the age of 10 were unable to speak English.[7] With this mix of immigrants all around him, America was a grand new experiment and Murphy wholeheartedly courted their votes.

In the end, Murphy received the most votes of any candidate and was the youngest person ever elected to the Recorder's Court.[8] As was predictable, he fared poorly in wards with native-born whites. He did the worst in Ward 4, a local in which fewer than 1 percent of the inhabitants were Black and nearly 78 percent were native-born whites.

Still, Murphy had some support from establishment figures. Murphy had ranked fifth among the 19 judicial candidates, and ahead of 3 of the sitting judges, in a pre-election poll conducted by the Detroit Bar Association.[9] His Army service helped him, as he drew the support of Legionnaires and various veteran groups. On the eve of the election in 1923, Murphy was the keynote speaker and addressed a raucous crowd of 4,500 veterans at Detroit's Light Guard Armory.[10]

And he had the support of women. Here, his work on the Lewen case paid dividends. Prominent Detroit clubwomen disliked the current crop of criminal court judges.[11] One of those judges they opposed was Judge William Heston, the one who presided over the Lewen murder case and had allowed in the testimony as to Lewen's bad character. These powerful women's organizations wanted this judge removed and threw their support behind Murphy.[12]

Murphy's desire to help women seemed sincere. Writing to his father before the passage of the Nineteenth Amendment, Murphy explained his support of the amendment in florid terms. The inability of women to vote was compared to "taxation without representation."[13] With the recent passage of that amendment, women had the vote on a national level, energizing them to act in local elections as well.[14]

The Detroit press tended to support the establishment figures, as their advertising dollars came from industrial and business concerns. This economic reality would lead to coverage that was biased, emphasizing any violence from the worker side during labor disputes, downplaying management-directed violence, and highlighting immigrant involvement in strikes.

However, this bad coverage was not universally true. Detroit had a new publication in 1923. The *Detroit Times* latched on to Murphy and used cartoons, editorials, and news columns to feature him. Murphy had cemented his relationship with the *Detroit Times* through his connection to Joseph Mulcahy, who had come to Detroit in 1921 to edit the newspaper after having served as managing editor of the *New York Evening Journal-American*. Mulcahy met Murphy at society functions and was impressed with the young attorney.[15] They were also both Irish American and both had a shock of red hair.

Mulcahy benefited from Murphy's political success as the *Times* trumpeted the victory. His newspaper became known in Detroit as one that promoted the Democratic Party's point of view. Following Murphy's victory in the Probate Court elections, the *Times* happily observed that the defeated interests included "Big Business," the Michigan Manufacturers' Association, and its rival newspaper, the *Detroit News*.[16]

During his campaign for the municipal criminal judge position in 1923, Murphy reminded the press of his youthfulness and good habits. He never drank or smoked, and his one indulgence, at least according to him, was an occasional insatiable urge for chocolate ice cream. He loved to ride horses and soon had a favorite named "Big Steve," which he rode with his companion Perry Meyers of Detroit's mounted police.[17]

His horse-riding exploits alienated him from certain colleagues later in his career. By 1939, Robert Jackson was the solicitor general (the Department of Justice attorney who makes arguments before the Supreme Court) and answerable to Murphy, then the Attorney General of the United States. Jackson complained that he could not secure a meeting with Murphy to discuss important cases, because Murphy was "merrily" horseback riding with young women when he should have been meeting with Jackson.[18]

But notwithstanding his attempts to project good health, soon after the election, Murphy became sick and entered a hospital in Detroit for the treatment of a sinus infection. He underwent two operations and was critically ill for a time. These debilitating illnesses, particularly after elections or important appointments, were to occur throughout Murphy's life. During Murphy's stint as Michigan governor, he admitted to missing 72 days during 1937, which he attributed to a combination of illnesses and obligations in Washington. By the time he was governor, he was in great demand as a national speaker and was also locked in around-the-clock meetings to resolve labor disputes roiling his state and the country.[19] Given his manic schedule, it appears he worked himself to sickness several times throughout his career. At one point, he offered to return a portion of his salary as Michigan governor when his rival complained about the number of days on the job he missed due to sickness.[20]

In January 1924, Murphy officially took the bench as a criminal court judge in Detroit. In the next five years, he paid his dues, handling routine matters, reviewing criminal complaints, issuing search warrants, convening grand juries, and holding trials for crimes of all sizes, from minor infractions to murder. One admirer wrote to him in broken English, "I [have] taken notice to the way treat peoples, white and black. . . it is time to take notice and say, there is still justice in the courts."[21]

In those same five years, Murphy effectively leveraged his position on this local court to gain a national profile. He did this by taking a clear side on two matters of growing importance in a rapidly industrializing and urbanizing country.

The first was in connection with the simmering disputes between labor and management playing out in local criminal courts such as the ones in Detroit. There, Murphy exercised his discretion to help workers, often immigrants, who were mistreated at work and heretofore had few allies in the court system. In the process, he gained a reputation as champion of the working man.

As already described, criminal court judges tended to side with management in labor disputes. Workers protested their wages and poor working conditions by picketing, which came to be interpreted under the law as infringements on the property rights of the owners and punishable as trespassing. Whenever fights broke out between management, private security forces, and union members, the union members were usually found to be guilty for provoking the fights.

Murphy had run for the judgeship with the promise that he would treat these labor disputes in a more even-handed way. He immediately signaled that he would follow through with his campaign pledge. In one early case, two unionists were brought before

Murphy on assault charges stemming from a clash between metal polishers' union pickets and company agents during a strike. Murphy remarked from the bench that he knew from experience that employers often charged workers with violence in labor disputes even when management was responsible for provoking the workers. He accused the prosecutor's office of acting in a biased manner, creating the impression that "the state is on the side of the employers."[22] This seemed to have had an effect on the prosecutor's office, which then brought an action against management for "felonious assault."[23] The Detroit Federation of Labor (DFL) stated in response that "labor men in general are pleased to have a judge with such a clear vision and the courage to state his view upon the bench."[24]

In addition to his duties as a judge, Murphy often sat as an arbitrator in labor disputes, and here too he made his mark as a pro-union judge. In one such arbitration, a railroad worker had been fired based on the secret testimony of five unnamed inspectors of the department's intelligence division that he had been derelict in his duties. The union had alleged that this was a pretext and had been fired because of his union activity.

The arbitration panel ruled in favor of the worker by a vote of two to one. Murphy wrote the opinion for the arbitration panel and stated that unsworn and unsigned complaints by the department's intelligence division had no probative value.[25] The union was delighted with the decision and its implied criticism of the "spy system" of the railways.[26] The union congratulated Murphy on "the wonderful service you rendered for mankind."[27] Further impressing the union, Murphy refused to accept the fee that the railway and union were to jointly pay the arbitrators.

Murphy's decision in 1926 in the *Detroit Stereotypers' Union No. 9 v. Detroit Free Press and Detroit Times* was even more influential with labor. A *stereotype* is a well-known word, but its origin refers to a long disused process. A stereotype was a solid plate of metal that was created from a cast of papier-mâché or plaster mold. That metal sheet was then used to print pages of books or newspapers. Stereotypers had their own unions.

One issue in this case was whether the union salaries should be tied to the financial health of the newspaper. Murphy found that the salaries should indeed be linked to the company's well-being, since it would be "unfair and unsound" to deny the wage earner "the opportunity of sharing in the results of the increased production and prosperity he helped to bring about." Murphy went further, stating that the worker was entitled to receive a living wage, which he defined as a wage that would permit the recipient "through frugality" to "earn sufficient to develop within reasonable limits his physical, spiritual, moral, and intellectual faculties, and in addition be able to set aside a reserve to provide for accident, old age, idleness, and misfortune."[28] A "careful study" revealed that a salary of $8 dollars a day, or $2,496 in a year consisting of 312 working days, falls short of what was necessary for a "comfortable and decent" support of a stereotyper's family living in Detroit.

In coming up with a proposed minimum wage for the stereotypers, Murphy's decision followed the guidelines promulgated by the Executive Counsel of the American Federation of Labor (AFL) only a few months before.[29] The stereotypers presented Murphy with a gold wristwatch after his decision.[30] The DFL's president Frank X. Martel was so taken with Murphy's decision that he tried to get Murphy to run for mayor of Detroit in both 1927 and 1929, offers that Murphy turned down.

Martel remained a key ally of Murphy's through the years, keeping up a steady stream of letters to Murphy asking him to run for statewide office in Michigan as Murphy rose in prominence. In 1934, while Murphy was stationed in the Philippines as an FDR appointee, Martel encouraged him to return to Michigan to run for senator or governor.[31] By 1936, Martel had grown more insistent, stating, "You are the only man that can return the Democratic Party to power in Michigan."[32] Later, Murphy failed to support Martel's AFL in its attempts to unionize auto plants, siding instead with the Congress of Industrial Organizations (CIO) and its UAW, but Martel did not hold this against Murphy. He subsequently supported an attempt by Murphy to unite the AFL and CIO during Murphy's stint as governor of Michigan.[33] As late as 1948, one year before Murphy's death, Martel can be seen at a labor dinner in Detroit, sitting between Murphy and President Truman.

Murphy's opinion on the minimum wage would be considered judicial overreach today, as the minimum wage is set by the federal and state governments and not by the courts. But his decision was even more radical at the time. In another case in 1923, just three years before Murphy's decision, the United States Supreme Court, the highest court in the land, held that states could not set minimum wage laws at all, on the rationale that such a worker protection would impede the freedom of contract between workers and their employers.[34] If legislatures had no power to set minimum wages under binding United States Supreme Court precedent, then certainly a local judge sitting on an arbitration panel had no right, especially as he set specific dollar amounts based on his own analysis of a living wage.[35] Murphy's decision was not appealed and so his statements about the minimum wage were never tested by a court of appeal.

As the *Stereotyper* case shows, Murphy applied his impartial decision-making to friends and foes alike. The press was a necessary ally of a publicity-hungry young politician. And Murphy credited his election in 1923 in part to the *Detroit Free Press* and his connection to Mulcahy, who played up the young and charismatic lawyer running for judge in part to boost newspaper sales. Yet Murphy ruled against the *Detroit Free Press* in the *Stereotyper* case.

Murphy soon obtained a reputation as a friend of unions and labor with this decision and others. The logic of collective worker organization was unassailable to him. It was a way of giving workers leverage in an age when large production lines made many craft industries obsolete. Workers who found value in being cobblers, carpenters, and printers were in many cases replaced by machines that could be run by uneducated and unskilled workers. These workers in turn were treated as replaceable cogs on a mass production line, working long and grinding hours doing repetitive activities under poor and dangerous working conditions.[36] Murphy, like FDR, never used Marxist terminology in describing labor struggles.[37] But workers needed a national advocate to fight for their rights against corporations with national scope, and national unions were the obvious choice to promote their rights.

In addition to labor issues, Murphy made his name as a judge in a second category, as he strove to make the court's sentencing procedures more uniform. The second area of his heavy involvement was in connection with "good government" issues as they related to the judicial branch. During his campaign for the Detroit criminal court, Murphy telescoped his desire to review biased court procedures and institute reforms, stating that courts could only work if they developed a "scientific administration of the criminal law."[38]

During his induction as a judge, Murphy remarked that punishment alone "too often crushes out what good there is left in the criminal and generates in him a rancor and a hatred and a fear." Criminals were released back into society "in a way that makes them much worse than at the time they first transgressed the law."[39] His statements were grandiose, his speech reading as though he had been elevated to a great position of power, instead of to an elected position as a local judge. But Murphy soon learned that he could use the position as a launching pad, and he delved into matters of administration designed to get him noticed by those prominent in the national penal reform movement. So Murphy demanded that the city's probation department gather and record information on the defendants brought before him, including such items as their previous offenses, their physical conditions as well as hereditary, psychiatric, and environmental factors such as their family situation.[40] A sentencing board was created, consisting of Murphy and the city's heads of the probation department and the psychopathic (now known as a psychiatric) clinic.

The board's role was to "minimize the effect of judicial temperament in passing sentence" by giving the judge the benefit of behavioral experts. Said Murphy, "[This] means neither severity [nor] leniency but a calm and scientific inquiry which is fair, not only to the defendant but the public."[41]

In one case before Murphy, two 19-year-olds were being tried for armed robbery. One entered a not-guilty plea and was tried. He made the wrong choice. He was convicted and received a 20- to 40-year sentence. The other took a different path, pleading guilty in Murphy's court. Murphy applied new sentencing procedures, and analysis convinced him that the criminal behavior of the man was unlikely to recur. This second one received two years in the reformatory.

As was his intention, Murphy became influential with this national group of criminal court reformers. The institutes being established in major cities such as Detroit served a dual purpose: to assist judges in devising a treatment appropriate for the individual and to conduct policy-shaping clinical research.[42] The most famous of these, Chicago's Psychopathic Institute, had been incorporated into that city's juvenile court close to 15 years before it was instituted by Murphy in Detroit.[43]

Murphy's crime clinic attracted attention outside of Detroit and was the subject of articles in the *Nation* and the *Literary Digest*. Murphy also became a draw in national gatherings by progressives. In a speech at a national governors' meeting, which he gave while still a local criminal court judge, he observed that the total number of arrests made in Detroit from 1921 to 1926 almost matched the city's population.[44] His point was that the police in Detroit routinely employed a strategy of harassment of certain groups of people and that some people were obviously being arrested numerous times as a means of intimidation.

In that same speech, he stated, "I am sure that statistics are used by a great many people who know nothing about them, to erroneous conclusions; and I think that they are likewise often prepared by people who have not any background. . . . But after all we need statistics."[45] Murphy had a boundless confidence before any group, in this case as a local criminal court judge speaking before a group of governors.[46] His invitation by this national group showed his outsized and growing stature. [47]

Murphy was also asked to speak before the National Association of Probation Officers during this time-period. Probation officers were increasingly professionalized and trained. He started by complimenting his audience as "far-visioned men and women, working with stout hearts and unfaltering purpose" and then made clear that their job was "to redeem and recall the wayward to the path of the wholesome social conduct through the probation system. The nation's richest resources are its healthy and happy men and women."[48]

Criminal court reform was a life-time passion. Later, as Attorney General in 1939, Murphy held a conference that called together judges, legislators, state attorneys general, prosecutors, police and prison officials, public welfare administrators, social workers, and educators as well as those directly engaged in parole work. FDR gave the opening speech as Murphy watched. "Well-administered parole is an instrument of tested value in the control of crime," said the president.[49] Although Murphy and FDR were interested in rehabilitation, they were aware that the parole process would more likely find political support as a crime-control issue.

Murphy was keenly interested in learning whether the financial costs of particular crime-control strategies justified the results. As the Attorney General serving under FDR in late 1939, directly prior to being appointed as a Supreme Court justice, he argued for less incarceration, pointing to the waste associated with the exorbitant cost of prisons in this country: "Every year the United States loses more money in its war on crime than the eleven billion dollars advanced to Europe during and since the war. The great industrial cities of the United States stagger under the burden of maintaining courts, police and corrective institutions."[50]

Yet Murphy never fully embraced science as the last word in the administration of justice. His moral beliefs always pervaded his decision-making. By 1927, a crime wave overcame Detroit and several newspapers called for a return to capital punishment. A few days after a Detroit police officer was murdered, Murphy participated in a radio debate on the death penalty. His opponent mocked hospitalization in mental institutions as the cure for crime, in an obvious reference to Murphy's reforms.[51] The implication was clear. Murphy was soft on crime and would have handed a light sentence to a police killer.

Murphy did not argue that some criminals are worthy of help or rehabilitation. "Thou shalt not kill," Murphy responded simply.[52] Murphy then asked his live radio audience whether supporters of the death penalty wanted to go back to "burning, drawing, and quartering, breaking on the wheel, crucifixion, suffocation, sawing asunder, flaying alive, burning alive, impaling, the drinking of molten lead?"[53] As became typical, he combined the facts with what he considered an appeal to the listeners' better angels. But he was also going to have to run for reelection, and he knew it. This position on the death penalty, when he was discussing the fate of a police killer, was courage, folly, or a combination of both.

Murphy was also developing a style on the bench that reflected his natural inclinations. Specifically, he tended to be forgiving toward those on the fringes. As one example, Murphy dealt leniently with prostitutes and demanded to know from law enforcement why it had selected "the most superficial and ineffective"[54] approach to the prostitution problem by arresting the women instead of padlocking the houses, prosecuting their proprietors, and arresting the male customers. Murphy believed that the prostitutes themselves should have been funneled into the rehabilitative wing of the penal system, using the assistance of social workers.[55]

Murphy softened the blow with humor and empathy even when ruling against someone. In one instance, Murphy was faced with a case of non-support by a husband. When a man named John Micalaces was brought before Judge Murphy, this defendant stated that the reason he had not given his wife money was because she had never asked him for it. Judge Murphy looked at Micalaces and remarked: "Either you are trying to impose on me or you have the strangest wife I've ever heard of." Judge Murphy ordered the defendant to support his family and placed him on probation for a year.[56]

Both of Frank's parents died during his years on the bench in Detroit. From his father, Murphy learned the crafts of law and politics. His father had been generous in promoting Frank's education and career, and eased Frank's entry into the professional world. Frank was happy that his mother had at least seen him sworn in as judge. Frank was at his mother's side when she passed away in Harbor Beach in 1924.[57] Murphy was exposed to various strands of Catholic thought from an early age because of his mother, and he assimilated those principles into his conception of social justice. Mary had instilled in him Catholic (both capital and small *c*) values in connection with moral issues.

As already mentioned, Murphy benefited from his status as an Irish Catholic with the Detroit electorate. He soon began to look nationally for similar benefits. In April 1927, Murphy spoke at the communion breakfast of the New York Fire Department's Holy Name Society, which included an audience with New York Governor Alfred Smith. Not coincidentally for Murphy, Smith was a national figure and soon to be the Democratic candidate for president. Murphy was savvy in finding points of entry with more powerful men. He would do so again when, as mayor of Detroit, he hired a cousin of FDR, who soon introduced him to the future president.

Murphy was a keen political observer and always seemed to absorb the best practices of those around him. Smith had enacted many economic and political reforms as the mayor of New York City and Murphy later adopted similar practices, particularly concerning "back to work" ideas during the Great Depression. As governor of Michigan in 1937, he quizzed Mary Dewson, a prominent feminist and activist and head of the Women's Division of the Democratic National Campaign Committee, about workman's compensation laws and procedures in New York state. "I want Michigan's administration of this and similar problems to be second to none in its efficiency and capacity to compete with modern conditions," he told her in a letter.[58]

Endnotes

1. Michael Willrich, *City of Courts: Socializing Justice in Progressive Era Chicago* (Cambridge: Cambridge University Press, 2003), 130.

2. The Republican Party abandoned Reconstruction after the Civil War, to Douglass's dismay. But Douglass felt he had no choice but to continue his support of the Republicans, given the lack of alternatives. "Five Myths about Frederick Douglas," *Washington Post*, Feb. 10, 2017, accessed Apr. 19, 2020, https://www.washingtonpost.com/opinions/five-myths-about-frederick-douglass/2017/02/10/0aaeb592-ea3b-11e6-bf6f-301b6b443624_story.html?noredirect=on&utm_term=.22bf3c4699d0. In the 1920s, Republican President Warren G. Harding, before a segregated crowd of 100,000 in Alabama, stated, "I would say let the black man vote when he is fit to vote; prohibit the white man voting when he is unfit to vote." His speech was met with cheers by Blacks and silence by the whites. John Herr, "President Warren G. Harding's Birmingham civil rights speech: Bold then, forgotten today, " *Alabama Newscenter*, Oct. 26, 2015, accessed Dec. 1, 2020, https://alabamanewscenter.com/2015/10/26/president-warren-g-hardings-birmingham-civil-rights-speech-bold-then-forgotten-today.

3. Murphy as mayor embodied many of these progressive ideals. In one instance, he commissioned reports from his Bureau of Governmental Research in an effort to make rubbish removal more cost effective. C.E. Righton, *Memorandum*, Detroit Bureau of Governmental Research, Jan. 5, 1932, FMP, reel 97.

4. Fine, *The Detroit Years*, 109.

5. Ibid, 110.

6. In one bizarre meeting, KKK members joined in a service of tolerance in Port Huron, Michigan, attended by a crowd of 10,000. The KKK members presented the flag to be hung at a church on a pole that was donated by a prominent Port Huron Jewish resident. The event was attended by "Protestants, Catholics, Jews, Negroes, veterans of American wars, representatives of local civic bodies and the Ku Klux Klan." United Press, "10,000 View 'Service of Tolerance,'" *THP*, Nov. 15, 1926, 5.

7. Fine, *Detroit Years*, 33. Howard noted that by 1925 less than half of Detroit's population was native born. Howard, *Mr. Justice Murphy*, 28.

8. Fine, *The Detroit Years*, 117.

9. Ibid, 107.

10. Ibid, 113.

11. Fine, *The Detroit Years*, 104.

12. Murphy made certain to personally respond to letters and inquiries from prominent female supporters throughout his career. In one letter to Mary W. Dewson, who once served as the head of the Women's Division of the Democratic National Campaign Committee, Murphy urged her to stay "in close contact with us on the subject of desirable protective legislation for women and children." Frank Murphy to Mary W. Dewson, Mar. 12, 1937, FDRL, Dawson Papers, Murphy file.

13. Frank Murphy, letter or memorandum on John Murphy letterhead, FMP, reel 91.

14. Women's groups were to continue their support for Murphy when he ran for mayor. FMP, reel 93.

15. Fine, *The Detroit Years*, 84, 110.

16. The *Detroit Times'* headline of Murphy's victory took a place of pride in his home. "Frank Murphy Leads Ticket, 'Big 4 Licked,'" *Detroit Times*, Apr. 3, 1923, 1.

17. "A Confidential Secretary Recalls: My 16 Years with Frank Murphy," *DFP*, Sept. 10, 1967, 140.

18. Jackson was enraged because Murphy was reported as cantering with beaus while horse-riding at Rock Creek Park. FDRL, Ernest Cuneo Papers, Box 113. ("Murphy and Jackson had an instant antipathy from the second they met at the Book Cadillac [hotel]. It did not improve when Murphy was attorney general and Jackson solicitor general. Jackson complained and angrily, that with 21 important cases coming up before the Supreme Court, he hadn't seen the attorney general.")

19. Associated Press, "Advance in Handling of Industrial Conflicts," *TENS*, Feb. 13, 1937, 7.

20. "Governor Offers Refund of Pay during Absence, Murphy Would Make 'Christmas Present' of Nearly $1,000 to Lieutenant Governor for Protracted 'Substitute' Service," *LSJ*, Dec. 22, 1937, 1.

21. Fine, *Detroit Years*, 145.

22. Fine, *The Detroit Years*, 145–146.

23. Ibid. Criminal judge Murphy would also chastise the prosecutor's office for failing to maintain files properly. "Checking Plan to Guard Files," *DFP*, Aug. 20, 1929, 1.

24. Ibid, 146.

25. Ibid, 181.

26. Ibid.

27. Ibid.

28. Ibid.

29. The *Stereotypers* decision is found in the Frank Murphy Papers, FMP, reel 93.

30. Fine, *The Detroit Years*, 181, 182.

31. Frank X. Martel to Frank Murphy, Apr. 4, 1934, WRL, Detroit AFL-CIO Collection Box 11, Folder: Murphy, Frank 1933–1936 (asking Murphy to return to Michigan to run for senator or governor and stating that the Democratic field is open to a newcomer).

32. Frank X. Martel to Frank Murphy, Feb. 6, 1936, WRL, Detroit AFL-CIO Collection Box 11, Folder: Murphy, Frank 1936; Apr. 28, 1936 (continues to urge Murphy to run for governor; mentions that George Murphy is doing an excellent job in the Recorder's Office) and June 10, 1936 (continues to urge Murphy to run for governor, states that George Murphy is still doing well, and signs off by wishing Murphy a pleasant stay in Hollywood).

33. Associated Press, "Labor Looks to Governor, Wants Murphy as Mediator to Unite C.I.O. and A.F. of L. Factions," *LSJ*, Dec. 2, 1937, 1. ("President Frank X. Martel offered a resolution that expressed regret over the continued struggle of the two organizations for the control of labor and declared that Governor Murphy was the "one who could settle the controversy.")

34. *Adkins v. Children's Hospital*, 261 U.S. 525 (1923) (invalidating a minimum wage law for women as a violation of the freedom to contract); *see also* per curiam opinions invalidating similar minimum wage laws on the authority of *Adkins*, like *Donham v. West-Nelson Mfg. Co.*, 273 U.S. 657 (1927) (Arkansas statute); *Murphy v. Sardell*, 269 U.S. 530 (1925) (Arizona statute).

35. This is so even though the publishers wanted Murphy and the arbitration panel to decide this issue as well, proposing their own numbers. FMP, reel 95 (opinion is found here).

36. In several addresses, Murphy presented the modern factory in these terms. Frank Murphy, address delivered before the National Conference of Social Work, Indianapolis, Indiana, May 28, 1937, *Murphy Collected Speeches, 1937–1938*.

37. Frank Murphy to Mary Murphy, probably 1919, FMM. (This is a letter from Murphy to his mother criticizing Bolshevism.)

38. Fine, *Detroit Years*, 142–143.

39. Addresses made at the opening of the Court and ascension of the Bench by the Honorable Frank Murphy, Judge of the Recorder's Court, Wednesday, Jan. 2, 1924, FMP, reel 141.

40. Fine, *Detroit Years*, 143.

41. Ibid, 143.

42. Willrich, *City of Courts*, 246.

43. Ibid.

44. FMP, reel 93 (citing statistics in a speech).

45. Ibid. (statistics quote in speech).

46. Fine, *Detroit Years*, 143.

47. Addresses made at the opening of the Court and ascension of the Bench by the Honorable Frank Murphy, Judge of the Recorder's Court, Wednesday, Jan. 2, 1924, FMP, reel 141.

48. Frank Murphy, "Speech before the National Association of Probation Officers," FMP, reel 93. ("The aspect of crass materialism which almost blankets the social order is less drab, less bleak, less repelling because of the humanitarian urge arising from the labors and sacrifices of far-visioned men and women, working with stout hearts and unfaltering purpose to redeem and recall the wayward to the path of wholesome social conduct through the probation system.")

49. FDR, "Speech before the Parole Conference," *Federal Probation* III, no. 1 (Feb. 1938) ("That is why Attorney General Murphy has invited judges, legislators, state attorneys general, prosecutors, police and prison officials, public welfare administrators, social workers and educators as well as those directly engaged in parole work" said the president.); Frank Murphy to Governor Herbert Lehman, Feb. 7, 1940, Lehman Collection, Columbia University Libraries (extending invitation to the New York State governor to attend parole conference).

50. Frank Murphy speech to probation officers (no date on draft), FMP, reel 93 (noting the prohibitive cost of the maintaining courts, police, and corrective institutions).

51. Progressive reforms in the criminal system fell under two main categories: law-and-order reforms and humane-treatment/rehabilitative reforms. Murphy was part of the latter reform movement. He would resist cries for retributive justice at every stage of his career.

52. Fine, *Detroit Years*, 137.

53. Ibid, 138.

54. Fine, *Detroit Years*, 142.

55. Ibid.

56. Article, *The Evening Sun from Baltimore*, Apr. 7, 1925, 25. Murphy's exploits would sometimes be picked up nationally.

57. Fine, *Detroit Years*, 192.

58. Frank Murphy to Mary Dewson, Mar. 12, 1937, FDRL, Dewson papers, Frank Murphy file.

CHAPTER 7

The Ossian Sweet Trial: A Black Defendant and a White Jury

Detroit was a segregated city in the early twentieth century.[1] Although the Northern cities did not have Jim Crow, they enforced strict residential racial separation through such means as restrictive covenants. The North also had active and large KKK chapters.[2]

Ossian Sweet's racially charged trial for murder in 1925 and 1926 electrified the city and became a national story, particularly in the Black press. The trial has been vividly recreated in various books such as Kevin Boyle's *Arc of Justice* and Donald McRae's *The Great Trials of Clarence Darrow: The Landmark Cases of Leopold and Loeb, John T. Scopes, and Ossian Sweet*. Murphy was the local criminal court judge who presided over the trial, and his role has been underappreciated.

In 1925, Ossian Sweet and his wife Gladys bought a house on the edge of a white neighborhood in Detroit for familiar reasons. They wanted better schools and higher-quality housing. Gladys had been raised in an upper-middle-class Black family in Pittsburgh. The contrast between husband, the son of a former slave, and his wife was described by a reporter covering the trial: "As a boy, Dr. Ossian Sweet plowed many a furrow behind scraggly mules . . . The Mitchells [Gladys' parents] were always in comfortable circumstances. They owned a car and a pleasant home. They respected themselves and were respected by their neighbors, all of whom, as it happened, were white."[3]

The purchase of the Detroit house by the Sweets infuriated the white neighbors.[4] In July 14, 1925, the local homeowners' association called a meeting and urged the residents to attend "in self-defense." In a pamphlet, they were asked, "Do you want to maintain the existing good health conditions and environment for your children? Do you want to see your neighborhood kept up to its present high standard?"[5]

Fearing an attack after he moved in, Sweet convinced his brother and numerous supporters to stay at his house.[6] Police officers were placed outside the Sweet residence to keep the peace as the white crowd, at times exceeding several thousand, waxed and waned in size over the course of several days.[7]

One night, as the white protesters and spectators outside Sweet's home grew restless, some began to throw stones at the house, eventually breaking an upstairs window. At that point, shots were fired from the house, hitting two white men. One of them, Eric Houghberg, was wounded in the leg. Leon Breiner was killed. Inspector Schuknecht, the head of the police detail, entered the house after the shooting and demanded to know, "What in Hell are you fellows shooting about?"[8]

"They are destroying my home," Dr. Sweet recalled at trial having told the inspector, "and my life is in imminent danger."[9] Sweet showed the inspector the broken window in his room, and the police officer, not yet knowing of the death, stated that he had not been aware that stones had been thrown and that he would put a stop to it.

Instead, the Detroit police arrested Sweet and his housemates, including Sweet's wife. The police interrogated each separately and vigorously. The defendants were not provided with an opportunity to consult with counsel.

The case initially appeared to be an open and shut one. In the preliminary hearing, the police and other witnesses testified for the state that the shooting had been unprovoked. "There were no unusual crowds, no disturbances, and no provocation prior to the shooting," the police officer testified.[10]

All the Black men in the house, including Sweet's brother and his friends, were suspects and all would be tried. Gladys did not escape detention initially but was soon released.[11]

As the chief judge for the Detroit Recorder's Office, Murphy could have avoided the headache of this case by assigning it to another judge. Instead, he gladly took the matter on himself. To Murphy, it was an "opportunity of a lifetime to demonstrate sincere liberalism and judicial integrity."[12] He had public opinion against him in this regard.[13] One mainstream Detroit newspaper, later recapping the day's trial developments, matter-of-factly described the Black defendants as "rioters."[14]

Murphy immediately made an impression on the women in attendance at the trial. Marcet Haldeman-Julius, the reporter, noted his commanding courtroom presence:

> In appearance he is tall, very good looking, inclined toward slenderness, with a long beautifully modeled head, thick curly, auburn hair and contemplative blue eyes. . . . Frank Murphy has the brooding imaginative temperament of an artist. And although his excellent features and splendid physique unquestionably convey an impression of strength, it is none the less of his finely tempered sensibility that one is most conscious. . . . He has both quality and presence. Dignity is an integral part of his nature and upon occasion he can be stern enough, but his most usual mood is one of tranquil thoughtfulness. When he smiles his face has the sparkle of a quiet river in the sunlight.[15]

The NAACP was interested in the trial but had limited resources. By October 1925, the organization had gone all in when its officials invited Clarence Darrow to join the Sweet defense team.[16] Darrow accepted; on October 15, it was announced he would be taking control of the defense.[17] Several consequences flowed from Darrow's decision. First, and most obviously, his presence ensured that the trial took on national significance.

Second, Darrow's request for a large retainer forced the NAACP to think about general ways of funding litigation in furtherance of its goals. The resulting campaign to raise cash empowered the NAACP to set its own long-term agenda, without having to rely on outside sources. The funds left over from collection efforts were used to start the NAACP Legal Defense Fund.[18]

Clarence Darrow was already well into a distinguished and controversial legal career, with a reputation for taking on unpopular clients, sometimes with extreme political leanings. Darrow's wit and eloquence made him one of the most prominent attorneys and civil libertarians in the nation. In 1911, he defended John and James McNamara, the brothers charged with dynamiting the *Los Angeles Times* building during a bitter labor struggle at that newspaper. Owing to a faulty timer, the bomb detonated prematurely, when the *Times* building was still occupied by employees, killing 21 and injuring 100 more. The unions supported the men, believing that the brothers had been framed. The case never went to trial as the brothers agreed to a plea deal.

Just one year before the Sweet trial, Darrow represented a substitute high school teacher, John T. Scopes, in the Scopes "Monkey" Trial in Tennessee. Scopes was accused of violating Tennessee's Butler Act, which had made it unlawful to teach human evolution in any state-funded school, including at the university level. In a trial that drew international attention, statesman and orator William Jennings Bryan opposed Darrow in a battle of legal heavyweights. The jury convicted Scopes but imposed a relatively nominal fine of $100. An appeals court upheld the conviction but overturned the fine. The Scopes Monkey Trial is known today as a hinge event. Based on that trial, many grew skeptical of the large place of religious beliefs in school science programs. The reality is more complex: The Butler Act stayed on the books until 1967.

On the morning of Friday, October 30, Clarence Darrow was ready for trial before Judge Murphy.[19] Almost from the start, Darrow focused on the size of the crowd surrounding the Sweet home. Specifically, he effectively exposed a coordinated attempt by the state's witnesses to vastly understate the size of the crowd. The state's strategy was to make it seem that Sweet and the other Black people in the house fired without provocation.

Darrow skillfully cross-examined Schuknecht, the police officer who had entered Sweet's house, who was sticking to his story
that there were no white mobs when Sweet or someone else shot
Breiner. "If the Sweets were not in danger," Darrow asked, "why
did you have a dozen [police officers] around the house and a
reserve squad at the ready? Why did you order Garland (the
street in front of the Sweet's house) closed to cars shortly before
the Negroes opened fire? If the shootings were unprovoked, why
was your first response to run straight toward the house filled
with homicidal colored men?"[20]

A key to the trial's outcome was Murphy's decision to let in
certain evidence that was not directly relevant to the shootings in
Detroit. Murphy permitted Sweet to provide details of his past as
a Black child growing up in the Deep South. Given this opening,
Sweet recalled to the jury how his own father was a slave. When
he was five years old, Sweet himself witnessed the lynching of
a Black male teenager named Fred Rochelle. Rochelle had supposedly admitted to attacking and murdering a white female. He
was pulled from jail by a white mob and burned at a stake. Sweet
recounted the smell of the kerosene, Rochelle's screams as he was
engulfed in flames, and the crowd's picking off pieces of charred
flesh to take home as souvenirs.[21]

A less sympathetic judge than Murphy might have declared
the story about this horrifying event in Sweet's childhood to be
irrelevant. The issue at hand was whether Sweet had shot Breiner
on a specific day in 1925. But Murphy allowed him to speak at
length about this childhood trauma, giving context to Sweet's
fears about the large white crowd outside his house.

Darrow was in top form in his summation to the jury after the
presentation of the witnesses and the evidence. He reminded the
jury that witnesses appeared to be coached to state that the white
crowds were not large and menacing. He asked the jurors, "Do you
remember the boy who came here, a 16-year-old boy or 17-year-
old boy, who was standing down on the corner of Charlevoix and
Garland on the next street waiting for a bus to go to his work. I asked
him what he saw. He said, 'When I came out I saw a great number
of—I saw a good many of—I saw a few people.' You remember him.
The poor little boy wanted to state the truth and didn't dare. I asked
him if he had been instructed to say 'a few,' and he said 'Yes.'"[22]

Darrow was not the only attorney to summarize matters on behalf of the Sweets. Another defense attorney was Thomas Chawke, known to represent Detroit mobsters. He told the jury that they knew, "the state knew, and everybody knew full well that if conditions had been reversed, if 11 white men were on the inside of the attacked premises, had defended themselves as the Sweets and their friends had done, there would be no trial."[23] Chawke would later be appointed by Governor Frank Murphy to a committee reviewing patronage appointments.[24]

Having received their instructions, Murphy sent the jury to deliberate. Most members of the jury came to an agreement that the eight defendants should be acquitted; there were, however, a few holdouts. At this point, Murphy dismissed the hung jury and declared a mistrial. The first trial of the killing of a white man by one of the Black defendants ended with a whimper and without a conviction. The all-white jury did not believe the police's version of events.

The second trial started on Monday, April 19, 1926.[25] For this trial, Ossian's brother, Henry Sweet, was the only defendant.[26] Henry had been the only one in the group willing to admit that he had fired a gun. The government had decided not to retry the others.

After the evidence was presented to the jury,[27] Darrow made many of the same arguments in his summation that he made during the first trial. The lawyer again criticized the prosecution's failure to introduce witnesses who had seen the large crowds congregating outside of Sweet's home. Darrow noted that his defense team had easily found witnesses who saw much larger crowds than the witnesses produced by the state, including an "honest old German woman," and questioned why the state had failed to find these easily identifiable witnesses.[28] On May 13, 1926, Murphy issued charges to the jury for the second trial that largely mimicked the instructions he gave in the first trial.

This time the jury took only four hours to return with an acquittal for Sweet's brother.[29] Ann Harding, a young woman sitting in the audience, leaped up and threw her arms around Darrow.[30] Harding was Murphy's on-again, off-again girlfriend.[31] They met in 1922, when she was a young actress getting her start in Detroit regional

theater. Since that time, she had often attended Murphy's court proceedings, sitting in the front row "flaxen-haired and cameo-faced, a
wind flower among pines."[32] As with all romantic matters involving Murphy, the situation with Harding remained fluid. Harding
eventually gave up on Murphy and moved to Hollywood, where
she became an accomplished actress and married another actor,
Harry Bannister.[33] In 1931, she was nominated for the Academy
Award for Best Actress in *Holiday*. Murphy and Harding renewed
their relationship in the 1930s after her divorce, and in a letter in
1932 she fantasized about growing old with Murphy.[34] But her letters to Murphy petered out and ended soon after.

The question of why a jury drawn from a group of whites in
segregated Detroit might refuse to convict Ossian Sweet and the
others deserves further explanation. While Darrow's eloquent
defense swayed the jury, Murphy's instructions to the jury arguably had a greater effect. Specifically, he made clear to the jury
that it had to consider the fear and terror of the owners of the
house as a white mob had gathered outside.

As with his evidentiary decisions, his instructions to the jury
proved crucial to the trial's outcome. We are fortunate to have a
transcript of his instructions in the Bentley Library, from which
the following section is drawn.

Murphy first outlined the prosecution's theory of the case, as
required in such instructions, but in a rather perfunctory manner.
According to Murphy, the state was asking the jury to believe that
Sweet and the other defendants "premeditatedly and with malice
aforethought banded themselves together and armed themselves
with the common understanding and agreement that one or more
of them would shoot to kill" if there was damage to the house or
one of them was injured.[35]

Murphy was saying that, to accept the prosecution's theory
of the case and to convict, the jury would first have to be satisfied that the group of men in Sweet's home discussed and plot-
ted among themselves that they would "shoot to kill" upon the
slightest provocation, a highly unlikely scenario given the police
presence and the large size of the crowd outside.

Murphy spent much more time in outlining the defendants' rights. He reminded the jury that "the accused in every criminal case is presumed to be innocent. He comes into court surrounded by that presumption; and, because of it, it is the duty of the people . . . to prove his guilt to each and every one of the essential elements of the crime. . . . by competent testimony, and beyond a reasonable doubt." As part of his instructions, Murphy discussed with the jury the fact that killing another human may not be a criminal offense, as when it is done in self-defense.

Here, assuming that Sweet was provoked by the crowd, didn't Sweet and his compatriots have a duty to retreat, for example, by leaving their house to avoid a deadly confrontation? Murphy answered his own question: "A man is not . . . obliged to retreat if assaulted in his dwelling but may use such means as are absolutely necessary to repel the assailant from his house, or to prevent his forcible entry, even to the taking of life."

On this point, Murphy stated that "if you find, from the facts of this case, that the accused fired a shot . . . under an honest and reasonable belief, based on the circumstances as they appeared to him and to them at the time . . . that he or they were in danger of losing his or their lives . . . or were resisting a forcible and violent felony . . . the defendant would be not guilty."[36]

Murphy continued that he was directing the members of the jury to set their prejudices aside: "Our Supreme Court has said all citizens, whether white or black, are equal before the law."[37] He reminded them that "Dr. Sweet had the right, under the law, to purchase and occupy" his house. A man's house is "his castle, whether he is white or black, and no man has the right to assault or invade it."

According to Murphy, the jury could consider Sweet's point of view as a Black man facing a white mob in deciding whether the killing of Breiner was a "justifiable."[38] In this regard, Murphy also reminded the jury of "other instances of recent occurrences in the city of Detroit . . . by mobs or assemblages of people against the property of colored people."[39] Murphy was asking the 12 men to place themselves in Sweet's shoes as a Black man at the time the unruly crowd was gathered outside his house.

Murphy also warned the jury not to use perfect 20/20 hindsight. It is quite possible that Breiner himself had no intention to storm the Sweet's house, but this was irrelevant. Murphy defined the standard to be whether Sweet, the defendant, believed himself to be "so menaced" regardless of the victim's intent.

In summary, Murphy's jury instructions provided a roadmap to acquit. A crowd had gathered outside Sweet's house, where he lawfully had a right to live. There, they threatened him and his family. The jurors would be able to relate to the "castle" metaphor. They would understand that there was no duty to retreat if a home were under attack.

And he concluded by appealing to the jurors' finer angels: "I consider it my duty to especially caution and warn you against prejudice or intolerance in your deliberations. . . . If you permit passion or prejudice, or hate or the like, to enter into your deliberations, reason will depart."

Following another acquittal, Murphy turned to the Sweet family, "I believe it is a just and reasonable verdict, and may God bless you."[40] Prominent Black leaders such as Walter White wrote to the two main Black newspapers in Detroit that Murphy had demonstrated with the Sweet trials that "justice has no color line." Black voters should show that they were "not forgetful or ungrateful" at the ballot box when Murphy was up for reelection.[41] It was the start of a strong and mutually beneficial relationship between Murphy and the Black community.

Why did the jury consist only of white males in both trials? Black adults lived as citizens in Detroit and voted. Women also now had the vote, at least on the national level, with the passage of the Nineteenth Amendment. An incomplete answer is that voting rights did not always translate into other rights that we now associate with full citizenship. During jury selection, the one Black candidate was excused because of his presumed bias in favor of Sweet and his compatriots.[42] So-called "preemptory challenges" that reject jurors simply because of their race or ethnic origin (or gender) are now forbidden under Supreme Court precedent[43] but were accepted at the time of the Sweet trial in the 1920s.

Murphy made clear that he did not like the present system of jury selection, which excluded members of the local community. When Murphy died, he was mourned by the future first Black Supreme Court justice, Thurgood Marshall, in a law review article. Marshall summarized Murphy's views that "if a jury is to be fairly chosen from a cross section of the community it must be done without limiting the number of persons of a particular color, racial background or faith—all of which are irrelevant factors in setting qualifications for jury service." This may result in the "selection of one, six, twelve or even no Negroes on a jury panel."[44]

Ossian Sweet indeed supported Murphy in his election campaigns as criminal court judge, devoting his time and "meager means" out of "appreciation and respect."[45] Sizing up Murphy, he stated, "I felt then as I feel now, that he is eminently qualified, both in temper[a]ment and educational qualification as well as by his socialistic outlook on life."[46] Sweet also provided financial assistance to his fellow defendants later in their lives and used his star power to buttress membership in the local NAACP.

But then Sweet failed to support Murphy when Murphy ran for mayor of Detroit a few years later. Sweet's logic was that Murphy had no executive experience. Sweet's position on Murphy put him at odds with the national branch of the NAACP, and Walter White in particular, who visited him in Detroit and accused him of ingratitude for backing another candidate for mayor.

As Sweet explained in a letter in 1930 to William Pickens, another powerful member of the NAACP and himself a son of former slaves, "[D]espite the love, respect and gratitude I had for him as Judge, when I began to think of him as Mayor, for a great industrial center like this, with unemployment at its zenith, lawlessness and murder stalking down the streets of this City, and the fact that we had elected another Judge who had about as much mayoralty experience as Judge Murphy, only to be re-called six months after he had taken the oath of office, because of his blunders and colossal mistakes, I knew then as I know now that the man who could lead Detroit's municipal affairs must of necessity, not only be honest, intelligent and willing but experienced and capable too."[47]

The Sweet family faced tragedy afterward. Dr. Sweet's daughter died of tuberculosis in 1926, and Gladys died of the same cause soon after. Dr. Sweet persevered, working as the supervising doctor at the Good Samaritan Hospital in Detroit.[48] In 1940, Sweet's brother Henry also died of tuberculosis. Sweet himself rose through the ranks, eventually becoming the superintendent of several hospitals. Then Sweet committed suicide in 1960 after suffering further personal and financial setbacks.[49]

Notwithstanding the electric results of this trial, Detroit remained a segregated city. In 1943, in the midst of World War II, when Detroit had converted all its factories to the production of planes and tanks for the war effort, race riots broke out along the border of the Black and white residential areas.[50] By then, the vast influx of Black residents into Detroit in the 20 years prior to and during World War II had created an untenable housing situation in the limited areas they were allowed to live in the city. A *riot* in the past usually meant that white people killed Black people. This race riot was different, with deaths on both sides. A few days later, Murphy, now a United States Supreme Court justice, recommended to FDR that "someone of tact, understanding and experience should be watching the race situation in Detroit, Michigan."[51] Murphy fit the description of his recommendation. He wanted FDR to appoint himself to deal with the problem. As will be seen, Murphy was strangely uncomfortable with his role as a United States Supreme Court justice, at least at the beginning, and sought out positions within the Roosevelt administration that he believed were more suitable for his abilities.

For Murphy, the separation of the races in Detroit was a galling reality for his entire political and judicial career. Despite the continuing segregation in Detroit, the trial marked a certain turning point in American history in that 12 white jurors could allow themselves to be swayed to acquit Sweet and other African Americans on trial. And now the NAACP had found its bearing, having established networks to fund its civil rights litigation. As for Murphy, he had secured the loyalty and gratitude of the Black community.

Endnotes

1. By the time Murphy took the Detroit criminal court bench, the Supreme Court had already decided in *Buchanan v. Worley* in 1917, ruling as unconstitutional state laws and local ordinances imposing residential segregation. The South simply ignored *Buchanan*, maintaining Jim Crow, with explicit laws that separated Black people from white people, buttressed by funding disparities in schools and infrastructure. The North enforced segregation through restrictive covenants and other means, condoned by the courts at the time. Rothstein, *The Color of Law* (describing how segregation persisted in the North through the use of these restrictive covenants and other means).

2. The KKK was powerful in the North. "Revival of Ku Kluxism Brings Terrorism and Lawlessness in Train," *DFP*, Sept. 28, 1921, 1.

3. The account comes from Marcet Haldeman-Julius's pamphlet on the Sweet (and Scopes) trials. Haldeman-Julius, *Clarence Darrow's Two Greatest Trials*, 22, https://archive.org/details/clarencedarrowst00hald/mode/2up.

4. Ironically, these neighbors did not know that the seller of the house to Dr. Sweet was also Black but with much lighter skin. Fine, *Detroit Years*, 148.

5. Boyle, *Arc of Justice*, 133.

6. Black people sometimes armed themselves in the absence of effective police protection. Later, Martin Luther King Jr. applied for a permit to carry a concealed firearm in 1956 after his house was bombed. King's application was denied, but from then on, armed supporters guarded his home. One advisor, Glenn Smiley, described the King home as "an arsenal." William Worthy, a Black reporter who covered the civil rights movement, almost sat on a loaded gun in a living room armchair during a visit to King's parsonage. Adam Winkler, "The Secret History of Guns," *The Atlantic Magazine*, Sept. 2011.

7. Mobs of white people menaced Black people in the North as well as the South. In 1926, in Carteret, New Jersey, about 20 miles from New York City, Black churchgoers were beaten and driven from a church, which was burned to the ground. "Mob Burns Church, Ejects All Negroes, 100 Families in Carteret, N.J., Are Herded from Homes after White Man Is Slain," *NYT*, Apr. 27, 1926. In Levittown, Pennsylvania, crowds formed outside a house and crosses were burned after a Black family bought a house in 1957. "Samuel Snipes, 99, Dies; Lawyer for First Black Family in Levittown, Pa.," *NYT*, Jan. 11, 2019.

8. Fine, *Detroit Years*, 150.

9. Ibid.

10. Fine, *Detroit Years*, 151.

11. Boyle, *Arc of Justice*, 227; Fine, *Detroit Years*, 151.

12. Fine, *Detroit Years*, 151.

13. Boyle, *Arc of Justice*, 184–185.

14. "Darrow in Final Plea for Rioters," *TNP*, Nov. 25, 1925, 10.

15. Haldeman-Julius, *Clarence Darrow's Two Greatest Trials*.

16. Telegram from W. E. B. Du Bois to Clarence Darrow, October 7, 1925. W. E. B. Du Bois Papers (MS 312). Special Collections and University Archives, University of Massachusetts Amherst Libraries.

17. United Press, "Darrow Pleads for 11 Negroes," *THP*, Oct. 30, 1925, 1.

18. Jeanne May, "The Call to Believers: Theme of NAACP's Convention is a Reminder of Its Origins in Bitter Conflict," *DFP*, July 9, 1989, 1L, 4L.

19. Boyle, *Arc of Justice*, 320.

20. Ibid.

21. Boyle, *Arc of Justice*, 68–69.

22. Clarence Darrow Closing Arguments, Douglas O. Linder, Famous Trials website, accessed Apr. 19, 2020, http://www.famous-trials.com/sweet/123-darrowargument.

23. Carrie Sharlow, "Michigan Lawyers in History: Thomas F. Chawke," *Michigan Bar Journal* (November 2015): 37.

24. Fine, *New Deal Years*, 217.

25. Associated Press, "Sweet May Go on Trial Second Time Tomorrow," *BCE*, Apr. 19, 1926, 7.

26. "Negro Lawyer, Sweet, Is Dead," *DFP*, Jan. 21, 1940, 7 (recalling trial).

27. Associated Press, "Jury Is Selected for Sweet Trial," *LSJ*, Apr. 24, 1926, 1. ("Judge Frank Murphy said that the jury will be kept locked up during the trial.")

28. Clarence Darrow Summation Transcript, FMP, reel 92, 16–17.

29. United Press, "Detroit Negro Is Not Guilty," *IDG*, May 14, 1926, 1.

30. O'Brien, *Ann Harding*, 84.

31. O'Brien, *Ann Harding*, 82. ("Ann championed the defense in the Sweet Trials, and followed the story in all its detail. She showed up for the proceedings whenever she could fit it into her hectic schedule.")

32. Haldeman-Julius, *Clarence Darrow's Two Greatest Trials*, 52.

33. O'Brien, *Ann Harding*, 86; "Ann Harding in a New Talkie," *NYT*, Jan. 11, 1930, 21 (listing her as acting with Harry Bannister).

34. Cartoon, "And your hair 'dear Ann' ["dear Ann" in Harding's hand-writing], I'll wager it still fetches to the knee." *New Yorker Magazine*, Apr. 15, 1933, FMP, reel 23. (In 1933, Harding sent a playful cartoon to Murphy in which they are now an elderly couple, with her handwritten additions, including: "Darling—Shall I wait for this? AH.")

35. Frank Murphy Jury Instructions, FMP, reel 92, 2.

36. Ibid, 11.

37. Ibid, 17.

38. Ibid, 21. A justifiable homicide in this context is one that occurs under the color of law, as when a police officer shoots a criminal in the scope of his or her duties or a soldier kills during wartime. Excusable homicide is when a person shares some fault, for example, starting a fight, but then seeks to withdraw and kills the other person because that person threatens his or her life.

39. Ibid, 26.

40. Ibid, 85.

41. Fine, *Detroit Years*, 184.

42. Fine, *Detroit Years*, 155.

43. Peremptory challenges cannot be used to systematically strike prospective jurors from the panel on the basis of race (*Batson v. Kentucky*, 476 U.S. 79 (1986)) or gender (*J.E.B. v. Alabama ex rel T.B.*, 511 U.S. 127 (1994)).

44. Thurgood Marshall, "Mr. Justice Murphy and Civil Rights," *Michigan Law Review*, 48, no. 6 (1950), accessed Apr. 19, 2020, https://www.jstor.org/stable/1284431.

45. Ossian Sweet to William Pickens, Dec. 20, 1930, University of Massachusetts, W.E.B. Du Bois Papers, 1803–1999, accessed Apr. 19, 2020, credo.library.umass.edu/view/pageturn/mums312-b060-i042/#page/1/mode/1up.

46. Ibid.

47. Ibid.

48. Ibid.

49. Fine, *Detroit Years*, 168–169; "Dr. Sweet—2 Bullets, 2 Tragedies," *DFP*, Mar. 21, 1960, 10.

50. "Martial Law at 10 P.M.," *DFP*, June 22, 1943, 1.

51. Frank Murphy to FDR, FDRL, Box 166, PSF, Supreme Court, 1938–1944 (referring to race riots in Detroit).

CHAPTER 8

Murphy as Mayor: Calling a Depression a Depression

Black Tuesday on Wall Street was October 29, 1929. To the modern reader, this was clearly the start of something new, the beginning of the Great Depression. At the time, however, many believed the downturn would be temporary. Republican president Herbert Hoover had offered soothing rhetoric after the initial panic a few days before: "The fundamental business of the country . . . is on a sound and prosperous basis."[1] The stock market had been on a nine-year run and some correction was expected before a return to the good times.

The *New York Times* was not unusual in its rosy predictions, reporting, "The smashing decline has brought stocks down to a level where, in the opinion of leading bankers and industrialists, they are a buy on their merits and prospects, and brokers have so advised their customers."[2]

The branches of government carried on the next few days like nothing happened after the massive one-day drop in the stock market. The Senate was focused not on the crash but on a tariff bill. Corporations continued to pay dividends to their shareholders, even as they started the process of laying off many workers. The day of the crash, directors of the United States Steel

Corporation and the American Can Company declared payments of dividends at their late-afternoon meetings.[3]

Murphy was still just a local judge in Detroit and was facing municipal elections in 1929. He was not particularly focused on the greater economic calamity engulfing his city and the country. As he did previously, Murphy actively campaigned, delivering a substantial number of his speeches before labor, Black, and ethnic groups.[4] As in 1923, the veterans gave him their support. He again won, this time the second-largest vote getter among the eight open positions for criminal judges.

Now his general electoral success drew the attention of Michigan Democratic Party leaders who wanted him to run for mayor of Detroit in 1930. A special election was being called because of the recall of the Republican mayor Charles Bowles. The KKK, operating openly and counting thousands of members in Detroit, had earlier thrown its support behind Bowles, helping fuel him to victory.[5]

Bowles was not recalled by the Detroit citizens for his ties to the KKK. Instead, he faced voter wrath for firing Police Commissioner Harold Emmons, himself a reformer. Bowles was accused of "tolerating lawlessness" by terminating Emmons, and a recall election was instituted barely six months after he had entered office.[6] This was the age of Prohibition, and crime was increasing as bootleggers fought each other. While Prohibition was disliked, particularly in the cities, many there also wanted an end to violent crime. On a more pedestrian level, respect for the law seemed to be on the decline as the wealthy and poor alike were finding ways of evading the law to get their liquor.[7] Bowles's termination of Emmons sent the wrong signal to the electorate.

Murphy had already turned down requests to run for mayor in 1927 and 1929, in part because he knew that the Detroit mayor's office had been controlled by Republicans since 1912. However, his latest win in 1929 as a criminal court judge filled Murphy with confidence. It seemed that Democrats could win in the city by appealing to the worker and ethnic bases.

Michigan was still a Republican state, but Republicans had two strikes against them in the upcoming local elections. First, they could not complain too much about the economy, as they were the party in power. Republicans did not wish to portray the economic deterioration as happening on their watch. Notwithstanding the sunny prognostication of President Herbert Hoover and the newspapers, and the continued payment of dividends by corporations to their shareholders, unemployment was skyrocketing. To name just one example, the Ford Motor Company, which in the spring of 1929 had employed 128,000 workers in the Detroit area, was hemorrhaging workers and was down to 37,000 employees by August 1931.[8]

Second, the incumbent Republican mayor had been recalled, casting a negative light on the party. And better yet from the Democrats' point of view, Bowles, tainted by the recall, had decided to run again. He was bound to split the Republican vote. Finally, the local Republican Party was thrown into total disarray with the murder of a radio commentator, Jerry Buckley, who had pressed for Bowles's recall.

A crowd of more than 100,000 people attended Buckley's funeral. Murphy was chosen to speak at the memorial, gaining this criminal court judge huge exposure in the city.[9] The *Detroit Times* reported that Murphy was now being besieged by requests to enter the mayoral race. From the *Times'* perspective, Murphy was the perfect candidate: As a judge, he had remained aloof from the recall fight, so he could not be charged with pushing for Bowles's withdrawal based on his own self-interest. And Murphy had championed some of the same causes as Bowles, such as old-age pensions and aid to the unemployed.[10]

The cries for Murphy to run for a city-wide office were not universal. Democrats feared that he would split the vote with the other Democrat who was running, thereby handing the election to Bowles or some other Republican. And several prominent Catholics, including the president of the University of Detroit—a school to which Murphy had strong ties—did not believe that Detroit was ready for a Catholic mayor.[11] While a judge, Murphy taught night school at University of Detroit Law School, offering a course in criminal justice. His students were mostly first-generation Americans.[12] The words of the university president must have stung.

In the end, Murphy was convinced to run. He announced his candidacy for mayor in August 1930. He immediately resigned from the Recorder's Office, even though there was no legal requirement to do so.[13] It was an act of confidence, probably not warranted given the Republican leanings of the city. In Murphy's last act as a Recorder's Court judge, he placed a defendant on probation rather than sentencing him to jail time. "I'm glad my last sentence can be one of mercy," he remarked.[14]

By now, Murphy knew the economy was in shambles, and he went all in criticizing the Republican incumbents. But he also made sure to give people hope. While warning of the grave economic conditions, Murphy exuded optimism during his campaign. He ran as the "dew-and-sunshine" candidate, with lofty and uplifting rhetoric in suffering Detroit. His ability to warn of the grave crisis and also instill hope in a demoralized public presaged FDR's own ability to do the same a few years later.[15] And echoes of Murphy's rhetoric were heard much later in Republican Ronald Reagan's "Morning in America" speeches.

Murphy constantly referred to those whose jobs were gone or who were not receiving a decent living.[16] Murphy understood at a visceral level that he should talk about the bad economic conditions and promote the idea that the city government could do something about it. This turned out to be a winning argument—focusing on the destitute and the benefits of government intervention—in this race and in several races to come.

Looking back, it might be an obvious proposition to focus on the economic downturn. Yet, he distinguished himself from his main Democratic rival, George Engel, who stressed crime as Detroit's main issue. Engel was a Catholic like Murphy and came from the large German community in Detroit. Engel therefore presented as a strong candidate. Because Murphy's focus was different from Engel's—economy versus crime—the voters had a real choice to signal what was important to them. Engel stated that it was a poor time for "fooling and experimenting" and trying out "idealistic [economic] theories."[17]

In the end, Murphy won the race for mayor by a plurality of about 40 percent of the total votes.[18] The Democrats had split their votes, as naysayers of Murphy's run had feared, but not enough to make a difference. Murphy's emphasis on the economic plight of Detroiters had resonated. Murphy's inauguration was delayed a week as Bowles called for a recount, but Bowles eventually conceded.[19]

One group threw its staunch support behind Murphy—the Black community voted overwhelming for him. NAACP representative Walter White attended much of the two Sweet trials and later tried to pressure Sweet to support Murphy's run. In a letter to the *Detroit Independent*, a newspaper that catered to the Black community, based on what he had seen at the Sweet trials, White heartily endorsed Murphy for mayor, referring to Murphy's "high character" and his "unquestionably fair attitude toward Negroes."[20] This relatively small population in Detroit may well have tilted the election in Murphy's favor. And Murphy never forgot it.

On September 23, 1930, at the age of 39, Murphy assumed the mayoralty of Detroit. By now, Detroit registered 120,000 unemployed in a city of 1.5 million. But much more menacing were the stories of starvation, some leading to deaths on the streets of the city. Parents were unable to provide for their children.

Murphy had no easy answers. The budget of the fourth-largest city in the country was wrecked, done in by falling revenue as its out-of-work residents stopped paying taxes.

Murphy chafed at the fiscal restrictions imposed by the state. In a letter to Detroit citizens delivered 90 days into his mayoral term, Murphy argued, proto-Keynesian style, that deficits should be allowed in extraordinary times, but "only those items which, because of an overwhelming necessity, cannot wait until the next budget-making period." He referred to Detroit as "this great city of plenty."[21]

This reference was a seeming paradox. But Detroit was a city of great wealth. Murphy's administration spent over $20 million in each of his first two years on mitigating the suffering of the unemployed in his city—not an insignificant sum, but still just a fraction of the yearly profits of large companies such as GM even in the depths of the Depression. GM had a net income of $248 million in 1929, $151 million in 1930, and $96 million in 1931, before falling to a mere $164 thousand in 1932.[22] Even in 1932, three years after the stock market crash, GM distributed over $9 million in dividends to its shareholders.[23]

Murphy's pleas for more funds for his city were largely ignored. The Republican governor of Michigan, echoing President Hoover, did not believe it was his state's role to help Detroit. This was not cold heartedness as such but more of a historical truism. State and federal governments were never the traditional sources of assistance for the cities' unemployed. Instead, private charities and sometimes the municipalities themselves provided the relief. And the programs tended to be stopgap in nature. The economy always recovered, and the unemployed found jobs or moved away, often westward.

Murphy made clear that any funds available to the city would go to the poor and destitute. In February 1930 alone, Detroit's city welfare department expended more than $1.7 million and cared for 50,858 families and a grand total of about 229,000 persons.[24] In the harsh winter of 1930–1931, free beds were given to 12,000 men. The city served three million free meals. Lunches were given to 10,000 school children.[25] Under Murphy, Detroit accounted for more than 25 percent of the public general relief dispensed in the United States in 1930, decreasing to a still significant 13 percent in 1931.[26]

In a critique of government benefits that would be recognizable today, the Detroit Board of Commerce complained about Murphy's efforts to help the destitute, asserting that "the openhanded, come one-come all welfare policy of Detroit" had "attracted . . . derelicts from all parts of America" who were being taught to live "without effort." Murphy's welfare program was "paternalism" inspired by Moscow and its recipients "midwestern derelicts" and "parasites."[27]

Murphy for his part did not accept the premise that he had to justify government payments to the poverty stricken, injecting his usual moral tone: "[L]et us worry over the forgotten and neglected ones and not consume ourselves in a fret over the few unfortunate misfits who cheat," he declared. In one interview, he stated, "If you want to call saving people from starvation and eviction a dole, that's what it is."[28] He also asked whether those criticizing the "derelicts" would be willing to repeat their remarks to families living on a few dollars a week. To the businessmen complaining about taxes, he wondered why they were not calling for austerity during the 1920s, when the city was engaged in spendthrift expenditures that lined their pockets.[29]

In the meantime, Murphy was open to any and all suggestions on how to raise funds for the city. To hit the ground running, Murphy established the Mayor's Unemployment Committee (MUC). Murphy thought that a new committee drawn from the diverse groups in the community was more likely to confront the plight of the newly poor with sympathy and understanding. The MUC was nimble, able to give rapid responses and assistance to public and private companies involved in relief efforts.

At times, the MUC had a carwash-fundraising, ad hoc quality to it, and that was the point: to try anything and everything to help the poor. This committee's most important initial proposal was the sale of apples by the unemployed, an enterprise soon to be adopted around the country. It also arranged for the cutting of cord wood from city lots not being used for other purposes.[30]

In 1930, a football game between Michigan and the already fading University of Chicago was a big draw and revenue generator for the MUC. The University of Chicago's long-standing coach Amos Alonzo Stagg brought excitement to the crowds with his many innovations, such as the Statute of Liberty play. The proceeds of the game, which Michigan won, went to fund projects in Detroit. The University of Chicago dismantled its football team a few years later, and its powerhouse image became just a distant memory.[31]

Murphy filled the MUC with key allies, including his friend Edward Kemp. Another appointee was G. Hall Roosevelt, the brother of Eleanor Roosevelt, and therefore also a more distant cousin of FDR.[32] Hall received an engineering degree from Harvard in 1914 and then made his way to Detroit in 1928 when he joined the Eastern Michigan Railways Company. The next year he became president of a bank in Detroit.[33]

Murphy was attracted to Hall for obvious reasons. The Roosevelt clan was already nationally famous and on top of this Hall, had a reputation of competence in his prior positions in Detroit. Less easy to explain was Hall's initial attraction to Murphy. Here, Murphy's charm and charisma must have played a prominent role. Then, once on Murphy's team, Hall was impressed enough with what he saw; he would soon broker introductory meetings between FDR and Murphy.

Murphy also placed powerful women on the MUC, including Beulah Young, an African-American publisher.[34] Another important member of the MUC was Josephine Gomon, who was also to become Murphy's executive secretary during his years in the mayor's office. Gomon's achievements for Murphy and later in her own right were considerable.[35] After graduating with a mathematics degree from the University of Michigan, she taught math and physics at what would become Wayne State University. She married and had five children but continued to work. She also taught in the Detroit public school system, wrote a child-education column for the *Detroit News,* and worked for the local Planned Parenthood league following the deaths of two of her friends during childbirth.[36]

Gomon may have become acquainted with Murphy during the Ossian Sweet trial. At those proceedings, Marcet Haldeman-Julius described Gomon, who was a regular attendee, as the "secretary of the Rationalist Society in Detroit."[37] Gomon was organized and constantly reminded Murphy of the need to attend to details. Murphy was interested in making a big splash, and sometimes he neglected following up on his own initiatives. For one of his many ideas, Murphy wanted to turn idle factories into residential shelters for the unemployed. In November, 1932, Gomon pointed out to Murphy that he could open a shelter in an empty automobile factory, without the need to submit the proposal to the city council, which would have delayed matters. The result, the aptly named Fisher Lodge, was a genuinely innovative space that housed the destitute[38] and produced one of the most famous pictures of Murphy: eating a meal on Christmas Eve of 1932, among the unemployed men now living at the factory.[39]

Murphy did divert funds to infrastructure. In Detroit, Hazen Pingree loomed large as a model for Murphy. When he entered the Detroit's mayor office around 1890, Pingree expressed dismay at the sorry state of Detroit's roads, which sometimes caught on fire because of the materials used in their construction, and he stressed the need to spend up front on roads and infrastructure to save money later on.[40] Pingree favored municipal ownership of light plants and street railways to break private monopolies and lower costs for the urban consumer.[41] Pingree's model was an entirely new one for local government, as the bureaucracy was mobilized to address the plight of those living in the teeming slums of the cities. Soon, other cities were copying him.

In the Pingree progressivist tradition, Murphy promoted city-funded projects within the severe constraints of the Great Depression. Murphy made a show of appearing at the opening of water treatment centers and other projects that would assist the common people.[42] He took prominent credit at the dedication of the Detroit-Windsor Tunnel, an impressive feat of engineering but one that was completed before he was elected and with largely private funds.

Mayor Murphy was always trying to wriggle out of Detroit's fiscal straightjacket. At times, the difference between servicing city debt and defaulting was a matter of a few million dollars. In 1931, Detroit met its debt obligations only when the indefatigable Gomon approached Henry Ford and convinced him that he would hate the idea of New York bankers having a stake in Detroit.[43] Ford ended up prepaying his taxes in the amount of $5 million.[44] In 1933, a $30 million hole was met through state legislation that allowed the issuance of $20 million in five-year bonds, with a group of influential citizens arranging for the sale. The bond sale, $7 million in economies, and the sale of $3 million from the sale of delinquent taxes addressed the deficit of $30 million.[45] To give this some context, GM reported having $186 million in the bank in 1932, even after the dividend payments had been made to shareholders.[46]

Quietly, Murphy acceded to the recommendations of an oversight board appointed by banks with the power to extend loans to Detroit. He began to lobby the Michigan legislature to raise debt limits for his city and frequently travelled to New York to negotiate with and cajole powerful banks to provide funds. The committee with so much power over his budget decisions was known as the Stone Committee, named after its head, Ralph Stone. Stone was a local businessman trusted by the New York banks. The purpose of the committee was to scour the city's budget and demand cuts and austerity and, in exchange, lend additional money as necessary, with significant strings. The irony, of course, was that these banks were soon to come under significant strain as the Great Depression of the 1930s kicked into high gear and required federal financial assistance to survive. As will be seen, one major bank would come "hat in hand" to Murphy, asking him to use his political connection with FDR to bail it out.

Although Murphy needed the banks, he also publicly attacked them as villains. In part, this was a function of Detroit's overall sour relationship with banks. Detroit's automobile industry grew largely without traditional financing from them. As Henry B. Joy, president of the Packard Motor Car company, said (as cited in Louis Brandeis's *Other Peoples' Money and How the Bankers Use It*): "It is observable facts of history, it is also my experience of thirty years as a businessman, banker, etc., that first the seer conceives an opportunity . . . The motor-car business was the same. When a few gentlemen followed me in my vision of the possibilities of the business, the banks and the older businessmen (who in the main were the banks) said, 'fools and their money soon to be parted, etc., etc.'"[47] Murphy found it easy to blame banks for Detroit's troubles as one who grew up in this anti-bank culture that even extended into the ethos of major car companies in Detroit.

Murphy had an ability to speak about his goals and ambitions, sometimes with extreme language to appeal to his base. At the same time, as with his negotiations with the oversight board, he could send the appropriate signals to those who might feel threatened by the implication that he was willing to work within the economic and political framework.

His various fights with business interests made good copy, and Murphy relished the publicity. Business interests had a natural advantage in publicizing their points of view on taxes and economic conditions generally, as they paid for advertisements in the newspapers. But Murphy also sprinkled city money on publications that provided favorable coverage. He cultivated the publishers and editors of the city's ethnic newspapers. For example, a newspaper with a German-immigrant audience had favored Murphy for mayor over his Democratic rival, an ethnic-German candidate. As Murphy's biographer Sidney Fine characterized it, Murphy "rewarded" the newspaper by appointing its business manager to the Water Board. Similarly, Murphy found a position in the city health department for Franz Prattinger, the editor of the *Hungarian News*.[48]

When a new daily, the *Detroit Mirror*, began publishing in 1931, Murphy quickly won the admiration of the managing editor, Frank Carson, who concluded that he had never encountered a public official who was "so much on the square." The mayor reciprocated by directing the city's official advertising to the *Mirror*.[49]

The African-American community had its own nationwide network of newspapers. As discussed, Murphy's most important connection to the Black press was with Beulah Young, in her capacity as the publisher of the *Detroit People's News* and the second vice president of the National Negro Press Association.[50] Young continued to provide editorial support to Murphy, later boosting his successful run for governor of Michigan. Young wrote to him she would "not only keep all the coloured peoples['] votes in Detroit sewed up," but she would also organize the state for him, and when he ran for president, she would "throw every worthwhile newspaper in the U.S. for [him]."[51] The community had not forgotten about his work on the Ossian Sweet trial.

Of the questions concerning Murphy's relations to women, his connection to Beulah Young, the Black publisher, is the most intriguing. Murphy's relationship with Young certainly exceeded professional boundaries.[52] This letter to him in early 1931 did not just contain political advice for retaining the support of the African-American community.[53] The letter started, "To the Garden of My Heart." An open relationship with this powerful (and married) African-American woman in segregated Detroit would have been explosive, and no doubt would have derailed the careers of both.[54] Young explicitly requested that Murphy burn the letter.[55] Murphy instead kept it, and the correspondence is now found in his archives in the Bentley Library.

A missive such as this might have caused Murphy to distance himself from Young, yet Young remained an advisor to Murphy long after it was written. Several years after she sent the letter, Murphy trusted her enough to send her to Washington, DC, to lobby Congress to supply Detroit with aid. Young suffered personal and professional setbacks a few years later. Her business was put into bankruptcy and her printing equipment was sold off. But she persevered. In the late 1940s and early 1950s, she threw her support to Charles C. Diggs, Jr., and is credited with helping him become the first Black Michigan state senator.[56] Diggs went on to serve 25 years in Congress, where he helped found the Congressional Black Caucus and rose to become chairman of the House District Committee. He died at the age of 75 in the 1990s after a stroke.[57]

Murphy would need all the support from the Black community and his other supporters because he was up for reelection less than a year into office, as he had been installed in a special election. He had competition for his position. As one columnist for the *New York Times* stated in the context of deteriorating economic conditions, the lucky candidates for mayor in Detroit were the "nine who fail."[58]

He campaigned energetically, again pitting himself as a compassionate overseer in a time of financial crisis. Murphy explicitly focused on the immigrant and minority vote. In his first election, the year before, Murphy had won on a bare plurality. But the 166,748 votes cast for Murphy on November 3, 1930, represented 64 percent of the total vote. He had easily dispatched the nine other candidates. As in other races, Murphy ran short in the wards with a high percentage of native-born whites of native-born parents and in the upper-income precincts. Murphy's support was overwhelming among other constituents. Murphy ran at 83 percent in Polish districts and did well in Greek, Hungarian, Italian, and Jewish precincts. The business interests had tried to portray Murphy as irresponsible, his programs to help the poor as corrupt giveaways. In the desperate economic environment, the voters did not care.[59]

Murphy's best showing in his reelection campaign was in the three Black wards, running up huge margins of up to 30 to 1 in his favor. This was a hinge event, signaling a shift of Black support from the Republicans to Democrats.[60] Soon, the Blacks in the North would reliably vote for the Democrat party candidates.

The Catholic press portrayed the election as free from religious issues: "Mr. Murphy, in his campaign, championed old age pensions and stressed the need for the solution of the unemployment problem. His appeal to the voters, the press reported, was not sectional."[61] This was not correct. The KKK had inserted itself into the mayoral election to stop this new rising ethnic star. The Klan dispatched senior officials from its executive offices in the nation's capital to deal with Murphy. About two weeks after their arrival, a pamphlet appeared that was published by the Citizens' Fact Finding Committee.[62] The pamphlet was entitled "How and Why are You Voting on November 3rd?" The purpose of the pamphlet was to demonstrate "an amazing political situation, showing how Catholic men and women, by exercising a plain political commonsense [sic] not displayed in the past by their Protestant brothers and sisters, have assumed control of our municipal government" by concentrating their votes.[63] When partisans sought to distribute the pamphlets outside Protestant churches on Sundays, many of the ministers denounced the document.[64] The inability of the KKK to gain traction reflected a change in the national mood. Before now, the KKK had brazenly operated in the open, with offices in Washington, DC. The organization had arguably tipped the scales at the 1924 Democratic presidential convention (forgotten because of the sweeping Republican national victories that year).

Soon after the election, the business interests in Detroit lobbied to lower city property taxes. Murphy saw these as blatant attempts to hurt the poor and railed against the perceived hypocrisy. "When I took office, the city was bonded up to the limit," he said. "Why? Partly to aid downtown real estate speculation . . . The special interests never said anything about a dole then."[65]

He noted that 20 percent of the welfare costs had been made necessary by ex-Ford employees residing inside the city limits, while the Ford headquarters and factories were all outside Detroit in Dearborn and Highland Park, thereby paying no taxes to Detroit. One of Murphy's ideas was to make Detroit a larger geographical entity, to allow the taxing of corporations that parked their headquarters just over city lines: "[W]e carry upon our welfare rolls [the former workers] while the community which receives the taxes does not have to bear the burden. It is a grave injustice to saddle the entire metropolitan area on 300,000 taxpayers."[66] Nothing came of this idea.

In the meantime, not getting the proper answer from Murphy in connection with a reduction in their taxes, large property owners within Detroit's borders decided they would take matters into their own hands. Their lobbies sought an amendment to the city charter that would limit property taxes. Under their proposal, Detroit could collect only $61 million for the 1932–1933 fiscal year. They obtained the requisite number of signatures for a vote on their initiative.[67]

Murphy had already won reelection, but with this end run by the real estate interests, his political agenda was in jeopardy. Would the voters favor lower taxes, as argued by the real estate industry, or did they want to ensure minimal services were met, which included assistance to the poor, as Murphy argued? Murphy went on the attack to stop this action by property owners. In one dramatic encounter, Murphy appeared at the Statler Hotel in Detroit where about 780 proponents of the initiative were meeting. At one point, Murphy started to speak. The hostile crowd tried to shout him down. "We are going to meet you with facts and figures in every corner," Murphy answered. "And the people of Detroit are not going to accept your boos, catcalls and hisses as arguments." There were cries of "Throw him out." The mayor, his jacket off and his sleeves pushed to his elbows, calmly continued. "You ought to listen to the facts whether you like them or not," he told the room, "and you won't like them." The booing continued to the end, but Murphy remained preternaturally composed. News of the Statler meeting made its rounds and Murphy was lauded for his calmness and persuasiveness.[68]

Detroit voters overwhelmingly sided with Murphy and rejected the initiative 126,578 to 40,050. The referendum, Murphy asserted, "was one of the most extraordinary political events which I can recall where a people on a technical question of taxation wisely showed sound discrimination, repudiating a proposal which on its face assured tax reduction."[69] He was partly correct because the reality was that the intricacies of the budget remained a mystery to almost all. More was at work than a simple rejection of a proposal that, if passed, would have resulted in fewer city services. Still, Murphy was able to counter arguments that tax cuts were universally desirable. In essence, the voters decided that his government was effective and provided services that justified the current tax rate.

Murphy clearly had persuasive abilities. But something larger was happening. The votes, first for Murphy's reelection, and next on the referendum relating to real estate taxes, were clear warnings that traditional politicians had misjudged the anger, frustration, and fear of the American public, and that business as usual was coming to an end.

Real estate and business interests actually did not give up in pressing for their tax cuts. And they found a political workaround even after this decisive referendum. Before long, the Republican-dominated state legislature voted to limit the ability of localities to tax real estate holdings in their jurisdictions. This had a profound negative effect on Detroit's budget.

Murphy had tried everything, cutting Detroit's city budget and squeezing out more money through tricks such as convincing wealthy citizens to pre-pay their taxes. But the New York and Detroit banks proposed onerous terms as a condition of extending loans, and the Michigan legislature proved stingy in loosening balanced budget requirements.

Murphy responded by trying to meet their respective demands. The economies implemented by the Murphy administration in 1931 and 1932 affected every phase of municipal government. Several thousand employees were laid off, working hours were reduced, maintenance costs were trimmed, restraints were placed on the use of city-owned cars, and the lighting in city offices and buildings was reduced. In 1930, the city spent about $14 million on unemployment relief. By 1931, in an attempt to balance the budget, that share was cut in half, to $7 million.[70]

In making cuts to city employees, Murphy looked for cover. He established commissions to shield him when he had to make difficult fiscal decisions. In early 1931, the official-sounding Detroit Bureau of Governmental Research recommended to the mayor he defer salary increases for teachers. The bureau stated in its report, "It must be born [sic] in mind at all times that the finances of the schools and all other city departments are a single, inseparable, interrelated subject . . . . Economic conditions affect the operation of schools no less than the police, fire and health departments . . . . Progress in the cost of education cannot exceed progress in the material welfare of those who bear that cost."[71] Murphy cited to the commission's findings in denying a pay increase for teachers. Despite his best efforts, all the economic forces were conspiring against Murphy in his attempt to meet Detroit's financial obligations.

Murphy was considering a radical step—leapfrogging over the state and appealing directly to the federal government for aid. A basic problem existed in this regard. The federal government was not a traditional source of assistance for cities. The federalist structure did not have a specific place for cities; the word *city* or *town* does not appear in the Constitution. Instead, according to the Tenth Amendment, all the powers not specifically outlined for the federal government are reserved for the states and the "people." When cities needed help from the federal government, they relied on the states in which they were located to promote their interests in the halls of Congress.[72]

Simply put, the founding fathers did not anticipate powerful cities of the size that had developed by the 1930s, nor did they consider how the interests of cities might diverge from those of the states in which they were located, which were largely rural, just a few miles out from the city centers. In 1930, the city of Detroit had a larger population than 18 states, including Florida. Nevada was the least populated state with about 90,000 residents. In fact, by the 1910s or 1920s, more Americans lived in urban areas than rural areas.[73] The political power had not caught up.

Murphy had a key insight. He realized that corporations were not mentioned in the U.S. Constitution. However, unlike cities, corporations were assumed to have a right to federal aid and largesse, particularly in downturns. Most recently, President Herbert Hoover signed the Reconstruction Finance Corporation (RFC) Act of 1932. This bill provided funding directly to the beleaguered railway lines and banks on the grounds that they were systemically important to the nation's economy. This big transfer of funds to prop up private companies was now squarely on Murphy's mind as he thought of creative ways to get funds directly to his city.

In October 1932, with Detroit on the verge of bankruptcy, Murphy sent a small team of close friends and advisors to Washington, DC, to lobby for federal aid. These advisors included Edward Kemp and Beulah Young. If there was any awkwardness about this combination, no one said anything, at least publicly.[74] Their efforts fell short, and Murphy needed another solution. He was on the right track, but he had employed the wrong type of pressure.

Endnotes

1. "President Hoover Issues a Statement of Reassurance On Continued Prosperity of Fundamental Business," *NYT*, Oct. 26, 1929, 1.

2. "Stocks Collapse in 16,410,030 Share Day, but Rally at Close Cheers Brokers, Bankers; Banker Optimistic, to Continue Aid," *NYT*, Oct. 30, 1929, 1.

3. Ibid.

4. Fine, *Detroit Years*, 183.

5. "Character of Michigan's 'Labor Governor' Analyzed," *TTH*, June 2, 1937, 5.

6. AP, "Detroit Votes of Recall of Mayor, Bowles Accused of Tolerating Lawlessness During Regime," *IDG*, July 22, 1930, 1.

7. Murphy as mayor would revoke the licenses of 175 "near-beer" establishments. "Mayor Revokes Near-Beer Licenses; Probes Delay in Getting Recommendation," *DFP*, Dec. 5, 1930, 20.

8. Zinn, *A People's History*, 387. The artist Thomas Hart Benton was one person who realized, suddenly, that this time was different. In 1930, one year after the stock market crash, he started to paint an epic mural cycle designed to celebrate life in 1920s America. Nine panels contained figures of farmers, coal miners, steelworkers, architects and builders, doctors, and teachers, representing a cross section of American life. The work, now on view at the Metropolitan Museum of Art in New York, is pulsing, sinewy, and giddy. The last panel, however, was an add-on in 1931, and in a poignant sign of the times, shows only hands reaching for bread and other hands holding money. "It wasn't clear there was a Depression until I was almost finished," Benton said later, "so I put that breadline over the door."

9. "Program for the Memorial of Gerald E. (Jerry) Buckley," listing Frank Murphy as a speaker, with the memorial to take place on Aug. 1, 1930, FMP, reel 93.

10. Fine, *Detroit Years*, 211.

11. Ibid, 212.

12. Ibid, 82.

13. Ibid, 214.

14. Ibid, 191–192.

15. "Detroit Finds Dole Has Left Coffers Empty," *The Baltimore Sun*, June 22, 1931, 1.

16. Fine, *Detroit Years*, 213.

17. Ibid, 219.

18. Ibid.

19. "Ends Mayoralty Fight; Bowles, in Detroit, Admits Defeat by Frank Murphy," *NYT*, Sept. 24, 1930, 2.

20. Speech or memorandum of Walter White, FMP, reel 92 (also recalling his impressions of Murphy at Sweet trials).

21. Fine, *Detroit Years*, 258.

22. Arlena Sawyers, "Even during the Depression, GM Managed to Make Money," *Automotive News*, Sept. 14, 2008, accessed Apr. 19, 2020, https://www.autonews.com/article/20080914/OEM/309149837/even-during-the-depression-gm-managed-to-make-money.

23. "Annual Report of General Motors Corporation [to Shareholders], Year Ended December 31, 1932," accessed Apr. 19, 2020, www.library.upenn.edu/collections/lippincott/corprpts/gm/gm1932.pdf.

24. Associated Press, "Mayor Irons Out Strife in Relief Ranks," *TNP*, Dec. 2, 1930, 11.

25. Raymond Clapper, "Relief Aims in Detroit Cited by Mayor Frank Murphy Who Dislikes 'Dole'—Word Picture Unfair," *TEC*, Nov. 19, 1931, 20. ("His critics said he was like the ancient Romans, giving the people free bread. His friends reelected him by the largest majority ever given to a Mayor in Detroit.")

26. Fine, *Detroit Years*, 307.

27. Howard, *Mr. Justice Murphy*, 40.

28. Raymond Clapper, "Relief Aims in Detroit Cited by Mayor Frank Murphy Who Dislikes "Dole- Word Picture Unfair," *TEC*, Nov. 19, 1931, 20.

29. Fine, *Detroit Years*, 305.

30. "Detroit's Relief Plans," *NYT*, Oct. 12, 1930, Section 3, 1. ("But [Murphy] has set manfully about the redemption of his pledge; and in no city in the country has a more systematic or sensible effort been set afoot to ameliorate the economic condition.")

31. Without its football team, the University of Chicago needed a use for its football field. During World War II, the field became the site of Fermi's lab and the first controlled nuclear reaction.

32. Fine, *Detroit Years*, 229.

33. Ibid.

34. Beulah Young to W.E.B Du Bois, July 15, 1924, University of Massachusetts, Amherst, James Aronson Collection of W.E.B. Du Bois, credo.library.umass.edu/view/pageturn/mums312-b027-i178/#page/1/mode/1up.

35. Gomon, Josephine (sometimes referred to as Josephine Fellows Gomon), *Encyclopedia of Detroit* (on the Detroit Historical Society website), detroithistorical.org/learn/encyclopedia-of-detroit/fellows-gomon-josephine.

36. Katie Vloet, "The Gladiator Outside the Spotlight," *Collections* (magazine of the Bentley Historical Library) (article on Josephine Gomon), bentley.umich.edu/news-events/magazine/the-gladiator-outside-the-spotlight.

37. Haldeman-Julius, *Clarence Darrow's Two Greatest Trials*, 53.

38. "City Schools Aid Welfare, 75,000 Persons to Be Fed in Cafeterias," *DFP*, July 2, 1932, 4 (with reference to Fisher Lodge).

39. Vloet, "The Gladiator Outside the Spotlight," *Collections*. Gomon deserves a much bigger place in the history books. She received only a few mentions in the formidable Murphy biographies by Professor J. Woodford Howard and Sidney Fine. In addition to her essential contributions during Murphy's mayoral term, she continued as a trailblazer in her career in government. She became the director of the Detroit Housing Commission, coordinating the building of residential complexes from federal and state funds. She allied herself with FDR's administration, and Detroit received some of the first funds for federal public housing because of her strong attachments to the administration. In one picture at the time, she is seen looking admiringly at Eleanor Roosevelt during FDR's visit to Detroit in 1935 to announce a well-intentioned new Detroit housing project for Black lower-income residents funded by the United States. That project, like many to follow around the county, backfired badly by reinforcing segregated housing patterns in Detroit. All Michigan politicians, including Murphy, had to answer for not doing more to desegregate Detroit, but this one housing project, supported by some of the biggest liberal names as a way of increasing the standard of living of African Americans, fell on the side of well-intentioned but horribly executed plans.

40. Holli, *Reform in Detroit*, 24.

41. Ibid, 120.

42. Photograph, "Mayor Frank Murphy and Commissioner Skrzycki at cornerstone laying, Springwells Station treatment plant," Detroit Public Library, Digital Collections.

43. "Social Reformer," *Daytona Beach Morning Journal*, Nov. 15, 1975, 2 (obituary of Josephine Gomon).

44. "How Detroit Surmounted Financial Perils in '30's," *NYT*, Sept. 7, 1975.

45. Fine, *New Deal Years*, 354.

46. Or in modern terms, a comparison can be made between the amounts held by Apple ($285.1 billion at the end of 2017) and the yearly NASA budget (approximately $20 billion a year). "Apple's Cash Pile Hits $285.1 Billion, a Record, as of the End of 2017." CNBC website, accessed Apr. 19, 2020, https://www.cnbc.com/2018/02/01/apple-earnings-q1-2018-how-much-money-does-apple-have.html.

47. Louis D. Brandeis, *Other People's Money and How the Bankers Use it*, (New York: Frederick A. Stokes Co., 1914), 148–149.

48. Fine, *Detroit Years*, 240.

49. Ibid, 240.

50. "Crowther, *The Political Activities of Detroit Clubwomen in the 1920s*, 136.

51. Beulah Young to Frank Murphy, Jan. 7, 1930 [but with a notation that the letter was actually from 1931], FMP, reel 148.

52. Crowther, *The Political Activities of Detroit Clubwomen in the 1920s*, 2, 136. Crowther described Young as having significant social connections in the Black community because of her education and her marriage to Detroit's first Black surgeon. As with other Black women in her circles, she was energetic in starting several newspapers to combat negative portrayals of Black people in the mainstream press.

53. Beulah Young to Frank Murphy, Jan. 7, 1930 [but with a notation that the letter was actually from 1931], FMP, reel 148.

54. Ibid.

55. Ibid.

56. Crowther, *The Political Activities of Detroit Clubwomen in the 1920s*, 2.

57. Richard Pearson, "Charles Diggs Dies at 75," *Washington Post*, Aug. 25, 1998, B06. ("Mr. Diggs was elected to the House in 1954. He was the first chairman of the Congressional Black Caucus, serving from 1969 to 1971, and from 1973 to 1978, he was chairman of the House District Committee. He also was chairman of the African affairs subcommittee of what was then the House Foreign Affairs Committee . . . He resigned from Congress in 1980, two years after being convicted of 29 counts of operating a payroll kickback scheme in his office. In 1978, he was stripped of his committee and subcommittee chairmanships. He also was censured by the House . . . During the trial and appeals, Mr. Diggs maintained that he was a victim of 'selective prosecution' and that he was held to standards different from white colleagues.")

58. Howard, *Mr. Justice Murphy*, 45.

59. Gladys H. Kelsey, "Detroit Creating Work for Jobless," *NYT*, Oct. 12, 1930, E5 ("Many citizens who did not believe he could make that promise [of finding work for the idle] are now finding admiration as they see a whole city organizing without partisan discord"); Raymond Clapper, "Relief Aims in Detroit Cited by Mayor Frank Murphy Who Dislikes 'Dole'—Word Picture Unfair," *TEC*, Nov. 19, 1931, 20 ("His critics said he was like the ancient Romans, giving the people free bread. His friends reelected him by the largest majority ever given to a Mayor in Detroit").

60. Data compiled by a prominent Black statistician found that Detroit had a Black population of 102,975 in 1929, and 40,000 were registered Republicans, while about 2,200 were Democrats (along with 1,174 independents). "Negroes Here Make

Progress: Recently Completed Survey Gives Interesting Data on Population Segment," *DFP*, July 9, 1929, 17.

61. "Catholic Mayor-Elect of Detroit, Defeating Former Klan Favorite," *The Catholic Transcript*, XXXIII, no. 16, Sept. 25, 1930, accessible through the U.S. Catholic News Service website.

62. Fine, *Detroit Years*, 438.

63. Pamphlet, FMP, reel 97. ("Detroit is predominately a Protestant city. Catholics dominate its elections only because they show fidelity to their duties of citizenship second only to their unswerving loyalty to their faith. They vote solidly, consistently, rain or shine, good times or bad, and their vote is always concentrated on selected Catholic candidates.")

64. Fine, *Detroit Years*, 439.

65. Raymond Clapper, "Relief Aims in Detroit Cited by Mayor Frank Murphy Who Dislikes 'Dole'—Word Picture Unfair," *TEC*, Nov. 19, 1931, 20.

66. Gladys H. Kelsey, "Welfare Problem Perplexes Detroit," *NYT*, May 3, 1931, 51.

67. Fine, *New Deal Years*, 355.

68. Ibid, 358. By Howard's telling, Murphy removed his jacket as if to fight. Howard, *Mr Justice Murphy*, 51.

69. Fine, *New Deal Years*, 359.

70. Raymond Clapper, "Relief Aims in Detroit Cited by Mayor Frank Murphy Who Dislikes 'Dole' —Word Picture Unfair," *TEC*, Nov. 19, 1931, 20 (describing financial plight of Detroit).

71. "Teachers' Pay Raise Opposed," *DFP*, Feb. 15, 1931.

72. The struggle between states and their cities for control over local financial resources continues to this day: "States like Ohio are placing their surpluses in rainy-day funds, but cities that have suffered because of cuts since the recession say it is time to loosen up." Timothy Williams, "Some States Sitting on Piles of Cash, and Cities Want a Cut," *NYT*, Aug. 17, 2018, A15.

73. Our World in Data website, sponsored by Oxford University and others, accessed May 3, 2020, https://ourworldindata.org/grapher/urban-and-rural-populations-in-the-united-states.

74. "Brucker Sure U.S. Will Give Aid to Detroit," *DFP*, Oct. 2, 1932, 1. (The committee sent by Murphy included "Edward G. Kemp, Charles M. Novak, Mrs. Josephine Gomon, Frank X. Martel, Dr. R.W. Woodroofe and Mrs. Beulah Young.")

CHAPTER 9

Mayor Murphy's Direct Appeal to Washington for Aid

Murphy was up for reelection less than a year into office. He again campaigned energetically as a compassionate overseer in a time of financial crisis. He won easily and settled in to running the city. Murphy was not willing to give up his idea to have the federal government assist localities in providing poverty relief. Having failed in all other efforts to raise federal money for his city, Murphy focused on uniting big-city mayors. If they banded together, large cities would have a better chance of convincing the federal government to start providing support directly to them, bypassing the states. To this end, he convinced 48 mayors of cities with populations in excess of 100,000 to attend a conference of mayors in Detroit.

The conference, scheduled for June 1932, was big news in the local newspapers around the country. People understood just how innovative Murphy's idea was. In Baltimore, the *Sun* announced that Mayor Howard Jackson would be attending, after receiving an invitation by Mayor Murphy, to discuss "federal aid for the unemployed." The meeting was necessary because "[t]he prolonged economic depression, the attending problems of unemployment and the curtailment of credit, have precipitated a serious social and financial burden which has fallen largely upon the municipalities which must organize."[1]

On June 1, 1932, Murphy gave the keynote address at the so-named Conference of Mayors. "We do not seek indiscriminate Federal Aid for local governments," he proclaimed. Instead, the federal government should recognize that "an unusual share of the general burden has been borne by the local governments until their resources have been exhausted." Now it was the job of the federal government "to assist municipalities to meet" their financial obligations, just as the federal government "is required to assist banks, railroads, insurance companies and other private corporations."[2] He wanted to project an air of reasonableness, but he was also issuing an implicit threat to publicize the government's efforts to prop up private companies if cities did not also receive funds to help the most desperate.

The cities faced problems due to factors beyond their control, including unprecedented deflationary pressures, making it harder to pay back debts. Financial obligations incurred during "the over-expansion period...must be paid with dollars worth more than when the debts were contracted."[3] Murphy recognized a basic problem that cities and other political entities identify with to this day: A debt load for a city is serviceable while the economy is growing. A fixed $20 million debt consumes 20 percent of a city's revenues if that city receives $100 million in revenues through sales taxes or property taxes. If tax revenue goes up to $200 million because of a booming economy or rising real estate values, the fixed debt of $20 million is only 10 percent of the city's revenue. If the economy sinks, and the city receives $50 million in tax revenue, then debt of $20 million is a whopping 40 percent of receipts, which would crowd out other payments such as to employees and upkeep of the local art museums and other amenities that make cities great. From there, a vicious cycle starts, as cuts in service make the city less attractive, leading to a rush to the door and then even more cutbacks.

Murphy also made a moral argument. Most of the suffering—and the unemployed—were in cities. Other parts of the country were offloading their problems to the urban areas, he informed his fellow mayors, as the workers without prospects in small towns moved to urban centers. Therefore, the entire nation had obligations to the big cities.

Finally, Murphy noted that legal limitations restricted cities attempting to raise revenue. Many cities and states had budget-balancing requirements imposed on them by the states.[4] Implicit in these laws was the assumption that the states would assist municipalities in times of economic strife, but this was not happening in the 1930s when the states faced their own massive problems.[5]

To his fellow mayors he stated, "Our Declaration of Independence declared us to be one people . . . Our Federal Constitution imposes the solemn obligation to promote the general welfare. The Federal government alone represents all the people."[6]

This speech to the mayors was a Murphy hallmark for at least three reasons. First, he spoke plainly about the challenges, giving the unvarnished facts but concluding as always with words of hope. Second, he appealed to moderation. Cities needed help, but only because of the unique times. Once this crisis passed, the options could be reconsidered.

Third, and most significantly, he boiled down the nation's foundational documents—the Declaration of Independence and the Constitution—into one or two sentences, and in ways that did not actually reflect the words of the documents, but rather his conception of American ideals. He was later to be criticized for ignoring the actual words in the Constitution in his Supreme Court decisions, but he was simply doing on the Supreme Court what came naturally to him. Murphy always defined the founding documents in his own terms. Just the year before, as mayor, he stated, "I read the Constitution of the United States that the Government is to promote the general welfare. I do not take that to mean the welfare of great property, or of any race or creed, but of all the people."[7]

The mayors spent most of their time at the conference drafting documents and planning a trip to Washington, DC, to lobby for aid. But the meeting was marked by several discordant interludes. During one session of the mayor's meeting, Murphy arranged for a debate on religion.[8] Clergy of all stripes faced off against Clarence Darrow, a well-known atheist and someone Murphy knew from the Sweet trial. Darrow made a presentation to the mayors that mocked religion—and he must have scandalized many in the room—although the transcript reflects applause from the audience after many of his statements. Murphy displayed tact and warmth as he sought to deflect Darrow's words. Recalling the Ossian Sweet trial to those "who are somewhat disturbed by what" Darrow had just said, Murphy related that "the situation [at the trial] was very tense. After some five hours of argument, [Darrow] shrugged his shoulders, looked at me and said, 'Now, judge, those are the facts, they are the real facts, the true facts in this case, and you know I wouldn't lie to you, unless I had to.'" After this statement that poked fun at his friend Darrow, the mayors applauded.[9]

A more cautious mayor would not have conducted a debate on religion, which was a predictable, and entirely avoidable, minefield. On this subject, like on all others, Murphy trusted his audience, whether they agreed with him or not. Vigorous debate was a hallmark of the American system. He never hid the salient points, both pro and con, or talked down to the people he sought to persuade. When discussing Detroit's problems in front of large groups of constituents, some with minimal education, Murphy did not hesitate to offer a blizzard of facts or to paint his point of view in the starkest of terms.

Some mayors had their ideas of fun. The conference was interrupted when some of the city leaders took a trip across the Detroit River to take advantage of the hospitality of the mayor of Windsor in Canada, which was not subject to Prohibition.[10]

In the end, Murphy succeeded in uniting the mayors. "It is a crisis, imminent and terrifying," the preamble to the mayors' closing resolution declared, and "the very foundations of our social order are imperiled." They lobbied for a $5 billion prosperity loan to be granted by the federal government, an extension of the RFC credit to the cities, and the use of these funds to pay maturing obligations of municipal governments.[11]

Before ending the conference, the mayors decided that they would send a delegation to Washington to appeal for direct federal aid. They were determined to seek an audience with President Hoover.

At the closing prayer, Murphy's friend Father Coughlin stated the case for the cities in stark terms: "We are here to say . . . our people are angry. . . . We cannot sit supinely by and wait for economic laws to operate magically into a solution. It is entirely within the power of enlightened human intelligence to ease and justly distribute the load, thus hastening the work of reconstruction and restoration."[12] Murphy and Coughlin often took steps to elevate the profile of the other at least early in their careers, and Coughlin would soon recommend Murphy for a position in FDR's administration.

On June 3, 1932, two days after the adjournment of the conference, Murphy appointed a seven-person commission of big-city mayors (including himself) and departed for the nation's capital. Hoover was still the president, and the 1932 elections had not yet taken place. This was a "what if" moment in history. What if Hoover had embraced the requests of the mayors and showed ideological flexibility by earmarking federal funds? Would he have captured the gratitude of the big cities? This was not to happen.

In this regard, other Republicans showed ideological flexibility. James Couzens, the Michigan senator and a Republican, showed that he would work with Murphy, shepherding him through various congressional offices to drum up support for Murphy's proposal. Couzens remained a Republican his entire career. He initially believed that the Great Depression's effects should be met through private charity but was chastened when other wealthy individuals could not or would not match his $1 million donation to the city of Detroit to alleviate its immediate financial troubles. By 1932, with the Republican Party still in control of the White House, Couzens agreed with Murphy's logic that the federal government was a place for cities to obtain these funds.

On June 6, Murphy and the other mayors met Texan John Nance Garner, then the U.S. Speaker of the House and soon to be the vice presidential choice of FDR. That same day, they met with the Republican Vice President Charles Curtis and Senate leaders. Finally, on June 8, 1932, Murphy and the colorful mayor James Curley of Boston met with President Hoover, who was at least initially unimpressed with the lobbying effort and indicated his opposition to the prosperity loan proposal of the mayors.[13] As attorney general, Murphy would later target Curley's political machine, an effort cut short by Murphy's elevation to the Supreme Court (which may not have been coincidental as a means of stopping Murphy's aggressive pursuit of corrupt politicians). For now, Curley and Murphy were on the same side.

Although Murphy was unafraid to blame the business community—sometimes virulently—for the financial woes of the cities, he believed it was important to acknowledge when they acted in what he considered to be a socially appropriate manner. He did not want to alienate them unnecessarily on his sojourn in Washington, DC, where Murphy went out of his way to praise the relief efforts of certain corporations in Detroit. He lauded Dodge, Cadillac, Packard, Briggs, and Hudson-Essex as companies that were working to care for their own employees and families.

But he singled out Ford as the exception to the rule of general corporate responsibility in dealing with the welfare of laid-off workers.[14] Murphy had his own reasons to dislike Ford. Just a few months before, on one of the coldest days of the year, 3,000 to 5,000 unemployed Ford workers and others marched from Detroit to Dearborn. This was the so-called "Hunger March." Murphy, as mayor of Detroit at the time, made clear that the march should take place and that the police should not intervene.

The context of this march was roiling labor unrest and growing expectations by workers that their former employers, many still profitable even in the depths of the Depression, had continuing obligations to the people they had fired. The Hunger Marchers had hoped to extract a pledge from Ford to help its former workers.

As soon as the marchers crossed into Dearborn, leaving Murphy's jurisdiction, police immediately fired tear gas to disperse the crowd. Dearborn police and Ford's own security force, under Harry Bennett, then shot and killed five marchers. Many more were injured. A number of the injured protestors were arrested and chained to their hospital beds.[15]

A grand jury appointed to investigate the violence issued a report a few months later. The report concluded, "After hearing many witnesses on both sides of the matter, this grand jury finds no legal grounds for indictments [of the workers who marched]. However, we find that the conduct of the demonstrators was ill-considered and unlawful in their utter disregard for constituted authority. We find, further, that the conduct of the Dearborn City Police when they first met the demonstrators, though well intended, might have been more discreet, and better considered before they applied force in the form of tear gas."[16]

One grand juror, a political ally of Murphy, dissented, calling the administration of the grand jury "the most biased, prejudiced and ignorant proceeding imaginable." This grand juror, Mrs. Jerry Houghton Bacon, said she "witnessed the most glaring dis-crimination on the parts of the prosecutors in the treatment of witnesses brought before the grand jury. Marked prejudice was voiced by the prosecutors which, without regard to its intent, impressed and influenced the minds of the jurors."[17]

As on other matters of criminal law, Murphy was later able to exert significant influence on national policy in his capacity as a Supreme Court justice. In this regard, Murphy ultimately decided that he did not like certain aspects of grand jury procedures. The case of *In re Oliver* came before the Supreme Court in 1948.[18] By now, he was an associate justice on the High Court and one year before his death. In *Oliver*, a witness who allegedly gave false or evasive testimony to a Michigan grand jury hearing was convicted and sentenced to jail without either notice or attorney assistance. Previously, under a law passed by progressivists in Michigan in 1917 to place a greater emphasis on investigative procedures, the local justices of the peace were given contempt power to vindicate their authority.[19]

Murphy was familiar with the one-man jury. He employed the procedure himself. But he also saw how grand juries generally can be abused. He would have remembered the Hunger March when, in his view, police were not held to account. In *Oliver*, the

Supreme Court overturned the conviction, and Justice Hugo Black, who wrote the decision, likened the Michigan grand jury's discretionary contempt convictions to the English Star Chamber (and for good measure, the French pre-Revolutionary *lettres de cachet*), allowing imprisonment without the opportunity for defense.[20] Murphy signed on to this opinion, overturning a state law that he never had enough power to address while a state official in Michigan.

Murphy learned something else from the Hunger March. He realized that companies would never assume the responsibility of caring for their laid-off workers, even when they returned to generating large profits. Not only that, management was willing to unleash violence against workers who raised this as an issue. For Murphy, this reinforced his perception that the government, and not private industry, was the vehicle to help these workers. Within the next few years, under the rubric of the New Deal, he and others of like mind helped usher in the era of government-run jobs programs and unemployment benefits, a system that survives to this day.

Murphy's idea to invade Washington, DC, with a group of mayors to plead for direct federal funding to cities was unprecedented. After all, this was an end-run around the states, the traditional forum for communicating local concerns to the federal government. And Murphy and his posse of mayors succeeded. The Emergency Relief and Construction Act passed in July 1932 despite some Democratic defections (mostly from senators and congressmen from the South who rationalized that funding cities directly on the federal level would take some control from the state leaders and thereby threaten Jim Crow). A band of 12 Republicans led by Fiorello LaGuardia, the future mayor of New York City and an ally of Murphy, spearheaded the passage of the legislation.

Hoover overcame his opposition to the idea and was the president who signed it. Ironically, in the end, Republicans took the lead in passing legislation to help localities, but this support by

Republicans was not to help their prospects in the 1932 national elections. And a more permanent result of Murphy's efforts was the creation of the Conference of Mayors, still in existence to this day.

Murphy always had a flurry of ideas, some of which he was less successful in implementing. He was unable to get legislation passed in Michigan to place a moratorium on city bond repayments and so, while he was in Washington, he appealed to Congress.[21] Congress likewise failed to act on Murphy's request.

In general, though, the trip to Washington, DC, was a success on a personal as well as political basis. Murphy had raised his national profile and was accepted into the inner corridors of power. He had impressed power brokers on both sides of the aisle. And he had succeeded with the Republican Party still in power. As such, he was a kind of scout for FDR and his New Deal. It was becoming more obvious that Washington, DC, was now ready to inject federal power and funds into local affairs. The relief for cities was one manifestation of this new attitude.

Murphy looked back at his time as mayor with pride that civility prevailed. Given the tinderbox conditions, it is a small miracle that widespread violence did not occur in Detroit, with its volatile mix of labor unrest and the desperation of many who had no ability to care for their families. In the late 1930s, already the U.S. Attorney General, Murphy recalled the dark days of 1932, when "the nation had reached the depths of the Great Depression."[22] He stated that in Detroit "resources had been virtually exhausted in an effort to protect the citizens from an economic collapse that had struck the city like a famine." But through it all there was not "a single untoward incident of major proportion."[23]

This was a tribute to the "great mass of people" to the ideal of civil liberties. "I doubt that there has ever been more convincing proof that the people of a democracy can keep their civil liberties in the bad weather as well as the fair," said Murphy. "Having stood that acid test, we should not fear any other."[24]

It is true that, like FDR, Murphy never urged people to take to the streets to confront the industrialists. But he was not afraid to use the threat of social disorder to get concessions from the more-conservative elements in society. Communists were trying to create "serious disorder," he declared in one speech as mayor, and he presented himself as a more moderate alternative. His goal was to scare people who were on the fence, whether businessmen or legislatures holding the power of the purse, to support him and, more to the point, provide funds or extend credit to the Detroit government during the financial emergency.[25]

In describing Ralph Stone and his banking oversight committee, Murphy stated, "I wonder if he knows of the weekly struggle between Communists and welfare workers for control of the City's welfare problems."[26] Murphy's tactics were like Roosevelt's. When confronting politicians or business owners skeptical of New Deal programs, he positioned himself as the reasonable one, far better to deal with than socialists and communists who were polling well.

At the same time, he employed populist language that is rarely seen today. During a battle over whether to cut city taxes in Detroit, as the business community wanted, he attacked businessmen in a way that he knew would be picked up by the press: "How dare you spend more money for each luncheon in this room than I need to feed a hungry child for a week!"[27] This combination of presenting himself to the general public as a moderate compared to others on his side, while showing his base the fire in his belly—all while pressing his goals—was a technique to be adopted by FDR, who pulled off the feat almost to perfection.

Endnotes

1. "Jackson to Attend Meeting of Mayors of Michigan," *Baltimore Sun*, May 26, 1932, 8. In smaller markets, newspapers covered the meeting by printing newswire stories. INS, "27 Mayors at Conference in Detroit Today: All Admit that Some Form of Federal Aid is Necessary Now," *The News-Messenger* (Fremont, Ohio), Jun. 1, 1932.

2. Frank Murphy speech, Conference of Mayors of the United States held in Detroit, Michigan, on or about June 1, 1932, FMP, reel 98.

3. Ibid.

4. Ibid.

5. Ibid.

6. Ibid.

7. Raymond Clapper, "Relief Aims in Detroit Cited by Mayor Frank Murphy Who Dislikes 'Dole'—Word Picture Unfair," *TEC*, Nov. 19, 1931, 20.

8. Article fragment, *LSJ*, Mar. 14, 1938, 2. (This article recalls the event but lists the wrong date of the event.)

9. Frank Murphy speech, Conference of Mayors of the United States held in Detroit, Michigan, on or about June 1, 1932, FMP, reel 98.

10. Fine, *Detroit Years*, 349–350.

11. Ibid, 350. The Denver mayor was the sole dissenter, stating that "no matter how much the cities borrow from the government, the citizens will have to pay it back." AP, "Citizens Will Have to Pay, Denver Mayor Voices Opposition to Federal Relief Plan," *The Spokesman Review* (Spokane, WA), June 2, 1932, 10.

12. Howard, *Mr. Justice Murphy*, 52.

13. Fine, *Detroit Years*, 351. Hoover initially told the group of mayors that he was sympathetic but thought the bond issue would do more harm than good. AP, "Group of Mayors Urges Hoover to Support Relief Bond Issue," *St. Louis Post-Dispatch*, June 9, 1932, 2.

14. "Murphy Tells of Aid Crisis; Reports on City Needs to Senate Body," *DFP*, Jan. 7, 1932.

15. Ford and Bennett later sent Frank Murphy a model of the B-24 bomber, being built at the rate of one an hour at Willow Run during World War II, showing there were no hard feelings, at least from their perspective. But there was a Murphy connection here as well. In 1941, Josephine Gomon was recruited by Henry Ford to the role of Director of Women Personnel at Willow Run for the duration of World War II. Murphy's political enemies had a grudging respect for his picks to assist him, and often hired them.

16. Maurice Sugar, *The Ford Hunger March* (Berkeley: Meiklejohn Civil Liberties Institute, 1980), 25.

17. Ibid.

18. *In re Oliver*, 333 U.S. 257 (1948).

19. Ibid, 261–262.

20. Ibid, 268–270.

21. Associated Press, "Detroit Mayor Seeks Support of President, Murphy Calls at White House to Urge Two-Year Moratorium on Cities' Debts," *BCE*, Mar. 22, 1933.

22. Frank Murphy, "Civil Liberties and the Cities," before the Joint Meeting of the United States Conference of Mayors and the National Institute of Municipal Law Officers at the Empire Room, the Waldorf-Astoria, New York City, May 15, 1939, United States Attorney General website, "Murphy speeches."

23. Ibid.

24. Ibid.

25. Fine, *Detroit Years*, 377.

26. Howard, *Mr. Justice Murphy*, 49.

27. Ibid, 51.

CHAPTER 10

The New Deal and Murphy

As mayor of Detroit, Murphy often came to New York City, hat in hand, trying to convince the New York bankers not to call in their Detroit loans. It was during one of these trips that Murphy met FDR for the first time. In June 1931, Murphy and Hall traveled to FDR's home in Hyde Park 70 miles up the Hudson River. The introduction was through G. Hall Roosevelt, then the Detroit city comptroller.[1] The three can be seen together in what was probably their first meeting together on the steps of the Roosevelt's mansion, FDR effortlessly holding himself up with his powerful arms and chest, his legs paralyzed by Infant Polio, Murphy gazing intently at him with a slight smile, and Hall standing behind the two of them.[2]

FDR and Murphy came from different social worlds. Roosevelt was of Dutch colonial stock on one side and a descendant from the Mayflower on the other. He went to exclusive East Coast private schools and had a famous cousin, Teddy Roosevelt. When FDR was a boy, his father had sufficient contacts to arrange a meeting with President Grover Cleveland. The tired and harassed president supposedly placed his hand on the child's head and said "Son, I'm making a strange wish for you. I wish that you may never be President."[3]

He attended private boarding schools and then finished his education at Harvard and Columbia. Consistent with his status,

Roosevelt had been handed a high-ranking position in the navy during World War I. In one photo taken around 1914, he could be seen symbolically laying the keel of the *Arizona*, the great battleship named after the newest state. The *Arizona* would later be sunk by the Japanese at Pearl Harbor, triggering Roosevelt's famous speech regarding the "day of infamy" that brought the United States into World War II.

Roosevelt had even been a vice presidential candidate on the unsuccessful Democratic ticket in 1920. Polio struck FDR in 1921 when he was 39, and after a harrowing recovery, he was to be paralyzed from the waist down for the rest of his life. When FDR had sufficiently recovered, he ran a successful campaign for New York State governor in 1928, the same year his fellow New Yorker Al Smith ran for president. A victorious Roosevelt showed that he could appeal not just to the traditional urban base of the Democratic Party, but also to the farmers and rural residents. In early 1931, shortly after his reelection as governor of New York, Roosevelt called for legislation that would enable the state to give immediate aid to unemployed New Yorkers, declaring that "the duty of the State towards the citizens is the duty of the servant to its master."[4] While Murphy was engaged in triage in Detroit simply trying to feed a hungry population, FDR was on the attack with new programs to lift his state out of the economic swamp.

Roosevelt's polio was widely acknowledged to have given him discipline and empathy. For FDR, a sense of noblesse oblige no doubt played a part, which his mother instilled in him. His wife Eleanor's influence was also decisive in explaining his political goals. She pushed him to appoint women to his administration and to consider the civil rights of Black people. She fought for better housing and the support of the arts through the Federal Arts Projects, a precursor of the National Endowment for the Arts. She championed workers' rights and lobbied for the NLRA demanding workers receive a living wage.

FDR and Murphy were natural political allies, given their sympathies to workers and their progressivist instincts. In early 1932, FDR invoked the "forgotten man" as a reason to rebuild the economy from the "bottom up."[5] This kind of rhetoric appealed to Murphy. In a radio address in November 1932, the day before the national election, Mayor Murphy declared, "The Forgotten Man on the farm, in the city, from the alley or the avenue, will have his day-in-court tomorrow as he exercises the right which is the proud duty of every freeman and citizen—to vote his conscience."[6] What Murphy probably did not know was that FDR's most famous phrase from his campaign, the "forgotten man" reference, was written by a newsman on a kind of dare from Roosevelt, after the reporters ribbed FDR for being too conservative on the campaign trail.[7]

And Murphy checked many boxes for Roosevelt as he sought to expand his own base in anticipation of his run for the presidency. One of Roosevelt's great gifts was his ability to incorporate ethnic groups into his coalition while maintaining the support of Protestant majorities. America was a place that just eight years before had passed the most restrictive immigration bill ever. Congress had passed the Immigration Act of 1924, in response to nativist pressure. The legislation set quotas at 2 percent of each nationality residing in the United States in 1910. By setting 1910 as the date for measuring relevant populations and not 1924, the year of the law, Congress further restricted the flow of Jews, Italians, Slavs, and Greeks—who had immigrated in large numbers during these intervening years.

In a bit of bigoted horse trading, support from the California congressional delegation was gained with a provision excluding from entry into the country any alien who by virtue of race or nationality was ineligible for citizenship. This was code for *Japanese Americans*, even though the words were not explicitly in the law: "Existing nationality laws dating from 1790 and 1870 excluded people of Asian lineage from naturalizing. As a result, the 1924 Act meant that even Asians not previously prevented from immigrating—the Japanese in particular—would no longer be admitted into the United States."[8]

FDR needed to acknowledge this nativist sentiment as he ran for national office. He threaded the needle by attracting the upstanding, Americanized citizens within various ethnic groups.

Murphy fit the profile. He was a Catholic who attended public school and was comfortable mixing with people from other ethnic and religious groups.

Murphy was to become utterly devoted to FDR. As we will see, he was willing to travel literally halfway around the world to please him. And FDR proved to be loyal to Murphy. When Murphy's star was fading in the late 1930s, Roosevelt never forgot his early support. He continued to reward Murphy with plum positions, out of line with Murphy's fading stature and to the general distain of others close to FDR. When FDR looked for a Catholic replacement to fill a Supreme Court justice's death, Murphy became an obvious choice.

Although FDR went into the Democratic National Convention in 1932 with a majority of delegates, his rival Alfred Smith hoped to deny him the two-thirds support necessary to win the party's presidential nomination. In a signal that Roosevelt was a new type of candidate, he tried to get the convention to change its rules to allow his nomination by a straight majority vote. The convention delegates refused to go along.[9] This would not be the last time Roosevelt attempted to move the goalposts when all else failed, sometimes failing miserably as he did with his Supreme Court packing debacle in 1937.[10]

FDR, with the help of Farley and others, then turned to influencing individual state delegates. As to the Michigan vote, FDR relied on people such as Murphy to sway that state's votes. On the first three ballots, Roosevelt had a majority of the national delegate vote but still lacked the two-thirds majority. Before the fourth ballot, Farley and his co-manager Louis McHenry Howe struck a deal with House Speaker John Nance Garner: Garner would drop out of the nominating race and support Roosevelt, and in return Roosevelt would agree to name Garner as his running mate. With this agreement, Roosevelt won the two-thirds majority and the Democratic presidential nomination. As it turned out, Roosevelt had nothing to fear from the Michigan delegation. The Michiganders voted as a bloc for Roosevelt on all four nominating ballots.[11]

It was now time to take on sitting president Herbert Hoover. One of FDR's political goals after winning the Democratic nomination was to incorporate traditionally Republican Western senators into his coalition, denying the traditional rural base of support to President Hoover. Here, Roosevelt succeeded. Senator George Norris, a Republican from Nebraska, had created the Nonpartisan League (NPL) in 1932 during the campaign season with the goal of helping FDR. The NPL appointed Murphy to its board, and then Murphy joined Senator Norris in his coast-to-coast tour to promote FDR. Murphy thereby played a significant role consolidating the urban and rural elements of the progressivist community.[12]

FDR's seduction of most of the progressives of stature in the Republican Party, and his convincing them to become Democrats, was another of FDR's "rabbit out of a hat" tricks. His future vice presidential pick, Henry Wallace, was a prime example. And a few progressives never left the Republican Party, even after Roosevelt's election, but they became staunch supporters of FDR nonetheless. Congressman Fiorello LaGuardia from New York City remained a Republican but also a staunch supporter of the New Deal. LaGuardia and Murphy were to form a close working relationship, joining forces to shore up support of liberals after a strong rebuke by voters during the 1938 off-year election, six years into FDR's presidency. Fatefully, the Democratic Party retained the most recalcitrant social conservatives from the South.[13]

In the national election held on November 8, 1932, FDR and his Texan vice presidential pick John Nance Garner received 22,821,277 votes, or 57.41 percent of the vote; Herbert Hoover and his vice presidential pick Charles Curtis from Kansas received 15,761,254 votes, or 39.6 percent of the vote[14]; and the socialist candidate Norman Thomas (after whom a public high school a few blocks from the Empire State Building was named) and his vice presidential pick of James H. Maurer received a respectable 887,000 votes.[15]

As for Michigan, Roosevelt did not have a problem carrying the state, with 871,700 votes versus 739,894 votes for the Hoover slate.[16] With one exception, every Democrat in the statewide ballot in Michigan won that year.

The idea that Roosevelt could reach into traditional Republican bastions such as Michigan and not only prevail but lift other Democratic candidates to victory was a terrifying prospect for the Republican power base. But many of the traditionally Republican states reverted to form in non-presidential election years, at least after 1936. Murphy, contending for reelection as governor in a Republican state, learned this the hard way in 1938. The one Republican to withstand the Democratic onslaught in Michigan was Frank Fitzgerald, who would emerge later as a major spoiler for Murphy's political ambitions in the state.

FDR, of course, did not immediately take office. The country descended into further economic turmoil between FDR's election in November 1932 and his inauguration in March 1933. For four months, Hoover remained encamped as the president, while the country waited on Roosevelt. In the meantime, the states were taking steps to protect their own populations as the economic crisis was worsening.

During this lame-duck period, many states were declaring bank holidays to prevent runs on deposits. Michigan was the first state to close all its financial institutions, although Murphy had no part in this decision. The immediate cause was the threat of Henry Ford to withdraw his money from Detroit's own Union Guardian Trust. At its core, Ford's bank had a liquidity problem. The Union Guardian Trust had many assets, but most were illiquid and unavailable on an immediate basis to cover Ford's withdrawals.

In one frantic weekend in 1933, Michigan senator Couzens urged President Hoover to inject outside money into Union Guardian Trust and other Michigan banks to meet withdrawal requests such as Ford's.[17] He argued that banks could look to the RFC Act, legislation that approved federal funds for large financial institutions. It will be recalled that Murphy pointed to this legislation as a basis for arguing that municipalities should also receive funding from the federal government.

Couzens failed in his last-minute attempts to obtain funding for the Michigan banks. Part of this may have been his own doing.

He had previously been critical of the secretive nature of some of the distributions from the RFC. He had argued that much of the federal funding went to prop up companies and banks without regard to prior malfeasance, and that some of the government relief went to repay irresponsible executives. Huey Long and Father Coughlin later characterized the RFC's lending policies in more conspiratorial terms. To them, the failure to lend to common citizens and only to the great financial institutions and industrial behemoths was an attempt to preserve these companies' hegemony on the backs of the working man.[18]

The Michigan bank holiday shocked the people of Detroit. Prices immediately started to increase on food and other staples. When reports reached Murphy of profiteering, he announced that he might appoint a "food dictator."[19]

Cash became hard to find. During the Michigan bank holidays, the big automakers paid their employees by shipping in currency on trucks from outside the city. Small business owners traveled to places such as Chicago with empty suitcases and came back loaded with cash. The bank closures were to prove disastrous to the 26,000 municipal employees who had no ability to travel outside the city to banks that may have still been open and not shuttered. Employees receiving their paychecks on March 1, 1933, were generally not able to cash them until April 25, 1933.[20] Now, because of the banks' temporary closing and the lack of physical currency, someone had to come up with another form of currency to keep the economy going. Thus barter became common in Detroit and other places around the country.

At the end of Murphy's first term as mayor in 1932, Detroit used scrip as a substitute for government-issued currency.[21] Murphy proposed that the scrip be supported by unpaid back taxes, but this plan was not met with enthusiasm from the business community. The scrip plan in Chicago, based on the same model, was seen as a failure because it allowed speculators to buy the scrip at a discount, later to be paid in full.[22]

While Michigan and several states had declared a bank holiday, other states seemed safe from the contagion for a while. This was not to last, as people lost their faith even in banks with ample reserves. They could observe the lines outside banks and worried that their own banks would not meet their obligations. The fear turned to panic as lines formed at banks around the country.

Further draining the economy was the United States' reliance on the gold standard, meaning a dollar could always be traded for a set amount of gold. The beauty of the traditionally strong American economy was that few bothered to trade their dollars for gold. Reflecting this fact, the Federal Reserve banks did not have enough gold to swap every dollar, maintaining reserves equal to only 40 percent of the paper currency they issued. But foreign and domestic holders of United States currency were rapidly losing faith in paper money and were redeeming dollars for gold at an alarming rate.[23] These exchanges were also sucking money out of the economy, reducing the money that consumers and business were putting in goods and upgrades to business.

On March 1, 1933, George Harrison, the head of the Federal Reserve in New York, sent an urgent message to Treasury Secretary Ogden Mills under President Hoover. He reported that the New York Reserve Bank's gold reserve had fallen below the legal limit. Harrison's communique to Washington bluntly stated that he would "no longer take responsibility" for running the New York Reserve Bank "with deficient reserves."[24] In his view, the best course for the country was a national bank holiday that "would permit the country to calm down and allow time for the enactment of remedial legislation."[25] But the initiative in declaring a bank holiday could only come from President Hoover, who refused to act. As more banks closed, and calls for a bank holiday increased, President-Elect Roosevelt stayed silent.

President Roosevelt's first inaugural speech in March 1933 is most famous today for his reassuring proclamation, "The only thing we have to fear is fear itself." In fact, Roosevelt's utterance did not draw applause at the time and did not become well-known until Roosevelt's reelection campaign in 1936. The part of the speech that resonated with the crowd most was when Roosevelt promised to use executive action if Congress did not enact his proposed legislation.[26]

Fortunately, FDR never exhibited authoritarian powers. He was, however, willing to use the levers of government in creative ways to help lift the country out of the Depression. Earlier, in a

Georgia campaign rally in 1932, he stated, "The country needs and, unless I mistake its temper, the country demands bold, persistent experimentation. It is common sense to take a method and try it: If it fails, admit it frankly and try another. But above all, try something."[27] These statements directly echoed Murphy's earlier "try any idea" approach with his MUC to alleviate starvation when he first became mayor of Detroit.

FDR's first substantial act was to deal with the bank crisis. At 1:00 AM on Monday, March 6, 1933, Roosevelt declared a national bank holiday, ordering the immediate suspension of all banking transactions. He had taken the oath of office only 36 hours earlier.

For an entire week, most Americans had no access to financial services. They could not withdraw or transfer their money, nor could they make deposits. In a swift chain of events, Congress dusted off a stalled bill from the Hoover era that required the Federal Reserve to extend credit to banks so that they could meet their immediate cash needs. After four days, banks started to reopen. And later that year, Congress passed a law creating the Federal Deposit Insurance Corporation (FDIC), giving a federal guarantee to bank deposits, a system in place to this day. These acts had a calming effect, and the run on banks stopped.

One of the goals of the new legislation was to replace sick banks with healthier ones. As for Detroit, the FDR administration now proposed eliminating the two major banks—the First National Bank and the Guardian National Bank—and replacing them with the new National Bank of Detroit. The officers of the established Detroit banks, having paid out dividends to themselves just the year before, were not too proud to appeal to Mayor Murphy to save them, asking him to go to the new President Roosevelt to save their institutions. Murphy refused to do so.[28]

Roosevelt also acted to revoke the gold standard. When people swapped their cash for gold, they were taking dollars out of circulation. This was causing deflation and making borrowers into paupers as they tried to pay back their debts over time. (A dollar is worth less in five years when there is inflation, and a dollar is worth more in five years when there is deflation.) Murphy had previously described a variation of this phenomenon at the meeting of mayors in Detroit in 1932. As told by Murphy, his city's debt load had turned into an unmanageable crisis as the city's tax revenue declined with growing unemployment and defaults in property taxes—deflation. But the same principle applied to any debtor, whether a business owner who took out a loan to fund operations or an individual who took out a mortgage. With fewer dollars in circulation, these debtors could not obtain cash to pay back creditors.

As president, Roosevelt had economic tools not available to Murphy to partly remedy the problem of insufficient cash in the economy. As already noted, Roosevelt could print money. And in April 1933, he issued another proclamation making it a crime to hoard gold. He also required people to turn in their gold for a set amount of dollars. This had the effect of placing more dollars into the economy. Several months after the fact, Congress followed with an actual law memorializing FDR's proclamation.

Roosevelt did not just bolster the financial system. He wanted to put people back to work in a more direct way. In 1933, Roosevelt's advisors developed the sprawling National Industrial Recovery Act (NIRA). NIRA absorbed 4 million unemployed people into industrial jobs. The country had about 120 million people, about a third of what it has today. Many people knew someone who was put to work by the federal government through these New Deal programs. This publicity was, of course, a boon to FDR and his fellow New Dealers.

NIRA reached into all aspects of the work environment. Companies were encouraged to sign agreements "to raise wages, create employment, and thus restore business."[29] Employers signed more than 2.3 million agreements, covering 16.3 million employees. Signers agreed to worker protections that included minimum wages and limitations on required work hours. Then-Alaska Senator Hugo Black was instrumental in inserting the shortened work.

Employers who signed the agreement displayed a "badge of honor," a blue eagle over the motto "We do our part." Though membership to NIRA was voluntary, customers often boycotted businesses that did not display the eagle. In Philadelphia, Pennsylvania, in 1933, the football team was named the Eagles in recognition of NIRA.

In a single stroke, NIRA radically restructured employer/
employee relations. The goal was to eliminate cut-throat competition by bringing industry, labor, and government together to create codes of fair practices and set prices. Roosevelt's aide Hugh
S. Johnson, one of the primary authors of NIRA, was *Time* magazine's Man of the Year for 1933. Murphy, as an arbitrator in Detroit
10 years before, had imposed a wage floor in the *Stereotypers* case.
NIRA was of an entirely different, and nationwide, scope.

The rhetoric of NIRA is jarring to the modern ear. Competition
is the keystone component to the free enterprise system. The
Supreme Court would overturn NIRA, as it did with many New
Deal programs, but surprisingly not for this reason. Rather, in
1935, Chief Justice Charles Evans Hughes wrote for a unanimous
court in *Schechter Poultry Corp. v. United States* that "the discretion of the President in approving or prescribing codes, and thus
enacting laws for the government of trade and industry throughout the country, is virtually unfettered. We think that the code-
making authority thus conferred is an unconstitutional delegation
of legislative power."[30] The technical reason for rejecting NIRA
was because it gave too much power to FDR and his administration. Congress should have been legislating instead of delegating.
Murphy harshly criticized *Schechter*, as did many others.

As we will see, given the Supreme Court's penchant for overturning New Deal legislation, Murphy thought it was time to consider a constitutional amendment to rectify the situation and provide workers with enshrined rights. As for FDR, he began to plot
ways to change the composition of the High Court. His actions
provoked a backlash, culminating in 1938 when a conservative
wave swept through the country, eliminating Roosevelt's majority in Congress and ousting New Dealers such as Murphy from
their perches in Congress and state capitols.[31]

All of this was in the future. In his first 100 days, FDR's administration was a beehive of activity. In addition to NIRA, the
administration introduced the Works Progress Administration
(WPA), emphasizing "shovel ready" projects. One of the biggest
projects was the Triborough Bridge,[32] designed to link the bor-
oughs of Manhattan, Queens, and the Bronx and to tie together
the expanding highway system in and out of New York City.[33]

The WPA funded innumerable road projects in Detroit, producing large buildings of lasting significance, such as the Board of Water and Light public utility building in Lansing in 1938–1939.[34] As can be seen, the projects were often local and solely within state lines, greatly expanding the reach of the federal government.

FDR's relationship with Murphy was not, in the end, just strategic. They both liked storytelling and socializing. They seemed to have a fondness for each other and spent social time together. In 1933, they attended a baseball game with an unusual guest. Patsy O'Toole had known Frank Murphy for at least three years before, when O'Toole started to act as a type of errand boy for him. He was more famous as a Tigers fan. To Detroit sports fans of the 1920s and 1930s, O'Toole was dubbed "The Human Earache" for his yells and taunts at Tiger Stadium.

The author Richard Bak described what happened when Murphy took O'Toole to meet the president. According to Bak, O'Toole accompanied Murphy to Washington, DC, where they and Roosevelt took in a World Series game between the Senators and New York Giants as guests of Senators' owner Clark Griffith. As O'Toole later described the scene, "I was in the box right next to the President, letting 'em have my best voice, never giving a minute's let-up."

O'Toole's blasts "nearly blew FDR out of his seat." A Secret Service agent hurried to O'Toole's side. "I'm sure you'd like to do the President a favor," the agent said. "He'd like you to move to the other side of the field, and Mr. Griffith has already made the arrangements." Far from being insulted, O'Toole was inspired. "From now on," he told reporters, "you can look—I mean listen—for my cheering at all the best box fights, football games, and sports shindigs all over the country. I'm in the big time now."[35]

Something intangible had happened between Roosevelt and Murphy, and Murphy was granted frequent access to FDR for the next several years. Looking back on it, one administration official noted that Murphy had a surprisingly earthy sense of humor, a weapon he wielded to subdue or charm those skeptical of his positions and a quality that President Roosevelt was said to appreciate.[36]

Even with their close political and personal connections, Roosevelt's policies sometimes let down progressives such as Murphy, who had distinct ideas of clean government and the injection of federal power and funds for better schools, health, and infrastructure. FDR freely gave money and sinecures to party bosses and Southern Democratic congressmen to do with as they saw fit, which was not necessarily consistent with good public policy or the principle of sound investments.

In the end, FDR adopted mostly progressive policies, but with a master politician's nod to maintaining the status quo in key respects. The urban bosses were corrupt, but they gave him votes. And so Roosevelt took care not to touch the Democratic Party bosses in most cities. He left alone the Jersey City mayor, Frank Hague, who died with an estate of $10 million even though he only held government jobs his entire life. In 1932, a Treasury Department official reported back that Louisiana's patronage system was "crawling." Huey Long and "his gang" were "stealing everything in their state." Yet, little was done about it.[37] FDR later paid a price for this neglect when Long consolidated his support and mounted a serious third-party run in 1935 before his assassination.

Murphy later became FDR's Attorney General. He never understood FDR's position in connection with tolerating the party bosses. Murphy targeted the traditional Democratic machines, some of which had been in existence in one form or another for more than 50 years. His most notable success was sending Kansas City boss Tom Pendergast, Harry Truman's benefactor, to jail for tax fraud. Murphy may have been given the Supreme Court job as a way of removing him as an overly zealous attorney general.

Still, Murphy was practical in backing legislative programs particularly important to Roosevelt, even if they contradicted Murphy's own values. The Agricultural Adjustment Act (AAA), yet another example of New Deal legislation, was introduced by Roosevelt in his first days in office to help the politically important agricultural sector. The idea was to boost agricultural prices by reducing the surplus of crops. The government paid farmers subsidies in exchange for allowing land to lie fallow.

In 1932, prior to the enactment of AAA, food prices were low, and farmers often could not sell their crops. The reasons for these depressed prices were complex. Poor distribution was a factor, as there was certainly a need for this food in cities such as Detroit.

Regardless of the reasons for the low prices, in the early 1930s, 70 percent of Americans still earned their living from the land, and protection of their economic interests was crucial to a Democratic or Republican win in future elections. The agricultural subsidies in AAA sealed the loyalty of major constituencies in the Midwest farm belt, transforming rural allegiances from the Republican Party to the Democratic Party for years to come.[38]

Roosevelt was choosing from bad options, whether to help the farmers or the unemployed or those who lacked income. The poorest of the poor were hurt when agricultural prices started to rise. Murphy's friend Father Coughlin hated AAA for this very reason. He found any attempts to raise food prices to be immoral. No doubt, Murphy would have sympathized with Coughlin. As mayor, Murphy stated often that the starving must be fed, even at the cost of a balanced budget. Later, he took time out of his duties as Supreme Court justice in 1942 to pen a note to Herbert Lehman, who had just resigned as governor of New York to accept an appointment as director of foreign relief and rehabilitation operations for the United States Department of State. Murphy stated that it was satisfying that Lehman was set to deploy his "demonstrated administrative abilities" to "handle the vast task of feeding helpless peoples."[39]

Overriding everything, however, was Murphy's unquestioning loyalty to FDR. If Murphy had misgivings about the philosophy of AAA, which increased the price of food, he never voiced these concerns publicly. Murphy's fealty to Roosevelt was one of his steady guiding principles. This made Murphy's break from Roosevelt in the Japanese-American internment cases 10 years later all the more traumatic.

Endnotes

1. "Nephew of T.R. Is Appointed," *Manitowoc Herald-Times* (Manitowoc, Wisconsin), Jan. 19, 1931.

2. Fine, *Detroit Years*, 443.

3. A.P., "Keeps Family Record Alive: Holds Up Tradition of Pioneer's Offspring," *DFP*, July 2, 1932, 4.

4. "A Farewell to Freedom Man,'" *Chicago Tribune,* Jan. 15, 1989, 58 (quoting FDR in the context of Reagan's presidency).

5. FDR, "Forgotten Man speech," Radio appearance for the Democratic Party on Lucky Strike Program, Apr. 7, 1932, accessed May 1, 2020.

6. Frank Murphy speech, "The Procession of the Forgotten Man," Address delivered over W J R Detroit, Nov. 7, 1932, FMM.

7. Hiltzik, *The New Deal*, 8–9.

8. "The Immigration Act of 1924 (The Johnson-Reed Act)," Department of State Website accessed May 21, 2020, https://history.state.gov/milestones/1921-1936/immigration-act.

9. "Old Democratic Two Thirds Rule Was Born One Hundred Years Ago," *LSJ,* June 24, 1932, 8 (giving background of two-thirds rule and explaining FDR's challenge to the rule).

10. As late as 1937, the Supreme Court was routinely finding New Deal programs unconstitutional, to the great frustration of FDR and Murphy. Although Roosevelt had been in office for more than four years, he had not had an opportunity to choose a new Supreme Court justice. To Roosevelt the time seemed right, after a smashing electoral victory in 1936, to do something about the recalcitrant court. On February 5, 1937, about three months after his reelection, President Roosevelt announced his controversial plan to expand the Supreme Court to as many as 15 judges, allegedly to make it more efficient. He ignored the advice of his closest advisors. Critics immediately charged that Roosevelt was trying to "pack" the court and thus neutralize Supreme Court justices hostile to his New Deal.

11. "Ballot Count at the Democratic Convention," *DFP*, July 2, 1932, 4.

12. "Norris Will Take Stump Soon for Gov. Roosevelt," *The Democrat-Argus* (Caruthersville, Missouri), Sept. 27, 1932, 1 (referring to Frank Murphy as another speaker on Norris's nationwide tour).

13. Segregationists and progressives came together to pass a bill that undeniably helped many poor farmers and miners, who received electricity for the first time in their lives, a full 25 years after the urban areas had mostly been electrified. The Democrat who sponsored the bill, Senator John E. Rankin, was a diehard segregationist. The Republican sponsor, George E. Norris, was a progressive.

Rankin was good at securing aid for his state, but he only went so far with his requests. FDR to Tennessee Valley Authority Chairman, Oct. 8, 1934, FDLR, PSF, Box 158, Rankin, John E. file. ("Congressman Rankin wants to know if we can start to clear the ground for the Pickwick Dam. He wants the Dam to go at Cooks Landing which he says is better than Pickwick Landing, as the Dam would be only two-thirds as long [otherwise].") Later he played a critical role in denying the benefits of the GI Bill to Black service members returning from World War II to the South. He fought against a bill that would have allocated fewer House seats to the South because the South denied the right to vote for Black people (the Fourteenth Amendment explicitly allows for this remedy in the event of voter suppression). In contrast, Norris was a champion for the working class (he would become an Independent after this vote, but never a Democrat).

14. The American Presidency Project, website hosted by UC Santa Cruz, accessed on June 1, 2020, https://www.presidency.ucsb.edu/statistics/elections/1932.

15. John Herling, "Where Is Norman Thomas When We Really Need Him?" *Washington Post*, Nov. 28, 1982, accessed June 1, 2020, https://www.washingtonpost.com/archive/opinions/1982/11/28/where-is-norman-thomas-when-we-really-need-him/09a1ef64-1148-4d9b-8fc9-d1b2c8dddfde/.

16. The American Presidency Project, website hosted by UC–Santa Cruz.

17. "Text of Testimony Given by Wilson W. Mills: He Describes Part Played by Couzens on Plea for Aid, Tells of Negotiations for R.F.C. Loan to Avert Closing of Union Guardian," *DFP*, Aug. 26, 1933, 2.

18. Brinkley, *Voices of Protest*, 153.

19. U.P., "Food Prices Being Raised in Detroit," Marshall Evening Chronicle, Mar. 9, 1933, 6.

20. Fine, *Detroit Years*, 377.

21. Ibid, 379. Examples of the scrip issued by the city are located in FMM.

22. "Murphy Plan Fails to Please," *DFP*, Mar. 7, 1933, 1. ("Difficulties which were encountered in Chicago and some other cities by issuance of public scrip, backed by delinquent taxes, was responsible for the lack of enthusiasm in the Murphy plan.")

23. Wheelock, David C., "Monetary Policy in the Great Depression: What the Fed Did, and Why," *Federal Reserve Bank of St. Louis Review*, March/April 1992, 19, accessed Apr. 20, 2020, https://www.federalreservehistory.org/essays/bank_holiday_of_1933.

24. George S. Eccles, *The Politics of Banking* (Salt Lake City: University of Utah Press, 1982), 85.

25. Helen M. Burns, *The American Banking Community and the New Deal Banking Reform, 1933–1935* (Westport: Greenwood Press, 1974), 36–37.

26. FDR, "First Inaugural Speech," Mar. 4, 1933. Roosevelt also stated, "These measures, or such other measures as the Congress may build out of its experience and wisdom, I shall seek, *within my constitutional authority* [italics added], to bring to speedy adoption. But in the event that the Congress shall fail to take one of these two courses, and in the event that the national emergency is still critical, I shall not evade the clear course of duty." One can listen to his speech, including the lack of applause after his "fear" statement, here: http://historymatters.gmu.edu/d/5057 (posted by the American Social History Project/Center for Media and Learning [Graduate Center, CUNY] and the Roy Rosenzweig Center for History and New Media [George Mason University]).

27. FDR, "Oglethorpe University Commencement Address," May 22, 1932, FDRL, Master Speech File, 1898–1945, Box 9.

28. Fine, *Detroit Years*, 374.

29. Jonathan Grossman, "Fair Labor Standards Act of 1938: Maximum Struggle for a Minimum Wage" (describing NIRA and other earlier New Deal programs), U.S. Department of Labor website, accessed May 1, 2020, https://www.dol.gov/general/aboutdol/history/flsa1938#6.

30. *Schechter Poultry Corp. v. United States*, 295 U.S. 495, 541–542 (1935).

31. The Fair Labor Standards Act in 1938 is recognized as the last major piece of New Deal legislation. In 1946, Murphy, now sitting as a Supreme Court justice, wrote the majority decision in *Anderson v. Mt. Clemens Pottery Co.*, 328 U.S. 680 (1946) (known

as the portal to portal case), when the United States Supreme Court held that preliminary work activities, if controlled by the employer and performed entirely for the employer's benefit, are properly included in the definition of compensable working time under Fair Labor Standards Act. This case probably represented the high-water mark of Supreme Court decisions broadly interpreting New Deal legislation. After that date, the court's composition changed.

32. Now officially the Robert F. Kennedy Bridge, but still known to New Yorkers as the Triborough Bridge.

33. Caro, *The Power Broker*, 386–395.

34. "WPA Projects in Michigan, 1935–1943," *Detroit News*, Oct. 6, 2018, accessed May 3, 2020, https://www.detroitnews.com/picture-gallery/news/local/michigan-history/2016/09/30/wpa-projects-in-michigan-1935-43/91340032/.

35. Bak, *A Place for Summer*, 159; Richard Bak, "Remembering Patsy O'Toole, 'The Human Earache' of Navin Field," Vintage Detroit Collection, Sept. 7, 2011, accessed Apr. 30, 2020, https://www.vintagedetroit.com/blog/2011/09/07/remembering-patsy-o%E2%80%99toole-%E2%80%9Cthe-human-earache%E2%80%9D-of-navin-field/.

36. Memorandum or speech honoring Frank Murphy upon Frank Murphy's death, FDRL, Ernest Cuneo Papers, Frank Murphy Folder.

37. Brinkley, *Voices of Protest*, 27.

38. Secretary of Agriculture Henry Wallace, still officially an Independent and later to be FDR's vice presidential running mate, oversaw the AAA program in his cabinet position. Wallace came from the politically formidable Wallace family of Iowa and was an example of the progressives now joining Roosevelt's cabinet. Wallace's father had been a cabinet member for Republican presidents in the 1920s, and his son was now comfortably working under a Democratic president. Like many others during Roosevelt's time and afterward, Wallace was liberal and progressive in supporting the working poor, except when doing so impacted on his voting base. Under AAA, Secretary Henry Wallace reviewed and approved agreements between agricultural producers and suppliers designed to prop up food prices under AAA. He signed one on milk with the following statement: "Its principles were proposed by the Michigan Producers Association, local dealers and others who considered it to be a fair proposal." The consumers were not listed in his statement. Propping up prices had the effect of placing the price of milk out of reach for certain consumers.

39. Frank Murphy to Governor Herbert Lehman, Nov. 26, 1942, Lehman Collection, Columbia University Libraries, Folder Number: 979, Document ID: ldpd_leh_0664_0012, accessed Apr. 19, 2020, http://lehman.cul.columbia.edu/document_id=ldpd_leh_0664_0012?&q=file_unittitle_t%3A%22Murphy%2C+Frank%22;&items=12&itemNo=11.

CHAPTER 11

Murphy to the Philippines

The Catholic priest Father Charles Coughlin was at the height of his influence when he met President-Elect Roosevelt in New York City in 1933. For now, Coughlin was urging his millions of radio listeners to support Roosevelt. Coughlin was also pressuring Roosevelt to appoint Catholics as ambassadors to Latin American countries. Roosevelt stated, "I'll tell you what I can do. I can give you the Philippines if you want it."[1] Roosevelt needed a place in his administration for Murphy anyway. Murphy had been an early supporter, and FDR was facing pressure from his cousin Hall, who was reporting that Murphy had "his heart set" on the Philippines.[2] The prestigious post had been held by luminaries such as William Howard Taft, and Henry L. Stimson. At 43, Murphy was the youngest to have ever been appointed governor general.[3]

Murphy came to the Philippines at a crucial turning point in that territory's history. First, the Islands were transitioning to independence from their status as a United States protectorate. Farmers in states such as Colorado believed they could not compete with the cheap labor of the Philippines. Philippine independence meant that states could pressure the United States to impose tariffs on the archipelago, something that could not be done if the Philippines remained a territory and within the U.S. taxation system. Many influential members of Congress and the Senate supported independence as a way of protecting their states' agricultural interests. Ironically, Colorado would soon have its own free labor, or something close to it, with the Japanese-American internees during World War II, about 10 years away. A young man named Fred Korematsu was one such Japanese American who worked on a beet farm in Colorado during his internment.

Regardless of the United States internal politics driving the decision, the Filipinos themselves were firmly behind the idea of independence. And Murphy gained the immediate approval of Filipinos in his inaugural address on June 15, 1933, when he proclaimed that he was leaving "this entire question [of independence] with you for your free determination, without interference and uncontrolled by any force or influence whatsoever." As will be seen, Murphy almost certainly had no power or authority to make such a grandiose statement.

Murphy's second major problem in his new role was dealing with the growing threat of the Japanese Empire. While the United States had turned inward with its own economic collapse, some in its government were starting to recognize the formidable military and industrial threat of Japan, which by now had fought and defeated Russia, a European power. Japan had significantly modernized its military since that time. Most recently, it had invaded mainland China and occupied numerous islands in the Pacific.

Japan was also undeniably an economic player in the Philippines, providing shoes to thousands who had never worn them before.[4] The Japanese had up to 14,000 citizens on the Islands and were active in developing the hemp trade.[5] In addition, some inhabitants had Japanese blood as a result of hundreds of years of trading contact.

Most, but not all, in the United States government assumed that the Japanese would not dare attack the Islands, basing their confidence on the mere fact that the Philippines was a protectorate of the United States. Murphy was not so sanguine and concluded after studying the situation that little could be done in the face of a concerted attack. He clashed with the chief military officer assigned to the Philippines, Douglas MacArthur, later of the "I shall return" fame. MacArthur believed the archipelago could be defended, and his confident assessment led to disastrous consequences for the troops who unconditionally surrendered to the Japanese.

During their time together on the Philippines, MacArthur competed with Murphy in all areas. MacArthur demanded and received a salary of $33,000 a year, one designed to match Murphy's.[6] MacArthur also received a fully air-conditioned penthouse atop the Manila Hotel, almost equal in size to Murphy's quarters at the palace.[7] In one area, they shared commonalities. Both liked to dress up. As told in Stanley Karnow's *In Our Image: America's Empire in the Philippines*, MacArthur "concocted a comic-opera uniform of black trousers and a white tunic filigreed with intimate designs. The ludicrous costume not only reflected his vanity but also caught the flavor of the Philippines, which then appeared to be devolving into a coconut republic."[8]

For his part, Murphy tried to eliminate MacArthur's position. Dwight Eisenhower was MacArthur's aide in the Philippines. As recalled by Carlo D'Este in *Eisenhower: A Soldier's Life*, "Murphy not only disliked MacArthur but was thought to have been behind an attempt to force the closure of the military mission and MacArthur's recall to the United States." And Eisenhower, "fed up with the intrigues," penned in his diary in 1937 that Murphy was "supposed to have written letters home to the President and the Secretary of War demanding relief of the mission. O.K. by me!! *I'm ready to go.* No one seems to realize how much energy and slavery Jim and I put into this d----- job."[9]

Murphy professed to live a spartan existence throughout his life. He refused to join social clubs, which he loudly claimed were breeding spots of social discrimination. He lived out of hotel rooms for long stretches of time.[10] Newspapers took him at his word that he was frugal and not prone to the highlife. "The [Michigan governor's] home should not be costly," he proclaimed later in his career when the legislature was considering a new chief executive residence. "It should be constructed on the American idea of simplicity. It should not be luxurious."[11] His allies in the press duly published his comments.

In the Philippines, though, he lived a life of luxury in the Malacañan Palace[12] in Manila and the summer palace in Baguio. He had access to a yacht and an entourage of Filipino helpers.

During these years, he earned significant sums, with many of his expenses covered by the United States government. His sister-in-law Irene, married to Harold, the eldest Murphy sibling, alluded to the opulence of Philippine surroundings when she wrote a letter to Frank and Frank's sister Marguerite, thanking them for their hospitality during her visit to Manila. She was having difficulty readjusting to the mundane realities of Detroit.[13] "It sounds perfectly spineless to say it, but, at first you get in a perfect panic when you see the multiplicity of household and personal tasks to be done and realize that the 'doing' is all up to you and not to a staff of silent, smiling houseboys. You don't realize how dependent you get on personal service until you get back here."[14] Irene divorced Harold a few years later, citing nonsupport.[15] In 1947, she was stationed by the United Nations in the Philippines as a social welfare advisor, where she helped develop village industries. She later developed a close relationship with Sidney Fine, Frank Murphy's biographer.

When Frank later ran for governor of Michigan, he was attacked by his rival for his personal extravagances in the Philippines. Murphy was indignant: "This is an absurdity as well as the fiction about my alleged Filipino valet, and the alleged salary paid to my sister, and my alleged yachts, and other antics of my opposition and his faithful press."[16] Yet his Republican opponent's charges were largely true.

Although Murphy lived opulently while in the Philippines, he was not corrupt in the way that governors general of other American territories were corrupt. According to Nelson Denis, in his book *War against All Puerto Ricans: Revolution and Terror in America's Colony*, a United States appointee in Puerto Rico of equivalent title to Murphy, serving at roughly the same time for him, later became a lobbyist for the United States corporations and sugar syndicates that "owned the economy of Puerto Rico."[17] By the standards of the day, Murphy could have pressed for shares of stock in agricultural interests on the Islands. Not only did he not do so, but he seemed to encourage independent Filipino economic development, as when he argued against the imposition of U.S. tariffs on Philippine beets in an "eloquent radiogram" in 1934.[18]

The move to the Philippines might have saved Murphy from an embarrassing electoral defeat back home in Detroit. Notwithstanding his own victory as mayor in 1930 and Roosevelt's triumph in 1932, Michigan trended Republican in both rural and urban areas, and the Detroit mayoralty went back to Republicans in the special elections that followed Murphy's departure for his new role in the Philippines.

Having little understanding of the political, social, and racial dynamics of the Philippines when he first arrived, Murphy chose very competent staff to bridge the gap. He convinced Joseph Ralston Hayden, a professor of political science at the University of Michigan, to be his vice governor. Murphy's choices of assistants reflected his persuasive powers and also his self-confidence that he would not be upstaged by strong-willed and intelligent subordinates. This was also in keeping with his "good government" approach that he adopted in Detroit, and which infuriated Democratic operatives there because Murphy refused to put in their cronies.

Hayden had an impressive resume, having already spent time in the Philippines as an exchange professor at the University of the Philippines in 1922–1923, as a newspaper correspondent in 1926, and most recently as the Carnegie visiting professor at the University of the Philippines. MacArthur, who otherwise butted heads with Murphy, recognized Murphy's choice and hired Hayden as his own special assistant during World War II.[19]

While in the Philippines, Murphy met another person who would remain at his side for the rest of his life. Eleanor Bumgardner was a graduate of the University of Michigan and became Murphy's secretary and special assistant. Starting in 1933, she was at Murphy's side as Murphy crisscrossed the globe.[20] When she later met FDR, he greeted her: "I remember you. You're the young lady who ran the Philippines."[21]

Bumgardner remained single throughout Murphy's life. She gave a detailed interview in the *Detroit Free Press* in 1967 about her 16 years with him, in which she described her role as gatekeeper for the "handsome" Murphy as young and old women confessed their amorous intentions with him.[22] When Murphy was featured on the cover of *Time* magazine in 1938, the accompanying article described a visit by Frank Murphy to the Green Inn in Narragansett, Rhode Island, with his secretary Eleanor Bumgardner and his legal assistant Edward G. Kemp. The article noted that they were assigned different rooms.[23] But his letters to her were quite affectionate, and he would sign off with "Love, Frank."

At Murphy's side, Bumgardner met political luminaries, celebrities, and heads of state.[24] "Often I'd do little things for them," she later said. "If they would ask Frank Murphy if there was something they could do to thank me, he would tell them about my doll collection, and they would often give me a doll."[25] Her doll collection kept growing. Later in her life, she recalled that she had dolls from 19 different presidents, sometimes given by family members. Amy Carter gave her a doll. After Murphy's death in 1949, Bumgardner remained with the United States Supreme Court as an executive secretary until her retirement in 1961.[26]

Frank also convinced his sister Marguerite Teahan (now married) to accompany him to the Philippines. She became his stand-in wife, attending many official functions with Frank. Marguerite named her adopted daughter Aurora after Aurora Quezon, the wife of the Philippine Prime Minister Manuel Quezon.[27] The baby naming reflected the strong bonds the families forged while the Murphys were in the Philippines. Their friendship seemed sincere but with a power imbalance. Prime Minister Quezon was answerable at all times to Murphy, the representative of the United States with troops to back its dominant power on the Islands.

Michigan newspapers were positive in their coverage of Murphy's sojourn abroad. A few months after he arrived in Manila, the *Port Huron Herald* gushed, "His adaptation as ruler of the Philippines is likened to the quick manner in which President Roosevelt started the United States back on the road to financial recovery."[28] Murphy made many comments that parroted FDR's, as though the New Deal model could be applied to the far less advanced Philippine economy.[29]

FDR and Murphy consulted frequently during this time. In a trip to the states in 1935, Murphy undertook two tasks unrelated to the Philippines at the president's request. First, he unsuccessfully tried to convince Michigan Republican senator Couzens to switch parties.[30] Back in 1932, Couzens had demonstrated his ideological flexibility by supporting Murphy's attempt to obtain federal funds for the large cities. Because of this, and because Couzens supported many of the New Deal initiatives, he was not particularly popular with the Republican leadership in Michigan.[31] Couzens was intrigued with the idea of switching parties but did not take Murphy's suggestion. He remained a Republican until his death a few years later.

Second, Roosevelt wanted Murphy to return to address growing concerns about Father Coughlin. In a few short years, Coughlin went from ally to strident critic of Roosevelt. Murphy teamed with Joseph Kennedy, the head of the Securities and Exchange Commission, and the two met Coughlin in Detroit to try to convince him to stop his increasingly frequent attacks on FDR's New Deal programs.

While Father Coughlin largely ignored Murphy's entreaties to support the sitting president, he remained on good enough terms with Murphy that he was among the well-wishers who bade Murphy farewell as he began the rail journey from Detroit to San Francisco and then on to the Philippines to resume his obligations as governor general. Kennedy was also to note that Coughlin had an ability to stay friends with those who had different political views.[32]

Philippine independence was on the horizon. When Murphy went to the Philippines in 1933, he was bound by the newly passed Hare–Hawes–Cutting (HHC) Bill, modified slightly in 1934. This United States congressional act provided a timeline, promising complete Philippine independence after 10 years.[33] The United States, with its immense power to dictate terms, reserved several military and naval bases for itself. One of these, Subic Bay, was a 262-square-mile base, about the size of Singapore, and it remained a main base for the Seventh Fleet until 1992 (with an interruption during World War II), when it was decommissioned.

As part of this move to independence, Filipino leaders drafted a constitution. One might assume that Murphy would have encouraged a document that mirrored the United States Constitution, but his suggestions diverged in significant respects. Specifically,

Murphy urged the establishment of a unicameral legislature.[34] As will be recalled, he and Nebraskan senator Norris embarked on a nationwide speaking tour to support FDR's presidency about two years before. Concurrently, Norris had promoted an amendment to eliminate Nebraska's bicameral house, which passed in 1934. To this day, Nebraska has the only unicameral legislative body in the country. This specific innovation may have been on Murphy's mind, based on his high regard for Norris.

Murphy similarly supported a six-year, one-term limitation as a check against the rise of a too-powerful president.[35] Quezon was a friend of Murphy, but, as always, Murphy did not let this personal relationship get in the way of what he perceived to be good policy. Murphy's suggestion of a one-term presidency was the equivalent of the founding fathers of the United States telling George Washington that specific presidential term restrictions were necessary on the presidency exactly because Washington was so popular in his own country. Notably, the Filipino constitution discarded an electoral system and placed the person with the most votes in charge.[36]

Murphy wanted women to have the right to vote in the Philippines. In one of his earliest acts as the new governor general there, he requested that the 1933 insular legislature enfranchise women.[37] This right was soon enshrined in the new commonwealth by popular vote.

Murphy also proposed specific protections for the traditionally disenfranchised. In a letter from Murphy to the labor leader Frank X. Martel back in Detroit in early 1934, Murphy expressed a desire to incorporate "the Mohammedan Filipinos with the other inhabitants of the Philippines."[38] Murphy stated that he was going to recommend that the Bureau of Non-Christian Tribes be consulted before significant policy changes were made in Philippine provinces.

He also addressed the court system. In his time in the Philippines, he converted death sentences to life in prison (he being opposed to the death penalty), introduced bills and appropriations for the "mentally afflicted," and enacted probationary law that replaced the "Spanish penology system."[39]

The completed draft constitution was approved by President Roosevelt on March 23, 1935,[40] and ratified by popular vote in the Philippines. In 1935, the Philippines officially became a commonwealth. Nearly 300,000 people attended the inauguration ceremonies of Manuel Quezon as president on November 15, 1935. Murphy was a guest of honor, along with a full American delegation that included the Vice President of the United States. However, Murphy again made sure that Quezon knew his place. Quezon wanted a 21-gun salute, the protocol reserved for a head of state. Murphy appealed to Roosevelt, and Quezon ended up with a 19-gun salute.[41] Because of the perceived slight, Quezon almost did not attend the ceremony but for "Murphian cajolery and a cablegram from Roosevelt."[42]

After the establishment of the commonwealth, Murphy was appointed by FDR as the high commissioner of the Islands. His job title changed, as did some of his functions, but the United States still had an effective veto power over the new republic during the 10-year transition period. Murphy remained in charge.

Murphy's friends later claimed that he considered his appointment as governor general and high commissioner of the Philippines as the high spot of his life. He kept his flag as governor general within his view in his private office when he became a Supreme Court justice.[43] He was distressed by the Japanese occupation during World War II and led several lobbying efforts for relief both during and after the war. He even tried to enlist as a soldier in the United States Army while he sat on the Supreme Court, and his stated goal was to help liberate Manila. In one speech before a lawyers' group in 1942, he mused, "Perhaps I am touched deeply because on those beautiful islands I spent three of the happiest years of my public service . . . For here was a democratic people coming into nationhood—a people that has shown a particular aptitude for self-government—attacked by a military autocracy with a record of harsh and unfriendly rule in every land it has conquered."[44]

In early May 1935, some 6,000 mostly illiterate, landless peasants rose up in the area around Manila. They converged on municipal offices and other government buildings and were met by withering gunfire by government forces. Over 100 died, and many were arrested. Murphy was not in the Philippines to witness the uprising. He had been delayed in returning from a trip to the United States because of an appendectomy.

Regardless of Murphy's own feelings on the subject, the United States allowed corruption by the Philippine government. Murphy's friend Manuel Quezon, by now the president of the commonwealth, controlled wages and prices and banned strikes and other "unwholesome agitation."[45] With Murphy in charge, certain landowners formed vigilante groups to crush the dissidents and directed their surrogates in the Philippine legislature to reject proposals aimed to address the concerns of the peasantry.[46]

Murphy expressed regret that he had not sufficiently addressed income inequality in the Philippines. He must have been reminded of the desperation he witnessed that led to the Ford Hunger March back in 1932. Eventually, his last official act before leaving the Philippines in 1935 was to release many of these rebels, now in jail under harsh conditions.[47] Murphy believed, a bit late in his tenure, that the Philippine government needed to adopt land reforms. His pardons had echoes of his last act as a judge on the Detroit criminal court, when he released convicts without requiring jail time.

Murphy took objects of national value back to Michigan. The scholar Sarita Echavez See reviewed the items currently in Murphy's home and museum in Harbor Beach, including paintings, clothes, and walking sticks.[48] She concluded that Murphy was oblivious to his power, with an entitlement to act as he wished and take what he wanted.[49]

The reality is that Murphy tried to protect cultural treasures. He created the Philippine Historical Research and Markers Committee to identify and record historic antiquities in Manila as a first step toward their preservation. Murphy and his family followed the latest protocols for removing items from the Philippines. For example, Murphy's former sister-in-law Irene sent andirons, used to hold the wooden logs for fires, back to Harbor Beach after World War II. She had retrieved the andirons from the partly destroyed summer palace in Baguio, sadly acknowledging that it was "American bombs that crushed it" during the campaign to retake the Islands from the Japanese. Before sending the items, however, she made it "official" when she "secured an official release from the District Engineer of Baguio, so they come correctly from the Philippine Republic."[50]

One also needs to think of the alternatives to Murphy's actions. The Imperial Japanese Army soon swept through the Philippines. Many national treasures disappeared during the harsh Japanese occupation.

Although Murphy was undeniably important as the Philippines moved to independence, he is rarely acknowledged in books describing that era. In the Pulitzer Prize–winning history of the Philippines, *In Our Image, America's Empire in the Philippines,* Stanley Karnow mentioned Murphy only in passing. Karnow focused instead on MacArthur, with Murphy no more than a passing foil, even during the four years that Murphy was in charge and MacArthur was the military attaché. For example, this is how Karnow described events leading to Murphy's appointment as high commissioner in 1935: "[MacArthur was] jockeying to be made high commissioner . . . Roosevelt seriously considered him until he overplayed his hand by reviling the incumbent [Philippine] governor, Frank Murphy, whose liberal opinions he detested."[51]

In reading Karnow's book, one can deduce that Roosevelt liked Murphy, so much so that a criticism of Murphy by MacArthur was not well received by the president. Why did Murphy have so much power over FDR, and why did Roosevelt choose him over MacArthur? Karnow provides no explanation whatsover.[52] And, as previously explained, Murphy was in charge of the Islands at a crucial time when they became a commonwealth. He presided over a peaceful transfer of power, although he had no model for doing so at the time. He grounded the Philippine Constitution on principles found in the U.S. Constitution, with modifications to make it even more Democratic. And he accurately predicted that the Philippines could not survive an attack by Imperial Japan. On every one of these points, Karnow did not mention Murphy, let alone give him credit.

On a larger level, Karnow's lack of attention to Murphy shows why Murphy is not better known today. At every stage of Murphy's career, it seemed that historians elevated others at Murphy's expense. Murphy came from the Midwest, out of the power structure of the East Coast. His parents were not well connected. He never attended any Ivy League school. These all account, in part, for the overall dismissiveness of his impressive record. Part of it was bad luck. He died young and did not have the post–World War II legacy of many of his peers that was fodder for many "greatest generation" biographies.

At the time, he was not dismissed by anyone. In 1941, FDR summoned Murphy to the White House. This was before the United States entered World War II and FDR understood that subjugated people around the world wanted hope. In his famous Four Freedoms speech he outlined his conceptions of American justice and individualism.[53] But FDR heard that the speech had largely fallen flat in Asia.

When Murphy arrived, he found Roosevelt in the company of Winston Churchill. There, the two world leaders proceeded to quiz Murphy about his time in the Philippines. Later, Murphy walked the streets of Washington, DC, with his good friend Ernest Cuneo,[54] fretting that he had been completely disrespectful for his candid advice: "I said directly to the President and Prime Minister Churchill, 'The Far East doesn't believe you. The reason the Four Freedoms Declaration made no impression on the Far East is that 400 years of bloody, rotten imperialism cannot be erased by a few paragraphs . . . and from my experience as governor general, I understand them enough to understand why.'"[55] For Murphy, a man brought up to despise the English domination of Ireland, his comments might have been sharper than usual in the presence of Churchill. But his criticism was not limited to British imperialism. He was also condemning the United States. He rarely kowtowed to anyone, and despite his misgivings, Murphy never revisited his comments with FDR.

Endnotes

1. Michael Beschloss, *Kennedy and Roosevelt: The Uneasy Alliance* (New York: Open Road Media, 2016), Kindle, 133 of 386, Loc. 2091 of 6904.
2. Howard, *Mr. Justice Murphy*, 57.
3. "Nomination of Frank Murphy as Governor General," Apr. 10, 1933, FMM.
4. Albert W. Herre, "Some Sources of Philippine Culture," *Mid-Pacific Magazine*, Jan.–Mar. 1936, 44.
5. "Murphy Aide Visits Home," *TTH*, Feb. 25, 1935, 10. (Kemp spoke to his local newspaper about Philippine issues.)
6. When Murphy won the race for governor in Michigan, newspapers at the time reported that his salary in the Philippines was only $16,000 and that this salary was being reduced to $5,000 as governor.
7. Stanley Karnow, *In Our Image: America's Empire in the Philippines* (New York: Random House, 1989), 275.
8. Ibid, 271.
9. D'Este, *Eisenhower*, 246 (italics in the original).
10. The wealthy and connected often stayed in long-term hotels. Such a practice was socially acceptable, more so than today. Still Murphy stayed in hotels in part to show his lack of interest in material possessions.
11. "Michigan's Homeless Governor," *Quad City Times* (Davenport, Iowa), Feb. 14, 1937, 16.
12. Fifty years later, in 1986, United States military helicopters airlifted Ferdinand Marcos from this location into exile.
13. "A Fantasy Life of Jungles, Palaces, Michiganian Led Filipino Society," *DFP*, Aug. 26, 1983, 17.
14. See, *The Filipino Primitive*, 70–71.
15. "Kin of Frank Murphy Is Divorced by Wife," *LSJ*, June 11, 1936, 11.
16. "Character of Michigan's 'Labor Governor' Analyzed," *TTH*, June 2, 1937, 5. ("Says Murphy in explanation of himself, 'I've never learned how to live. People like my brother George much better than like me. You see, George knows how to live.'")
17. Nelson Denis, *War against All Puerto Ricans: Revolution and Terror in America's Colony* (New York: Bold Type Books, 2015), loc. 1089, Kindle.
18. Murphy was unsuccessful in his request to remove the beet tariffs. Friend, *Between Two Empires*, 142–143.
19. Joseph Ralston Hayden authored a book on the Philippines, based partly on his experiences as an assistant to Murphy, entitled *The Philippines: A Study in National Development*. By then, the Philippines was under Japanese occupation during World War II.
20. Photograph, "At the Palace in the Philippines, a picture of Murphy was taken with his staff, including Edward Kemp, Joseph Ralston Hayden and Eleanor Bumgardner." Truman Archives, Library, accessed Apr. 18, 2020, https://www.trumanlibrary.gov/photograph-records/2017-3544.
21. James M. Haswell, "Detroiter Works for Nine Bosses," *DFP*, Apr. 18, 1955, 5 (also noting she was the confidential secretary for all nine Supreme Court justices at the time, substituting as needed when they needed assistance.)

22. "A Confidential Secretary Recalls: My 16 Years with Frank Murphy," *DFP*, Sept. 10, 1967, 140. In the early 1930s, Murphy had a connection to a young Ann Walker. FMP, reel 148.

23. "The Cabinet: Lay Bishop," *Time*, Aug. 28, 1939.

24. Celebrities generally knew of Murphy. Walt Disney was in contact with a local Michigan Mickey Mouse club that wanted to honor Murphy and discussed the design of a plaque in Murphy's honor. "Murphy Rallies Mickey Mouse's Knee-Pant Vote," *DFP*, Aug. 13, 1936, 1.

25. Martha Gross, "Singer's Get-Well Gift Starts Doll Collection," *Fort Lauderdale News*, Aug. 9, 1987, 5E.

26. Ibid.

27. "Baptism of Marguerite Murphy Teahan," *Philippine Free Press*, Aug. 14, 1937.

28. "Philippine Newspapers Praise Governor, Former Thumb Boy," *TTH*, Aug. 25, 1933.

29. Ibid.

30. Fine, *New Deal Years*, 223.

31. Ibid.

32. Michael Beschloss, *Kennedy and Roosevelt: The Uneasy Alliance* (New York: Open Road Media, 2016), Kindle, 133 of 386, Loc. 2091 of 6904.

33. Friend, *Between Two Empires*, 97-98.

34. "Character of Michigan's 'Labor Governor' Analyzed," *TTH*, June 2, 1937, 5.

35. Frederic S. Marquardt, "Quezon and Osmeña," *Philippines Free Press Online*, Dec. 15, 1962, accessed Apr. 19, 2020, https://philippinesfreepress.wordpress.com/1962/12/15/quezon-and-osmena-december-15-1962/. ("I covered the constitutional convention for the *Free Press*, and attended many of its sessions. It was always my opinion, although I could never prove it, that Governor General Frank Murphy, who later became a justice on the US Supreme Court, planted the seed of the single six-year term. He also was responsible for the unicameral legislature that was written into the Philippine Constitution—and abandoned shortly after he left the Philippines.")

36. Maximo M. Kalaw, "The New Constitution of the Philippine Commonwealth," *Foreign Affairs* 13, no. 4 (July 1935): 687–694.

37. Associated Press, "Murphy May Retain Island Women's Vote," *Oakland Tribune*, June 29, 1935, 2.

38. Frank Murphy to Frank X. Martel, Aug. 5, 1935, WRL, Detroit AFL-CIO Collection Box 11, Folder: Murphy, Frank 1933–1936.

39. Ibid.

40. Photograph, "Signing the Constitution of the Philippine Commonwealth, 23 March 1935," Murphy is standing, Mar. 23, 1935, accessed July 10, 2020, https://commons.wikimedia.org/wiki/File:Signing_the_Constitution_of_the_Philippine_Commonwealth,_23_March_1935.jpg#filelinks.

41. Karnow, *In Our Image*, 255.

42. Friend, *Between Two Empires*, 185.

43. John P. Frank, "Justice Murphy: The Goals Attempted," *Yale Law Journal* 59, no. 1 (1949): 10.

44. Frank Murphy speech, "The Challenge to Our National Character," Address delivered to the Lawyers Association of Missouri and broadcast over the Blue Network, Jan. 23, 1942, reproduced in *Vital Speeches of the Day* 7: 272–275, accessed July 10, 2020, http://www.ibiblio.org/pha/policy/1942/1942-01-23a.html.

45. Fine, *New Deal Years*, 55.

46. Ibid, 274.

47. Ibid, 89.

48. See, *The Filipino Primitive*, 58–59.

49. Ibid, 70–74.

50. Irene Murphy to George and Brigid Murphy, May 6, 1947, FMP, reel 87.

51. Karnow, *In Our Image*, 270.

52. Paul Kriesberg, "The Accidental Colony," *NYT*, Apr. 2, 1989. ("Henry Stimson, the Governor of the islands in 1927 and 1928, became President Herbert Hoover's secretary of state and President Franklin Roosevelt's secretary of war, and Frank Murphy, the governor from 1933 to 1935, was later elevated to the Supreme Court.") In this review of the Karnow book, Kriesberg makes the same omission about Murphy's two additional years on the Islands as the high commissioner, while at least acknowledging Murphy's leadership role.

53. Leonard Lyons, "The Lyons Den," *Washington Post*, July 22, 1949. The Four Freedoms speech, delivered during the dark early days of World War II before the United States joined the fight, described the president's vision in which the American ideals of individual liberties were extended throughout the world.

54. Cuneo is credited with helping to establish the Office of Strategic Services, the forebearer of the CIA. He seemingly knew everyone, but among his acquaintances was Ian Fleming, who gave Cuneo credit for coming up with part of the *Goldfinger* plot. Cuneo was the most obvious link between Drew Pearson, an influential newspaper columnist who often wrote favorably about Murphy. A good narrative of Cuneo's rich life was penned by Michael W. Williams, "FDR's Confidential Crusader: Ernest Cuneo Helped the Roosevelt Administration with Little Fanfare Before, During, and After World War II," War History Network, accessed May 3, 2020, https://warfarehistorynetwork.com/2019/01/22/fdrs-confidential-crusader-2/.

55. Ibid; Memorandum from Ernest Cuneo recalling the event, FDRL, Ernest Cuneo Papers, Frank Murphy Folder.

Murphy, held by his mother Mary, was born in 1890 in the town of Sand Beach, Michigan. Frank Murphy papers, Bentley Historical Library, University of Michigan.

Murphy's younger brother George (right) had a career that closely tracked Frank's, becoming a lawyer and later a criminal court judge in Detroit. Frank Murphy papers, Bentley Historical Library, University of Michigan.

Murphy was close with his sister Marguerite and niece Sharon throughout his life. Frank Murphy papers, Bentley Historical Library, University of Michigan.

Murphy, pictured with his mother, volunteered for the Army Reserves within a week after the U.S. declared war against Germany in 1917. Frank Murphy papers, Bentley Historical Library, University of Michigan.

Murphy befriended Father Charles E. Coughlin in the 1920s, before the priest rose to national fame as a radio personality. Walter P. Reuther Library, Archives of Labor and Urban Affairs, Wayne State University.

Mayor Murphy hoists a glass of beer with Michigan Governor Fred W. Green. Walter P. Reuther Library, Archives of Labor and Urban Affairs, Wayne State University.

Mayor Murphy attends the dedication of the Detroit-Windsor tunnel with Windsor Mayor Cecil E. Jackson. Walter P. Reuther Library, Archives of Labor and Urban Affairs, Wayne State University.

Mayor Murphy meets with President Herbert Hoover. Murphy lobbied Washington to provide Detroit with federal aid after the Great Depression. Frank Murphy papers, Bentley Historical Library, University of Michigan.

Murphy watches presidential candidate Franklin D. Roosevelt make a speech in Detroit. Walter P. Reuther Library, Archives of Labor and Urban Affairs, Wayne State University.

Governor Murphy meets with police officers in Monroe, Michigan. The city's mayor, Daniel A. Knaggs, asked Murphy to send in the National Guard to break a sit-down strike at a steel plant. Frank Murphy papers, Bentley Historical Library, University of Michigan.

Attorney General Murphy
meets with FBI Director
J. Edgar Hoover. Walter P.
Reuther Library, Archives
of Labor and Urban Affairs,
Wayne State University.

Murphy loved riding horses, which gained him some notoriety later in life, when he
was often seen riding in the company of young women in the Washington, DC area
when he should have been attending to official duties as attorney general. Frank Murphy papers, Bentley Historical Library, University of Michigan.

Attorney General Murphy meets with New York City Mayor Fiorello La Guardia and Chicago Mayor Edward Kelly. Despite different politics, the three men became strong allies in their support of the New Deal. Frank Murphy papers, Bentley Historical Library, University of Michigan.

In 1939, while serving as U. S. Attorney General, Murphy learned that he was Roosevelt's choice to fill the Supreme Court vacancy left by the death of Pierce Butler. Frank Murphy papers, Bentley Historical Library, University of Michigan.

Murphy's on-and-off girlfriend, Ann Harding, eventually headed for Hollywood and was later nominated for an Academy Award. Frank Murphy papers, Bentley Historical Library, University of Michigan.

Murphy and Edward Kemp
were companions from their
college years until Murphy's
death. Frank Murphy
papers, Bentley Historical
Library, University of
Michigan.

Murphy died July 19, 1949. More than 10,000 people attended his funeral in Detroit.
Frank Murphy papers, Bentley Historical Library, University of Michigan.

CHAPTER 12

The Campaign for Governor

On January 7, 1936, Murphy was in the Philippines when he received a letter from Roosevelt marked *Personal*. The first-term president was focused on his own reelection. Michigan, then as now, was a key battleground state, and Roosevelt had an idea.

In the letter, the president foresaw "a battle such has not been seen waged in the United States since 1861."[1] FDR continued, "You are familiar with the demoralized state of the Democratic organization in Michigan. We have been studying the problem for months and no solution has been offered other than for you to assemble the discordant elements. No one has been able to suggest a candidate for the Governorship who shows the slightest likelihood of a successful outcome with the exception of yourself."[2]

The situation was indeed grim. The Democratic Party in Michigan was in its usual state of disarray and, additionally, had suffered recent electoral defeats. The mayor of Detroit was now Republican, as was the governor and both senators. Roosevelt pegged his own chances of winning the state in 1936 as only a 50/50 proposition.[3] Michigan had few Democrats with stature, and Murphy was one such figure.

Murphy's opponent would be the formidable incumbent Republican governor Frank Fitzgerald. When elected Michigan secretary of state in 1932, Fitzgerald was the only Michigan

Republican with a statewide office to survive the Democratic onslaught led by President Franklin D. Roosevelt. In 1934, Fitzgerald resigned as Michigan secretary of state to run for governor as a Republican. He was elected in a year FDR was not running, defeating the Democratic opponent Arthur J. Lacy. During Fitzgerald's term, he balanced the state budget and introduced reforms such as consolidating state agencies to reduce waste and overlap.

The president laid the groundwork for Murphy's run before Murphy made his decision. FDR had chosen Murphy's campaign manager, G. Donald Kennedy, who happened to be the business manager to the Michigan State Highway commissioner, who in turn happened to control about 20 percent of the state government's jobs. In his letter to Murphy, FDR acted like a political consultant, noting that there were many "constructive moves that should be made" before Murphy's return, "such as to secure the support of the University Regents."[4]

Roosevelt meant that Murphy should start making promises to reward these groups for their political support. The Michigan State Highway Commission and the University regents parceled out contracts around the state, and a savvy governor could funnel these projects to gain votes. Murphy never showed an interest in pulling levers of this kind, and his later defeat in 1938 could be attributed in part to this failure to reward political allies in the manner that FDR was explicit in suggesting.[5]

The president assured Murphy that "if you should fail and this Administration continues, your work would obviously be recognized."[6] Murphy was enjoying himself in the Philippines, and FDR must have wondered whether Murphy was willing to leave his responsibilities behind.[7]

In February 1936, after FDR's letter, Murphy wrote to the labor leader Frank X. Martel, demonstrating a hesitancy about engaging in Michigan politics.[8] He wanted "to know the real facts" before agreeing to run for governor. But Martel had previously made his views known. As early as 1934, Martel had requested that Murphy return to Michigan, suggesting that a Senate seat or the governorship was his for the taking.[9] Murphy was nothing if not loyal to FDR, and his decision to run was never really in doubt. And once he was all in, Murphy did not hesitate to tie his fortunes to those of the president as he campaigned across Michigan. Appearing before large audiences, he praised FDR and the New Deal, and he sought to bring Michigan "a modern, progressive, kindly government, conducted in the interests of the public."[10]

The New Deal programs, firmly associated with FDR, were putting many people to work. It is not surprising that, in 1936, the Democrats ran on that issue whenever possible. In their 1936 national platform, drafted in part by Murphy, they alleged that "12 years of Republican leadership left our Nation sorely stricken in body, mind, and spirit; and that three years of Democratic leadership have put it back on the road to restored health and prosperity."[11]

Murphy complained on the campaign trail that the current Republican governor did not take sufficient advantage of the new federal programs, such as Social Security. The Social Security Act of 1935 established a permanent system of universal retirement pensions, unemployment insurance, and welfare benefits. It established the framework for the United States welfare system as we still know it today.

Like many other New Deal programs, Social Security was at first run through the states' bureaucracies and not from Washington, DC. This was done as a carrot to get state elected officials— whether Democrat or Republican—behind the new federal benefits. The states (and their leaders) would receive federal funds if their public assistance plans met federal requirements. The local leaders could take credit, thereby strengthening the legitimacy of these brand new programs originating from Washington, DC. In certain ways, the strategy for popularizing Social Security resembled that of President Obama in connection with the Affordable Care Act (ACA), which requires states to meet certain minimal program requirements as a condition of receiving federal funds.

But Murphy had an advantage over his Republican adversary in a way that a Democrat running on the benefits of ACA did not. Prior to 1932, the states had few programs to assist the elderly and others in desperate straits. In many states, the Social Security Act was not replacing something else; it was an entirely new benefit. Other New Deal programs that pumped money into the states were firmly associated with the Democrats. The WPA benefited upward of 75,000 families in Michigan.[12] Murphy argued that with his strong ties to FDR, he was in a position to maximize the benefits of these new federal programs for his state. [13]

Murphy's standing within his state party was far more elevated than in 1932, when he could not even convince the Michigan Democratic Party bosses to incorporate his ideas into their state-wide platform. This time, he was returning from a position as an FDR appointee, and this fact alone swept aside most internal resistance. A few grumbled that he was stepping into a slot that belonged to local politicians who had worked their way up in the state ranks, but these malcontents never gained traction.[14] While this bitterness did not hurt Murphy during his run, he continued to largely ignore these local functionaries after he became governor, rather than addressing their parochial needs. He did not take FDR's advice to use his power to reward supporters with jobs in the highway department and other state agencies.

Roosevelt was not just facing Republican opposition in the 1936 election but also discontent from the left for not going far enough with his economic programs. Although Murphy's loyalty to Roosevelt was ironclad, he drew the attention from the populists, hoping he might leave the New Deal fold and join them for more radical programs. Louisiana senator Huey Long was one such office-bearer who courted Murphy. Long is widely believed to be the model for the Governor Willie Stark in Robert Penn Warren's *All the King's Men*.

In 1934, Senator Long established a movement known as Share Our Wealth, which had specific political goals that could compete with the New Deal. He advocated giving all families a guaranteed annual income of $2,000. Long's motto was "Every Man a King," and he sold it with a folksy delivery. He was someone who cut across party lines and appealed to the poor rural whites and Catholics, and also the urban poor. He had formed his own party, the Union Party, and convinced Father Coughlin to join him.

At one point, Long wrote a fictional account of his first few days as president of the United States in which he mentioned

Murphy by name. The book was entitled *My First Days in the White House*, published in 1935.[15] Long's biographer T. Harry Williams described the book as "curious" and "a mixture of nonsense and wisdom, of frivolity and gravity," and he believed that "Huey must have thoroughly enjoyed writing it."[16] Long portrayed his ideal cabinet, which "was truly a ministry of all the talents. He sought out the best man for each position, regardless of party, and persuaded the individual that he had to accept the appointment as a patriotic duty."[17]

In this novel, Long called Murphy into the Oval Office and asked him to be the Attorney General. The two engaged in a prolonged discussion about the unfairness of the legal system, and both agreed that no man should be in jail if his crime was committed in an attempt to feed his family. President Long asked if Murphy wanted a sentencing board in every federal court, "to sentence intelligently, after compiling an accurate record of the man's life." Murphy answered, "Yes. And that [criminal] record should go to the penal board. . . . in accord with the recommendations of the sociologists and psychiatrists who have joined in sentencing him." Their conversation ended with Murphy accepting Long's request to serve in Long's cabinet, saying, "Mr. President, we shall restore Justice in America."[18] In this fictional account, Long had felt Murphy's "piercing eyes boring into my soul."[19]

Long's description of Murphy's charisma and interests is on point and supports the theory that the two men met and discussed joining forces. Murphy had a lifetime interest in making justice fairer and less retributive, and had introduced a parole board to give sentencing recommendations when he was a local criminal court judge in Detroit. And five years later, as Roosevelt's Attorney General, Murphy did in fact convene a conference made of national experts to discuss sentencing reform. Plus, Long and Murphy might have bonded over a shared love for college football. Murphy was a cheerleader for the University of Michigan, while "the Kingfish" led the band and gave pep talks to the football team at Louisiana State University (LSU).

In 1935, the time of this possible meeting with Long, Murphy was seeking a position in the Roosevelt cabinet and might have expressed his desire for such a position to the senator from Louisiana, thereby placing the idea in Long's head. It is also

possible they never met—Long may have gleaned this information about Murphy's inclinations from their mutual friend Father
Coughlin.[20]

On September 8, 1935, just a few months later, Long was shot
by an assassin, the son-in-law of a political enemy; he died two
days later. His supporters' dreams of a third party died with
him, but he had inspired a wide range of people. A Black couple
from Louisiana named their seventh child Huey in honor of the
Louisiana governor. Huey Newton later became the founder of
the Black Panthers.

Coughlin drifted after losing his main avenue to renewed
power. His third-party run had been effectively destroyed with
Long's assassination. In a move that must have wounded Murphy
greatly, Coughlin threw his support behind Murphy's Republican
rival in the local state race.[21]

While running for governor of Michigan, Murphy found time
to go to the Democratic national convention in 1936. He was an at-
large delegate for Michigan and a member of the platform committee. With his input, the Democratic written platform reflected
a progressive approach. The platform reminded the country that
the Democrats had "given the army of America's industrial workers something more substantial than the Republicans' dinner pail
full of promises." (The "dinner pail" reference was a metaphor for
the blue-collar worker.) "We have increased the worker's pay and
shortened his hours;" ran the manifesto, "we have undertaken to
put an end to the sweated labor of his wife and children; we have
written into the law of the land his right to collective bargaining and self-organization free from the interference of employers;
we have provided Federal machinery for the peaceful settlement
of labor disputes." It went on, "We will continue to protect the
worker and we will guard his rights, both as wage-earner and
consumer, in the production and consumption of all commodi-
ties, including coal and water-power and other natural resource
products."[22] The platform tracked many of Murphy's comments
on the campaign trail.

It was at the convention that Murphy probably first met Senator Hugo Black of Alabama, who was to become a close friend and ally of Murphy on the Supreme Court. The youngest of eight children of a farmer in rural Alabama, Black attended local schools but did not graduate high school. He briefly attended Birmingham Medical College at age 17, then entered the University of Alabama Law School, earning a bachelor of laws degree in 1906. They bonded over their common histories as trial lawyers and local judges and together fought for a wage-hour plank in the committee. They convinced the party elders to do something on the party platform about "minimum wages, maximum hours, child labor and working conditions."[23]

In 1936, Black was one year away from his appointment by FDR as associate Supreme Court justice, the first of eight choices that FDR would use to reshape the Court. Murphy later claimed credit for influencing FDR's decision to choose Black. When Murphy joined the High Tribunal as an associate justice, they fought rearguard actions to protect the achievements of the New Deal and laid the seeds for the Warren court with its emphasis on civil liberties.

Roosevelt's statements in support of the Democratic Party platform helped save the two-party system as the Democrats continued to absorb many of the independents calling for radical changes to the American political system, most notably in the areas of workplace relations and Social Security. By now, most progressives realized that they had a friend in FDR. This sizable group would have otherwise migrated to third parties—such as the Communist Party or Labor Party, which were now common features in European politics.

But who was behind this flanking move by FDR, pushing and prodding him? It was men such as Murphy who did not abandon Roosevelt for third parties and instead insisted on certain progressivist benchmarks in the platform.

Although Roosevelt ran for a third term, mooting any presidential run by Murphy, it is intriguing to note that Murphy had an ability to connect with southern politicians, a crucial attribute for any Democrat seeking the party's nomination. Murphy's bond with Black was strong, but he also had other contacts among southern politicians. Murphy's greatest friend on the Supreme Court was Justice Wiley Blount Rutledge, a Kentucky native who was the son of a Baptist minister. Murphy was a liberal from Michigan who made friends with a diverse group of politicians, including rural and conservative ones. He could have mounted a credible national presidential campaign if Roosevelt had not run.

Endnotes

1. FDR to Frank Murphy, Jan. 7, 1936, FML, reel 106. Fine, *New Deal Years*, 216.
2. Ibid.
3. David Lawrence (syndicated columnist), "Today in the Campaign," *RG*, Oct. 17, 1936, 25.
4. FDR to Frank Murphy, Jan. 7, 1936, FML, reel 106. Fine, *New Deal Years*, 216.
5. Dudley W. Buffa, *Union Power and American Democracy: The UAW and the Democratic Party, 1935–72* (Ann Arbor: University of Michigan Press, 1984), 11. ("Murphy was elected [Michigan governor] and did little to create [a strong party] during his single two-year term as governor.")
6. FDR to Frank Murphy, Jan. 7, 1936, FML, reel 106.
7. Preston Grover (syndicated columnist), "Washington Daybook," *CDS*, July 21, 1936, 6. (The press at the time showed Murphy as hesitant to run. "Those intimate with Murphy said he was adverse [sic] to quitting the $18,000 a year high commissioner post in the islands, with a large executive mansion.")
8. Murphy remained coy about his intentions well into 1936. Associated Press, "Murphy to Visit with States Democratic Chiefs Next Week," *THP*, June 9, 1936, 4. ("County Auditor Edward H. Williams . . . returned to Detroit and said Murphy insists it was not politics which brought him back to the United States but Philippines Trade conferences at Washington.")
9. Frank X. Martel to Frank Murphy, Apr. 4, 1934, WRL, Detroit AFL-CIO Collection Box 11, Folder: Murphy, Frank 1933–1936.
10. Fine, *New Deal Years*, 239.
11. 1936 Democratic Party Platform, June 23, 1936, accessed Apr. 19, 2020, http://www.presidency.ucsb.edu/ws/index.php?pid=29596.
12. Fine, *New Deal Years*, 244.
13. Moreover, only part of the United States, chiefly in the urban areas, resembled modern America, with electricity and plumbing. Roosevelt deliberately targeted areas without these conveniences and necessities for large infrastructure projects. A young Lyndon Johnson won his first House race in 1937 by promising to work directly with FDR to bring electrification to the Hill Country of Texas. Johnson was a national sensation when he beat his Democratic rivals who did not stress the benefits of the New Deal. When the upgrades to infrastructure (such as electricity and water) came, his constituents were grateful and often attributed the upgrades to Roosevelt himself. These improvements also allowed radios to operate, which brought FDR's actual voice to rural Texas. Republicans at first had great difficulty in countering the appeal of the New Deal money, leading to their widespread losses in the election in 1936.

14. "Murphy Unopposed on September Ballot," *DFP*, July 27, 1938, 11.

15. Williams, *Huey Long*, 845.

16. Ibid.

17. Ibid.

18. Huey Pierce Long, *My First Days in the White House* (Harrisburg: The Telegraph Press, 1935), Kindle, Loc. 538 of 1474.

19. Ibid.

20. Fine also speculated on whether the two men met. Fine, *New Deal Years*, 221.

21. Associated Press, "Highlights in Michigan Politics over Weekend," *IDG*, Oct. 19, 1936, 1.

22. 1936 Democratic Party Platform, June 23, 1936, accessed Apr. 19, 2020, http://www.presidency.ucsb.edu/node/273216.

23. Frank, *Hugo Black*, 92.

CHAPTER 13

A Governorship Dominated by Labor Strife

Murphy won the election as Michigan's governor on November 3, 1936. From his crowded suite in the Book-Cadillac Hotel, Murphy lauded the "plain people's faith in intelligent, progressive leadership" and promised to address their "desire for clean, honest and enlightened government."[1]

Murphy had been recalled from the Philippines to run in Michigan. Roosevelt's men believed that Murphy would bolster Roosevelt's chances there, but the results showed that it was Roosevelt who carried Murphy on his coattails. In Michigan, President Roosevelt prevailed by 300,000 votes over the Republican presidential candidate Alf Landon.[2] Murphy's margin of victory in the state was much smaller, winning by a mere 30,000 votes. This tight victory in the gubernatorial race signaled trouble for Murphy, who would have to run two years later without the benefit of Roosevelt on a national ticket to draw in the Democratic voters.

Murphy then promptly went on vacation. He claimed that he needed rest as a result of unspecified illnesses. This was the first documented time that he took time off for health issues, which was to become a recurring background issue throughout the rest of his career. He essentially severed all connections with his staff, exposing him to charges that he was not serious in solving Michigan's looming problems.[3]

Of note, Murphy was ensconced in Florida at Joseph Kennedy's estate,[4] where Murphy would have presumably spent time with a young John Kennedy. Joseph Kennedy's children would have seen in Murphy a powerful example of a Catholic Irish American who had scaled to the heights of power, perhaps reinforcing their confidence that they could do so as well.

Upon his return to Michigan, Murphy no doubt would have relished working with Roosevelt on the big-ticket items outlined in FDR's second inaugural address to the American people. In his January 1937 speech, Roosevelt channeled the late Louisiana governor Huey Long when he urged Congress to enact more comprehensive New Deal programs for "ill-housed, ill-clad, ill-nourished" Americans.

But Murphy had more immediate issues on his desk. Specifically, labor strikes had swept through the state of Michigan and were threatening to cascade into violence and extremism. Whatever the reasons for his earlier absences, he returned to Michigan with worker unrest on his mind. He was fully aware of the possible harm to his legacy as a man who sought to lift up the dispossessed if these issues were not addressed to everyone's satisfaction.

As it turned out, at the exact moment that Roosevelt was delivering his famous inaugural speech, Murphy, already governor of Michigan, was in a meeting with Secretary of Labor Frances Perkins and executives from automaker General Motors as they attempted to settle a major strike. GM, the largest company in the country, had essentially been shut down because of the novel use of a particularly potent brand of worker protest, the sit-down strike. In addition, the strike took place in an important location. Any action that affected a major facility in Detroit had a significant effect on the country because the Detroit area was the country's leading industrial center.

A sit-down strike is what it sounds like—workers stay at their workstations during the labor action to prevent any other workers, presumably non-union strikebreakers, from taking their place. They camp in the factories overnight, and sometimes for weeks on end.

The sit-down strike was therefore different from a traditional strike picket line, where the company could continue to operate with workers willing and able to cross the lines. With the sit-down, management did not have this choice and instead had to decide whether it could endure the economic losses of a shutdown or the political costs of ejecting the workers either through legal process or, as was frequently done, by private police they had hired.

Perkins's presence in this meeting pointed to the national implications.[5] She had already developed a positive impression of Murphy because of his support for Social Security during his campaign for governor.[6] The two would work closely on labor issues and remain friendly over the next several years. Murphy served as Perkins's escort on several occasions at Washington soirees. Murphy's election had encouraged general worker activism. As described by Henry Kraus, the union chronicler who lived through the events of that year, the workers perceived that the new governor was in their corner, which emboldened them to go on strike.[7] On December 30, 1936, just a few days before Murphy took office, employees at the GM Fisher Number One Plant began their sit-down, and this seminal event dragged on for about seven weeks.

In hindsight, Murphy's election was only a contributing factor to the worker activism, as the strike had started earlier that day in a Fisher plant in Cleveland, Ohio.[8] Nevertheless, the workers closed plants in Michigan where "most of the bodies for all GM cars, and all the engines for [GM's] biggest money-maker, Chevrolet, were manufactured."[9] Upwards of 100,000 workers were idled, and factories around the country were completely closed by the workers' action.

By now, strikes had appeared as a major phenomenon in the United States. In 1937, 477 sit-down strikes occurred, a vast increase from previous years.[10] To give this festering labor unrest in the mid-1930s some context, in the year 2017, there were only seven total work stoppages involving 1,000 or more workers lasting at least one shift.[11] Further, in 1936, the United States had a population of 128.1 million, compared with a population of 330 million in 2019. The strikes therefore invaded the public consciousness in a way they do not today.

Detroit alone accounted for almost half the sit-down strikes in the nation in February and March 1937.[12] By the time Murphy became governor, a *Detroit News* reporter observed, "Sitting down has replaced baseball as the national pastime, and the sitter-downers clutter up the landscape in every direction."[13]

The GM strike was big even by the standards of the day. The strike went down in history as the "Flint strike," but the strikes against GM took place across the country and essentially shut down all production.

As governor, Murphy was sworn in to uphold the law and to vindicate the power of the courts when they made rulings. But he faced a dilemma. At the time, courts generally treated picketers as trespassers. Businesses successfully argued in court that the workers were blocking or occupying private property: the factory sites. Trespass was a crime, and court subpoenas and orders were often served by as many as 100 heavily armed sheriffs in quasi-military actions. The sheriffs may not have been trained to deal with employees, and violence often ensued as workers were removed. Many times, the governors would send conspicuous and heavily armed state militias to surround the facilities as workers were being evicted. And if local police forces could not handle the tasks, governors mobilized the national guard in a show of force.

GM acted in the traditional manner and took the striking workers to court, fully expecting the support of Michigan's judicial system regardless of Governor Murphy's point of view. As early as January 2, 1937 (about three days into the sit-down strikes), GM obtained an injunction from State Circuit Judge Edward D. Black, but after it was read to the sit-down strikers by county authorities, no action was taken to enforce it. The UAW then discovered that Judge Black held over $200,000 in GM stock. Maurice Sugar and other UAW attorneys took full advantage, requesting the judge's removal and delaying enforcement of his injunction that would have ended the strikes. As previously discussed, Murphy had represented Sugar early in the careers of both men. Sugar had been disbarred for failing to register for the draft following the entry of the United States into the World War I. Murphy, an eager proponent of the war, nevertheless thought he had an obligation to represent a colleague standing on principle.

By February 2, 1937, another judge had been assigned. Circuit Judge Paul V. Gadola of Genesee County, where Flint is located, duly granted another injunction restraining strikers staying in two GM plants in Flint. The order required the workers to abandon the properties within 24 hours.[14]

The workers ignored this order as well.[15] Now Murphy faced enormous pressure to vindicate the power of the court by enforcing the order to evict the sit-down strikers. But Murphy still resisted calls for the use of force on the strikers and instead offered to mediate a global resolution.

To complicate Murphy's task, the workers were not acting as a monolithic bloc. Moderates mixed with revolutionaries, and various unions vied for supremacy. The CIO had been founded in May 1935 in Detroit under the auspices of the AFL, and the UAW in turn operated under the auspices of the CIO. Recently, the AFL and CIO had split.

Murphy tipped the scales in this internecine union fight. He chose to bring the UAW into negotiations, ensuring that the CIO would be the most important union in the battle to secure better wages and benefits for auto workers. The CIO's strategy of inclusion influenced Murphy's decision to back this horse. The AFL generally allowed only skilled workers to enter its ranks. In addition, the AFL generally adopted the philosophy that immigrants threatened the wages of its members. Samuel Gompers, the founder of the AFL, supported the draconian restrictions on new arrivals to the country in the Immigration Act of 1924 because he opposed the cheap labor that immigration represented.[16] AFL unions locals were often "whites only," mixing prejudice and a desire to limit the pool of qualified workers. Given this reality, Murphy's preference of the CIO was natural. And the CIO in turn supported Murphy. The "Hand of God," a statute outside the criminal courthouse in Detroit, was later commissioned and paid for by the UAW in Murphy's honor.

As the weeks in early 1937 passed and there was no resolution to the sit-down strikes, pressure increased on Murphy to finally enforce the injunction order obtained by the auto companies. The Detroit city manager at one point stated that he had decided to organize a 500-person army, in the form of a special police reserve. His intention was to eject the sit-downers from Fisher No. 1.[17] "We are going down there shooting," he declared. "The strikers have taken over this town and we are going to take it back."[18] He never followed through, but the message had been sent to the striking workers.

Murphy was conflicted. He took his oath of office seriously, and his job was to enforce the law. But he hesitated, seeing the possibility of a blood bath. "My God," Murphy said to Perkins, "it seems an awful thing to shoot people for . . . trespass."[19]

Murphy was an outlier even among New Deal governors for having such thoughts. His fellow governor Martin L. Davey, a Democrat in Ohio, sent in troops to suppress a strike of steel workers at about the same time. During the labor unrest, Davey issued a proclamation calling forth the militia "to execute the laws of the state, to suppress insurrection and repel invasion."[20] The workers were no less than foreign agents, and unsurprisingly the steel strike in Ohio was soon over. This action shows that, even among New Deal Democrats, Murphy was unique in his effort to protect workers.

Murphy also rejected requests for troops by local authorities in more rural areas to resolve other labor disputes. The mayor of Saginaw called Murphy in early February 1937 and requested that the state of Michigan send four companies of militia to deal with a strike at a local factory. Murphy refused. The Saginaw mayor later related with bewilderment that "Governor Murphy advised against interfering with the [union] meeting. He told me that when he was Mayor of Detroit, he always preserved the right of free speech and thought that the best policy."[21]

Similarly, in Monroe, Michigan, Mayor Daniel A. Knaggs asked Murphy to send in the National Guard to open a steel plant that was the subject of a sit-down strike. When Murphy demurred, Knaggs deputized more than 300 men. In the resulting violence, numerous picketers were beaten. Later, at a congressional hearing,

Knaggs admitted that some of the special police officers sworn in for strike duty were armed with baseball bats. Contemporaneous photos at the time in fact showed his men armed with rifles.[22]

GM could not get Murphy to enforce the injunction, so it tried to increase the pressure on the workers in other ways. GM cut the plant's heat and electricity and prevented food deliveries.

In response, Murphy ordered the State Welfare Department to provide food to the striking workers, thereby removing them from the shadows of starvation. He was signaling GM that the workers would be provided with minimal sustenance even as they received no money while out on strike, an unprecedented move by the state and a great moral booster for the laborers.[23]

GM loyalists remained active against the union. A group with strong ties to the KKK, rather ironically known as the Black Legion, threatened and terrorized union members.

The Flint Alliance, which was mostly made up of GM supervisors and hired strikebreakers, was also formed by GM, or at least with GM's blessing.[24] Supervisors went to plants that were not on strike and forced workers to sign membership cards for the Flint Alliance.

Murphy met with representatives from the Alliance in late January 1937 and then blamed them for the continuing unrest. He declared, without backing the claim, "Had it not been for the Flint Alliance, all General Motors employees would likely be back at work today."[25] In response to questions posed by the Alliance, he stated, "I want no inflammatory actions to bring the militia into this dispute. There must be law and order. I am going to see to it that this strike is settled without violence and bloodshed."[26]

The auto workers were camping in the factories and were out of the public view, except when violence flared. But others seeking better pay and working conditions took note of the sit-down tactics. Woolworth employees in Detroit conducted sit-down strikes,[27] and this made the unrest more manifest to the public. Murphy's hand was seemingly behind some of these strikes. Murphy appointed Myra Wolfgang, about 23 years old at the time, to the Michigan Employment Security Commission. Concurrently, Wolfgang also served as the recording secretary of Detroit Waiters Local 705. During this time period, she helped organize the Woolworth strikes in Detroit.[28]

The public was split, then as now, about these worker actions, and the sit-downers received bad press. The specter of foreign influence in the strikes loomed large in the public imagination. In March 1937, Senator J. Hamilton Lewis of Illinois, the Democratic whip, told the United States Senate the sit-down strikes would lead to "Hitlerism." Lewis was a relic, born in Virginia during the Civil War. Now he cautioned: "The time has come when [Congress] would be justified in imploring the president to intervene in this lawlessness created by conflicts between employers and employees that may lead to ruin."[29]

But most who believed foreign influence was at play thought the Soviet Union and communists, rather than fascists, were behind the strike. For his part, Alfred Sloan, the president of GM, declared in a letter to stockholders that the CIO union movement, if successful, would result in "economic and political slavery of the worker." The union movement threatened to create an "economic political dictatorship." There was "little at issue in the whole argument" by unions that "directly affected worker interests."[30]

Newspapers, their revenues dependent on advertising dollars from businesses, portrayed the striking workers in a negative light. They ran stories about how housewives became reluctant to travel downtown to shop near the factories. They described people preparing for the worst, hoarding food. Stores, clubs, and other establishments took measures to protect themselves from the rabble taking over private property.

For Murphy, time was running out. He reminded the union of his legal obligations to enforce the law, to cajole the unions to settle. Murphy threatened the union in a way designed to be picked up by the press: "We have [the] means to enforce respect for public authority and propose to use them with proper vigor if need be."[31] Murphy collected a military force of startling strength. In addition to 1,300 troops already in Flint, Murphy authorized an additional 1,200, including light artillery and cavalry.[32]

On the last night before the GM strike settled in February 1937, Murphy was said to have had a heated exchange with John L. Lewis, the head of the CIO. Murphy had awoken Lewis and told him that he was ordering in the National Guard to evict the strikers because it was his duty to uphold the law. According to Saul Alinsky,

> Lewis fixed a stony stare on the Governor . . . 'Uphold the law? You are doing this to uphold the law? . . . You, Frank Murphy, by doing this are giving complete victory to General Motors and defeating the hopes and dreams of these men.'" Just getting started, Lewis continued, "Governor Murphy, when you gave ardent support to the Irish Revolutionary movement against the British Empire you were not doing that because of your high regard for law and order. . . . When your father, Gov[ernor] Murphy, was imprisoned by the British authorities for his activities as an Irish revolutionary, you did not sing forth hosanas and say 'The law cannot be wrong.' . . . And when the British Government took your grandfather as an Irish revolutionary and hanged him from the neck until dead . . . you did not glory in the purity of the law, the law that must be upheld at all costs!
>
> "But here, Gov[ernor] Murphy, you do. You want my answer, sir? I give it to you. Tomorrow morning, I shall personally enter General Motors Chevrolet Plant No. 4. I shall order the men to disregard your order . . . . Then when you order your troops to fire mine will be the first breast those bullets will strike." Then Lewis lowered his voice, "And as my body falls from that window to the ground, you listen to voice of your grandfather as he whispers in your ear, 'Frank, are you sure you are doing the right thing?'" Gov. Murphy, white and shaking, seized the order back and tore out of the room. The order was not issued.[33]

At times these accounts of almost cartoon-like episodes do not ring true (the Irish sergeant who tested Murphy's eyesight was another example). Murphy was certainly proud of his Irish past, but he was not often swayed by such calls to sentimentality. After all, he fought with the British during World War I and was prepared to do so again in World War II.

Murphy desperately needed to convince the workers to compromise. As described by the historian Christopher Johnson, in one meeting with the union leaders, Murphy told the labor representatives that they could turn the country against them if they pressed too hard. In this meeting, Murphy was in his bathrobe and slippers, lounging in a deep chair as he spoke. He related that he had been eminently fair to the union but the time had come for a change and the union would have to make an important concession if it wished to avoid an attack of volcanic proportions upon itself, the Democratic Party, and him. Putting his hand on Maurice Sugar's knee, he asked, "Morrie, what do you think about that?"[34]

Murphy's threats and legal positions often irked the labor leaders. Sugar, by now a leftist attorney and legal advisor to the UAW (he became the union's general counsel in 1939), took offense at Murphy's challenge to the legality of the sit-down strikes. "This is not a contest between workers and the law," Sugar wrote to the governor shortly after the meeting. "It is in reality a contest between the industrialists and the law, a contest between greed on the one side and humanity on the other."[35]

But the stakes were too high for both sides to remain at a stalemate. The Flint strikes settled in February 1937.[36] Under the terms of the settlement, the workers agreed to vacate the plants and GM recognized the UAW as the worker's collective bargaining unit.[37] This recognition, while seemingly almost a technical point hardly worthy of celebration, was in fact a seismic event. In today's environment, most people recognize worker unions as the entity that bargains with employers. But in the late 1930s, this was not the case at all. Recent legislation had passed establishing a procedure for industrial collective bargaining (the NLRA, otherwise known as the Wagner Act), but its constitutionality was in doubt. Murphy's perseverance helped create the union system we recognize today.

All sides initially gave Murphy a great deal of credit for resolving the dispute. Most significantly for Murphy, FDR sent him "hearty congratulations" for his "splendid work." Roosevelt stated that "an acute situation which threatened serious disorder and dislocation has been amicably adjusted through negotiation." Roosevelt extended the "thanks of the nation."[38] And during Murphy's reelection campaign a year later, Franklin Roosevelt was only too happy to remind the industrialists that they had praised Murphy's performance at the time, including "Mr. Sloan and Mr. Knudsen of General Motors, . . . Mr. Chrysler of Chrysler Motors, and . . . the Fisher Brothers of the Fisher Body Corporation, . . . Mr. Barrett of Hudson Motors and Mr. Graham of Graham Motors."[39]

Murphy became a de facto mediator in many labor disputes while he was governor, and not just in the auto industry. He spent many days and nights negotiating with top corporate leaders and worker activists. With most of these strike settlements, he proved not to be a shill of the unions and developed a reputation as someone who would work with the industrialists. The Chrysler strike was settled when Murphy convinced the striking workers to leave the plants and instead to pursue their grievances in court. Here Murphy had a long history with the Chrysler family. Murphy was the godfather of Walter Chrysler's granddaughter, and Walter had once offered Murphy the job of general counsel. The newspapers at the time of the sit-down strikes did not make a note of this connection.[40] But Walter certainly knew, and he in fact became disillusioned with Murphy after he realized that the close family connections did not place Murphy completely on his side during the tense labor negotiations.

A common theme emerged about Murphy's approach in resolving the strikes roiling a wide range of industries in Michigan. Murphy wanted to secure for workers the right to collectively bargain and to join unions. He was willing to have them surrender the most potent weapon in their arsenal, the sit-down strike, in exchange for this right. The UAW agreed with this strategy, and this was a reason he favored the UAW over other labor groups (another being its relative openness to accepting minorities and workers not generally accepted in the more elite trade unions associated with the AFL).

Murphy knew that the legal system had been stacked against workers, with its emphasis on treating strikes as violations of the owners' property rights and not as an issue of free speech. And with the Depression, workers were more replaceable than ever. With Murphy's assistance, they had gained a seat at the negotiating table. Under the circumstances, this was a great advance even as they gave up their right to sit down.[41]

During the labor strife in his state, Murphy acted on two principles. First, he feared extremism and the threat of violence. If the labor disputes were not settled peacefully, the New Deal was at risk. Second, he feared the outcome of the matter if it reached the Supreme Court. If history was a prelude, the Supreme Court was likely to overturn the Wagner Act (otherwise known as the NLRA of 1935), and with it the legal framework for collective bargaining. Because of this legal uncertainty, Murphy's limited goals for the workers are more understandable. Under the regime negotiated by Murphy, even if the Supreme Court overturned the Wagner Act and the National Labor Relations Board (NLRB) established thereunder, the contracts between the UAW and the car manufacturers would have survived, as they were private contracts and therefore would be enforceable in the courts. Murphy was thereby protecting the right of the workers to collectively bargain, regardless of the constitutionality of the Wagner Act.

Murphy's intuition about the Supreme Court was correct but not in the particulars. The Supreme Court upheld the constitutionality of the Wagner Act, and specifically "the right to self-organization, to form, join, or assist labor organizations, to bargain and to engage in other concerted activities for the purpose of collective bargaining or other mutual aid or protection," as well as the right "to refrain from any or all such activities."[42] However, a few years later, the Supreme Court struck down the use of the sit-down strike.

The Supreme Court's pronouncements about the Wagner Act did not happen in a vacuum. Murphy's skillful resolution of the strikes may have made the collective bargaining regime more palatable to the High Court by showing that workers could be reasonable, contributing to the decision by the Supreme Court to uphold the statute.[43] While the right to collectively bargain was now safe, certain work actions were outlawed. In 1939, now as

FDR's Attorney General, Murphy informed FDR in a routine memo that the Supreme Court had done away with the sit-down strike.[44] The legacy of the sit-down strike would live on, however, adopted by the civil rights movement. The sit-ins at luncheonette counters were direct descendants of the factory sit-downs in the late 1930s.

The strikes in 1937 were to have lasting consequences, not only in setting up a structure for settling labor disputes, but by also establishing clear winners and losers in the union movement. The UAW was transformed from a collection of isolated locals into a major organization, extending its reach to large sectors of the United States automobile industry. Surprisingly perhaps, Murphy retained his good standing with the AFL. During efforts to combine the AFL with the CIO, the Detroit and Wayne County Federation of Labor voted unanimously in December 1937 for a resolution proposing Murphy as a mediator between the two groups because his "reputation for fairness and friendliness to the labor movement" was recognized by "leaders of both factions."[45] Frank X. Martel remained his friend, and later became a bridge between Murphy and President Truman.

Many believed that unions would come to dominate the American workforce and become co-equal with corporations in forging the nation's industrial policies. That did not happen for a variety of reasons. New Deal government programs, such as Social Security and unemployment insurance, addressed some of the biggest demands of the unions but outside the context of collective bargaining. The Wagner Act's NLRB had the effect of channeling disputes to the courts and the labor board, making the union picket line during strikes less central. The Wagner Act also dissipated the growing power of third parties that explicitly promoted worker interests, such as the Socialist and Communist Parties.

On the other side of the ledger, the relationship between management and labor had changed. The "freedom of contract" regime, which in practice meant that workers were free to work unlimited hours in sweatshop-like conditions, was gone. Unions were now established facts, and they had the right to collectively bargain. The idea that pickets were a form of criminal trespass that could subject prosecution largely ended. The use of brute force in quelling worker actions was abandoned, at least in major population centers where the press was active.

Murphy was now as close as ever to FDR and officials in his administration. He developed a particularly close bond to Labor Secretary Frances Perkins during the strikes and traveled to Washington, DC, to meet with her during particularly tense moments.[46] Later, Murphy accompanied Perkins as a kind of escort at official Washington events.[47]

More important, he had secured the gratitude of President Roosevelt. Murphy's settlement of the strikes relieved the immense political pressure that FDR faced from both within his party and business interests during the labor unrest. FDR later told his advisor Samuel Rosenman that "it took real calm not to call out the troops. Little do people realize how I had to take abuse and criticism for inaction at the time of the Flint strike. I believed, and I was right, that the country including labor would learn the lesson of their own volition without having it forced on them by marching troops."[48]

Later, after Murphy lost his governorship to a Republican challenger, many questioned why FDR then gave Murphy such high-ranking positions in his administration. While FDR never kept a diary and rarely explained the reasons for his actions, he no doubt remembered how Murphy addressed the labor strife in Michigan without violence.

Murphy's mediation efforts were not completely successful even at the time. One car company took a far different approach with Murphy, refusing his offers to help. Henry Ford and Murphy had squared off before during the Ford Hunger March in 1932. Now Ford was prepared to move aggressively against the unions even after the strikes against GM and Chrysler were settled by Murphy. The UAW knew that Ford's workers were afraid of Ford's private police force, in part remembering the great violence in front of Ford headquarters during the Ford Hunger March.

So UAW officials decided to come to the Ford plants themselves to try to organize the workers. Walter Reuther, a UAW official, obtained a permit to leaflet a Ford plant. Anticipating a violent response from Ford's police force, the labor leader invited ministers, journalists, and staffers of the Senate Committee on Civil Liberties to join him.

Calling for "Unionism, Not Fordism," the UAW now demanded that Ford provide a pay raise and shorter hours. Ford was paying $6 for an eight-hour day, and the UAW demanded $8 for a six-hour day. This was a widespread demand during the 1930s, the shorter work week designed to spread work around to more of the nation's unemployed. France took up the idea of a 35-hour work week within the last 20 years, with decidedly mixed political results.[49]

As Reuther and other UAW organizers, around 50 in total, walked toward the plant to leaflet for the six-hour day, *Detroit News* photographer Scotty Kilpatrick asked them to pose for a picture with the Ford company sign in the background. As they did so, Harry Bennett, the head of Ford's private police force, and around 40 from his force, attacked them.[50] This force also assaulted women who had arrived to help pass out leaflets. They confiscated all the cameras of the media, except for one, which they missed. Kilpatrick managed to hide photography plates under his car seat. When the photographs came out, public outrage ensued. But Ford initially suffered little from what became known as the Battle of the Overpass. The newly formed NLRB ordered him to stop violating the Wagner Act, a demand that was ignored by Ford—and Ford was not unionized for several more years.

Murphy's term was dominated by labor woes, but he did manage to pass certain bills. Under his watch, the Michigan legislature adopted a relief appropriation bill, provided funds for a housing program, and instituted a moratorium on mortgages. These advances showed that the country had moved politically to an acceptance of government aid for the poor and those struggling to meet their expenses, even in a Republican-dominated state. This change was a watershed, signaling a far different environment than Murphy faced in addressing starvation in Detroit at the beginning of his first mayoral term a scant eight years before.

Murphy tried to create a less corrupt government. To this end, he convened a 90-person bipartisan commission to examine reforms to the Michigan state government (headed by his

Philippines assistant Hayden, now a political science professor at the University of Michigan). Some of their suggestions were implemented.[51] While the effects of these changes were limited, they signaled Murphy's continued interest in progressivist ideals.

But Murphy was distracted from his core functions as governor and not just because of the labor strife. He was a national figure and in demand for speeches around the country. He had built a nationwide network of supporters and was a natural organizer, putting together the Conference of Mayors five years before and becoming its first chairman. As one of the more stylish figures in American politics and an orator of renown, Murphy had been in demand nationwide as a speaker.[52]

His popularity outside of his state may have led him to miscalculate his electoral prospects. He opened himself up to charges that he should pay back a portion of his salary for missing so many days, to which he sanctimoniously proclaimed, "I'd rather give up all my salary than have a cent of it incorrectly."[53] Like a glamorous politician sometimes does when he or she has an eye on a bigger office, Murphy may have ignored local affairs in Michigan too much.

Endnotes

1. United Press, "'Plain People Have Shown Faith'—Murphy," *TSB*, Nov. 4, 1936, 7.
2. "Justice Murphy of the Supreme Court Dies," *NYT*, July 20, 1949 (citing the margin of victory for both FDR and Murphy in Michigan).
3. Fine, *New Deal Years*, 264.
4. Ibid.
5. Alinsky, *John L. Lewis*, loc. 2192 of 6973, Kindle.
6. Political commentators often got the power dynamics in Washington, DC, wrong. In one syndicated column in 1935, it was reported that "Miss Perkins has been out of the picture as an important labor advisor [to the President] for months" and that she was to be replaced by Frank Murphy as Secretary of Labor. Drew Pearson and Robert S. Allen, "Merry-Go-Round," *The Scranton Republican* (Scranton, Pennsylvania), Apr. 3, 1935, 8. Drew Pearson was a friend and admirer of Frank Murphy and wrote a heart-felt tribute to Murphy upon Murphy's death in 1949.
7. Kraus, *Heroes of Unwritten Story*, 187–188 (recounting supportive speeches by Murphy to labor unions and their positive effect on the workers).
8. Ibid, 245–248.
9. Ibid.

10. Howard, *Mr. Justice Murphy*, 145. The level of strike activity for the years prior to 1939, showing large increases in 1937, was summarized in a Department of Labor report. "Strikes in 1939," *Monthly Labor Review of the Bureau of Labor Statistics, United States Department of Labor,* May 1940, 3 ("In this report no distinction is made between strikes and lock-outs . . . As in former years, the figures do not include stoppages which lasted less than a full working day or shift, nor do they include those involving fewer than six workers.").

11. "Major Work Stoppages in 2017," Bureau of Labor Statistics, accessed Oct. 25, 2019, https://www.bls.gov/news.release/pdf/wkstp.pdf.

12. Fine, *New Deal Years*, 326.

13. Ibid.

14. Article fragment, *TON*, Feb. 3, 1937.

15. Strikers at the No. 2 Plant to Frank Murphy, Feb. 3, 1937, WRL, Maurice Sugar Papers, Box 25, Folder 2. ("Governor, we have decided to stay in the plant. We have no illusion about the sacrifices that this decision will entail. We fully expect that if a violent effort is made to oust us many of us will be killed and we take this as a means of making it known to our wives, to our children, to the people of the State of Michigan and of the country that if this result follows from the attempt to eject us you are the one who must be held responsible for our deaths.")

16. Lipset and Wolf, *It Didn't Happen Here*, 132.

17. Fisher was a division of GM.

18. Fine, *New Deal Years*, 310.

19. Fine, *New Deal Years,* 299.

20. Proclamation of Governor Martin L. Davey in Connection with Ohio Steel Strike, June 21, 1937, Kent State Libraries, Special Collections and Archives, accessed Apr. 19, 2020, https://www.library.kent.edu/special-collections-and-archives/ohio-steel-strike-proclamation.

21. Article fragment, *San Francisco Examiner,* Jan. 29, 1937, 2. ("Fear of new violence in Saginaw was expressed today by Mayor Frank Marxer who phoned the governor and received assurance troops would be sent there Sunday if the rally of union men should cause trouble.")

22. Photograph, "Baseball bats used by police in strike duty in Michigan town." Photograph with the caption, Washington, DC, Aug. 1, 1937. National Library of Congress, Prints & Photographs Online Catalogue.

23. Alinsky, *John L. Lewis,* loc. 2141 of 6973, Kindle.

24. "Murphy in Clash," *San Francisco Examiner,* Jan. 29, 1937, 1 (quoting Murphy about the Flint Alliance).

25. "40,000 Return," *San Francisco Examiner,* Jan. 29, 1937, 1.

26. Ibid.

27. "Five and Ten Girls Start Hunger Strike," *San Francisco Examiner,* Mar. 18, 1937, 3.

28. The two could be seen in photos at the time. Blog post, "(31514) Myra Wolfgang, Frank Murphy, ca. 1930s," WRL, accessed July 20, 2020, https://reuther.wayne.edu/node/11220.

29. "Warning Given," *San Francisco Examiner,* Mar. 18, 1937, 3.

30. Associated Press, "Sloan Attacks Latest Mass Labor Movement," *LSJ*, Apr. 2, 1937.

31. Alinsky, *John L. Lewis*, loc. 2348 of 6973, Kindle.

32. Ibid.

33. Ibid; also recounted in an article, *DFP,* Nov. 6, 1949, 19.

34. Johnson, *Maurice Sugar*, 269.

35. Sugar to Murphy, Mar. 22, 1937, WRL, Maurice Sugar Papers, Box 3.

36. The actual settlement date is subject to some debate. Contemporaneous accounts show that the announcement of the settlement predated the finalization of the terms. Associated Press, "Advance in Handling of Industrial Conflicts," *TENS,* Feb. 13, 1937, 7. ("The red-haired Michigan chief executive, visibly wearied from the strain of sleepless nights in his role as peace maker, spoke from the courtroom where less than an hour before the agreement was signed. . . . There was a slight delay before the microphone was brought before the desk at which Murphy sat. The governor looked tired. He covered his face with his hands and dropped his head to the desk. He appeared almost asleep, but roused himself to make the short address.")

37. "Bargain Clause Straight," *LSJ,* Apr. 2, 1937, 6.

38. FDR to Frank Murphy, telegram Feb. 11, 1937, FDRL.

39. Photograph with caption, "Left to right (seated): Alfred P. Sloan, Jr.; President General Motors; Secretary Perkins; Governor Frank Murphy; and William S. Knudsen. Back Row: John Thomas Smith; (left) Chairman Finance Committee, General Motors." Library of Congress Prints and Photographs Division, Washington, DC.

40. "Strikes, Many Other Issues Will Be Aired, President Invites Congressional Leaders to Meet with Him Late This Afternoon to Discuss Critical Problems—Urged to Break General Strike Silence," *TBES,* Mar. 27, 1937, 1.

41. United Press, "Approve Plan to Ban GM Sit-Down Strikes," *IDG*, Sept. 16, 1937, 1. (Revisions to the agreement resolving the sit-down strikes were being discussed by the executive board of the UAW as late as September 1937.)

42. *National Labor Relations Board v Jones & Laughlin Steel Corporation,* 301 U.S. 1 (1937), was the United States Supreme Court case that upheld the constitutionality of the National Labor Relations Act of 1935, also known as the Wagner Act. The quoted items are from the Wagner Act itself.

43. Michael Goldfield, "Worker Insurgency, Radical Organization, and New Deal Labor Legislation," *American Political Science Review* 83, no. 4 (1989): 1257–1282. (He argued that many industries, like the miners in West Virginia, unionized without formal federal action. With or without the Wagner Act, workers would have organized.)

44. In a February 1939 letter, Murphy provided FDR with a "Supreme Court roundup" of important cases. First on the list was *NLRB v. Fansteel Metallurgical Corp.,* decided in 1939, in which the Supreme Court upheld the firing of workers for participating in sit-down strikes. The outcome of this Supreme Court case vindicated Murphy's hunch that trading away the right to sit down in exchange for the tangible benefit of a collective bargaining regime that gave the union a seat at the table was a good one for labor.

45. Associated Press, "Labor Looks to Governor, Wants Murphy as Mediator to Unite C.I.O. and A.F. of L. Factions," *LSJ*, Dec. 2, 1937, 1.

46. Photograph, "Auto strike problem brought to Washington for conference by Governor of Michigan. Washington D.C. In an effort to settle the strike of automobile workers in Detroit, Governor Frank Murphy came to Washington today to confer with Secretary of Labor Perkins and Labor Officials. This picture, made at the Labor Department after a six-hour meeting, shows left to right: John L. Lewis, Head of the CIO; Secretary Perkins; Governor Frank Murphy; and James F. Dewey, Conciliator of the Labor Department," Library of Congress Prints and Photographs Division, Washington, DC, accessed Apr. 19, 2020, https://www.loc.gov/item/2016871168/.

47. Nancy Randolph, "Frank Murphy's [the] Lion of Washington Whirl," *Daily News* (New York), December 17, 1939.

48. Howard, *Mr. Justice Murphy*, 183, citing FDR to Rosenman, Nov. 13, 1940, FDRL, PPF-64.

49. "French Candidates Divided on Future of 35-Hour Work Week," *France 24*, Apr. 13, 2017, accessed Apr. 19, 2020, https://www.france24.com/en/20170413-french-presidential-candidates-divided-35-hour-week-economy-employment.

50. The Henry Ford, a museum, has a digital archive containing details of those events. The attacks on the labor organizers can be found in these four sequential pictures, accessed Apr. 19, 2020: https://www.thehenryford.org/collections-and-research/digital-collections/artifact/253992; https://www.thehenryford.org/collections-and-research/digital-collections/artifact/316203; https://www.thehenryford.org/collections-and-research/digital-collections/artifact/34144; https://www.thehenryford.org/collections-and-research/digital-collections/artifact/275276.

51. "Must Go Slow Reorganizing State Gov't," *Marshall Evening Chronicle* (Marshall, Michigan), Oct. 13, 1938, 1.

52. Fine, *New Deal Years*, 484.

53. "Governor Offers Refund of Pay during Absence, Murphy Would Make 'Christmas Present' of Nearly $1,000 to Lieutenant Governor for Protracted 'Substitute' Service," *LSJ*, Dec. 22, 1937, 1. (The article also observed that Murphy "said that he had asked Edward R. Kemp, his legal counsel, to investigate legal aspects of the situation.")

CHAPTER 14

Murphy's Ineffective Reelection Campaign

In 1938, Governor Murphy faced reelection in a tight two-year election cycle. On the surface, Murphy had reason to be optimistic about his political future. President Franklin Roosevelt had carried him to victory two years before in his own landslide victory. The two remained close, having coordinated responses to the labor issues in Michigan. All had been settled without violence and with the seeming consent of the major constituencies.

There were some storm clouds. At its core, Michigan was still a Republican state. Murphy was admired and loved in Harbor Beach, but it was well known that even his neighbors there, primarily Republican loyalists, did not vote for him.[1] To win in Michigan, a Democrat had to catch significant breaks. Perhaps a Republican candidate was wrapped up in a scandal—Murphy had won his race for mayor in part because of the recall of Republican mayor Charles Bowles.[2] Perhaps a Republican candidate had refused to fully acknowledge the reality that the Great Depression was different from other downturns, with the 30 percent unemployment rate and the misery on the streets.

Murphy now had a national reputation for his loyalty to Roosevelt. He was described in *Fortune* magazine as FDR's *Airedale*, a type of terrier favored by hunters. Murphy's campaign strategy focused in large part on basking in the reflected glory of

Roosevelt. After all, even in a Republican state, FDR was hugely popular.

But Murphy was not a pragmatist in the FDR mode. Roosevelt made sure the money flowed to powerful Democratic interests, such as party bosses and segregationist Democrats from the South. In this way, he kept their loyalty at election time. Murphy failed to organize his party in his home state. He refused to parcel jobs out to Democratic Party insiders, which cost him enthusiasm and votes with the state apparatus. His bi-partisan commission (see Chapter 13) was not beloved by Democrats who wanted the spoils of victory. By way of an example of a lost opportunity, he appointed a Republican, Ralph H. Ferris, as the State Probation and Paroles director. Ferris was a competent choice without regard to political considerations, and he served in that role for about 10 years.[3] But he was not a Democrat.

Compounding Murphy's problems, FDR largely abandoned him in the off-year election. It was not that the two men were not close. Rather, FDR was suffering from some self-inflicted wounds that cost him in popularity and prestige and largely kept him off the campaign trail in 1938. Most notably, FDR took two strong positions that backfired badly. His miscalculations, ironically, could be said to have resulted from his overwhelming victory in 1936. Roosevelt had been elected by a large margin, receiving 61 percent of the vote. His margins of victory in the South were even more impressive. Of the 11 former Confederate states, only 1 failed to give Roosevelt over 70 percent of the vote. In Georgia, the home of Hot Springs, Roosevelt's second home and the place of his death, FDR won over 81 percent of the vote.[4] As already noted, he easily carried Michigan, traditionally Republican. And on his coattails, Democrats, who already held the majority of seats in both the United States House and Senate, gained even more in the 1936 election.[5] In the Senate, the increases were especially impressive. The Democrats picked up five seats, and this margin was made even larger because certain elected Republicans switched parties. The Republicans were reduced to holding 16 seats, the most lopsided Senate since Reconstruction.

Roosevelt interpreted the significant Democratic majority in Congress as an affirmation of his policies and an opportunity to reinforce his gains. His first target was the Supreme Court. In Roosevelt's view, the United States Supreme Court had not been receptive to his New Deal initiatives. After five years in office, Roosevelt had been unable to appoint even one justice, and much of his legislation had been ruled unconstitutional. Against the advice of key advisors, he mused publicly about adding more justices, in what became known as his court-packing scheme. In 1937 he introduced the ill-fated Judicial Procedures Reform Bill. The central provision of the bill would have granted the president power to appoint up to a maximum of six Supreme Court justices for every sitting member of the court over the age of 70 years and six months. Upon hearing of Roosevelt's desire to "pack" the court, critics accused him of wanting to create a dictatorship. His court-packing scheme went down as a dismal failure.

Then, in a June 1938 fireside chat, Roosevelt announced his intentions to campaign for liberals in selected Democratic congressional primaries, and specifically to inform Americans which candidates supported his New Deal programs. Roosevelt's targets for defeat were not Republicans but Democrats from his own party whom he perceived as being not liberal enough. As the Democratic Party leader, he declared, "I feel that I have every right to speak in those few instances where there may be a clear issue between candidates for a Democratic nomination involving those principles or involving a clear misuse of my name."[6]

In this vein, he backed only 21 of the 31 Democratic senators seeking reelection. The rest he opposed, with varying degrees of involvement. And he was humiliated as the liberal candidates he proffered overwhelmingly lost their primary races. Most alarming to the Roosevelt administration was the poor showing of his favored candidate in Georgia, Lawrence Camp. This federal attorney secured less than 5 percent of the vote that determined the Democratic Party nominee. True, the incumbent Democrat Walter George appealed to the racist tendencies of the electorate,[7] but the *New York Times* also made the point that the incumbent generally had a favorable New Deal voting record.[8] Stung by these losses, some very recent, FDR refused to take to the campaign trail for the general elections.

Murphy had what he thought was the perfect idea to repair any damage from Roosevelt's missteps. He publicly invited Roosevelt to come to Michigan for the Blue Water Bridge opening in Port Huron: "I'd like him to come out here and make a speech for me even if he doesn't dedicate the Port Huron Bridge and I'd like to see him in advance and tell him a few things."[9]

It was a clever request, designed to highlight the projects that FDR and Murphy relied on to show that government can deliver. The bridge itself was impressive, a silver arch of steel standing out like a rainbow in the sky above the St. Clair River that connected the United States to Canada. It was a time of impressive public works that were conceived and built on compressed time schedules, not burdened by all the bureaucratic scrapes that might delay matters today. The project was conceived just a few years before, in 1935, when the Michigan legislature (Republican through and through) passed a law creating a State Bridge Commission to finance the design and erection of the main bridge structure of the Blue Water Bridge. The commission was approved by the United States Congress in August 1935. The law permitted it to sell bonds that would be repaid by the revenue from the tolls ($0.25 per vehicle) collected within 30 years.[10]

All told, the occasion provided ready examples of toughness and metaphors about the need for cooperating in the face of adversity. Roosevelt would have received accolades throughout the state if he had attended the opening of this bridge, with its pomp and circumstance.

But Roosevelt did not come. And when he did not, certain papers portrayed Roosevelt's failure to take this opportunity as a sign of a falling out with Murphy. In a conversation with Roosevelt's assistant Harry L. Hopkins on September 1, 1938, Murphy very much sounded the supplicant, praising Roosevelt and trying to determine whether the newspapers' portrayals had any merit.[11] In that same conversation, Murphy blamed behind-the-scenes machinations of Hall Roosevelt, who was "on the payroll of the finance companies . . . and they of course are controlled by the automobile industry and consistently opposed to the President." Murphy was showing a churlish side, dangerously accusing the relative of FDR who had introduced him to the president of disloyalty. Ultimately, FDR did not seem to take any offense, if he heard about these accusations from Hopkins.

FDR's failure to appear in Michigan was not the only setback for Murphy in his reelection campaign. Murphy had run as an unabashed admirer of Roosevelt's economic programs. In campaign speeches for governorship two years before, he lauded the policies of Roosevelt that were designed to prevent future depressions. Yet, the country was now in another downturn, particularly discouraging for the New Dealers. With the paucity of jobs, newly empowered unions lost their leverage. And because tax revenues depended on economic activity, the state now ran at a deficit, weakening the incumbent governor.[12]

Six years before, the Republicans, as the party in power under President Hoover, had trouble countering the Democrats' forceful arguments that the economy needed serious repair with the assistance of government. In 1938, it was the Democrats, including Murphy, with myopia over how bad the economy was at that moment. Consistent with this downturn, unemployment jumped almost 5 percent in two years, to 19 percent in 1938. Manufacturing output fell to 1934 levels. Political adversaries to the president may not have had better solutions, but at least they could argue that the economy was on the wrong course under FDR, a sweet reversal of roles from six years ago when FDR was running and pinned the bad economy on Republicans.

More than this, the Republican Party had grown nimble in countering the New Deal juggernaut, with its promise of large public works projects and sustenance for the needy. Republicans now sometimes grudgingly—and sometimes enthusiastically—supported government programs to help the destitute and put people to work. In Murphy's home state, James Couzens, the Republican senator who made his fortune as an aide to Henry Ford and who later had introduced Murphy to his colleagues in the U.S. Senate when Murphy was a mayor seeking direct federal aid for cities, consistently voted in favor of New Deal proposals. In a tribute to the survivability of the two-party system, the Republicans accepted the role of central government in local matters; from now on, the fight would be over the scale of that involvement. Murphy could not now successfully run, as he had done as mayor and as governor the first time, simply by stating that the Republicans did not support government intervention to help the most desperate and that they were hopelessly out of touch with the fact that the country was in the Great Depression and not simply in a market correction. As already noted, the Republican majorities in Michigan's legislature had promoted and supported the building of the Blue Water Bridge, notwithstanding Murphy's desire to snap up credit.

Murphy had other problems. He had been praised just a year before for his settlement of strikes. But now, Murphy became the poster boy for conservative attempts to paint pro-labor politicians as communist, or more charitably as communist dupes. In this case, the most energetic accusers were fellow Democrats and not Republicans. The Dies Committee, otherwise known as the House Committee on Un-American Activities (HUAC), was created in 1938 by Texas congressman Martin Dies, Jr. The committee's most publicized investigations were those of Joseph McCarthy and Richard Nixon in the 1950s, but the committee existed before that. Congressman Dies was an enthusiastic supporter of these highly publicized investigations well before the McCarthy era, and Murphy became an early target.

Vice President John Nance Garner, also from Texas, was a power behind the committee. He and Dies fully supported the New Deal in its early stages as it aimed to provide relief for the distressed rural areas in Texas and elsewhere. But the focus of the New Deal changed, and with it, Southern Democratic support largely evaporated.

The Wagner Act was especially disliked by Southern politicians, upon whom FDR relied, because it protected labor organizing. Those same politicians also disliked the WPA relief program (which made the federal government by far the largest single employer in the nation), the Social Security Act, and new programs to aid tenant farmers and migrant workers. These politicians saw these programs as taking away local power and nefariously undermining the Jim Crow power structure of the South with its clear rules against worker (and specifically Black) activism.

Dies's targeting of Murphy was logical. Roosevelt was too popular to attack head-on, and so an appropriate surrogate was chosen.[13] But FDR did not shy from this fight. To his great credit, he defended Murphy, and he did it in his usual dramatic way. At a press conference on October 25, 1938, one of the reporters asked the president what he thought of the Dies Committee charging Murphy with "treasonable" activities in the settlement of the sit-down strikes in Michigan two years prior.[14] With a flair for the dramatic, Roosevelt told the questioner that he wished to think about the question.

When FDR's answer came a few days later, he was unequivocal in his response. He issued a press release in which he stated that he "was disturbed not because of the absurdly false charges made by a coterie of disgruntled Republican officeholders against a profoundly religious, able and law abiding Governor; but [also] because a Congressional Committee charged with the responsibility of investigating un-American activities should have permitted itself to be used in a flagrantly unfair and un-American attempt to influence an election."[15]

Specifically, the committee "permitted a disgruntled Republican judge, a discharged Republican City Manager and a couple of officious police officers to make lurid charges against Governor Frank Murphy, without attempting to elicit from them facts as to their undeniable bias and their charges and without attempting to obtain from the Governor or, for that matter, from any responsible motor manufacturer, his version of the events."[16] Here, he blamed Republicans first, even though they were not the main instigators of the attacks on Murphy. As this episode demonstrated, the president did not try to distance himself from his surrogate. He stated that "Murphy had been in touch" with him "on an almost daily basis about the status of the strike" at the time.[17] If Murphy was a communist dupe, then Roosevelt was saying that he was in the same boat. Further, all the important car manufacturers involved, all of whom initially praised Murphy, were also dupes.

As to the court order to evict the sit-down strikers from the GM plants, Roosevelt noted, "Governor Murphy always insisted that the lawful order of the court must be obeyed. But knowing that negotiations for settlement were proceeding and that precipitous efforts to enforce the court order would result in violence which would disrupt peaceful negotiations, he requested the sheriff to postpone the enforcement of the court order over the weekend."[18]

Roosevelt continued, "For that act a few petty politicians accuse [Murphy] of treason; for that act every peace-loving American should praise him." Because of Murphy's calm, "the most alarming strike which ever occurred in this country"[19] concluded without the loss of a single human life.

Roosevelt had two trump cards in defending Murphy, even in the president's weakened political state. First, while communist infiltration in American life was a constant fear that could be exploited since the foundation of the Soviet Union, the country was beginning to fear fascism even more, with the belligerent acts of Hitler and Mussolini in Europe and their immediate threat to United States' allies.

But second, Roosevelt's full-throated endorsement of Murphy could also be seen in the context of a politician who may have believed that he was not running again, and therefore could lash out at enemies without fear that the American public would not support his assessment. Roosevelt was approaching the end of his second term.

Nevertheless, the attacks on Murphy had their desired effect in weakening the incumbent in Michigan. Murphy was increasingly portrayed as a communist sympathizer and someone who encouraged lawlessness. In a sign of trouble to come, fellow Catholic Father Joseph Luther, the head of Student Activities at the University of Detroit, where Murphy had taught law to immigrant students, refused to shake Murphy's hand due to "weak characteristics" in connection with the Michigan strikes.[20]

As previously discussed, although sometimes accused of being a communist by his political opponents, Murphy was never to turn radical or adopt Marxist terminology, even though he had frequent contact throughout his life with firebrands of diverse types, and he himself expressed anger at the working conditions of the average laborer. He pushed back hard against those who accused him of being a stooge for Moscow when he advocated for worker rights. At one point, he argued: "The persons who utter these fictions [about me] either cannot or will not appreciate the fact that, allowing for the undoubted presence of a few selfish and insincere members in the labor unions, there is in back of them a substantial mass movement based on natural causes."[21] He considered his contact with labor radicals, including Earl Browder of the Communist Party USA, to be a price he had to pay as part of his efforts to help the working man. But Earl Browder was also useful as a foil, and Murphy was able to paint himself as a moderate in comparison.[22]

President Roosevelt also used communists and other radicals as foils to show the American public that he was a moderate. Before signing the Fair Labor Standards Act (FLSA) of 1938, he warned, "Do not let any calamity-howling executive with an income of $1,000 a day . . . tell you . . . that a wage of $11 a week is going to have a disastrous effect on all American industry."[23] Both men did what they had to in order to rile up their working-class base, whether that meant demonizing executives or expressing sympathy for radicals.

Governor Murphy's opponent on the campaign trail was Frank Fitzgerald, the former governor he had defeated two years before. Fitzgerald proved to be a canny campaigner. This should not have been surprising, notwithstanding his defeat two years before. He painted Murphy as being a tool of the communists. "Michigan's shame is being paraded before the nation again," Fitzgerald declared, referring to Dies Committee testimony. "The sordid story of what happened here when a spineless government let the Reds have their way is being paraded across the land. . . . A public official who gives aid to Communists is far worse than an avowed Communist," he said. "It matters not that my opponent is or is not a Communist. The fact is he has given aid to that party."[24]

Murphy did his best to obtain support throughout the state. He claimed that New Deal programs helped farmers and his rural constituents.[25] And Murphy again threw his lot in with the workers as he did in every election. In his speeches on the campaign trail, Murphy mentioned the continuing employer violence against the workers: "Somewhat like the person who at one time believed it perilous to give the masses education, they say that labor must be put in its place."[26]

On the night of the election in 1938, Murphy went to see a version of *Pins and Needles* in Detroit. The successful Broadway play, now running in Detroit, looked at current events from a pro-union standpoint. Skits spoofed everything from fascist European dictators to bigots in the Daughters of the American Revolution. One scene satirized Murphy's friend Father Coughlin, along with the German-American Bund leader Fritz Kuhn and Robert Reynolds, the Democratic Party senator from North Carolina. Audience members cheered wildly when they realized Murphy was sitting in the audience.[27]

Even some Republicans supported him. Chase Osborn, the governor who had united Murphy and Kemp during their college years, had stayed a Republican all these years. He vowed to vote Republican in this election, but with one important exception: "I am for Governor Frank Murphy but I am not going to leave the Republican Party for him. I wish the entire Republican ticket success except Frank D. Fitzgerald."[28] Osborn thought that Fitzgerald's attacks that Murphy was a communist sympathizer were grossly unfair.[29]

Fitzgerald defeated Murphy, becoming only one of two governors in Michigan to serve non-sequential terms. Murphy lost by a large margin, over 60,000 votes. Only two and a half months after retaking office, Fitzgerald died at the age of 54.[30] Murphy for his part lost in his bid to become the first Democratic governor to win reelection in Michigan since the Civil War.[31]

This was Murphy's first political defeat since his ill-fated run for Congress in 1920. He put on a brave face, stating, "Defeat is good for the man occasionally." A true believer of the rightness of his approach to the end, he added, "But in the case of the welfare laws, it was a defeat for the state."³² He took a call from the president on election night, considerably lifting his spirits.

On paper, the Democrats continued to hold large majorities in the U.S. House and Senate after the 1938 election cycle. But they had won only a plurality of the total national vote in the 1938 elections. The vagaries of the electoral system, which awards a minimal number of congressional seats to states with small populations and two Senate seats per state regardless of population, worked in the Democrats' favor in the 1930s and 1940s, just as it works in the Republicans' favor today. For example, the Democrats won the U.S. Senate seat in Nevada with a grand total of less than 28,000 votes for the incumbent Pat McCarran.

But within a few days after the elections, it was clear that the New Dealers had lost significant ground around the country. Big states saw Democratic gubernatorial seats turn Republican.³³ Voters knew who was a New Deal Democrat and who was not, and the identifiable New Deal Democrats were overwhelmingly met with defeat. At least in Congress, this meant that the rubber-stamp approval of the blitz of litigation by the New Dealers came to an end. Following the 1938 election, a conservative coalition controlled both the Senate and the House. The conservative coalition proceeded to dominate Congress for the next 20 years, until the election of 1958.

For many Black people in the South, the elections of 1938 accelerated their Great Migration to Northern cities. Southern Democrats now had more leverage over FDR than ever due to the other Democratic losses around the country. Many Black residents in the South moved because they quite literally feared for their lives and had little hope that the situation might change any time soon in the Jim Crow South.

Within a week after the election, the New Dealers had partially regained their equilibrium and engaged in a post-game analysis.

Mayor LaGuardia of New York, a Republican but a firm New Dealer, proposed a meeting of progressives in Washington, DC, to to solidify their forces. He invited the people he perceived as the leaders of the progressive movement: Senator Robert LaFollette of Wisconsin, Senator George W. Norris of Nebraska, and also Frank Murphy.[34]

At least three of the four men—LaGuardia, Murphy, and Norris—knew each other. Murphy had barnstormed across the country with Norris as they gave speeches in support of FDR during his first presidential run. And Murphy and LaGuardia were linked through Ernest Cuneo, an official with the National Democratic Committee. Cuneo had been Murphy's campaign advisor when Murphy ran for reelection as governor of Michigan in 1938.[35] Cuneo had also served as LaGuardia's aide when LaGuardia was mayor of New York City.

In a letter dated December 2, 1938, Murphy provided his own roadmap to the president, with a full-throated endorsement of a progressivist agenda even in the face of his own defeat: "I know that you will not be persuaded by recent events either to compromise or temporize about the great things for which you stand. For our democracy to go ahead and the progressive cause to remain a vigorous force . . . the battle must go on with continuing spirit and enthusiasm."[36]

In spite of FDR's "courageous" recovery measures that "six years ago saved the nation's manpower and averted bankruptcy for municipalities and states," the "great, underlying problem of unemployment" remained.[37] Murphy then recommended that the president double down on a progressivist wish list, including a job and a "living wage" for any person willing to work, and health care for all, with an emphasis on the construction of labs that could solve major medical issues.

He ended his letter with a hint of flattery to the man who might yet employ him: "I am supremely confident that under the leadership of a President whom I deem the greatest ever to occupy the position, the American people will continue to move forward in the pathway marked out by democracy."[38] Murphy, at least, remained an unbowed liberal.

Endnotes

1.   Frank Potts, Jan. 8, 1965, transcript of interview conducted by Sidney Fine, Frank Murphy Oral History Project, FMP, 5.

2.   United Press, "Ends Mayoralty Fight, Bowles, in Detroit, Admits Defeat by Frank Murphy," *NYT*, Sept. 24, 1930, 2.

3.   "As We See It," *DFP*, Aug. 3, 1949, 8.

4.   McGillivary, Alice V., and Richard M. Scammon, eds., *America at the Polls: 1920–1956, A Handbook of American Presidential Election Statistics* (Washington, DC: Congressional Quarterly, 1994). This referred to a Gallup Poll from 1938 showing strong support in the South for FDR. "July 20, 1938, President Roosevelt's Voter Appeal: If Franklin Roosevelt were running for President today, would you vote for or against him?" Middle Atlantic, For = 54%, Against = 46%; South For = 67%, Against = 33%.

5.   "Franklin Roosevelt Re-elected in Landslide," *NYT*, Nov. 3, 1936.

6.   FDR Radio Address from the White House, "On Party Primaries," June 24, 1938, accessed May 1, 2020, http://docs.fdrlibrary.marist.edu/062438.html.

7.   "Senator Certain He'll Win Despite Uneven Contest," *The Atlanta Constitution*, August 16, 1938.

8.   "Yes-Men Wanted," *New York Times*, August 12, 1938.

9.   Summary of Conversation with Frank Murphy [unknown author], Sept. 1, 1938, FDRL, PSF, Frank Murphy Folder.

10.   History, Blue Water Bridge, Michigan Department of Transportation website, accessed June 1, 2020, https://www.michigan.gov/mdot/0,4616,7-151-87728_11070-22062--,00.html.

11.   Harry Hopkins to FDR, memorandum, on or about Sept. 1, 1938, FDRL, PSF, Frank Murphy.); "Blow Dealt to Murphy; Roosevelt Cancels Visit," *DFP*, Sept. 1, 1938, 1.

12.   Ex-augural message of Frank Murphy, governor of Michigan (speech he gave upon leaving the governorship). ("During the present biennium the government has been obliged to contend with three factors of an adverse nature which have made the task of fiscal administration very difficult. The first of these was the action of the legislature in voting appropriations for each year that were $15,000,000 in excess of actual revenue estimates. The other two factors were the severe decline in state revenues [amounting to more than $10,000,000 in sales tax receipts for the calendar year 1938], and the large increase in relief expenditures brought about by the recession in business.")

13.   "Campaign on Labor Issues, Murphy and Fitzgerald Scrap over Sit-Down Guilt," *TTH*, Oct. 25, 1938, 14. (Former Republican governor Osborn threw in his lot with Murphy, while staying a Republican and otherwise supporting the Republican state ticket.)

14.   "Press Release [of FDR] re Dies Committee vs. Governor Frank Murphy," Oct. 25, 1938, FDRL, Master Speech File, Box 42, No. 1176 (the "Dies Committee Press Release"); "A Confidential Secretary Recalls: My 16 Years with Frank Murphy," *DFP*, Sept. 10, 1967, 140. ("Worse yet, the Dies Committee in Washington declared that the strikes were communist inspired and accused the Governor of using treasonable tactics.")

15. The Dies Committee Press Release, 17.

16. Ibid.

17. Ibid.

18. Ibid.

19. Ibid.

20. "Murphy Defended on Red Charges," *DFP*, Nov. 3, 1938.

21. Ibid.

22. "Browder Assails Murphy at Rally," *NYT*, Jan. 23, 1940 (part of the headline read, "19,000 Communists and Their Friends Give Leader Five-Minute Ovation at [Madison Square] Garden"). Browder believed that Murphy abandoned him, for the "opportunity to join the most exclusive old men's club in America."

23. Jonathan Grossman, "Fair Labor Standards Act of 1938: Maximum Struggle for a Minimum Wage," Department of Labor Website, accessed June 1, 2020, https://www.dol.gov/general/aboutdol/history/flsa1938.

24. "Campaign on Labor Issues," *TTH*, Oct. 25, 1938, 14.

25. "Eyes of Nation on Michigan Voters," *TTH*, Nov. 6, 1938 (noting Murphy's wooing of the rural vote by emphasizing that he brought rural electrification to Michigan).

26. Fine, *New Deal Years*, 491–492.

27. "Murphy Is Applauded by Theater Audience," *DFP*, Nov. 9, 1938.

28. "Osborn Votes G.O.P. But --," *TTH*, Oct. 25, 1938, 14.

29. "Campaign on Labor Issues," *TTH*, Oct. 25, 1938, 14.

30. Dan Austin, "The Day Michigan's Governor Died in Office," *DFP*, accessed Mar. 3, 2021, https://www.freep.com/story/news/local/2015/03/16/michigan-governor/24844109.

31. "No Deal Chief Admits Defeat, Executive Dejected; 9 Congressmen Ride to Victory with Winner," *The Akron Beacon Journal*, Nov. 9, 1938, 6.

32. Article fragment, *DFP*, Nov. 11, 1938, 1. ("Murphy lamented the defeat of the proposed welfare reorganization program in Tuesday's referendum, asserting 'that was the real loss of the election; it was a tragic thing.'")

33. Alfred L. Morgan, "The Significance of Pennsylvania's 1938 Gubernatorial Election," *The Pennsylvania Magazine of History and Biography* 102, no. 2 (1978): 184–211, accessed May 2, 2020, www.jstor.org/stable/20091255.

34. Article fragment, *DFP*, Nov. 11, 1938, 2. ("A call for a conference of the Nation's progressive political leaders to solidify their forces was sounded by Mayor Fiorello H. LaGuardia.")

35. Draft of an article or book, FDRL, Ernest Cuneo Papers, Miscellaneous Articles, Folder entitled the "Mind of the President."

36. Frank Murphy to FDRL, Dec. 2, 1938, FDRL, PSF, Frank Murphy Folder.

37. Ibid.

38. Ibid.

CHAPTER 15

Murphy as Attorney General of the United States

Murphy professed a desire to leave public life after he lost his reelection campaign for governor of Michigan, announcing that he and Edward Kemp would start a law practice in Detroit. "The only thing to which one can go back with dignity in this world of ours is private life," said Murphy. He scoffed at rumors that he would become a federal Circuit Court judge.[1]

Yet matters were proceeding behind the scenes. Before long, Murphy learned that he was President Roosevelt's pick to be the U.S. Attorney General. The rumors had been circulating for several months, and Murphy knew this even as he made his announcement to return to private practice.

It may seem surprising that FDR installed a failed governor in a prominent cabinet position. If FDR believed he had some reason to reward Murphy for his past loyalty, he could have sent him as an ambassador to an obscure Catholic country or some other similar role. FDR did in fact find an overseas assignment for Paul McNutt, the telegenic former Democratic Indiana governor. But perhaps not coincidently, McNutt was making waves about running against FDR in 1940.[2]

It is likely that Murphy or Murphy's allies had convinced Roosevelt to send a signal to their political enemies by choosing him for this cabinet position. The archives at the Walter Reuther Library at Wayne State University show that Frank X. Martel and the AFL generally sent out numerous letters to labor organizations pressuring them to contact their senators to confirm Murphy as the U.S. Attorney General.[3]

With Murphy's appointment, every single one of FDR's cabinet members was a New Deal advocate.[4] The same day Murphy was confirmed, Felix Frankfurter, the liberal icon who had defended Nicola Sacco and Bartolomeo Vanzetti, was approved by the Senate for the Supreme Court.[5]

Officially, at least, the reason for Murphy's appointment was his managerial skills as the governor of Michigan. In announcing the selection, Stephen Early, the president's press secretary, stated that the president was deeply impressed with Murphy's reorganization of the state government in Michigan.[6] Early expressed a desire for Murphy to revive a federal government reorganization bill that Congress had "shelved."[7]

Murphy replaced Homer Cummings as the U.S. Attorney General. Cummings was a product of Yale College and Yale Law School, and had been with Roosevelt from the first days of his presidency. Washington insiders such as Cummings often took a disdainful view of Murphy, painting him as regional and ethnic. Later, when Murphy was promoted to the Supreme Court, Cummings would say that "with Murphy's appointment, the number of Justices would be increased to twelve since Murphy would 'bring with him as colleagues Father, Son and Holy Ghost.'"[8]

Cummings may have changed his opinion of Murphy if he had known that Murphy was now in charge of an investigation into Cummings relating to a certain land deal in Connecticut. Upon his appointment, Murphy personally quashed the investigation. Murphy often acted on principle, but he demonstrated at times an ability to protect FDR from embarrassment. An ethical scandal involving his longstanding attorney general fit the description of something that needed to be swept under the rug.

Murphy was accompanied by his brother George and sister Marguerite to Washington, DC. Marguerite assumed her role as confidant and hostess. George was by now an elected judge in the Detroit Recorder's Court, Frank Murphy's first elected position several years before. The Murphy brothers remained popular in their home state, now otherwise Republican in voting patterns, and George won his seat on the criminal court in election after election, even as he echoed Murphy's sympathetic views relating to labor.[9]

Frank was sworn in on January 2, 1939.[10] Then, two weeks later, Murphy easily received Senate confirmation of his appointment.[11] Murphy was approved with 59 Democrats and 16 Republicans voting in favor.

The Southern Democratic senators were notable in their unanimous "aye" votes. Certain Southerners such as Congressman Dies may have cost Murphy the governor's seat in Michigan by painting him as a communist sympathizer. Now, without fanfare, conservative senators approved his appointment as the nation's top enforcement officer.

Murphy was unapologetic about his past, recalling his role during the great sit-down strikes during his time as governor of Michigan: "[These] hard-working citizens had determined that their right to bargain collectively should be recognized . . . They were thousands of honest citizens . . . who believe that they were only defending their own rights against . . . the lawless refusal of their employers to recognize their unions."[12]

A combination of factors worked in his favor. First, the senators respected the political power of FDR, who remained immensely popular throughout the country in both Republican and Democratic districts despite the significant electoral setbacks in 1938. Second, President Roosevelt had the power over vast flows of federal funds, with the ability to divert federal money from or to senators' favored projects, a reason to support his picks.

But Murphy did face some opposition within his party. Vice President Garner from Texas was known to oppose the pick, pivoting on the charge that Murphy, as governor of Michigan, had improperly countenanced unlawful sit-down strikes during the

CIO attempts to organize automobile workers. Garner was isolated within the administration, but still powerful as the pre-
sumptive frontrunner of the Democrats if Roosevelt chose not to
run for a third term. FDR's great advisor Harry Hopkins, concurrently being considered for secretary of commerce, faced similar
allegations of being a communist sympathizer, but he too was
confirmed by the Senate.

Among the senators who did not vote for Murphy was
Arthur Vandenberg, the Republican from Murphy's home state
of Michigan, who was known for his switch from isolationist
before World War II to cold warrior (the big California military
base is not, however, named after him). The Michigan voters had
decided against Murphy's reelection, and Vandenberg therefore
felt he could not support Murphy for Attorney General. Prentiss
Brown, the Democratic senator for Michigan, however, rose to
Murphy's defense and called Murphy "a great Christian and a
great Catholic," and the victim of "baseless charges," no doubt a
reference to the communist label.

The House of Representatives, although not part of the confirmation process, had its own hearings in connection with Murphy's
appointment. Here, he was received less kindly. Certain representatives, including Representative Clare Hoffman of Michigan,
used the hearing as a platform to blast Murphy.[13]

Hoffman griped that, as mayor, Murphy did not adequately
protect the property of owners of factories back in 1932 during
the Ford Hunger March. Hoffman also referred to the more recent
sit-down strikes at Flint and Lansing in 1937, which Murphy as
Michigan governor had settled. "Frank Murphy," he said, "did
not ask those violators of the law who were in possession of those
factories to abandon their lawless activities. On the contrary, he
asked, he insisted, that the Sheriff of the county and the peace officers of the city refrain from their lawful duty and that they permit
the violators of the law to remain in possession of the factories."[14]
This was all political theater as the House of Representatives does
not confirm Cabinet appointees and could not change the outcome of Murphy's appointment as U.S. Attorney General.[15]

Once in the nation's capital, Murphy the bachelor passed as a desirable suitor in the Washington power corridors. The "Irishman of strawberry-colored eyebrows" was the "answer to ladies' prayers and the big news of the social season" in Washington, DC, at least according to Nancy Randolph in December 1939, who wrote the society column of the *New York Daily News* during that newspaper's heyday. Randolph, a pseudonym for the prolific Inez Robb, was a serious newspaper reporter.

Randolph reported that "here in Washington . . . you can't go to any of the snootier hang-outs or attend any of the more uppity parties without running smack into 'General Frank' ladling out gallant gestures and pleasant conversations."[16] After an impressive White House function in which Murphy "solemnly" escorted Labor Secretary Frances Perkins, the first female cabinet member, into the Red Room, he raced across Lafayette Square and squired his new beau Ann Parker, "a vision of loveliness." Her father was the "Commander of the Department of the Philippines when Murphy was the Governor-General there."[17] Murphy had been seen at the opera stroking the hair of the young Ms. Parker. By now, they had known each other for at least six years. Parker may have been dismayed by the next words of this columnist. Randolph wrote in this article that the status of Murphy's various female friendships "is a favorite indoor sport" in Washington.

As described in George Chauncey's book *Gay New York*, the *Daily News* had a documented history of innuendo when describing gay men in society columns.[18] The stroking of Parker's hair by Murphy seemed to be a deliberate, conspicuous act. And perhaps the *Daily News*' description of this detail was code as well.

Although Murphy's tenure as the nation's top law enforcement official was short—just over a year—he pursued an activist agenda, particularly in weeding out political corruption and staking a claim in the area of civil rights. Murphy had a history of ferreting out graft, starting with his first job out of the Army when as an assistant United States attorney, he targeted World War I profiteers.[19] As a criminal court judge, he launched grand jury investigations into monopolistic syndicates within his city.[20] His even-handedness in dealing with wrongdoers, regardless of party affiliation, should have been a warning to the Democrats who supported his appointment. Indeed, as the U.S. Attorney General, he attacked Roosevelt's most important allies, consisting of the Southern Democratic establishment and the city bosses.

By the time of Murphy's appointment, Huey Long, the senator from Louisiana and erstwhile presidential candidate, had been dead for four years. Long had a reputation for corruption but for covering it well. Long's successors were equally compromised but not as careful.[21] Knowing that they were in his gunsights, the leaders of Louisiana invited Attorney General Murphy to receive an honorary degree at LSU graduation ceremonies in 1939. Murphy accepted the invitation and came to Baton Rouge. Prior to his arrival, however, he made sure that the local newspapers covered his meeting with J. Edgar Hoover, the director of the Federal Bureau of Investigation (FBI), to discuss the coming trip.[22]

Murphy's visit to the LSU campus was separately documented by Robert Penn Warren, the author of the novel *All the King's Men*. In a 1981 *New York Times* article, Warren recalled the visit by Murphy to the graduation ceremonies at the LSU campus, which he had attended as a student. At the time of Murphy's visit in 1939, Warren was drafting his soon-to-be-famous novel. Where faculty, graduates, and fond parents had been waiting under the floodlights, Warren saw "Murphy march across the sacred greensward, a thin, tense man with the gaunt aquiline look of a 16th-century Inquisitor."[23] When it was Murphy's turn to speak to the graduating class at LSU, he focused in his speech on the spread of corruption in state governments. Murphy "deplored" the connection between crime and politics. Serious, intense, and undistracted, he was speaking truth to power in the lion's den. It was reminiscent of a younger Murphy as he calmly spoke in a Detroit banquet hall filled with businesspeople who opposed his budget and who were trying to shout him down.

Robert Penn Warren was captivated by Murphy's performance at LSU. "As I sat through the commencement I had the odd impression that I was looking at an epilogue of my own project,"

Warren noted.[24] As was typical of articles or books mentioning Murphy, the attorney general was not the focus of Warren's article in the *New York Times* (in this case, the protagonist was the long-deceased Huey Long). Clues about Murphy's strong presence at important historical events must be gleaned in passing references to him in stories about others. But this article leaves no doubt about the strong impression Murphy made on Warren and also of Murphy's sense of timing and the dramatic.

The New Orleans *Times-Picayune* was instrumental in pressuring Murphy to act. The editors baited Murphy, wondering "whether the close social and political ties between the administration which Attorney General Murphy serves and the Louisiana government will save the tolerated rackets in this state from his pursuits." Murphy almost immediately reached out with a handwritten note to the newspaper's editor-in-chief, George William Healey, asking for further proof of the graft. Healey "assured him that [the *Times-Picayune*] could supply evidence of corruption and leads to additional evidence to anyone authorized by the attorney general to make a serious investigation."[25]

The information provided by the *Times-Picayune* and others on Louisiana graft was sent to O. John Rogge, who was in charge of Murphy's criminal division.[26] Several senior Louisiana government officials, including Governor Richard W. Leche, subsequently went to jail for fraud associated with federal projects. The Attorney General then wrote another letter to Healey's senior correspondent in Washington in language we have come to expect of Murphy, "There is no more satisfying task than freeing our people from the loss of morals."[27]

No character in *All the King's Men* can be tied directly to Murphy. But Warren based his novel in part on Murphy's visit to the state and the subsequent prosecution of Huey Long's successors by the Department of Justice. In the plot of *All the King's Men*, Tiny Duffy, large and untrustworthy, became governor after Stark's assassination. Like Leche, the actual governor of Louisiana, the fictional Duffy ended up in jail for his financial crimes.

Murphy attacked other party bosses with zeal. He successfully presented charges of graft and corruption against the Pendergast machine in Kansas City. Murphy fully backed Maurice Milligan, the local United States attorney in Kansas City in his pursuit of this Democratic Party city boss. Milligan eventually convicted Pendergast, along with 259 of his colleagues, for crimes ranging from vote fraud to income tax and insurance frauds.[28]

The Pendergast prosecution by Murphy may have been the last straw for Roosevelt, who relied on the party bosses, with their extraordinary vote-gathering abilities. Pendergast often had turnouts of well over 100 percent. And Murphy had already complicated FDR's life by supporting the prosecution of the Louisiana Democratic machine at a time when the two Democratic senator votes from that state were meaningful to the president.[29]

In the end, Frank Murphy may have failed up, elevated to the Supreme Court from his perch as U.S. Attorney General, to stop his pursuit of the party bosses.[30] One thing is certain. Other prosecutions of party bosses "largely ceased" upon Murphy's appointment to the Supreme Court.[31]

While he attacked corruption with a religious zeal, Murphy's probes sometimes coincided with Roosevelt's needs. In 1936, Moses "Moe" Annenberg purchased the *Philadelphia Inquirer*, the third-oldest surviving daily newspaper in the United States. Roosevelt did not like Annenburg, who declared war on the New Deal and its Pennsylvania mouthpiece, Governor George Earle (Earle had also been defeated by his Republican rival in 1938). After receiving encouragement from Franklin Roosevelt, Treasury Secretary Morgenthau started a review of Annenberg's tax returns.

On April 21, 1939, Murphy announced that Annenberg was being investigated by his department and explained that now "two lines" of inquiry were being pursued. Morgenthau complained to the president about Murphy's invasion of his turf, but the Department of Justice continued its investigation. The tax case brought against Annenberg was the largest tax evasion case the Justice Department had ever prosecuted to date.[32] On April 4, 1940, in a case filed under Murphy's watch, Annenberg pleaded guilty, to Roosevelt's great satisfaction.

FDR may have encouraged Murphy to aggressively pursue certain crime bosses to upstage Thomas Dewey, the Republican

New York district attorney, who was being spoken about as the Republican challenger to FDR in 1940 and who was tracking higher than FDR in some head-to-head polls. But some articles portrayed the real competition as between Murphy and Dewey, who themselves might have been adversaries in the 1940 presidential race if FDR had decided not to run.[33]

Separately, Murphy voiced his desire to keep his department clean of scandals. He made a speech to a new FBI training class that its graduates should not cavort with the criminal element, even if the sole motivation was to get close to rogue elements to obtain their cooperation in FBI investigations.[34]

Murphy could sound wounded and petty in connection with accusations of bias in his review of corruption cases. To the charges that he had suppressed proceedings against the Chicago mayor and the Jersey City mayor, among others, he moaned, "Such stories and such statements are not true—I resent them and the implications arising from them."[35]

Murphy was also active in the promotion of civil liberties during his year as the U.S. Attorney General. To date, the Fourteenth Amendment and associated federal statutes had rarely been used for their clearly intended purpose—to protect Black civil rights. Murphy wanted this to change. He pressed his Department of Justice to bring cases challenging the status quo and specifically to find ways to apply federal laws to state and local actors. In line with his view of government's role as protector of individual liberties, Murphy established a Civil Liberties Section in the Criminal Division of the Department of Justice. Murphy was explicit in explaining its role:

> The maintenance of civil liberties of the individual is one of the mainstays and bulwarks of democracy. It is fundamental that in the United States certain civil rights are guaranteed by the state governments, while others are assured by the Federal Government. In respect to the latter group the Department of Justice

has an important function to perform. With that end
in view, I caused to be organized a Civil Liberties
Unit in the Criminal Division of the Department. One
of the functions of this unit is to study complaints of
violations of the Civil Rights Act and to supervise
prosecutions under those statutes.[36]

Thurgood Marshall expressed appreciation for Murphy's work
as U.S. Attorney General. In a tribute to Murphy in 1950, Marshall
wrote that Murphy "will always be remembered for having set up
and put into motion the Civil Rights Division of the Department
of Justice for the purposes of enforcing the civil rights statutes of
the United States and of protecting the civil rights of Americans
throughout the country."[37]

Murphy had a target-rich environment. The South was segregated, with lynchings and violence against Black people, and
with laws that were baked in to ensure inequality. The North in
many ways was no better, segregated by tradition and by law.
Redlining, wherein Black people were steered to certain neighborhoods, was prevalent. And the federal government itself was
segregated. The armed forces famously had all-white and all-
Black units (and would soon have segregated Japanese-American
units).[38] But separation of the races was also the norm throughout
the federal workforce going back to the time of President Wilson
(who had actually *reimposed* segregation in the federal bureaucratic ranks). Also, federal contracts allowed contractors to create
segregated work environments.

Murphy had a basic problem in changing practices. The federal
laws on the books to stop discrimination were not entirely clear in
their specific application and, in any event, had rarely been used.
Murphy directed lawyers assigned to the new section he created
to undertake a comprehensive study of the existing statutes the
federal government could use to prosecute civil rights violations.
They then vigorously applied these laws, even when those laws
did not seem to strictly apply to the facts at hand.

In *Screws v. United States*, 325 U.S. 91 (1945), Murphy's strategy on civil rights was the issue before the Supreme Court.
Specifically, the Department of Justice had used an imperfect law

to try to address an injustice of the Jim Crow South. The justices heard a case in which Claude Screws, a white sheriff, arrested Robert "Bobby" Hall, an African American, on January 29, 1943. Hall had allegedly stolen a tire. Hall was arrested at his home and brought to the local jail: "After Hall, still handcuffed, had been knocked to the ground, [police] continued to beat him from fifteen to thirty minutes until he was unconscious. Hall was then dragged feet first through the courthouse yard into the jail and thrown upon the floor, dying."[39]

A white jury empaneled by a state court quickly acquitted the police officers of murder, outraging many. This was exactly the type of case that Murphy wanted his team at the Department of Justice to take on. The federal government would prosecute wrongdoers if the states were unwilling to do so. It would do so by applying civil rights laws, passed by Congress, even if they were not a perfect fit. In the absence of a specific anti-lynching law, Screws was tried under a Reconstruction-era civil rights law—Section 20 of the United States criminal code—that made it a crime for anyone acting "under color of any law" to deprive any inhabitant of the United States "of any rights, privileges, or immunities secured or protected by the Constitution and laws of the United States." Section 20 was one of a panoply of laws designed to give effect to the Thirteenth Amendment outlawing slavery. It, along with many of the other Reconstruction-era laws, were largely ignored until they were dusted off by the Department of Justice starting under Murphy's watch in the late 1930s.

The conviction of Screws showed that Southern juries could convict white men, even law enforcement officials, in the death of Black people. But it should also be noted that while the case was moving through the courts, Screws was reelected as sheriff by a very wide margin.

The conviction was upheld by the Circuit Court and then appealed to the Supreme Court. The High Court, in a decision authored by William O. Douglas, acknowledged that the case involved "a shocking and revolting episode in law enforcement"[40] but ruled that the federal government had not shown that Screws had the intention of violating Hall's civil rights when he killed him.

Douglas approached his ruling from the perspective of protecting defendants' rights to due process. Any criminal law must give a defendant fair warning that his or her conduct is the subject of a crime. A specific anti-lynching law would have given this notice to the Georgia sheriff and his men—a more general statute as was used by the government did not fit the facts. But anti-lynching legislation had been hopelessly stalled in Congress for decades.

By now, Murphy was a justice on the Supreme Court, in essence ruling on the legal strategy he had developed as an attorney general. In dissent, Justice Murphy raged, "Knowledge of a comprehensive law library is unnecessary for officers of the law to know that the right to murder of individuals in the course of their duties is unrecognized in this nation. No appreciable amount of intelligence or conjecture on the part of the lowliest state official is needed for him to realize that fact; nor should it surprise him to find out that the Constitution protects persons from his reckless disregard of human life, and that statutes punish him therefor."[41]

As later chapters show, Murphy has been criticized by legal scholars over the years for not hewing to precedent and for lacking a narrow focus when he wrote opinions. And *Screws* is as good a case as any to make this point. In *Screws*, Murphy did not cite even one case of legal precedent. But the bigger picture is relevant. Murphy's statements would not require case law today. They would be self-evident. For many years after his death, however, his decisions were seen as unduly provocative and off-the-cuff, and the substance of his opinions have largely been forgotten.

"Robert Hall, a Negro citizen,"— Murphy used his full name to humanize, as he often did in his Supreme Court decisions—"has been deprived not only of the right to be tried by a court, rather than by ordeal. He has been deprived of the right to life itself. That right belonged to him not because he was a Negro or a member of any particular race or creed. That right was his because he was an American citizen, because he was a human being. . . . He has been cruelly and unjustifiably beaten to death by local police officers acting under color of authority derived from the state."[42]

Murphy could not change the fact that the High Court had ruled against his Department of Justice. This failure to impose liability as Murphy would have liked had direct consequences for the civil rights movement. Throttled with the *Screws* decision, the Department of Justice hesitated to take on civil rights cases. It did not press charges in connection with the 1955 lynching of Emmett Till in Mississippi after suspects were cleared by an all-white jury. The failure of the federal government to act in that lynching helped galvanize civil rights activists in the South.[43]

As the U.S. Attorney General, Murphy had another problem in promoting civil rights. Even when his department acted aggressively, he needed grand juries willing to indict. This remained difficult in the South, notwithstanding the occasional success, as in the *Screws* case.

One of the best accounts of the early years of the Civil Rights Division was by an attorney in the division, Eleanor Bontecou.[44] Bontecou described the basic dilemma, "If the grand jury wouldn't indict, we couldn't go any further. And with very clear evidence and all, they still wouldn't indict. We were trying to overcome a popular attitude as well as the crimes. We had one case of a group of Negroes being run out of town. That was a very interesting case, but I don't know how you'd classify that exactly, except the right to live in peace." As she stated, "We also had jurisdiction over lynchings in which we never got beyond attempting an indictment. We couldn't." In spite of the problems, she believed that the Civil Rights Division had some effect. "We did feel that the threat of the Federal law hung over people all the time and that was a restraint."

Murphy was ahead of his time in sounding the alarm about the Axis powers. Before the attack on Pearl Harbor, most in the United States were not keen about going to war. The memories of being "played" by the European powers during and after World War I were still strong, and created isolationistic streaks. "We are frankly determined to have peace at any price," said a *Harvard*

Crimson editorial appearing in the fall of 1939. "We refuse to fight another balance-of-power war."[45]

On Capitol Hill, a combination of Republicans and Democrats, isolationists and anti-communists, teamed to stop the FDR administration in its efforts to arm the British, Soviets, and Chinese nationalists (at war with the Japanese) and to grow the paltry American military.[46]

As Attorney General, Murphy tried to find legal justifications for FDR's Lend-Lease program and other attempts to help China, the Soviet Union, and Britain. Legally, he had little to work with. Congress and its Neutrality Act had prohibited overt aid by the United States to the European powers.

On September 1, 1939, Germany invaded Poland. FDR was awoken at 2 AM with the news. He understood immediately that this meant a larger war, as England and France had pledged to come to Poland's aid.[47] Murphy understood as well. Later that month, Murphy, along with Secretary of State Cordell Hull, prepared a report for FDR outlining the limited actions that he could take to help countries under attack while still abiding by the law requiring him to respect the neutrality of the United States.[48] Given the reality, Murphy instead tried to build political support for action against the Axis powers.

Most striking was Murphy's early and forceful condemnation of the growing discrimination against the Jews in Europe. As governor, Murphy stated, "We are not here, certainly, to interfere in the affairs of other nations. However, you can't remain silent in the face of evil."[49] As Attorney General, he often spoke before Jewish groups. He decried the existence of an estimated "800 organizations in the United States [that] are carrying on definite anti-Jewish propaganda. All told, they claim in the neighborhood of six million followers—no doubt a considerable over-statement." But, regardless, "we face the fact that a large number of our people subscribe to the philosophy that has reduced the Jews of Central Europe to a condition of misery seldom equaled in the world's history."[50] He stated that as a child he was brought up to revere the Bible as the "book of books" and that "Palestine is not simply a distant country, nor are the people [who] first made it the Holy Land, simply another race." In support of a Jewish homeland, he proclaimed that "America itself came into being at the hands of harried and homeless people, searching for the blessings of peace and freedom."[51]

Murphy deserves credit for recognizing the threat posed by fascist regimes ahead of most others in this country. But the reality remains that he did little to move the needle. Hitler's atrocities and invasion of Poland, and Japan's occupation of substantial portions of China, including Shanghai, did not arouse the ire of the American public. "Hitler's attacks on the Jews did not bring the United States into World War II, any more than the enslavement of 4 million blacks brought Civil War in 1861," said Howard Zinn in *A People's History.*[52]

Murphy had to deal with FDR's obvious desire to seek a third term. As troubling as this break with the two-term tradition was, life without FDR seemed scarier to those in the progressive wing of the Democratic Party. The political strength of Vice President Garner from Texas loomed large. Murphy and other liberals feared that Garner would seize the Democratic mantel. In cabinet meetings, Garner expressed his hostility to New Deal programs, particularly those after 1936 that tended to promote government intervention into areas such as management/labor relations. Garner and his like were concerned whenever the central government imposed minimal standards for workers, as this was seen as a threat to the status quo in the South, with its unequal treatment of Black employees in workplace environments.

In late December of 1939, Murphy was part of a coordinated attempt to build legitimacy for a third term. Here, he worked with New York City Mayor Fiorello LaGuardia and Harold Ickes. That month, LaGuardia visited FDR with great fanfare to discuss the upcoming national elections. At that meeting, LaGuardia asked FDR to consider a third term. Following LaGuardia's press conference, Murphy held his own press conference and stated that "LaGuardia should be welcomed into the Democratic Party. We should seek him with outstretched arms" in part for his support of FDR's third term. Murphy was followed by Harold Ickes, FDR's great strategist, who went on record that he considered it imperative that a liberal be elected, "or we may run into an internal situation as disastrous as what happened in certain European countries."[53] The decision by Roosevelt to run for a third term traumatized many of his closest supporters. James Farley, one of Roosevelt's top advisors, and the man most responsible for brokering the Democratic Convention in 1932 that led to FDR's first nomination, now opposed Roosevelt for breaking with tradition. Farley decided to challenge Roosevelt in the Democratic primary in 1940, placing a distant second.[54]

As with earlier entreaties by Huey Long and Father Coughlin, Murphy decided to reject Farley, throwing his full support behind FDR. Once again, Murphy was proving his worth to FDR. And FDR was soon to reward him with a bigger prize: a seat on the Supreme Court.

Endnotes

1. "No Bench for Murphy," *NYT*, Nov. 11, 1938.
2. Dr. George Gallup (pollster), "McNutt Gains in Support of Nation-Wide Survey of 1940 Possibilities," *Tampa Bay Times*, Sept. 14, 1939, 4.
3. The AFL's support Murphy showed that Murphy's support of the rival CIO and its UAW during the sit-downs did not cause permanent harm. But Martel also beseeched Murphy to appoint his allies if elected. These statements continued after Murphy was appointed attorney general. The Metropolitan Detroit AFL-CIO Collection, Box 11.
4. "Murphy Is In; Cabinet Now All New Deal," *DN*, Jan. 3, 1939, 2.
5. Associated Press, "Frankfurter and Murphy Receive Senate Approval, Supreme Court and Attorney Voted in—Long Debate Features Murphy Decision," *MMT*, Jan. 17, 1939, 1.
6. "Governor Says Goodbye," *DFP,* Jan. 2, 1939, 7.
7. The stated reason for Murphy's selection as Attorney General was likely a pretext. An attorney general did not typically oversee government reorganization efforts. Nor did Congress randomly "shelve" Roosevelt's 1937 bill. The legislation was not put on hold on the merits but as part of Congress's pushback to FDR's court-packing scheme and his purge of Democratic candidates seen by him as insufficiently loyal to New Deal principles. The reorganization legislation would have passed if not perceived as part of an overall power grab by Roosevelt.
8. Fine, *Washington Years*, 138.
9. Like his brother Frank, George Murphy volunteered to serve in World War II. In 1942, he was given a leave of absence from his position on the court to allow him to report to the Naval War College in Rhode Island. Untitled article, *TNP*, June 26, 1942, 12. Unlike Frank, perhaps George was drawn to the sea by his childhood upbringing in a port town on the shores of Lake Huron.

10. "Appointee," *DN*, Jan. 3, 1939, 22.

11. This was a reversal of the usual order. Confirmation by the Senate precedes the appointment. But Murphy was confirmed on January 17, 1939.

12. Harold Norris, *Mr. Justice Murphy and the Bill of Rights* (Dobbs Ferry, New York: Oceana Publications, 1965).

13. Clare Hoffman, "In Bed with the Reds," *TNP*, Oct. 13, 1938, 12. In a letter to the editor before the elections in 1938, Clare Hoffman wrote of his belief that Murphy had sided with communists and acted as a stooge for Earl Browder, the Communist Party head in the United States.

14. Ibid.

15. Associated Press, "Frankfurter and Murphy Receive Senate Approval," *MMT*, Jan. 17, 1939, 1.

16. The General is a reference to attorney general. He was also referred to as Gigi when he was the governor general in the Philippines.

17. Nancy Randolph, "Frank Murphy's [the] Lion of Washington Whirl," *DN*, Dec. 17, 1939.

18. Chauncey, *Gay New York*, 54 (describing a profile of entertainer Harry Richman).

19. "Before Death Took Toll of Murphy Family" from "Murphy Souvenir Section" of newspaper, probably from *DFP*, Apr. 23, 1933, FMM.

20. "Graft Warrants Being Prepared for Detroiters; Judge Murphy Finds Evidence of Wholesale Practice of Fraud in the City, *TTH*, Apr. 27, 1925, 1. ("Judge Murphy's recommendations were made in a 47-page report on the grand jury investigation he conducted into alleged irregularities and extravagance in several city and county departments that cost the tax payers hundreds of thousands of dollars.")

21. Healey, *A Lifetime on Deadline*, 95.

22. "Group Charged with Using the Mails to Defraud," *Messenger-Inquirer* (Owensboro, Kentucky), July 18, 1939, 11.

23. Robert Penn Warren, "In the Time of 'All The King's Men,'" *NYT*, Sunday, May 31, 1981.

24. Ibid.

25. Healey, *A Lifetime*, 95.

26. Rogge, *Our Vanishing Civil Liberties*, 14 (recalling his appointment by Murphy).

27. Healey, *A Lifetime*, 95.

28. "The Missouri Compromise," Drew Pearson, "Merry-Go-Around," *The Town Talk* (Alexandria, Louisiana), July 22, 1944, 6. Articles on Pendergast started to appear in 1944 as Truman was being considered FDR's vice presidential candidate.

29. O. John Rogge, Nov. 13, 1965, transcript of interview conducted by Sidney Fine and Robert M. Warner, Frank Murphy Oral History Project, FMP, 4.

30. Drew Pearson, "Washington Merry-Go-Round," July 23, 1949 (reprinted in *Florence Morning News*, Florence, South Carolina); FDRL, Ernest Cuneo Papers, Box 113 (stating that Murphy preferred to be secretary of war).

31. Drew Pearson, "Washington Merry-Go-Round," July 23, 1949 (reprinted in *Florence Morning News*, Florence, South Carolina).

32. Folsom, *The Money Trail*, 289 (describing Attorney General Murphy's investigation of Moe Annenberg).

33. Frank Kluckhohn, "Federal War on Crimes Aims at Basic Causes," *NYT*, Aug. 27, 1939 (with a cartoon of Murphy staring down Dewey, both with guns in their hands, and Louis [Lepke] Buchalter, "one of the country's foremost racketeers," drawn as a duck in the pond; the article noted that Lepke surrendered to federal agents in New York City). This surrender to the federal authorities was victory for Murphy in a turf fight with New York local prosecutors.

34. "Head G-Man Applauds Attorney General," *TTH*, July 9, 1939.

35. "Statement by Retiring Attorney General Frank Murphy," Jan. 18, 1940.

36. "Annual Report of the Attorney General of the United States for the Fiscal Year Ending June 30, 1939," (Washington, DC: U.S. Government Printing Office, 1939), 2.

37. Thurgood Marshall, "Mr. Justice Murphy and Civil Rights," *Michigan Law Review* 48 (1950): 745.

38. Eleanor Roosevelt to FDR, memorandum, probably Sept. 1940. ("There is a growing feeling amongst the colored people, and they are creating a feeling among white people. They feel that they should be able to participate in any training that is going on, in [] aviation, army and navy.")

39. *Screws v. United States,* 325 U.S. 91, 93 (1945).

40. Ibid at 92.

41. Ibid at 136–137.

42. Ibid at 134.

43. Jeff Zillgitt, "Kareem Abdul-Jabbar Honors Those Who Inspired Him on MSNBC Show," *USA Today,* Sports, Dec. 10, 2016. ("For me, it was especially so. I remember the Emmett Till murder in 1955. I didn't understand why it happened, but it had a profound effect on me. I couldn't get it. It really bothered me. It made me pay attention to the Civil Rights movement. I was only 8 years old when it happened, but it still got to me.")

44. "Eleanor Bontecou Oral History Interview," Harry S Truman Library, accessed Apr. 19, 2020, https://www.trumanlibrary.org/oralhist/bontecou.htm.

45. "From Soldiers to Scholars," *The Harvard Crimson,* June 4, 1996, accessed June 1, 2010, https://www.thecrimson.com/article/1996/6/4/from-soldiers-to-scholars-pwhen-world/.

46. Eric Pace, "Hamilton Fish, in Congress 24 Years, Dies at 102," *NYT,* Jan. 21, 1991, Section 1, 26 (describing how Congressman Hamilton Fish, who held the seat that covered FDR's home in Hyde Park, was a staunch opponent of United States involvement in World War II right up until the attack on Pearl Harbor).

47. Handwritten memorandum of FDR, reflecting his conversation with Francis Biddle ("In bed, 3:05 a.m."), Sept. 1, 1939, FDRL, PSF: Diplomatic Correspondence—Poland, 1933–1945; Collection.

48. The reference of the memorandum of Hull and Murphy is found in the FDR papers. FDRL, PSF, Raw Folder (containing summary of memoranda).

49. "5,000 in Detroit Ask Bank on Reich Trade, German Persecutions Not 'Will of the People,' Murphy Says," *NYT,* Nov. 21, 1938.

50. Frank Murphy, "Civil Liberties and the Cities," before the Joint Meeting of the United States Conference of Mayors and the National Institute of Municipal Law Officers at the Empire Room, the Waldorf-Astoria, New York City, May 15, 1939, United States Attorney General website, "Murphy speeches."

51. Frank Murphy, "The Challenge of Intolerance," at the National Conference for Palestine, Washington, DC, Jan. 7, 1940, United States Attorney General website, "Murphy speeches."

52. Zinn, *A People's History*, 410.

53. Clifford A. Prevost, "Roosevelt Backers Start Drive to Halt Garner Nomination; President Hears LaGuardia's Ideas; Murphy Says Mayor Should Join Hands with Democrats; Ickes Draws Up Plans for Parley of Liberals," *NYT*, Dec. 22, 1939.

54. In 1947, President Harry S Truman appointed James Farley to serve in a senior post as a commissioner on the Hoover Commission, also known as the Commission on Organization of the Executive Branch of the Government. Farley's work on the commission led to the development and ratification of the Twenty-Second Amendment of the Constitution, establishing the modern two-term limit for the chief executive. The passage of the amendment was viewed by many, including Farley, as vindication for his public opposition to Roosevelt's third term.

CHAPTER 16

The Supreme Court: Murphy's Initial Years

In November 1939, while serving as the U.S. Attorney General, Murphy learned that he was the president's choice to fill the Supreme Court vacancy left by the death of Pierce Butler. Murphy and Butler were both Catholics from the Midwest but otherwise shared few similarities. Butler was a social and economic conservative. In 1938, he refused to sign on to the Supreme Court decision of *Gaines v. Canada*,[1] which stood for the rather limited proposition that a state-sponsored law school catering to white students must also admit Black students if the state had no "separate but equal" facility for those Black students. Butler disagreed, joining a dissent by James McReynolds, who concluded that a desegregated law school in Missouri would "damnify both races."[2]

Butler was also a reliable vote to overturn FDR's New Deal legislation. From the outset of his presidency in 1932, FDR knew that four of the sitting Supreme Court justices—Pierce Butler (whom Murphy replaced), James McReynolds, George Sutherland, and Willis Van Devanter—would vote to invalidate New Deal programs. They were known by their enemies as the "Four Horsemen," an explicit reference to the book of Revelations. In the spring of 1935, a fifth justice, Hoover-appointee Owen Roberts—at 60, the youngest man of the nine men on the Supreme

Court—began casting his swing vote to create a conservative majority. This seeming conversion by Roberts panicked Roosevelt and his staff, and was the genesis of Roosevelt's ill-fated scheme to "pack" the Supreme Court.

The Supreme Court problems for Roosevelt resolved themselves not through amendments, legislation, or political machinations, but through departures and deaths on the court, much like the collapse of a "one-hoss shay."[3] In May 1937, one of the Four Horsemen opposed to New Deal legislation, Justice Van Devanter, announced his retirement from the court, which gave President Roosevelt the opportunity to appoint a Supreme Court justice with views more similar to his own.

In quick succession, FDR appointed four new justices before appointing Murphy to the High Tribunal. One can instantly see how these choices collectively changed the court from a conservative outpost to one in full support for FDR's programs. Hugo Black, the Alabama senator, was Roosevelt's first pick for the Supreme Court. He was a drafter or promoter of much of the New Deal legislation. There was little doubt Black would uphold the Democratic economic initiatives.

Second came Stanley Reed, the administration's solicitor general.[4] Reed had argued for the constitutionality of FDR's legislation before the Supreme Court. He was reliably in the president's corner. Third was Felix Frankfurter, a close advisor to Roosevelt, who would veer off from Roosevelt's worldview in unexpected ways, but at least at the beginning approved of FDR's economic agenda as being consistent with his general deference to the decisions of political branches of government. Fourth came William Douglas, who headed FDR's Securities and Exchange Commission, itself another New Deal creation.

And fifth was Murphy. In short, the court that Murphy entered, consisting of nine justices in total, was now squarely on the side of Roosevelt and his economic programs. The justices appointed by Roosevelt later diverged in their assessments of the appropriate limits of the New Deal–era legislation. For now, however, many detractors saw Murphy as another cog in the new majority that would bless the new administrative state that FDR was creating. And with Murphy's appointment, a voice supporting Jim Crow and segregation was also replaced by a proven champion of religious and racial minorities.

Murphy at first resisted the call to serve on the Supreme Court. In a letter to Roosevelt dated December 9, 1939, Murphy provided a list of candidates to replace Butler. His name was notably not on his own list. In the letter, he sanctimoniously admonished the president, "Members of the Supreme Court are not called upon nor expected to represent any single interest or group, area or class of person. They speak for the country as a whole. Considerations of residential area or class interest, creed, or racial extraction, ought therefore to be subordinated if not entirely disregarded."[5] Despite his lofty words, Murphy's candidate list consisted exclusively of male, white senators and assorted allies of FDR. Some names on the list we recognize today, and others have disappeared from the national stage. None were identifiable as Republican.

Certain members of Roosevelt's staff were opposed to Murphy's appointment, raising his lack of scholarly experience as a basis (and ignoring his work as a professor at the Detroit School of Law and his briefings to the president on legal matters).

They also believed he was an ineffective attorney general. Murphy had been a bull in the china shop, with his emphasis on ferreting out graft and creating a civil rights division. But regardless of his effectiveness, he had the most important qualification—his appeal to the president. Ironically, Republicans grasped this reality better than some in Roosevelt's administration. "If Murphy is as bad as you now say he is," a Republican reporter answered one grumbling aide of Roosevelt, "and the President agrees with you about him, why did not the President merely ask for Murphy's resignation instead of putting him on the Supreme Court?"[6]

Murphy ultimately acquiesced, as always, when FDR pushed him to take the job.[7] Privately, Murphy expressed humility. To a friend, he stated that the cases on the High Court were "beyond his grasp" and he "fear[ed] that my work will be mediocre up there."[8] Part of this was no doubt designed to elicit reassurance. Murphy rarely felt overwhelmed in prior jobs, and he had some reason for actual confidence. As the Attorney General, he had briefed the president on important Supreme Court decisions. He was familiar with constitutional law. But he also knew how to employ staff and clerks to produce sophisticated finished legal products.

He quickly warmed to the idea. He was downright giddy in a press conference in early January 1940 when he took questions on his new appointment, bantering and joking with the full assembly of reporters at his office.[9] His appointment was met with cheers by many on the outside. Murphy was "one of the most favorably received judicial appointments of the century"—a "splendid selection," said Arthur Krock, an influential *New York Times* columnist. Krock had previously identified Murphy as "one of the most earnest, interesting and able men in public life" even after Murphy's defeat as governor in 1938.[10]

By historical standards, Murphy's appointment process was lightning fast, with the announcement on January 4, 1940, and the confirmation by the full Senate 12 days later with a decisive vote of 69 in favor and 23 opposed.[11] He never had to appear before a Senate screening committee, as he was considered fully vetted based on his prior experience in the federal government. FDR swore him in, starting a tradition in which presidents swore in Supreme Court justices.[12]

Almost everything about Murphy's past would have instilled confidence in Roosevelt that Murphy would faithfully uphold his New Deal legislation while on the bench. Murphy was an early convert to the might of the federal government to improve lives when charities and the state failed to deliver answers to the misery, poverty, and starvation in Detroit in the late 1920s and early 1930s. Murphy believed that the national government alone had the resources to solve the problems of an increasingly complex society. As governor, he once said, "Since the turn of the century and especially since the [First] World War, the development of large industrial units with their mass production and the trend of population from rural to urban areas, there has come a gradual change in the economic and social status. . . . It is important, therefore that our laws and political institutions keep steady pace."[13]

Here it must be noted that Murphy had previously been heavily involved in a movement to change the Constitution in response to the Supreme Court's string of decisions overturning FDR's New Deal legislation. Murphy's solution at the time was to support an amendment to the Constitution to enshrine worker rights. In February 1937, while Murphy was governor of Michigan, he appeared before the National Conference for Clarifying the Constitution by Amendment. The conference was called because, according to Murphy, with "the Court's outlawing of effective regulation," Roosevelt's recovery program was in jeopardy.[14]

In his speech in Detroit, Murphy mocked the 1935 Supreme Court *Schechter* case, which rendered the National Industrial Recovery Act of 1933 (NIRA) unconstitutional (this was the "Eagle Seal" statute from which the Philadelphia Eagles name was derived).[15] In that case, the federal government had used the authority under NIRA to try to impose minimum wages and maximum hours for employees of a chicken slaughterhouse located in Brooklyn.[16] The slaughterhouse was mostly a local affair, but it did buy chickens from out of state. Because of this limited interstate commerce, FDR's lawyers argued that the federal government had a right to impose minimal work condition standards to protect the employees. In response, the Supreme Court declared NIRA to be invalid: "If the commerce clause were construed to reach all enterprise and transactions which could be said to have an indirect effect upon interstate commerce, the federal authority would embrace practically all the activities of the people, and the authority of the State over its domestic concerns would exist only by sufferance of the federal government."[17]

Murphy and others saw a benevolent federal government trying to protect workers, thwarted on a legal technicality. According to Murphy, the Supreme Court had taken it on itself to declare that not even the states "could protect wage earning women and minors against starvation wages and sweatshop conditions. The job was complete. The handcuffs had been put on both wrists."[18] Ultimately, the Supreme Court reversed its viewpoint as men such as Murphy entered its ranks. What was unconstitutional several years before, and what caused FDR so much consternation and led him to try to pack the court, became constitutional according to the newly appointed members. Once on the Supreme Court,

Murphy never once raised the issue that the proper way to protect workers was not to go to the courts but to seek an Amendment to the Constitution. He found reasons to uphold worker protections every step of the way.

Murphy entered the court with experience in two professional arenas that would define his tenure. First, he had vast experience as a lawyer and judge who conducted actual trials. Lawyers come in all types. Some never enter the courtroom in their careers, and others only practice at the rarified federal appellate level. Murphy had spent time in the trenches, trying and deciding cases large and small, and dealing with people during the worst time in their lives. And others on his High Court were similar in this regard. Hugo Black had been a trial lawyer from a small town in Alabama. Wiley Rutledge, Murphy's great friend on the Court, was a high school teacher and trial lawyer.

Second, Murphy was a politician with executive experience. He had to propose budgets, deal with subordinates, field constituent questions, and ultimately face the voters at the ballot box. Over the years, he had made many speeches and learned to express his point of view in ways that ordinary people could understand. One of Murphy's clerks opined that he was not a great legal scholar, but "he took a back seat to no one in his knowledge of how government actually works and the interplay between the government and its people."[19] He generally believed that government had a wide-ranging right to intervene in the affairs of the people, but he was aware that government often fell short.

This was a different time and the standards were different for Supreme Court justices. In contrast, no current member of the Supreme Court has tried a lawsuit before a jury except for Justice Neil Gorsuch. No justice other than Justice Sonia Sotomayor has been a trial-level judge, required to take cases as they come. And, likewise, due to the nature of the Supreme Court pipeline today, no current justice has experience as an elected official on the state or national level. None has headed an administrative agency, as either a cabinet member or otherwise. Since Murphy's time, only one justice has served as a governor of a state. That justice—Earl Warren—was a rough contemporary of Murphy. Hugo Black, also his contemporary, held state office as a senator of Alabama and outlived Murphy by many years.[20] Murphy's tenure on the Supreme Court must be seen in the context that he brought with him trial-court experience and executive experience.

Until this time, Murphy and Kemp, Murphy's longtime friend and colleague, had been virtually inseparable. In *Courting Justice: Gay Men and Lesbians v. The Supreme Court*, written in 2001, Joyce Murdoch and Deb Price declared as "highly likely" that Murphy was the first gay Supreme Court justice. They noted that Kemp, like Murphy, was a lifelong bachelor. From college until Murphy's death, the two men "found creative ways to work and live together."[21] They met as undergraduates at the University of Michigan and then attended law school there. They then continued their studies in England. "After returning [from abroad], they shared an apartment with a friend, starting a pattern of shared living quarters in ways unlikely to raise eyebrows. After World War I broke out, Murphy and Kemp served together, and after became law partners."[22]

Certainly, there is much to support their conclusions about Murphy and Kemp. Murdoch and Price could have also noted other times the two men were together: When Murphy went on to become the governor general of the Philippines, Kemp became his legal advisor. Edward Kemp had a desk in Murphy's own office when Murphy was Michigan's governor.[23] Kemp joined Murphy as a special assistant when Murphy became the Attorney General. Finally, Kemp and Murphy were so intimate that Kemp had a hand in drafting Murphy's decisions when Murphy sat on the Supreme Court.

Murphy and Kemp were also travel companions. In 1925, the *Detroit Free Press* recited on its "Society" page that Murphy was taking a "European sojourn of six weeks' duration" with Edward Kemp.[24] This was during a time period when Murphy was supposedly courting Hester Everand, one of several women with whom he also had a long-term relationship.[25]

And their choice of Europe as a destination may not have been coincidental. By 1925, when Murphy and Kemp set sail for Europe after the Great War, they both would have known about the cultural offerings of Paris and Berlin. As George Chauncey in his book *Gay New York* explained, World War I took many provincial and isolated homosexual American men from their small midwestern towns and sent them to Europe. The accepting cultural and political climate for homosexuals in France was eye opening for these young soldiers from the States.[26] Both Murphy and Kemp were World War I Army veterans from small midwestern towns.

They took long trips together later in life as well. In 1935, when Murphy was the governor general of the Philippines, he and Kemp traveled together from Manila back to Michigan, a journey of several weeks that involved significant boat travel and then train travel from the West Coast.[27] In their trip back to the Philippines, where Murphy resumed his duties, Kemp was again listed in newspaper articles as accompanying Frank.[28] In pictures of Murphy's funeral in 1949, Kemp can be seen as a pallbearer.[29]

Murphy had the money and resources to pay for large hotel suites that could hold several members of his staff (although he left some outstanding hotel bills upon his death). The press often reported that his staff lived close by. He could use his money and resources to hide a certain lifestyle.

Of course, Murphy and Kemp had ample reasons to keep their relationship private and not write letters to each other and the like. Sexual relationships between men were often prosecuted under a variety of criminal statutes ranging from loitering to sodomy. And blackmail or discrimination against homosexuals was not out of the question. In 1950, one year after Murphy's death, a Senate committee published a document entitled *Employment of Homosexuals and Other Sex Perverts in Government*.[30] With a focus on Washington, DC, where Frank Murphy spent most of his time in his later years, the report noted that "between January 1, 1947, and August 1, 1950, approximately 1,700 applicants for Federal positions were denied employment because they had a record of homosexuality or other sex perversion." The labeling of homosexuality as a type of sex perversion by a congressional body and its rabid efforts to root out applicants highlighted the perils to gays in government.

What were FDR's views on homosexuality? FDR likely could have confirmed any rumors about Frank's sexual orientation and then sidelined Murphy if he were so inclined. It is likely he did not particularly care, based on his treatment of another official facing rumors of homosexuality. In 1940, one of FDR's most trusted aides, Sumner Welles, was rumored to have drunkenly propositioned a male Black Pullman car porter. Welles was the son of a prominent New York family and had proven himself to be a brilliant assistant secretary of state, especially in keeping Latin American countries in line during World War II.

As recalled by Welles' son Benjamin,[31] the incident was generally known in political circles, but not spoken about, until 1943, when Secretary of State Cordell Hull, who had policy differences with Welles and resented that he had FDR's ear, threatened to go public with the allegations if FDR did not fire Welles. FDR complied with Hull's request, fearing Hull might turn Southern Democratic senators against him. Welles related how his father remained FDR's close advisor even after details of that drunken night in 1940 spilled out. The idea that Welles was a homosexual or a bisexual did not seem to bother FDR: "Roosevelt chose to ignore the incident, believing it was a momentary lapse triggered by alcohol and fatigue and felt confident the incident would soon be forgotten."[32]

On the other hand, he seemed to jettison Welles when it was politically expedient to do so. As to FDR's general views on the subject, we are hobbled by FDR's notorious failure to keep diaries or allow people to take notes during their meetings with him.

One interesting side note is that Hull apparently went to FBI director J. Edgar Hoover for the file on Welles, and Hoover refused to turn it over.[33] Hoover faced rumors about his own sexuality, and he and Murphy had a close working relationship when Murphy was the U.S. Attorney General. In this regard, Hoover had the ability to expose Murphy (or Welles) if there was any evidence in his files. Although he was ruthless in the compilation and use of information of a personal nature, Hoover did not do so with either of these two men.[34] This could mean that the information truly did not exist or that Hoover suppressed the information.

Murphy knew Welles, as he seemed to almost everyone of consequence at the time. A photograph exists of the two men leaving

St. Patrick's Church in Washington, both nattily dressed, following a Pan-American Thanksgiving Day Mass on November 21, 1940. This photograph was taken about two months after the alleged incident on the Pullman train.

Welles donated his papers to the FDR library. These papers contain letters he wrote to various leaders and others informing them of his dismissal in 1943. As might be expected, there is nothing in his papers hinting at Hull's threat. Even one of the best known stories in the Washington, DC rumor mill, that of Welles, contained little in the way of definitive proof.

In the end, the facts that people point to in establishing a romantic relationship between Murphy and Kemp—that they lived in close proximity their entire lives and that both were bachelors—do not actually establish a romantic relationship, and many plausible alternative scenarios exist.

Murphy and Kemp may have formed what was simply a strong friendship based on common political beliefs, sealed by their connections to Michigan. They initially bonded in college when they worked on the campaign for progressivist Chase Osborn. Once they knew each other, they had reason to stay in touch as young, ambitious lawyers entering the Detroit legal and political community. Kemp was an extraordinary talent in his own right. He showed early promise as an associate editor of the *Michigan Daily* and the *Michigan Law Review*.[35] Murphy and Kemp complemented one another's legal and political talents.

Kemp's intellectual firepower cannot be understated. In early January 1940, the press reported that Kemp was being considered for a District of Columbia district court judgeship.[36] Eventually, Kemp found a home as the general counsel of the Bureau of the Budget. Roosevelt was personally involved in Kemp's transfer to the Bureau, which also required Senate confirmation.[37] It was a prominent post, especially because the Government Reorganization Act of 1939 placed the Budget Bureau directly under the control of the president and not with the Department of Treasury where it had previously resided. With this switch, the Bureau became a nerve center for implementing the vastly expanded initiatives of the New Deal. Kemp's appointment is a testament to his skills as a lawyer and advisor, deeply impressing those holding powerful positions.[38] True, Murphy may have suggested that Roosevelt find a place for Kemp as a condition for taking the Supreme Court position (no written evidence of this exists), but if so, Roosevelt had no reason to place Kemp in such an important position just to placate Murphy.[39] Kemp was undoubtedly a talent in his own right and was a key to Murphy's personal success, at the very least.

Sidney Fine's third book on Murphy, *The Washington Years*, was published in the mid-1980s. Fine wrote that, other than one letter received near the close of his tenure as the Attorney General, there is "no other evidence in the written record pointing in the same direction, nor was friend or foe of Murphy when questioned on the matter inclined to believe that he was other than heterosexual."[40] By now, Fine had devoted more than 30 years to the study of Murphy's life, starting around 1952 with his first interview of Murphy's Supreme Court law clerk, Eugene Gressman. Between the years of 1963 and 1968, Fine conducted no fewer than 30 interviews with friends and colleagues of Murphy, including top government officials and justices active in the 1930s and 1940s. As a University of Michigan professor, Fine had access to the private papers of Frank Murphy, stored at the Bentley Library.[41]

Intriguingly, however, Fine tended to shy away from asking direct questions in this regard. A review of oral histories at the Bentley Library shows that Fine rarely asked about the subject of Fine's personal relationships with Kemp and other men. The closest Fine came was in this elliptical exchange with a close family friend of Murphy's:

> *Fine*: You say [Murphy] was trying to protect the inner man from public scrutiny. What was this inner man that he was protecting?
>
> *Frank Potts*: It was nothing he was hiding.
>
> *Fine*: I understand that. I don't mean there is anything undesirable about it.[42]

Fine, a sharp and incisive interviewer, in this instance moved on to other questions. He could have pressed Potts, a family friend, on his defensiveness in connection to the question. More to the point, he could have asked whether Potts knew of the rumors of Murphy's sexuality. He could have asked this question of any of the many interviewees as part of his oral histories, and perhaps sealed the record if the answers were too explosive for his times. He did not, at least not as reflected in the transcripts.[43]

Leslie Woodcock Tentler, professor emerita of history at Catholic University, was a graduate student at the University of Michigan, and while there had an occasion to ask Sidney Fine about Murphy's sexuality. In an email, Tentler has confirmed that "he answered, rather primly, that he did not regard it as appropriate for a biographer to speculate on such things, especially given the lack of definitive evidence." She continued, "I also asked my mother, who was active in the labor movement in Detroit in the 1930s and was in later life a friend of Josephine Gomon. She remembered Murphy showing up for public events locally with gorgeous women on his arm, but never with any apparent romantic entanglements. So naturally she wondered, and assumed that others did, too. Detroit had an aggressive vice squad in those days and any hint of scandal would have ended Murphy's career."

Murphy encouraged others to worship him, and it may be that Kemp had unrequited romantic feelings for Murphy. Murphy was eccentric, receiving people in his private suite in his bathrobe and slippers, as when he welcomed labor leaders during the great sit-down strikes.[44] He was physical, seen holding the hands of young women,[45] touching Maurice Sugar on his knee during labor negotiations, and hoisting Kemp onto his shoulders when the two men were soldiers in England following World War I. Murphy may have encouraged Kemp, while never allowing sex to intrude in their relationship. If any definitive proof of a sexual relationship exists, it has not been found, and the question will not be answered in this book.

New justices are traditionally allowed to select their initial writing assignment, and Murphy chose *Thornhill v. Alabama*, a labor case.[46] His decision came out in April 1940, just a few months after his appointment. Murphy started his opinion by citing the full name of the petitioner, Byron Thornhill. This was a conscious Murphy trait, as he humanized the picketer by naming him. Resounding support of the employees in labor disputes would also become a regular feature in Murphy's decisions.

Thornhill was an employee of the Brown Wood Preserving Company in Alabama and the president of a local union to which all but 4 of the company's 100 workers belonged. The union had gone on strike, and Thornhill was arrested "on the picket line."[47] Thornhill was charged with the violation of an Alabama statute making it a misdemeanor to "loiter" or "picket" for the purpose of "inducing other persons not to . . . have business dealings with, or be employed by" the picketed firm.[48]

Murphy needed a constitutional hook to side with the employees. He got it by citing the First Amendment's protection of freedom of speech, a "fundamental personal right" secured by the Fourteenth Amendment against abridgment by a state.[49] Murphy wrote that freedom of speech "embraces at the least the liberty to discuss publicly and truthfully all matters of public concern, without previous restraint or fear of subsequent punishment."[50]

This seemingly matter-of-fact statement by Murphy in *Thornhill* was radical at the time. Yes, the First Amendment explicitly applies to actions the federal government might take to stifle criticism. But Thornhill worked for a private company and was prosecuted under state, and not federal, law. Did the United States Supreme Court have a right to inject itself into a local battle?

In support of his argument about the broad scope of the First Amendment, Murphy left the four corners of this amendment's text. Instead, he quoted from a letter sent by the Continental Congress to the "Inhabitants of Quebec" (October 26, 1774, before the official outbreak of the American Revolution and the drafting of the Declaration of Independence), which proclaimed that the freedom of the press exists for the "advancement of truth, science, morality, and arts in general, in its diffusion of liberal sentiments on the administration of Government, its ready communication of thoughts between subjects, and its consequential promotion of union among them whereby oppressive officers are ashamed or intimidated into more honourable and just modes of conducting affairs."[51]

From this, he jumped to the present situation: "It is recognized now that satisfactory hours and wages and working conditions in industry and a bargaining position which makes these possible have an importance" of the kind to society that the founding fathers would have embraced as needing an open and fulsome debate. Further, the "present generation and of those as yet unborn may depend on these matters."[52]

The language is stirring. But the First Amendment has nothing to say about "satisfactory hours and wages" at work or about picketers in front of a factory. For that matter, neither did the 1774 letter to the inhabitants of Quebec. Although Murphy brought almost the entire court with him in an 8 to 1 decision, this was more out of respect for a new member and agreement with the result than for Murphy's logic. Soon he would have members complaining bitterly about his writing style, his failure to stay on point, and his inability to cite Supreme Court precedent to support his decisions.

As noted, the law that the Supreme Court was questioning in *Thornhill* was a state law and not federal one. This fact bears emphasizing because the Supreme Court is the top federal court. States have their own systems of courts and laws. Before the 1940s and decisions such as *Thornhill*, the Supreme Court largely avoided comment on state laws, and everyone knew the implications of this failure—the South's segregationist laws had been left intact by the Supreme Court.

Murphy and his colleagues on the Supreme Court were starting to deploy the Fourteenth Amendment in a new way, using a concept called "incorporation." The Fourteenth Amendment requires states, and not just the federal government, to provide "equal protection under the law." The original intent of the Amendment was to help solidify the rights of the newly freed slaves, making clear that states could not create laws that discriminated against their Black residents. *Thornhill* and the others were at the vanguard of the use by the Supreme Court of this Civil War–era amendment to review and strike down state laws in the employment area. From then on, the Fourteenth Amendment would become the lynchpin in court rulings that expanded the rights of various groups that faced discrimination or unfair treatment. Ironically, the Fourteenth Amendment was not yet being deployed for its original purpose, as Jim Crow prevailed in the South.

For his entire Supreme Court tenure, Murphy assumed the federal courts had this right to intervene on matters traditionally left to the highest state courts. If Murphy's view had not prevailed, *Brown v. Board of Education* could never have been decided as it was, because in *Brown*, the Supreme Court struck down a state, and not a federal, law. The Supreme Court needed cases such as *Thornhill* as a building block to its civil rights decisions in the 1950s and 1960s.

The lone dissenter in *Thornhill* was McReynolds, the last of the Four Horsemen on the Supreme Court. He complained that the Supreme Court was intruding on state rights. To him, this was not a First Amendment case. The picketers in front of the store were trespassing under state law. This was a simple property law case. The factory owner had a right to enjoy his property, free from harassing picketers.

His opinion was certainly the traditional view. But McReynolds was fighting a rearguard and ultimately losing battle. As a Supreme Court justice, McReynolds was a relic in labor and racial issues. He turned his back on Thurgood Marshall when Marshall was arguing a case before the Supreme Court. McReynolds was the one who wrote the Supreme Court dissent that the desegregation of a law school in Missouri would "damnify both races."[53]

Murphy and other FDR appointees continued their assault on this traditional idea that labor activism was a violation of the property rights of factory owners. In fact, matters progressed to such a point that the *employers'* speech could be interpreted as illegal threats. Justice William O. Douglas later wrote: "As Justice Murphy said in *Labor Board v. Virginia Power Co.*, 314 U.S. 489, 477 . . . 'conduct, though evidenced in part by speech, may amount, in connection with other circumstances, to coercion.'"[54] In this case, Murphy, writing the opinion for the Supreme Court, found that certain statements by the employer about a proposed contract, although an exercise of speech, could violate relevant labor laws.

It should be noted that Frank's brother George was continuing the Murphy legacy on a local level back in Detroit, having won a feat as a criminal court judge in 1935, and then running for reelection periodically. The brothers were simpatico on labor issues.

For example, in campaign literature at about the same time as the *Thornhill* decision, George advertised that he was "the first judge of a court of record in Michigan to hold that peaceful picketing [of workplaces] was legal."[55]

Justice Murphy got along well with some of the other justices. In fact, he had a hand in picking at least two of his colleagues. Murphy had known Hugo Black from the days when they were both on the drafting committee for the Democratic platform in 1936. He offered his positive opinion to FDR, although he retracted that opinion and told a reporter that Black was "judicially unqualified" after his Klan membership became public.[56] That negative assessment would change with Black's decisions on the Court, and the two men became close. And as Attorney General, Murphy escorted William O. Douglas to a Senate hearing in connection with Douglas's consideration for the Supreme Court, and was in the room when members of the executive branch gathered to celebrate Douglas's confirmation.

Hugo Black and William O. Douglas were no doubt aware of Murphy's involvement in their appointment. Now on that High Court, the three men were friendly and usually came down on the same side of issues. In an interview in 1964, Douglas described Murphy as "like a brother" to him.[57] When Murphy was ill in 1948, one year before his death, Douglas would send him ribald notes to buck up his spirits.[58]

But not everyone shared their views of Murphy. As Justice Douglas described in his diary Murphy's appointment to the Supreme Court:

> I like Frank. I think he has good instincts, tho he is
> not learned in the law like [Justice Frankfurter] . . .
> I like [Frank] for his stamina, integrity & courage.
> Some of his friends on the hill tell me he is 'whacky.'
> They think he is a lousy administrator & a loose
> witted fellow, full of indiscretions. The department
> heads at Justice share that view. They are delighted
> that he is leaving & express great sympathy for those
> on the Court who will receive him. They say he is
> irresponsible & a publicity hound. . . I do not share
> their views.[59]

Justice Felix Frankfurter was different. Murphy was seen by Frankfurter as not sufficiently obsequious. The editor of the *Court Diary* gave the following explanation as to why Frankfurter, almost from the start, disliked Murphy: "Frankfurter first wooed and only later disparaged Murphy" when he found he could not control him. Justice Douglas confirmed that Frankfurter "started his poisonous whispering campaign on Frank's incompetence & stupidity." Murphy's former law clerk stated that the two would diverge philosophically and this explained their dislike for each other. Frankfurter was an advocate of judicial restraint, and Murphy was an activist bent on achieving justice as he defined it.[60]

As an early fig leaf to Frankfurter, who came on to the court with a towering intellectual reputation, Murphy accepted Frankfurter's recommendation for a law clerk. Soon, however, Murphy became convinced that Frankfurter was using this law clerk as a spy. From then on, Murphy only picked University of Michigan graduates as clerks.[61] He did not seem to care about their political persuasion as long as they came from his alma mater. He even selected one clerk who had voted for Roosevelt's 1940 Republican challenger, Wendell Willkie.[62]

Murphy was used to charming people. He could awe them, project his physicality upon them, or flatter them. He could be self-disparaging about his own intellectual abilities, as a means to disarm them. Frankfurter, however, refused to take the bait. By 1943, Murphy knew he could not break through, and he referred to Frankfurter as a "shit" to his new law clerk.[63]

Because of Frankfurter's web of contacts and because he out-lived Murphy by some 15 years, he could effectively convey all of Murphy's faults and shortcomings to the crucial generation of legal scholars after Murphy's death.[64] By 1957, nine years after his death, Murphy had a toxic reputation in elite legal circles. A "word-of-mouth tradition" took hold "in law school circles that the Justice was a legal illiterate."[65] As Ernest Cuneo stated, Murphy "was unpopular with the Harvard cadre and the allied intellectuals. They were cruel about his abilities."[66]

It is important to dwell on this common perception of Murphy in legal circles. By the time he was on the High Court, Murphy was a man of many accomplishments: a big-city mayor, an administrator in the Philippines, a governor of Michigan, and a

New Deal ally of the president. But a person is often judged by how he fulfilled his last job. The harsh judgments of Supreme Court Justice Murphy by academics, starting before his death and continuing many years thereafter, were largely unwarranted, but they go a long way in explaining why Murphy is less than well known today.

In *Police Interrogations and Confessions, Essays in Law and Policy*,[67] Yale Kamisar's definitive book on the 1960 Supreme Court decisions relating to police interactions with criminal suspects, the Michigan law professor said little about Murphy at all, except that he never failed to "gag at Justice Murphy's dissent"[68] in a 1947 case called *Adamson v. California*.[69] The offensive passage penned by Murphy was as follows: "Much can be said pro and con as to the desirability of allowing comment on the failure of the accused to testify. But policy arguments are to no avail in the face of a clear constitutional command."[70]

In *Adamson*, the Supreme Court upheld a state law that allowed prosecutors to argue that a criminal defendant's silence could be used as evidence of his guilt. And Murphy was unquestionably on the wrong side at the time, dissenting with the Court's conclusion and earning him dismissive scorn.

But the conclusions of *Adamson* also sounds backward to the modern ear. A defendant's silence *cannot* be used against him. And indeed that is the case. As Kamisar acknowledged in a footnote, "Eighteen years later the Court did vindicate Justice Murphy's opinion, although it was not content to rest on a 'plain reading' of the Constitution."[71]

Frankfurter agreed with the now obsolete *Adamson* decision. Specifically, Justice Frankfurter took the dissenting justices including Murphy to task, stating that "between the incorporation of the Fourteenth Amendment into the Constitution and the beginning of the present membership of the Court—a period of seventy years—the scope of that Amendment was passed upon by 43 judges. Of all these judges, only one, who may respectfully be called an eccentric exception, ever indicated the belief that the Fourteenth Amendment was a shorthand summary of the first eight Amendments theretofore limiting only the Federal Government, and that due process incorporated those eight Amendments as restrictions upon the powers of the States."[72]

Frankfurter was criticizing incorporation, an idea that was gaining momentum in the Court. Here too, Murphy was on the right side of history (and Frankfurter was on the wrong side) as the Fourteenth Amendment was later deployed by the Supreme Court as a basis to overturn state laws that buttressed segregation, the most notable example being *Brown v. Board of Education*. But as this passage reveals, Frankfurter had a cutting, intellectual quality that captivated.

Regardless of the overturning of *Adamson*, isn't it completely valid for legal historians and law professors to criticize Justice Murphy for not putting specific constitutional provisions first? After all, justices take an oath to defend the Constitution. Law students take classes entitled Constitutional Law or variations thereof. Wasn't Murphy supposed to base his decisions on the Constitution, come what may? To Justice Frankfurter, Murphy nearly always sided with the following: "Reds, Whores, Crooks, Indians and all other colored people, Longshoremen, M'tgors and other debtors, R.R. Employees, Pacifists, Traitors, Japs, Women, Children and Most Men."[73] Frankfurter was mocking Murphy's humanitarian instincts but also signaling how far removed, in his view, Murphy was from the other justices because Murphy followed his gut and not the Constitution.

If this is a fair criticism, however, then Murphy is far from alone in looking outside the Constitution for inspiration and guidance. Justices most celebrated for their stands on civil liberties also failed to ground their philosophies in specific provisions of the Constitution. Justice Louis D. Brandeis is a notable example. In his famous dissent in the wiretap case of *Olmstead v. United States* in 1928, he postulated that "the makers of our Constitution undertook to secure conditions favorable to the pursuit of happiness. They recognized the significance of man's spiritual nature, of his feelings and of his intellect. They knew that only a part of the pain, pleasure and satisfactions of life are to be found in material things. They sought to protect Americans in their beliefs, their thoughts, their emotions and their sensations."[74] He defined the "right to be left alone" (itself not a right found in the Constitution) as "the most comprehensive of rights, and the right most valued by civilized men."[75] Murphy would have agreed with all of these statements and their conclusions.

And if Supreme Court justices do not allow their personal feelings to interfere with their decisions, how does one explain the diametrically different opinions by Supreme Court members on fundamental issues in American society? The Supreme Court decided *Plessy v. Ferguson*, which entrenched segregation and established "separate but equal" as the standard in local public and private institutions. Without any changes to the Constitution, the Supreme decided *Brown v. Board of Education*, thereby effectively outlawing separate but equal. Obviously, society had changed since *Plessy*, and a half-century later the Supreme Court justices had changed with it. Without any changes to the Constitution, the Supreme Court decided it could, in fact, reach in and declare invalid a California law allowing a defendant's silence to be used against him. In the end, great justices decide cases based on their conceptions of American ideals.

In spite of their differences, Frankfurter and Murphy maintained some grudging respect and even fondness for each other. As Murphy's biographer J. Woodford Howard described it, "Both were liberals and sensitive to their minority status. Both were passionately devoted to idealized versions of the American dream. And no matter how heated their disputes, they managed to maintain a uniquely personal, almost love-hate understanding filled with frank discourse and frequent jokes about their personal idiosyncrasies and ethnic origins."[76]

Frankfurter was generous at times with his praise for Murphy. After the sit-down strikes of 1937, Frankfurter sent a personal note to Governor Murphy congratulating him for his work in resolving the labor disputes. Now at the beginning of World War II, Frankfurter wrote to the president on Murphy's behalf stating that Murphy had expressed his desire to try to resolve some of the strikes in Detroit that were hindering the armament effort.[77]

And although Frankfurter never spoke about it, he must have appreciated Murphy's strong support for Jewish causes. Frankfurter's appointment to the Supreme Court was highly symbolic, coming as it did in 1939. Hitler was making Jews pariahs.[78] In an elegant rebuke to such intolerance, FDR appointed an accomplished Jew to the highest court in the land. Frankfurter later became a strong advocate for the State of Israel. In this regard, Murphy was fully aware of the slaughter of Jews taking place during World War II. He suggested, with sincerity, that the United States establish temporary havens for Europeans fleeing from the war. The "free port," where customs fees are waived, was thought to promote commerce. Under his idea, refugees would be free to circulate within these camps. "I am sure application of this principle to the transport of refugees will be found equally helpful . . . Surely we have not become so calloused to human suffering, so inured to brutality and bestiality that we can stand idly by and refuse to initiate this simple plan which will save thousands of human lives and in the bargain not cost the taxpayers of our country a cent." Murphy believed the refugees would develop the land they were on, thereby paying for themselves through their productive capabilities.[79]

Regardless of the internal machinations of the Supreme Court, Murphy was often the toast of parties, appearing in society pages in Palm Beach, Florida, and elsewhere.[80] He had a long list of social engagements during his first few years on the Court, including with Mrs. William Randolph Hearst, Crown Princess Martha and Prince Olaf of Norway, and Mrs. Cornelius Vanderbilt.[81] He was always in the company of interesting people, as when he took a cruise with Charlie Chaplin.[82]

During his Washington, DC years, he was a frequent companion of Evalyn Walsh McLean, the owner of the Hope Diamond. Murphy referred to one luncheon at her estate at which "no one else was present but Mrs. McLean, the Hope Diamond, and myself."[83] Murphy served as godfather to three of Mrs. McLean's grandchildren.[84]

Evalyn was the subject of the Hope Diamond curse. Among other things, McLean's first son was killed in a car accident. Her husband Ned ran off with another woman, inconveniently occurring only after she was memorialized as "Mrs. Ned McLean" in a Cole Porter song. She was about five years older than Murphy; they never considered marriage, and she passed away in 1947.[85]

Murphy then moved on to the parties of Gwendolyn Cafritz, which she gave at her white brick mansion on Foxhall Road. She provided an environment conducive to socializing, permitting guests to gather for cocktails on the outside terrace with a magnificent view of the nation's Capitol looking southeast to the Washington Monument.[86] During this time, Murphy courted younger women such as Cafritz. Joseph Kennedy, the father of the future president, wrote to Murphy, "By the way, I've yet to meet a girl in New York or Washington who doesn't know Frank Murphy."[87] But his friend from Harbor Beach had a caveat: "[I]t was the in-between, it was the contemporaries, that he was scared to death of, you know," Frank Potts confided.[88]

The *Palm Beach Post*, for its part, reported that eligible women had given up on Murphy. But his colleagues persisted in trying to get him to settle down. President Roosevelt and Jim Farley tried to intervene by introducing him to a Tennessee widow.[89] Congressman John Dingell of Michigan, a "father of three," stated, "You're 50 years old. And if you wait much longer it may be too late. I'd hate to see you grow old alone."[90]

In September 1940, Murphy went on vacation to Los Angeles with his sister Marguerite.[91] Its local newspaper reported that he used to come through on his way to the Philippines and was "still a bachelor."[92] Starting with his days as governor general, he relied on his sister to host or accompany him on his holidays and vacations.[93] Eleanor Bumgardner recalled that Murphy was a good uncle. On the night before he was going to leave for the Philippines to assume his new job there, he lingered outside his house "because he could not bring himself to say goodbye to Sharon, his three-year-old niece, who was one of the few joys in his life."[94]

Even as a Supreme Court justice, Murphy continued to advise FDR, as the justices met with the president with some frequency. Justice Frankfurter was said to have tipped off the president of the *Korematsu* decision the day before it was issued. And as for Murphy, in one letter to the president, he criticized an assistant United States attorney for straying outside his duties in court and commenting on state matters.[95] He did so without a sense of the irony of his advice.

At this time, rumors of Murphy's bad health started to surface in newspapers. This was not by itself alarming. In 1944, the papers also reported that justices Stone and Black would miss some court sessions because of colds.[96] More unusual, in 1943, the papers reported that Murphy had a nervous breakdown in Dallas on his way to San Francisco to visit his brother George, now in the Navy.[97] However, he did have reason to be supremely worried about his brother. George, now on leave from his court position in Detroit, had injured his spine in a training accident (or perhaps a fall downstairs) and his well-being was in doubt.[98]

As Frank departed to the West Coast, he wrote of this event to the president, reminding FDR that he would be available if the president needed to speak to him.[99] FDR was moving away from him, and Murphy felt this keenly. He was no longer a favorite of the president, and his letters to FDR, like this one, became more beseeching as time went on. In the 1940s, he constantly requested an audience with the president, offering bullet points on various political or policy issues, even as he sat on the Supreme Court. Ironically, Murphy's influence on events in the United States was growing ever larger because of his position on the High Tribunal, even if he did not fully recognize it.

Murphy was not immune to the larger global events. With the entrance of the United States into the war against Germany, Japan, and Italy, Murphy, by now about 50 years old and a sitting member of the Supreme Court, expressed a desire to join the United States infantry. He trumpeted that he was fit and wanted to serve. He had served his country in the past, during World War I. Then, while a judge in Detroit, he again applied to serve in the officer reserve. He wanted to serve again and still entertained hopes that FDR would recognize his gumption and perhaps appoint him to an important cabinet position.

By now he was far beyond the age of the typical soldier. Because he was a man of stature, Murphy had to be treated gingerly by the military command. He made his first request right after the attack on Pearl Harbor. In a letter to Murphy on December 13, 1941, George C. Marshall, then the chief of staff of the Army and later the secretary of war and author of the Marshall Plan, acknowledged Murphy's "generous offer of service." Marshall indicated that he was forwarding an appropriate application for Murphy to complete and emphasized, "It is reassuring . . . to have such a distinguished American available for duty in the Army."[100]

One can wonder how Marshall must have felt about having to devote attention to this self-important person about one week after the Japanese Empire's attack on United States territory. Marshall had known Murphy for several years and respected his positions on civil liberties, sending Murphy a complimentary letter when Murphy was the U.S. Attorney General.[101] He probably assumed he could dissuade Murphy from pursuing his quest.

Murphy persisted. In an act of bravado that was reminiscent of his efforts to fight during World War I, Murphy stated that "it would serve no good purpose to leave my present duties unless I could be assigned to active duty and sent to the front."[102]

In response, Marshall noted that he was delayed as he had only arrived from England that day.[103] He was trying to fight a war. Even so, he "had talked to several members of [his] staff concerning this matter," and "we had all agreed" that the offer to serve was "one of the finest expressions we have received since the war began. It is characteristic that you strictly limit your offer to duty with a combat unit." He further praised Murphy, stating that he could not "find a more potent candidate," as demonstrated by his "splendid" war record. Nevertheless, Marshall gently observed that officers who wished to enter training could not be older than 47 and that "[w]e feel that the policy is sound and it was established only after serious consideration." Then, Marshall stated that Murphy's duties as a Supreme Court justice "far exceed in importance, both to the nation and to the Army, any position which the War Department can offer." Finally, he said, "[Y]ou can be assured that I will treat the matter as confidential."

Murphy did not take the hint and continued to press for a military appointment. Marshall next tried to appeal to Murphy's sense of ethics. "I had first thought that we could place you on an active duty status if you were willing to forego your pay as Justice of the Supreme Court. The Judge Advocate General, however, has given me an opinion to the contrary."[104] Such an appeal might have worked with Murphy in another context but not here.

Murphy eventually enlisted in the infantry with the salary of a Supreme Court justice. Apparently in specific response to Murphy's maneuverings, the Department of Justice soon after issued guidance that barred sitting federal judges from serving in the Army or Navy.[105]

In the Army, Murphy was required to get out of bed anywhere from 3:30 AM to 6 AM. He washed his own socks and underwear. More substantively, he made speeches while wearing his soldier's hat and demonstrated a grasp of the strategic situation. In one lecture in Detroit in September 1942, Murphy told a labor group that the United States wartime industrial production was soon to pass the combined production of all the Axis powers put together.[106] Many political scientists look at such a factor—the ability to mobilize industrial might to the war effort—as the key to winning a war. For instance, person to person, Civil War Confederate soldiers were as good as the Union soldiers, but the Union was able to overwhelm the South through its sheer industrial productive capabilities.[107]

Murphy trained at Fort Knox in Kentucky, where he delivered the commencement address in front of 500 members of his class. In a fawning article on its favorite son, the *Port Huron Times Herald* stated that "Frank Murphy is determined to help get [the Philippines] back, even if it means that he will never again return to his beloved boyhood home," as though he were going to personally storm the Islands.[108] His fellow justices teased him for joining the Army. Justice Byrnes sent him a letter, "When you return, I promise to salute you and if I were large enough to wear your uniform, I would borrow it from you."[109]

This was not Murphy's only attempt to volunteer for active service, although it was the one time he was successful. Murphy often felt restless on the court, particularly early in his tenure, and peppered FDR for assignments. In 1941, already on the bench, Murphy asked Roosevelt to send him to Detroit to try to resolve the Ford auto strike, citing his experience as governor.[110] On May 17, 1943, in a letter to the president, Murphy plaintively wrote that "should the War Department find it impractical to send me to the Philippines [at the time occupied by the Imperial Japanese Army] . . . I do hope you will bear in mind my experience in colonial administration. If I can help you in any way in India or Africa or any type of field duty in Russia, I am at your call. Let me assure you again that I am not disturbed by the possibility of personal danger and prepared as far as physical conditions and training are concerned to undertake any assignment."[111]

In 1944, Murphy yet again pestered FDR to drop him behind enemy lines in the Philippines on a secret mission. Chief of Staff Marshall wrote a memo to FDR, informing him that Murphy would be an attractive target for the increasingly desperate Imperial Japanese Army, and that such an assignment was not a good idea.[112] By now, FDR had little time or patience for Murphy's requests for special assignments. On Marshall's memo, FDR wrote a note to Grace Tully, his assistant, "Grace—Break this to Murphy."[113] The two men would have little personal contact in the last years of FDR's life.

Endnotes

1. *Missouri ex rel. Gaines v. Canada*, 305 U.S. 337 (1938).
2. Ibid at 353. Simon, *FDR and Chief Justice Hughes*, 358–359 (describing opinion).
3. Frank, *Hugo Black*, 123.
4. Murphy was still governor of Michigan at this time when his name circulated as a possible candidate for the Supreme Court. If he was picked instead of Stanley Reed, he would have been Roosevelt's second appointment and also would have been the swing vote on the High Court for New Deal legislation. *See* Associated Press, "New Deal Due for a Majority in High Court," *DFP*, Jan. 6, 1938, 1.
5. Frank Murphy to FDR, Dec. 9, 1939, FDRL, PSF, Justice Murphy Files; also found here: http://www.fdrlibrary.marist.edu/_resources/images/psf/b-psfc000052.pdf.
6. Carter Field, "Mainly Politics," *Valley Morning Star*, Mar. 19, 1940, 4.
7. "Murphy's Career One of Activity," *NYT*, Jan. 5, 1940, 10.

8. Fine, *Washington Years,* 133.

9. "Murphy Attends Roosevelt Press Conference, Appointment to High Court Due This Week," *NYT,* Jan. 3, 1940, 1.

10. Howard, *Mr. Justice Murphy,* 217, n. 68 (citing Arthur Krock, *NYT,* Nov. 21, 1939, 22:5; Arthur Krock, "The Nature of Mr. Murphy's Unfinished Business," *NYT,* Jan. 4, 1940.

11. R. Sam Garret and Denis Steven Rutkus, "Speed of Presidential and Senate Actions on Supreme Court Nominations, 1900–2010," Aug. 6, 2010, Congressional Research Service, accessed Apr. 19, 2020, https://fas.org/sgp/crs/misc/RL33118.pdf.

12. "Presidential Involvement with Supreme Court Oath Ceremonies," Supreme Court website, accessed Apr. 19, 2020, www.supremecourt.gov/about/oath/presidentialinvolvementwithoath.aspx.

13. "Address of Frank Murphy Delivered at the Annual Patriots' Day Dinner of the Knights of Columbus," Boston, Massachusetts, Apr. 18, 1937, *Murphy Collected Speeches, 1937–1938.*

14. "Address of Frank Murphy Delivered before the National Conference for Clarifying the Constitution by Amendment, over CBS Nation-Wide Network," Detroit, Michigan, February 1, 1937, *Murphy Collected Speeches, 1937–1938.*

15. NIRA was discussed in a prior chapter, as one of the bright New Deal programs. *A.L.A. Schechter Poultry Corp. v. United States,* 295 U.S. 495 (1935) was a unanimous decision that rendered a main piece of New Deal legislation unconstitutional.

16. *Schechter,* 295 U.S. at 524.

17. Ibid at 546. As with the cases to follow, the intention here is not to provide a full recitation of the facts and a broad legal analysis, but to give the reader some context for Murphy's thought process.

18. Ibid.

19. Thomas Pickering, "A Tribute to Frank Murphy," *University of Detroit Law Review* 73 (1996): 703, 705.

20. In *Nine Men against America,* Rosalie M. Gordon critiqued Murphy and the other justices appointed by FDR and subsequent presidents. Among her policy proposals to fix perceived problems with the court was to require 10 years of prior court experience as a prerequisite to a justice's appointment. "If we apply some such rule to the members of the Supreme Court appointed since 1937, when packing began, we can see how far short they fall on judicial experience. . . . Their total previous judicial experience amounts to thirty-seven and half years—and that includes Justice Black's eighteen months as a police-court judge and Justice Murphy's service . . . If we assume each should have had at least ten years of previous experience—a total of 170 years [she was counting the 17 justices after 1937 at the time of her book in 1958]—we can see that our last seventeen justices have fallen short of that logical minimum by 132 ½ years"; Gordon, *Nine Men against America,* 114.

21. Murdoch and Price, *Courting Justice,* 18–21.

22. Ibid.

23. "Limited Parking Space at Capitol Allotted," *LSJ,* Oct. 14, 1937, 14 (describing parking spots for Governor Murphy and his "legal advisor" Kemp).

24. "Society," *DFP,* Apr. 21, 1925, 8.

25. *Girlfriend* or *boyfriend* is a word that describes the perception of the outside world and was how Murphy and Hester described their own relationship.

26. Chauncey, *Gay New York*, 144.

27. "Kemp, Legal Advisor to Governor Murphy, Will Visit Mother, *TTH*, Feb. 21, 1935, 14.

28. "Off to the Philippines," *DFP*, May 15, 1935, 9 (giving the list of advisors accompanying Murphy back to his post after a visit in Michigan, including Kemp, Hill, and Bumgardner).

29. Article fragment, *DFP*, July 23, 1949, 10 ("Bearing the coffin were Circuit Judge Ira W. Jayne, James Lincoln, Edward Kemp, and Norman Hill, among others").

30. *Employment of Homosexuals and Other Sex Perverts in Government*, Interim Report submitted to the Committee on Expenditures in the Executive Departments by its Subcommittee on Investigations pursuant to S. Res. 280 (81st Congress) (1950).

31. Welles, *Sumner Welles*, 582–583.

32. Ibid, 582.

33. Ibid.

34. To this author's knowledge, the FBI files on the sexual preferences of Murphy (or Welles) such that they exist have not been made public.

35. Kemp was a member of the glee club and an associate editor of the *Michigan Daily* and the law review. "Death Takes E.G. Kemp," *TTH*, Nov. 23, 1962, 2.

36. "Edw. Kemp Expected to Be District of Columbia Judge, Second Thumb Native Slated for U.S. Appointment," *TTH*, Jan. 8, 1940, 10.

37. Associated Press, "Edward Kemp Shifted to Bureau of Budget," *THP*, Mar. 25, 1940, 4.

38. "These Are Michigan Men at Work in Washington," *DFP*, Dec. 28, 1941, 81.

39. "Kemp New Budget Counsel, President Praises His Work," *TTH*, Mar. 25, 1940, 10.

40. Fine, *Washington Years*, 9.

41. Frank Murphy Oral History Project, FMP. ("Transcripts of oral interviews conducted by University of Michigan history professor Sidney Fine in cooperation with the Michigan Historical Collections with individuals on the subject of the life and times of Michigan governor and U.S. Supreme Court Justice, Frank Murphy; and sound recordings of the interviews.")

42. Frank Potts, Jan. 8, 1965, transcript of interview conducted by Sidney Fine, Frank Murphy Oral History Project, FMP, 12.

43. The unpleasant prospect of whether Sidney Fine suppressed or destroyed certain correspondence must be raised. In a letter from Irene Murphy to Joan Cuddihy in 1967, Irene described Sidney Fine as follows: "He sorts out the junk from the historical stuff . . . or abstracts or personal letters for the one or two paragraphs of merit . . . . and returns or destroys the rest. I find him sensitive, discreet and trustworthy." Irene Murphy to Joan Cuddihy, JC, Correspondence from friends and Murphy family 1945–1972. This author has reviewed much of the material at the Bentley and has found the Fine citations in his prior biographies to be impeccable. This, letter however, raises the issue of what was included in the Bentley donations in the first place. I did not find certain letters of a personal nature in the Bentley archives (like the "lover's lane" letter to his mother or the reference to the one letter received by Murphy that seemed to imply a sexual relationship). I have attributed this failure to my own research shortcomings, rather than an absence of these documents in the files.

44. Kraus, *Heroes of Unwritten Story*, 269.

45. Fine, *Washington Years*, 9.

46. *Thornhill v. Alabama*, 310 U.S. 88 (1941).

47. Ibid at 94.

48. Ibid at 91–92.

49. Ibid at 95.

50. Ibid at 101–102.

51. Ibid at 102.

52. Ibid at 103.

53. Simon, *FDR and Chief Justice Hughes*, 358–359.

54. Douglas, *The Right of the People*, 56.

55. "Memorandum of Recorders Court Candidates from 1941," WRL, AFL-CIO Metropolitan Detroit, Box 30, Folder: Wayne County Court. (Included in the memorandum is a biography of George Murphy, stating that "Judge Murphy has been called upon to serve as arbitrator and conciliator in several labor disputes between local unions and employers. Significantly, he has won high praise from both groups for his fair and impartial decisions.")

56. Fine, *Washington Years*, 156.

57. William O. Douglas, Oct. 22, 1964, transcript of interview conducted by Sidney Fine and Robert M. Warner, Frank Murphy Oral History Project, FMP.

58. Fine, *Washington Years*, 483–484.

59. John H. Pickering, "A Tribute to Justice Frank Murphy," *University of Detroit Mercy Law Review* 73 (1996): 703–704.

60. Ibid.

61. Ibid.

62. John H. Pickering, Oct. 19, 1964, transcript of interview conducted by Sidney Fine, Frank Murphy Oral History Project, FMP. (When interviewing for his clerkship on the Supreme Court, John H. Pickering recalled that he had been a supporter of Wendell Willkie, Roosevelt's Republican challenger in the 1940 election: "I think, maybe perhaps, I may have told him that. It made no difference to him.")

63. Pickering, "A Tribute," 703.

64. "School Plans Frankfurter Chair of Law," *Harvard Crimson*, Apr. 29, 1963, accessed Apr. 19, 2020, https://www.thecrimson.com/article/1963/4/29/school-plans-frankfurter-chair-of-law/. ("Frankfurter also sent to Roosevelt a number of his best law students, who manned many of the top administrative posts in Washington during the 1930's and '40's. Known collectively as 'The Little Hot Dogs,' they included Tommy Corcoran and Ben Cohen.")

65. John P. Roche, "The Utopian Pilgrimage of Mr. Justice Murphy," *Vanderbilt Law Review* 10 (1957): 369.

66. FDRL, Ernest Cuneo Papers, Box 105, Frank Murphy File. ("He was one of the best Attorney Generals as a Justice of the Supreme Court, often brought Liberal applause where his chief detractor, Justice Frankfurter brought groans.")

67. Yale Kamisar, *Police Interrogation and Confessions: Essays in Law and Policy* (Ann Arbor: University of Michigan Press, 1980).

68. Ibid at 44.

69. *Adamson v. California*, 332 U.S. 46 (1947).

70. Kamisar, *Police Interrogation*, 44.

71. Ibid, 238, n. 17 (citing *Griffin v. California*, 380 U.S. 609 (1965) (Douglas, J)).

72. *Adamson*, 332 U.S. at 62.

73. Fine, *Washington Years*, 259.

74. *Olmstead v. United States*, 277 U.S. 438, 478 (1928).

75. Ibid.

76. Howard, *Mr. Justice Murphy*, 268.

77. Memorandum of James Rowe to President, Apr. 2, 1941, FDRL, PSF, Strike problem folder (recalling that Murphy had appealed through Frankfurter to the President, "referring to the Ford Strike situation" to allow him to "straighten the matter out because of his previous experience with Michigan labor problems when he was governor").

78. Lash, *Diaries of Felix Frankfurter*, 73.

79. "Murphy Group Backs 'Free Port' Proposal, Anti-Persecution Committee Says Thousands Can Be Saved," *NYT*, May 29, 1944, 9. It is unclear why Murphy stated this proposal would not cost any money. He might have been referring to an earlier proposal to use Alaska as a place to settle immigrants who would jump-start development in that territory, thereby paying for themselves.

80. "Palm Beach Scene of Many Parties," *NYT*, Jan. 27, 1940, 15, 16. (Mrs. Diana Guess gave a reception for Murphy at the Chambord.)

81. Fine, *Washington Years*, 200–201.

82. Charlie Chaplin and Frank Murphy aboard the S. S. Coolidge, June 4, 1936, FMP, Box 95, Folder: Governor General, Philippines II, accessed Apr. 19, 2020, https://quod.lib.umich.edu/b/bhl/x-bl000137/*.

83. Fine, *Washington Years*, 200–201.

84. Ibid.

85. "Mrs. McLean Buried beside Her Daughter," *NYT*, Apr. 30, 1947, 23 (noting that Frank Murphy attended her funeral).

86. Bart Barnes, "D.C. Hostess Gwendolyn Cafritz Dies," *Washington Post*, Nov. 30, 1988, accessed Apr. 19, 2020, https://www.washingtonpost.com/archive/local/1988/11/30/dc-hostess-gwendolyn-cafritz-dies/1ce03124-db68-459f-85c9-61d0d94ac47c/?utm_term=.05184732d3f4.

87. Michael Beschloss, *Kennedy and Roosevelt: The Uneasy Alliance* (New York: Open Road Media, 2016), Kindle, 133 of 386, Loc. 2091 of 6904.

88. Frank Potts, Jan. 8, 1965, transcript of interview conducted by Sidney Fine, Frank Murphy Oral History Project, FMP, 16.

89. Frank Murphy to FDR, Mar. 20, 1940, FDR Archives, PSF, Box 166, Supreme Court, 1938–1944. (Murphy responded mysteriously, stating "I don't want to lose the Tennessee widow because of laches.")

90. Article fragment, "Bachelor Frank Murphy," *Palm Beach Post* (West Palm Beach, Florida), May 3, 1940, 4.

91. "Associate Justice Murphy Here for Southland Vacation," *Los Angeles Times*, Sept. 13, 1940, 39 (Section C1).

92. Ibid.

93. "Justice Murphy in Detroit," *TTH*, Dec. 24, 1942, 1.

94. "A Confidential Secretary Recalls: My 16 Years with Frank Murphy," *DFP*, Sept. 10, 1967, 140.

95. EMW to FDR, Jan. 19, 1940, FDRL, PSF, Supreme Court.

96. Associated Press, "Price and Rent Control Upheld," *Los Angeles Times*, Mar. 28, 1944, Part I.

97. "Justice Murphy in S.F. to See Brother," *Oakland Tribune*, Feb. 21, 1943, A–11.

98. "Justice Is Taken from Plane in Dallas in Nervous Collapse," *NYT*, Feb. 17, 1943, 26.

99. FDR Archives, Personal Files, Memorandum from a "TOI," Feb. 13, 1943. (By now, Murphy was unable to get regular time with the president. Perhaps knowing this, he tried to pique FDR's interest: "There are several other matters he [Murphy] wishes to discuss and he promises that he won't even sit down.")

100. George C. Marshall to Frank Murphy, FMP, Dec. 13, 1941, reel 91.

101. George C. Marshall to Frank Murphy, Apr. 7, 1939, Papers of George Catlett Marshall, Volume 1, accessed Apr. 19, 2020, https://www.marshallfoundation.org/library/digital-archive/to-frank-murphy/.

102. Frank Murphy to George C. Marshall, Apr. 15, 1942 ("My dear Chief of Staff"), FMP, reel 92.

103. George C. Marshall to Frank Murphy, Apr. 20, 1942, FMP, reel 92.

104. George C. Marshall to Frank Murphy, May 19, 1942, FMP, reel 92.

105. "Biddle Rules Judges Leave Posts at Once on Taking Pay as Military Officers," *NYT*, Oct. 23, 1942.

106. "Murphy Sees Large U.S. Production Front," *The Herald Press* (St. Joseph, Michigan), Sept. 29, 1942.

107. By 1946, he was convinced that the United States had global responsibilities. "Because of atomic energy, the radio, and the airplane, the world is much smaller today," he warned residents in his hometown of Harbor Beach. The problems of the world were their problems. "A Man of Faith," *TTH*, Sept. 18, 1946.

108. "Justice Murphy in Detroit," *TTH*, Dec. 24, 1942.

109. James F. Byrnes to FM, June 17, 1942, FMM.

110. Memorandum of James Rowe, Jr., Apr. 2, 1941, to the President, FDRL, PSF, Strike problem folder (recalling that Murphy had appealed through Frankfurter to the president, "referring to the Ford Strike situation" to allow him to "straighten the matter out because of his previous experience with Michigan labor problems when he was governor").

111. Frank Murphy to FDR, May 17, 1943, FDRL, PSF, Box 166, Supreme Court 1938–1944.

112. Memorandum to FDR, Mar. 16, 1944, FDRL, PSF, Box 166, Supreme Court, 1938–1944 online archives (with FDR's note to Grace Tully).

113. Ibid.

CHAPTER 17

The Japanese-American Internments and the Supreme Court Curfew Cases

On December 7, 1941, the Japanese Empire launched a surprise attack on Pearl Harbor. The United States declared war on Japan, Germany, and Italy the next day. Soon after the Declaration of War, the United States rounded up thousands of Americans of German, Italian, and Japanese descent, utilizing lists that had previously been drawn up and periodically updated.[1] This was the first of a series of steps by the United States that would eventually lead to the incarceration of 120,000 Japanese Americans.

From the start, the choices on these initial lists made little sense. Minoru Yasui, an American-born lawyer, described how on December 13, 1941, about a week after the Pearl Harbor attack, the authorities took his father, a store owner in Oregon, without any attempt to show he violated any laws or had even voiced any pro-Japanese sentiments. His children, U.S. citizens all, included a son and daughter at the University of Oregon, another son at the University of Michigan, and two children at the local high school. For two weeks, Minoru's mother had no information on what had happened to her husband.[2] For now, the government seemed to limit its targets on leaders in these communities, and not the entire population.

Frank Murphy's initial lack of interest in this trampling of civil rights is disappointing given his early and loud warnings about the dangers of intolerance in Europe and his traditional focus on minority rights. For the first few years of his Supreme Court tenure, he was distracted generally from his duties as a Supreme Court justice, hoping for some other appointment in FDR's cabinet. There was also his sincere, but utterly misguided, attempt to serve in combat in World War II.

Following this initial limited sweep of individuals, federal government leaders pondered their next steps. The decision to evacuate all the Japanese Americans from the West Coast came despite obvious evidence that there was no need for such a drastic step. The logical time for Japanese Americans to cause mischief was in the days after the Pearl Harbor attack, when the United States was stunned by the blow and before the lumbering giant started to get its bearings. Yet, not one act of sabotage occurred. Newspapers, intent on selling copy, had every incentive to root out any act of disloyalty and publicize it on the front pages. They could find nothing (but did occasionally run with stories that proved to be false). At the beginning of February 1942, FBI Director J. Edgar Hoover "stood right up, read his own memorandum and said, 'This evacuation isn't necessary; I've already got all the bad boys.'"[3]

In spite of this reality, during a two-week period in February 1942, the attitude in Washington, DC, hardened against Japanese Americans and officials coalesced behind a decision to order a mass evacuation of Japanese Americans. The reasons for this change in heart remain obscure and have a similar quality to the ad hoc decision-making errors by the European powers that led to the calamitous outbreak of World War I.[4]

But it seems clear that FDR did not seriously question the necessity of the evacuations when the executive order was placed before him to sign on February 19, 1942, a little over three months after the surprise attack on Pearl Harbor.

Even after the executive order was signed, the evacuation of the Japanese-American population was not a foregone conclusion.

The executive order did not require the internment of Japanese Americans. Instead, under the language of the order, the president deputized "the Secretary of War, and the Military Commanders whom he may from time to time designate, *whenever he or any designated Commander deems such action necessary or desirable*, to prescribe military areas in such places *and of such extent as he or the appropriate Military Commander may determine*, from which any or all persons may be excluded, and with respect to which, the right of any person to enter, remain in, or leave *shall be subject to whatever restrictions the Secretary of War or the appropriate Military Commander may impose in his discretion*" (emphasis added).[5]

Like the president, Congress had the basic facts before it, which was a lack of disloyal acts by Japanese Americans combined with an admitted swirl of hysteria. Congress's response, Public Law 503, was approved with almost no debate after only an hour of discussion in the Senate and 30 minutes in the House. Authored by War Department official Karl Bendetsen—who would later be promoted to director of the Wartime Civilian Control Administration and oversee the incarceration of Japanese Americans—the two-page Public Law 503 made violations of military orders in connection with the expulsions punishable by up to $5,000 in fines and one year in prison.[6] On March 21, 1942, a full month after the issuance of Executive Order 9066, President Roosevelt signed Public Law 503. Although Executive Order 9066 became synonymous with the injustices perpetrated against Japanese Americans, Public Law 503 was the enabling statute.

Japanese Americans inclined toward disloyalty now knew of FDR's executive order and also were aware of the passage of a law that specifically targeted them for exile. In spite of this, the historical record shows that Japanese Americans committed no acts of disloyalty during this time period.

The internments did not happen immediately. Rather, the Japanese Americans were subject to restrictions that became incrementally more onerous. First they were subject to curfews, requiring them to remain at home in California, Oregon, and Washington during designated hours.[7] The lack of outrage in the greater public over the curfews—which would prove to be among the lesser-known injustices initiated against those of Japanese origins—gave authorities the confidence to take the next step of outright banishment of this group.

Why were German Americans and Italian Americans not targeted in the same way? As stated, some were rounded up as part of the initial detentions.[8] In fact, of the 12,071 aliens arrested during the first year of the war, "almost ten thousand were either Germans who belonged to pro-Nazi groups such as the German-American Bund or the militaristic Kyffhauserbund,"[9] or Italians who were members of fascist organizations. Fewer than half of these individuals were interned after receiving individual hearings.[10] More generally, the fate of Americans who immigrated from Germany and Italy diverged from those who originated from Japan. As to the general population consisting of German and Italian descendants, the U.S. government made great efforts to portray them as loyal United States citizens. Their sons and daughters served in the United States armed forces and were sent where needed, including to the European theatre, where they faced German and Italian soldiers.

But Japanese Americans themselves faced vastly different destinies depending on their location. Indeed, the largest number of Japanese Americans, about 150,000, were located on the territory of Hawaii, the site of the Pearl Harbor attack. While facing harsh treatment under military law in Hawaii, those of Japanese ancestry on the islands were not subject to mass internment. And at least all residents in Hawaii, including Caucasians, were subject to military law as well. Far from worrying about their loyalty, many businesspeople in Hawaii wanted Japanese Americans to remain free because of a labor shortage on the islands.

Non-Hawaiian Japanese Americans—those living in California, Oregon, and Washington—were the ones subject to mass incarceration.[11] They were shipped to locations far from their homes, places such as Manzanar and Tule Lake in California, Gila River in Arizona, and Heart Mountain in Wyoming, among other places. They were called "relocation camps" at the time by the federal authorities, but in 2018 Chief Justice John Roberts correctly called them "concentration camps."[12] Photos from the camps survive to this day and are frightening in their black-and-white power. In some, armed troops stand next to long rows of men, women, and children, suitcases at their sides. In others, the prisoners were now in their remote relocation points doing the ordinary, sweeping the floors of their temporary homes or hanging out clothes. Here they were playing baseball, a birthright of all Americans, with guards lazily looking on. There was a picture of a mother in a camp grasping a framed photograph of a young Japanese-American man in a United States Army uniform. As jarring as these pictures are, they were sanitized products. The army made great efforts to censor the pictures, for example, not allowing photographers to capture the barbed wire and guard towers.[13]

The matters finally landed at the Supreme Court's doorstep in 1943, when it decided to take up the subject of the Japanese-American curfews. This choice was a curious one. Most notably, the curfews, even if wrong at the time, no longer affected the 120,000 Japanese Americans. After all, they were no longer on the West Coast and therefore no longer subject to the curfew.

The two men who were the named plaintiffs in the 1943 curfew case bear some review. The first plaintiff was Gordon Kiyoshi Hirabayashi. A United States citizen, he was born in Seattle and was a student at the University of Washington when General John DeWitt issued the relevant expulsion order, as authorized under Executive Order 9066 and Public Law 503.[14] Hirabayashi faced the Hobson's choice typical of Japanese residents on the West Coast. As a college senior, he needed to complete his education. But if he did not comply with the order, thereby stopping his education, he would be considered a criminal. That is, he would be found guilty of being a Japanese-American citizen on the West Coast.

Hirabayashi disobeyed the nighttime curfew and then turned himself in at the FBI's Seattle office on May 16, 1942. Although the basic facts were not in dispute, FBI agents rifled through his diary to find evidence of wrongdoing. They discovered entries in which he discussed his decision not to obey the curfew. Based on the undisputed evidence, Hirabayashi was indicted on May 28, 1942. He was found guilty—his crime was being a Japanese-American citizen on the streets of Seattle after curfew—and sentenced to two concurrent 90-day sentences, both for violation of the curfew and the expulsion order.

Minoru Yasui, the other plaintiff challenging the curfew (and the internment), was a lawyer and the first Japanese-American member of the Oregon State Bar. Yasui too was a United States citizen, born in the United States. In college, he had served in the ROTC. He had also been commissioned as a second lieutenant in the United States Army Reserves after graduating from the University of Oregon Law School. He had rushed back to join his unit after the Japanese attack on Pearl Harbor.

As he stated in a later interview, Yasui urged other Japanese-American residents in his town to challenge the expulsion orders so that he could represent them. He found them to be naturally reluctant, given the possibility of large fines and jail time under Public Law 503. In the end, he decided to challenge the laws himself.[15]

He described parading up and down the Portland streets after curfew hours, assuming he would be arrested. After several hours with no result, Yasui approached a police officer and insisted that he be arrested for violation of the nighttime curfew, showing the officer a copy of the Public Proclamation and his birth certificate to prove that he was of Japanese ancestry. The patrolman told him to go home. But soon after, military police arrived at the Yasui family home in Hood River and escorted Yasui back to Portland, depositing him in the North Portland Livestock Pavilion, which had been hastily fortified and renamed the Portland Assembly Center.[16] There, he lived with some 3,000 other Japanese Americans as he awaited his trial.

Yasui was a lawyer, and his trial for violating the curfew attracted the attention of the highest authorities. Tom Clark, the civilian coordinator of the Alien Enemy Control Program, flew up to Portland to personally witness the trial. Clark was later appointed to the Supreme Court, taking Murphy's place.

In September 1942, while waiting for the results of his trial, Yasui was sent, by military transport, to the Minidoka Relocation Camp in Idaho, where he joined other Japanese Americans from the Portland area. In November 1942, Yasui was then returned, under armed guard, from Minidoka back to Portland, to hear the decision of Judge James Alger Fee the United States District Court. Judge Fee ruled that the curfew order as it applied to American citizens was unconstitutional. But he then ruled that Minoru Yasui was not a United States citizen, concluding that Yasui's prior work for the Japanese consulate in Chicago effectively resulted in a renunciation of his United States citizenship. Therefore, according to Fee, Yasui disobeyed a lawful regulation governing enemy aliens and was found guilty as charged. He was sentenced to the maximum penalty: one year in jail and a $5,000 fine.

A United States citizen, born on United States soil, had now lost his citizenship for the twin acts of remaining in the state of Oregon and legally working for a Japanese consulate. From November 1942 to August 1943, Yasui spent nine months in solitary confinement, in a six-by-eight-foot windowless cell in Multnomah County Jail, where he awaited the results of his appeal.

On May 10 and 11, 1943, the Supreme Court heard oral arguments in connection with the cases of *Hirabayashi* and *Yasui*. Again, the issue was the curfew and not the internment. Justice Stone was now the chief justice of the court. He was a holdover from pre-Roosevelt days, installed on the High Court by Republican Calvin Coolidge, his Amherst classmate. To lock up Stone's loyalty, Roosevelt tried to flatter and reward justices who supported his positions, and on June 12, 1941, nominated Stone to become chief justice.

Stone was not known for his consensus-building abilities on the bench. In the instance of the Japanese curfews, however, he succeeded in uniting the court. Writing for the Supreme Court in favor of curfews of Japanese Americans, he grounded his opinion on the "war powers" of the executive and legislative branches.[17]

Under the court's analysis, these war powers were expansive:

> The war power of the National Government extends
> to every matter and activity so related to war as
> substantially to affect its conduct and progress. The
> power is not restricted to the winning of victories in
> the field and the repulse of enemy forces. It embraces
> every phase of the national defense, including the
> protection of war materials and the members of the
> armed forces from injury and from the dangers which
> attend the rise, prosecution and progress of war.
> . . . Since the Constitution commits to the Executive
> and to Congress the exercise of the war power in
> all the vicissitudes and conditions of warfare, it has
> necessarily given them wide scope for the exercise of
> judgment and discretion.[18]

As the author of this unanimous decision, Stone stated that "the aim of Congress and the Executive [in imposing curfews on the Japanese Americans] was the protection against sabotage of war materials and utilities in areas thought to be in danger of Japanese invasion and air attack."[19]

This statement contains a large proviso to the government's war powers. These powers extend to the homeland, but only if two conditions are met. First, there must be "danger of sabotage," and second, there must be a "danger of Japanese invasion and air attack." The Supreme Court never did answer whether the two conditions were met, even as it found the curfews to be legal.

Rather than addressing his own questions, Justice Stone cited the concentration of the Japanese Americans living in strategic areas, the large numbers of Japanese Americans who were not U.S. citizens in senior positions in their community, and Japanese-American communities' failure to integrate. From this, a leap was made: "We cannot say that these facts and circumstances, considered in the particular war setting, could afford no ground for differentiating citizens of Japanese ancestry from other groups in the United States."[20] From this statement, a further leap was made: The curfew on the entire population was considered appropriate.[21]

As a foundational matter, the three factors listed by Stone were not within the power of Japanese Americans to change. Those of Japanese origin owned land in strategic areas near ports and in border lands, not because of some plot they had hatched but because they were restricted from buying land in more attractive areas by law and by prejudice. These legal restrictions on land ownership by Japanese Americans would be the subject of Supreme Court review and scathing criticism by Murphy, but only after World War II. This inability to buy land in prime locations also sometimes prevented Japanese Americans from integrating into the larger community. Many of the older Japanese were "aliens" only because they had no path to citizenship under the laws as they stood at that time. Although the word seems derogatory today, non-citizens were often referred to as aliens, and statutes used that terminology. In 1922, Justice George Sutherland (one of the Four Horsemen already described), writing for a unanimous Supreme Court in *Ozawa v. United States*, concluded that Japanese-American residents actually born in Japan could not become United States citizens under the plain terms of the Naturalization Act of 1906, which allowed only "free white persons" and "persons of African nativity or persons of African descent" to naturalize and become United States citizens.[22] Reviewing case law precedent, The Supreme Court concluded that Japanese Americans were neither white nor Black.[23]

The leaders of the Japanese-American community were typically non-citizens, as Japanese immigration had halted with the Immigration Act of 1924. The older Japanese Americans tended to be non-citizens, and the younger ones, born in the United States, were citizens by birthright. Many of these Japanese American "aliens" had lived in the United States for many years, had children who were American citizens, and in many cases had completely severed ties with Japan. Because the laws did not allow these Japanese-born residents to naturalize, they had no path to citizenship even if they had no memories of Japan.

Hindsight is 20/20. It is easy today to criticize the High Court for upholding the curfew, operating as it was in the fog of war. But it should be noted the fog was not very thick, particularly to members of the well-connected Court. Justice Owen Roberts had been appointed by President Roosevelt to head the Roberts

Commission, as it was known, to do a postmortem and review the reasons why the United States had left itself so vulnerable to an attack on Pearl Harbor. He had the duty to review allegations of Japanese-American treachery as part of his wide-ranging mandate and to publish any positive results.

Indeed, in the report he published in late January 1942, well before the 1943 decision of *Hirabayashi* came before the Supreme Court, Roberts specifically stated that his commission had heard "much testimony as to the population of Hawaii, its composition [40 percent of Japanese-American origin] and the attitude and disposition of the persons composing it in the belief that the facts disclosed might aid in appraising the results of the investigative, counter-espionage and anti-sabotage work done antecedent to the attack."[24] At the time Roberts was reviewing the causes of the surprise attack on Hawaii, anti-Japanese fervor in the United States was riding high. Yet his report contained not one instance of Japanese-American disloyalty.

The report was public and available for anyone to review. But the Supreme Court justices were not part of the ordinary public. Any Supreme Court justice could have wandered down the hallway to Roberts to ask if anything was missing from the report. The Supreme Court justices, Murphy included, were politically connected and friends of many of those directly involved with the mechanics of the internments. These justices could confirm facts about the internments, including whether Japanese Americans were showing signs of disloyalty or treachery. For example, General John DeWitt was placed in charge of the expulsions of the Japanese Americans. This Alabama native had once roomed with Supreme Court Justice Hugo Black, and Black had access to him to ask for his candid assessment.[25]

In addition, many members of the Supreme Court had direct access to FDR and his top aides. They could have asked their highly placed sources for information. Frankfurter, for one, met with the president on a regular basis; Murphy also had this ability to confirm facts from FDR himself or his highest aides during his frequent meetings with them. Murphy was himself was perhaps in the best position to know. As the U.S. Attorney General, he met regularly with J. Edgar Hoover to discuss national security and espionage threats. In the Bentley Library, certain sensitive attorney general files became publicly available in 2015. These files showed concern about the German American Bund and fascist and communist organizations located in the United States. They did not focus at all on the threat of Japanese Americans or Japanese spies.[26]

But the Supreme Court members did not just collectively bury their heads in the sand. They misrepresented the contents of reports that were a part of the record before them. In *Hirabayashi*, the Supreme Court stated that, in connection with Public Law 503, "Congress also had before it the Preliminary Report of a House Committee investigating national defense migration, of March 19, 1942, which approved the provisions of Executive Order No. 9066, and which recommended the evacuation, from military areas established under the Order, of all persons of Japanese ancestry, including citizens."[27]

A reader would be hard pressed to translate this sentence. Nevertheless, from its tenor, that reader might conclude that Congress had some compelling evidence before it in considering legislation (Public Law 503) to implement FDR's executive order. At least three factors should have been red flags for the High Tribunal.

First, and regardless of the report's contents, the date of the report in question (as recited in the *Hirabayashi* decision) was March 19, 1942, which was after the signing of Executive Order 9066 (on February 19, 1942). So, even if the report had conclusive evidence about Japanese-American treachery, FDR did not review it before signing his order.

Second, March 19, 1942, was the very same day that Congress voted to pass Public Law 503. If Congress considered the report, it processed the report's conclusions very quickly, as it took a full vote on Public Law 503 on the very day the report was issued. As a precursor to the full Congress's approval, both the Senate Military Affairs Committee and the House Committee reviewed matters. They recommended that the full Congress pass the bill, without the benefit of the report, which had not yet been issued.[28]

Third, the report in question was the Tolan Report, which came out in several versions and was issued by the Tolan Committee, a congressional committee originally called upon to investigate whether Japanese-American internment was appropriate. The committee's work was upended when the evacuation order was issued before its work was complete (again, Executive Order 9066 was issued in February 1942, and the report in question was issued on March 19, 1942). The Tolan Committee therefore shifted its focus to mitigating the effect of Executive Order 9066. In this regard, the report never recommended evacuation. Rather, the select committee that created the Tolan Report had sidestepped the issue, saying, "The committee does not deem its proper province to encompass a judgment on the military need for present (and any subsequent) evacuation orders," but concluded, "We earnestly hope that every effort will be made by the Federal Government to resettle them in normal and productive ways of living."[29] The Tolan Report was clear on one matter: It cited not one instance of Japanese-American spying or sabotage. So, contrary to the Supreme Court's summary, the report never recommended evacuation.

In one poignant section of the report, a Japanese-American organization noted that Japanese Americans had physical features that made them undesirable as spies. Specifically, unlike German and Italian spies, Japanese saboteurs were readily identifiable if they were found in sensitive areas.[30]

Politicians lead in many ways. They push for certain statutes, and they also use their bully pulpit. Their words matter, sometimes even more than the legislation they actually sign. Supreme Court justices are different. Their opinions are their most important legacies. They sometimes send letters or make speeches to explain why they make certain decisions, but their opinions are what is binding until overturned by an amendment or a subsequent Supreme Court ruling.

To this author at least, the correspondence of Supreme Court members to each other, or to others, is only mildly interesting from a historical perspective, as is whether the Supreme Court justices received help from a clerk or another justice in drafting their opinions.

In the end, the justices are the ones who sign the opinions. In this vein, Murphy must be held to historical account like the other justices for voting to uphold the curfews in *Hirabayashi*.

Still, it is interesting to note that Murphy did not just sign Stone's majority opinion. Instead, he filed a concurrence, indicating he had more to say on the subject. In this decision, he was not kind to the president, Congress, and the military establishment. He observed that the curfew, depriving citizens of liberty "because of their particular racial inheritance[,] . . . bears a melancholy resemblance to the treatment accorded to members of the Jewish race in Germany and in other parts of Europe."[31]

As his biographer Sidney Fine discovered, Murphy's concurrence was won with a great deal of arm-twisting by Frankfurter and others on the Supreme Court. Frankfurter was concerned about how claims of "racism" in the United States might be used by America's enemies abroad. He convinced Murphy to change his dissent into a concurrence. Murphy had wanted to dissent, and his concurrence reads like one.

Murphy was troubled by Stone's comments concerning the alleged failure of Japanese Americans to assimilate. "To say that any racial or cultural group cannot be assimilated," Murphy wrote in a note to Justice Stone, "is to admit that the great American experiment has failed, that our way of life has failed when confronted with the normal attachment of certain groups of people in other lands."[32] To Murphy, America was a shining city on the hill because it accepted all and made disparate groups a part of its fabric.

In *Hirabayashi*, Murphy also revealed his belief that the Supreme Court had a muscular role during wartime as a coequal to the other two branches of government: "While this Court sits, it has the inescapable duty of seeing that the mandates of the Constitution are obeyed. That duty exists in time of war as well as in time of peace, and in its performance we must not forget that few indeed have been the invasions upon essential liberties which have not been accompanied by pleas of urgent necessity advanced in good faith by responsible men."[33] His position on the Supreme Court's role as a counterweight to the other two branches was no small matter, and it is a discussion to which we will return.

Murphy was not the only justice to file a concurrence. Justice Douglas had some stirring words in *Hirabayashi* when he said, "I think it important to emphasize that we are dealing here with a problem of loyalty, not assimilation. Loyalty is a matter of mind and of heart, not of race. That indeed is the history of America.

Moreover, guilt is personal under our constitutional system. Detention for reasonable cause is one thing. Detention on account of ancestry is another."[34]

But then he dismissed his own eloquent words as completely irrelevant. "Hirabayashi," he said, "tendered by a plea in abatement the question of his loyalty to the United States. I think that plea was properly stricken; military measures of defense might be paralyzed if it were necessary to try out that issue preliminarily."[35]

Hirabayashi's conviction stood. The Supreme Court had ruled against him. But even if the Supreme Court had ruled in his favor on the issue of the curfew, it is unclear how it would have helped Gordon, who in 1943 was now in exile in Arizona.

In *Hirabayashi*, the Supreme Court justices, including Murphy, assumed the good faith of the United States government in imposing curfews on Japanese Americans. That is, they supposed that there must have been some compelling reason for the draconian decision. Otherwise, the government would not have done it.

The justices showed a lack of curiosity about the facts on the ground, as shown in all their opinions associated with that case. The justices did not stop to create a timeline between when Public Law 503 was passed by both houses of Congress and when the Tolan Report was actually issued. The justices likewise were not focused on any specific piece of evidence, or lack thereof, such as the fact that no Japanese Americans had committed treason or sabotage. This was a defining trait of the Supreme Court members of the time. They had a faith in the other branches of government, and they had a confidence that the military was telling the truth about its inability to sort the "good" from the "bad," necessitating the removal of all Japanese Americans from the West Coast.

In fact, United States officials had engaged in a vast propaganda effort to create an impression that Japanese Americans presented a threat to the country's war effort, and that their exile was necessary to protect the homeland. As part of this propaganda campaign, these officials also sought to tamp down the anxiety of the American public that the wholesale removal of an entire group based simply on their national origin was wrong and against core beliefs.

The educated elite in this country, even while starting to recognize the systemic biases in the American legal and economic system against Black people, were holding on to their virulent anti-Asian rhetoric and views.

Murphy was not immune from the use of racist terminology when describing those of Japanese origin. In 1942, while volunteering to serve in the Army, Murphy remarked that he had grown to love the Philippines. "Now they're in the hands of the Japs."[36] The Japanese triggered a special category of prejudice in the United States, which contributed to the expulsion of this group during World War II.

As to *Yasui*,[37] the less-famous companion case to *Hirabayashi*, the Supreme Court issued a cursory decision that failed to recite the dramatic history of this imprisoned lawyer. Referring readers to *Hirabayashi*, issued that same day, Chief Justice Stone declared that the curfew was valid in this case as well. The Supreme Court described Yasui as follows: "Appellant was born in Oregon in 1916 of alien parents; that when he was eight years old he spent a summer in Japan; that he attended the public schools in Oregon, and also, for about three years, a Japanese language school."[38] One can see that much of this description is wholly irrelevant but paints Yasui as something foreign, even though in fact he was a United States citizen.

If there was one positive to the *Yasui* case, it was that the Supreme Court restored United States citizenship to this Oregon-born Japanese American.[39] The lower court had stripped him of his citizenship because he had worked for the Japanese consulate in Chicago prior to volunteering for the United States Army.

The Supreme Court also reversed the district court findings that the curfew could not apply to United States citizens.[40] In short, Yasui was still guilty of violating the curfew simply by virtue of being a Japanese-American citizen on the streets after 6 PM. The Supreme Court, including Murphy, again completely ignored the fact that Yasui could no longer violate the curfew even if he wanted to, as he had been shipped to an internment camp in the meantime.

After World War II, Yasui was released from the internment camp. He passed the Colorado bar but was denied admission due to his wartime conviction for violating the curfew (people with criminal records sometimes cannot become members of the bar). But eventually, he was admitted as an attorney and was a founding member of many civil rights organizations in the Denver area. He fought to overturn his conviction his entire life but died in 1986 before his rights were fully restored.

Endnotes

1. Daniels, *Concentration Camps U.S.A.*, 34.

2. John Tateishi, ed, *And Justice for All: An Oral History of the Japanese American Detention Camps*, 64.

3. James H. Rowe, "The Japanese Evacuation Decision," in *Japanese-American Relocation Reviewed*, vol. 1, Decision and Exodus, the Earl Warren Oral History Project (Berkeley: University of California, 1976), 29, accessed May 3, 2020, http://texts.cdlib.org/view?docId=ft667nb2x8&doc.view=entire_text.

4. Barbara W. Tuchman wrote the definitive book on the process that led to World War I in *The Guns of August*. Several books, including Peter Iron's *Justice at War*, Roger Daniels' *Concentration Camps USA: Japanese Americans and World War II*, and Michi Nishiura Weglyn's *Years of Infamy: The Untold Story of America's Concentration Camps*, have covered the major events covering the time period when the federal government went from dismissing cries to ban the Japanese Americans to ordering the expulsion of every man, woman and child.

5. Executive Order 9066, Feb. 19, 1942; General Records of the Unites States Government; Record Group 11; National Archives.

6. In hindsight, this blessing by Congress of Executive Order 9066 may have seemed like a formality, but it was at least respectful of a process that sometimes allows a president to act alone in a perceived emergency, with the expectation that the chief executive would limit his or her actions and expeditiously seek approval from the legislative branch. But the lack of debate showed that Congress was not concerned by the president's actions.

7. *Hirabayashi v. United States*, 320 U.S. 81, 88 (1943) (describing curfews).

8. Irons, *Justice at War*, 24.

9. Ibid.

10. Ibid.

11. Relatively small Japanese-American populations lived in other parts of the country.

12. *Trump v. Hawaii*, 585 U.S. 2392, 2423 (2018).

13. Milton S. Eisenhower, the brother of the Supreme Allied Commander Dwight D. Eisenhower, narrated one such film entitled *Japanese Relocation*. In the film, Eisenhower explained that the government "tried to do the job as a democracy should, with a real consideration for the people involved." The film is available on CSPAN, accessed October 4, 2020, https://www.c-span.org/video/?323978-1/japanese-relocation.

14. Gordon Hirabayashi had to report to a Civil Control Center at the Christian Youth Center in Seattle as the first step to his expulsion.

15. His story was recounted by his daughter Holly Yasui in her 2018 documentary *Never Give Up! Minoru Yasui and the Fight for Justice*, available on her website at https://www.minoruyasuifilm.org/film.

16. Nishiura, *Years of Infamy*, 79 (this was the sole assembly camp for all the Japanese-American residents in the state of Oregon).

17. *Hirabayashi v. United States*, 320 U.S. 81, 93 (1943). The United States Constitution assigns specific war powers to the executive and legislative branches. In summary, Congress is explicitly granted the sole authority to "declare war," "make Rules for the Government and Regulation of the land and naval Forces" (Article I, Section 8), and to control the funding of those same forces, while the president has inherent authority as commander in chief (Article II, Section 2).

18. Ibid.

19. Ibid at 101.

20. Ibid at 101.

21. Ibid at 105.

22. *Takao Ozawa v. United States*, 260 U.S. 178, 198 (1922) ("The briefs filed on behalf of appellant refer in complimentary terms to the culture and enlightenment of the Japanese people, and with this estimate we have no reason to disagree; but these are matters which cannot enter into our consideration of the questions here at issue. We have no function in the matter other than to ascertain the will of Congress and declare it.").

23. Ibid.

24. "Negligence of the Two Highest Officers in the Pacific Is Blamed for Losses at Hawaii," *NYT*, Jan. 24, 1942 (full text of report is published in this *NYT* article).

25. Dennis J. Hutchinson, "Hugo Black among Friends," *Michigan Law Review* 93 (1995): 1885, 1890.

26. Memorandum from J. Edgar Hoover to Attorney General Murphy, Mar. 16, 1939, FMP, Box 89 (and generally Boxes 87–89).

27. *Hirabayashi,* 320 U.S. at 91.

28. Irons, *Justice at War*, 64–68.

29. "House Select Committee Investigates Japanese Evacuation and Relocation," *History, Art and Archives* (blog), The House of Representatives, accessed Apr. 18, 2020, https://history.house.gov/Blog/2018/May/5-8-tolan-committee/.

30. *Report Submitted to Tolan Congressional Committee on National Defense Migration,* Feb. 28, 1942. Special Collections and Archives, UC Irvine Libraries, Main Library, accessed Apr. 18, 2020, https://oac.cdlib.org/view?docId=hb8s2008kv&brand=oac4 &doc.view=entire_text. (In this report, the Japanese American Citizens League noted, "Among Axis enemies, the Japanese are the worst possible people to select as saboteurs, spies, and fifth columnist. A Japanese can be distinguished from a considerable distance because of Oriental facial characteristics which set him apart from the general mass of people. Enemies with Caucasian faces can mix with crowds anywhere and carry out their nefarious missions.")

31. *Hirabayashi*, 320 U.S. at 111.
32. Fine, *Washington Years*, 442–443.
33. *Hirabayashi*, 320 U. S. at 111.
34. Ibid at 107–108.
35. Ibid at 108.
36. Arthur Tholen, "Murphy between Jobs," *TTH*, Sept. 21, 1942.
37. *Yasui v. United States*, 320 U.S. 115 (1943).
38. Ibid at 116.
39. Ibid at 117.
40. Ibid.

CHAPTER 18

Murphy's Supreme Court Confronts the Expulsions

In 1944, the Supreme Court addressed the expulsions of the Japanese Americans from the West Coast, a full two years after the evacuations took place. By now, even if the High Court decided that the president and Congress had overstepped their authority, any relief would be tempered with the knowledge of this delay. The lives of 120,000 people had been inalterably disrupted. People had lost their homes, businesses, and bonds with neighbors.

The court reviewed the legality of the internments through the review of the cases of Fred Korematsu and Mitsuye Endo, two young Japanese-American citizens of the United States.

The first internee, Fred Korematsu, was born on June 30, 1919, in Oakland, California. His loyalty was never a question for the lower courts that had upheld his banishment from the West Coast. As Justice Jackson summarized the matter, "Korematsu was born on our soil, of parents born in Japan. The Constitution makes him a citizen of the United States by nativity and a citizen of California by residence. No claim is made that he is not loyal to this country."[1]

Korematsu had violated the military expulsion order and remained in California, leading to his conviction. He was not testing the law's legality, as Gordon Hirabayashi and Minoru Yasui had done. Rather, he simply wanted to be with his girlfriend, who happened to be white. "I stayed in Oakland to earn enough money to take my girl with me to the [Midwest]," Korematsu told an FBI agent, according to an affidavit he signed. That way, he thought, he could live freely and not be concerned with being sent to a camp. Questioned about scars on his nose and forehead, he said he had plastic surgery with the goal of "changing my appearance so that I would not be subject to ostracism when my girl and I went East."[2]

Prosecutors and the press stressed the detail that he had sought cosmetic surgery as evidence that he was trying to evade the evacuation laws.[3] This argument completely ignored the real and sad reason for his surgery, which was to avoid the inevitable discrimination against him because of his appearance.

On September 8, 1943, Korematsu's one-day trial took place and he was found guilty under the military orders implementing Executive Order 9066 and Public Law 503. It was a classic open-and-shut case. His presence in California was illegal: "Korematsu . . . has been convicted of an act not commonly thought a crime," Supreme Court Justice Robert Jackson later wrote. "It consists merely of being present in the state whereof he is a citizen, near the place where he was born, and where all his life he has lived."[4]

Korematsu was never seen as a threat to the United States government. Starting in November 1942 (even before his one-day trial and conviction), the government allowed this young man to leave the barbed-wire fences of his camp in Utah to take on odd jobs. Korematsu picked sugar beets,[5] worked at a construction company, and obtained a welding job in Salt Lake City. "I don't even know how it is to have a home," Korematsu wrote his lawyer. "I feel like an orphan or something."[6] In January 1944, the government granted Korematsu indefinite leave from the camp in Utah, before his case was heard before the Supreme Court.[7]

Mitsuye Endo, the subject of the other Supreme Court case issued on the same day as *Korematsu* in 1944, was born a United States citizen on May 10, 1920, in Sacramento, California. She was the daughter of Japanese immigrants and the second of four children. After graduating from Sacramento Senior High School, she went to secretarial school and obtained work as a clerk with the California Department of Employment. In the weeks after the

Japanese attack on Pearl Harbor, the California State Personnel Board took "a variety of steps that led to the ultimate dismissal of all Japanese-American state employees." [8] By the spring of 1942, Endo was among the dismissed.[9]

Mitsuye was one of the 63 California state employees who sought to challenge their firings with the aid of the Japanese American Citizens League (JACL). The JACL was the major organization representing Japanese-American interests since 1929. It had become controversial in the Japanese-American community for initially failing to oppose the expulsions. The JACL leaders were uncertain of the intentions of the United States government in the immediate aftermath of the attack on Pearl Harbor. Government officials had threatened harsher treatment if the Japanese Americans did not peacefully relocate.[10] The JACL had elected to cooperate with the United States government while seeking concessions on camp conditions and the like.[11]

By 1943, the JACL had reasserted itself and was supporting litigation challenging the expulsions. Japanese-American lawyers who could have ably handled the cases, such as JACL National President Saburo Kido[12] and past president Walter Tsukamoto,[13] were confined in camps, far from law libraries and proper office facilities. The JACL therefore enlisted a lawyer by the name of James C. Purcell. He came to believe that Mitsuye was a very good choice to challenge the incarceration. She was a Methodist, had a brother in the Army, and had never been to Japan. As she told an interviewer many years later, "I agreed to do it at that moment, because they said it [was] for the good of everybody, and so I said, 'Well if that's it, I'll go ahead and do it.'"[14]

She filed a challenge to the expulsion. In the meantime, she began her exile. She was sent with her family to the Sacramento Assembly Center, a temporary location; to Tule Lake for one year; and finally to Topaz in Utah for two.[15]

Unlike Mitsuye, Korematsu initially had trouble finding legal representation after his arrest. The ACLU, founded in part by the now Supreme Court Justice Frankfurter, was a natural choice, with its absolutist views on issues of free speech and its inherent suspicion of the government restrictions on personal freedoms. However, the ACLU decided not to challenge the expulsion policy. At the time, the ACLU leadership consisted of an unlikely coalition that argued in favor of deferring to the president and the military, and leftists whose priority was to throw their full support behind the war effort to defeat totalitarianism.

The Northern California (NC) branch of the ACLU accepted Korematsu's case only by violating the direct orders of the national group not to challenge the order's constitutionality. In 1942, Wayne Collins was recruited to represent Fred Korematsu on behalf of the NC-ACLU. During preparations for the trial, the national ACLU office maintained its policy of not directly challenging the constitutionality of Executive Order 9066.

Collins argued the case before federal judge Adolphus F. St. Sure, who found Korematsu guilty of violating the expulsion order (again, he was in California, an illegal act for a Japanese American), and sentenced him to five years of probation. During 1943–1944, Collins represented Korematsu in his appeals, first to the Court of Appeals for the Ninth Circuit[16] and then before the Supreme Court.

The government could not simply cite the Executive Order for the expulsions. It needed a better reason and pressed for an expansive reading of the war powers of the president and Congress as a justification—specifically, the clear and present danger believed to be posed by the Japanese in the United States in the days immediately following Pearl Harbor. The authorities had no time to separate the good Japanese from the bad, so they all had to go. This had been a winning argument in *Hirabayashi*. And it was again a winning argument.

The *Korematsu* Supreme Court ruled in favor of the government in a 6–3 decision. This was a shift from the year before, when the *entire* court, including Murphy, ruled that the curfews placed on the Japanese Americans were constitutional. But *Korematsu* was still a decisive win for the government.

As an initial matter, the Supreme Court attacked the terminology used by counsel for the Japanese-American plaintiffs. Justice Hugo Black wrote in his opinion that "we deem it unjustifiable to call them concentration camps, with all the ugly connotations that term implies."[17] But this was a gratuitous statement. As will be seen, adopting the government's "relocation center" terminology would not have swayed the results.

In a reprise of *Hirabayashi* the year before, the *Korematsu* majority focused on the obligation of the High Court to defer to the executive and legislative branches in times of national emergencies.[18] Congress needed the expansive power to fund wars, and the president required discretion in how he pursued war aims, justifying even the lifting of individual due process if that is what it took.[19]

The "military imperative" of the early war years precluded the possibility of individualized due process, wrote Justice Black in his majority decision. The emergency of the situation "answers the contention that the exclusion was in the nature of group punishment based on antagonism to those of Japanese origin."[20] Further, "in time of war and when military necessity requires," the president can order the wholesale evacuation of persons deemed to be potentially dangerous to the national security.[21] In other words, in this case, U.S. citizens were not entitled to trials to establish their guilt or innocence.

The High Court cited *Hirabayashi* as a building block in the *Korematsu* decision. Specifically, Justice Black relied on that case to conclude, as a factual matter, that there was no time to investigate and separate the "good" from the "bad" Japanese residents in the immediate aftermath of the attacks on Pearl Harbor. As Justice Black explained, "[T]he petitioner [Korematsu] challenges the assumptions upon which we rested our conclusions in the *Hirabayashi* case. He also urges that, by May 1942, when Order No. 34 was promulgated, all danger of Japanese invasion of the West Coast had disappeared. After careful consideration of these contentions, we are compelled to reject them."[22]

Justice Black then repeated the government's version of events and adopted it wholesale, stating that "we cannot reject as unfounded the judgment of the military authorities and of Congress that there were disloyal members of that population, whose number and strength could not be precisely and quickly ascertained. We cannot say that the war-making branches of the Government did not have grounds for believing that, in a critical hour, such persons could not readily be isolated and separately dealt with, and constituted a menace to the national defense and safety which demanded that prompt and adequate measures be taken to guard against it."[23]

Because the *Hirabayashi* court never cited an actual instance of betrayal by a Japanese American, Black, possibly sensing the weakness of his arguments, next offered the following after-the-fact justification for the expulsions: "That there were members of the group who retained loyalties to Japan has been confirmed by investigations made subsequent to the exclusion." By definition, "investigations made subsequent to the exclusion" were not considered in the decision to expel the Japanese Americans from the West Coast. There is no basis under United States law to lock someone up without any suspicion whatsoever and then try to find some proof of malfeasance after the fact. Yet here Black was stating that not just one but 120,000 people, including children and the elderly, could be imprisoned, without any evidence at all.

If the High Court wanted to do an ex post facto review, it should have looked at all the evidence. Instead, the *Korematsu* court took no notice of the changed fortunes of the United States since the beginning of World War II. The United States, stunned by the Pearl Harbor attack, was now fully engaged and on the offensive in the Pacific.[24] The threat of a Japanese invasion of Hawaii or some other United States territory was negligible. By 1944, United States Marine Corps had landed on Saipan and, with that, American heavy bombers had a forward base that put them within range of mainland Japan. The Battle of the Philippine Sea (June 19–20, 1944) was known as "the greatest carrier battle of the war," ending in a complete United States victory. United States airmen shot down more than 300 planes and sank two carriers, and as the Japanese fleet retreated northward toward Okinawa it lost another carrier and 100 more planes. But more than this, many of Japan's highly trained and elite airmen were now dead, with no pipeline of replacements. And Japan had no industrial capacity to replace its carrier losses even as United States production was ramping up. At the start of the war, the United States had seven carriers, and by the end, it had 28.

And by now, young Japanese Americans were demonstrating their loyalty through their service in the United States armed forces. Specifically, Japanese Americans served with great distinction in the U.S. Army. In 1943 and 1944, the government assembled combat units of Japanese Americans for the European theatre. The 442nd Regimental Combat Team, composed exclusively of Japanese Americans, became one of the most highly decorated units of World War II. Perhaps the best-known soldier was Daniel Inouye, who became the U.S. senator from Hawaii from 1963 to 2012. He was a member of the Democratic Party and was president pro tempore of the Senate (third in the Presidential Line of Succession) from 2010 until his death in 2012.

Among its heroics, Inouye's segregated unit rescued the "Lost Battalion" in 1944. A group of about 800 soldiers originating from Texas had become trapped behind German lines in the Vosge Mountains in France near the border of Germany. During that battle, Inouye was almost killed when he was struck by a bullet. As legend had it, he was saved when two lucky silver dollars in his pocket stopped the bullet. In fact, "in recognition of Inouye's courage and leadership during the battle, he was given a rare battlefield commission that made him a second lieutenant. Second Lieutenant Inouye also received the Bronze Star Medal for his heroism."[25] But his luck would not hold out, and he was grievously wounded in another battle, losing his arm.

One Japanese-American soldier described the devastating losses to Inouye's unit after the battle to free the Lost Battalion. "The normal strength of the squad [he was joining] is twelve men, and there were just two people left before we came." John Kanda was this soldier and later told his story in an oral history. His parents were uprooted from their home and farm. He himself had lived in Tule Lake, an internment camp, before entering the Army.[26]

One other story of note (among many) is that of Clarence Matsumura, who with his Japanese-American unit liberated the Dachau Death Camp in Germany. Matsumura had himself been forced into a relocation camp at Hart Mountain in Wyoming. His father had lost his life savings when, given six days to evacuate, he sold his grocery store in Hollywood, California, to Caucasian owners, who ultimately never paid him. The irony of Matsumura then being someone who entered Germany and provided assistance to the emaciated survivors was recounted by a grateful survivor, Solly Ganor, in *Light One Candle: A Survivor's Tale from Lithuania to Jerusalem*.[27]

Japanese-American soldiers were not permitted to openly fight in the Pacific theatre, as U.S. officials decided that Japanese Americans could not be trusted to combat the Imperial Japanese Army. As many Japanese Americans noted at the time, this concern was absurd: The Japanese Empire's troops would have treated any captured Japanese Americans far worse than other United States soldiers. In reality, up to 6,000 Japanese Americans were secretly serving as translators and intelligence officers for the United States in the Pacific theatre.[28] The Supreme Court did not know the specifics of Japanese-American heroics, but the existence of Japanese Americans fighting in Europe was well known.

And what about the Japanese Americans in Hawaii? Justice Black had been quick to conclude that the internments were necessary because of an inability to separate the good from the bad in the Japanese-American community. He ignored the parallel reality in Hawaii. There, as already noted, the Japanese-American population of 150,000 in this concentrated area exceeded the entire West Coast population. It was the site of Pearl Harbor. Yet, those of Japanese origin were not placed in internment camps, as they were needed by the business community.[29]

Justice Black knew that life was continuing in the United States in 1944, without an overt fear of sabotage by those of Japanese descent. Just three weeks after the attack on Pearl Harbor, on December 31, 1941, upwards of 500,000 people gathered in Times Square in New York City for an enormous New Year's Eve celebration. There had been some talk of canceling due to a fear of an air raid (by Germany, not Japan), but the gathering was held as scheduled. These New Year's celebrations in Times Square and other high-profile locations continued throughout the war.

In the end, Black did not seem to struggle with his decision to uphold the internments and Korematsu's detention. In joining Black, Justice Frankfurter added, "To recognize that military orders are 'reasonably expedient military precautions' in time of war and yet to deny them constitutional legitimacy makes of the Constitution an instrument for dialectic subtleties not reasonably to be attributed to the hard-headed Framers, of whom a majority had had actual participation in war." Frankfurter further posited: "To find that the Constitution does not forbid the military measures now complained of does not carry with it the approval of that which Congress and the Executive did. That is their business, not ours."[30]

Disregarding the facts, he used the case as an opportunity to espouse his general philosophy of judicial restraint. The expulsion order was issued by the military, under the authority granted by Public Law 503. Frankfurter believed that once the executive branch and the legislative branch agreed to a law, it was not the judiciary's place to disturb that finding absent some exigent circumstance.

Peter Irons, in his book *Justice at War*, explained that Justice Frankfurter was close to many in the administration. He may have tipped off his friends in the executive branch that the Supreme Court was considering whether to overturn the statutes authorizing the Japanese-American internments.[31] Irons noted that the Supreme Court decision upholding *Korematsu* came just one day after the FDR administration announced that Japanese Americans could return home to the West Coast. Seen in this context, the Supreme Court majority may have made an implicit pact with the president: "Release the Japanese Americans, and we will not embarrass you with a bad decision."

Three justices dissented in the *Korematsu* decision. Owen Roberts, the one who headed the Roberts Commission charged with investigating the causes of the Pearl Harbor disaster, filed a separate dissent. He started his opinion with the unambiguous statement that Korematsu's constitutional rights were violated. Korematsu was convicted "as a punishment for not submitting to imprisonment in a concentration camp, based on his ancestry, and solely because of his ancestry, without evidence or inquiry concerning his loyalty and good disposition toward the United States.

If this be a correct statement of the facts disclosed by this record, and facts of which we take judicial notice, I need hardly labor the conclusion that Constitutional rights have been violated."[32]

He did not explain why "imprisonment" by sending Japanese to internal camps was constitutionally improper, while "imprisonment" through a curfew was allowed. After all, in *Hirabayashi*, he had voted with the court for upholding the curfew. Roberts also failed to refer to his eponymous report critiquing American readiness in the face of the Japanese attack on Pearl Harbor, which was submitted to FDR and published in major newspapers and which also notably failed to cite an instance of Japanese-American treachery.[33]

Regardless of his logic, Roberts was on the right side of history with his initial statement. But then, Roberts garbled his position. He analyzed various evacuation orders issued by General DeWitt under the authority of Public Law 503 and concluded that Korematsu could not abide by all the orders even if he wanted to. One order required him to stay on the West Coast while another required him to go: "The predicament in which the petitioner thus found himself was this: he was forbidden, by Military Order, to leave the zone in which he lived; he was forbidden, by Military Order, after a date fixed, to be found within that zone unless he were in an Assembly Center located in that zone."[34]

What would have happened if General DeWitt had issued one, unambiguous order? What if the order stated that Korematsu and Japanese Americans had to evacuate from the West Coast? Would Roberts have decided the same way? Roberts did not say, and it is impossible to know the answer.

Justice Jackson's dissent in *Korematsu* had some eloquent language. He wrote, "However well-intentioned may have been the military command on the Pacific Coast, [it] is to adopt one of the cruelest of the rationales used by our enemies to destroy the dignity of the individual and to encourage and open the door to discriminatory actions against other minority groups in the passions of tomorrow."[35]

But Jackson's dissent was deeply flawed and internally inconsistent. Jackson was not objecting because the courts were trampling civil rights. Rather, he was troubled that a district court and later the Supreme Court, both Article III courts, had reviewed and enforced a *military* order. Article III courts had no place interpreting or enforcing military orders. "I should hold that a civil court cannot be made to enforce an order which violates constitutional limitations even if it is a reasonable exercise of military authority," Jackson wrote. "The courts can exercise only the judicial power, can apply only law, and must abide by the Constitution, or they cease to be civil courts and become instruments of military policy."[36]

Jackson's conclusions are unsettling. If the Supreme Court and the lower courts, Article III courts all, have no say over military orders, as Jackson theorized, it follows that the military would have carte blanche. Frankfurter, to his credit, rejected this blanket statement. In his *Korematsu* concurrence, whatever else its flaws, Frankfurter at least stated his belief that the military must follow the Constitution.[37]

Jackson had no immediate solution if the military were to issue an order that conflicts with constitutional principles: "If the people ever let command of the war power fall into irresponsible and unscrupulous hands, the courts wield no power equal to its restraint." Rather, those military leaders would be judged by history: "Those who command the physical forces of the country, in the future as in the past, must be their responsibility to the political judgments of their contemporaries and to the moral judgments of history."[38]

As previously stated, the Supreme Court cited Justice Jackson's dissent in overturning *Korematsu* in 2018. It is likely that the High Tribunal majority simply liked Jackson's poetic language. The majority decision in *Hawaii* does not otherwise endorse Jackson's views about the need to maintain a strict separation of military and civilian courts, or his statements that the Supreme Court has no jurisdiction to review military court orders.

Murphy demonstrated repeatedly that he would not compromise his values for political expediency, even when they were not completely aligned with those of his constituents. As a Detroit criminal court judge, Murphy upheld the rights of Black defendants before an all-white jury in the Ossian Sweet trial, even though he would soon be up for election in a segregated city with a relatively small Black population. And even when running for criminal court reelection, he refused to cancel a radio debate on the death penalty right after a Detroit police officer was killed in the line of duty. He did not pander or hedge, instead repeating his per se position during the debate about the efficacy of capital punishment, "Thou shalt not kill."[39]

In *Korematsu*, Murphy followed the facts and drew his conclusions, oblivious to the political consequences. He was the only justice on the court to challenge the government's heretofore unopposed factual assertions, most notably the prosecutors' contentions that (a) some of the Japanese Americans on the West Coast were probably disloyal and might engage in sabotage or espionage, and (b) the large size of this group made it impossible to sort the loyal from the disloyal.

For the rest of the justices, the government's claims about the Japanese-American threat to the American homeland were lazily taken as fact. Once these "facts" were established, many other conclusions flowed, most notably that the government had a right to treat the situation as an emergency and to restrict individual rights of all Americans of Japanese origin.

This desire to dig into the facts reflected Murphy's past as a trial-level attorney and criminal court judge. Murphy read (or had his clerks read) all the reports submitted by the government, scouring them for specific examples of misconduct by Japanese Americans. Murphy first observed, "In support of this blanket condemnation of all persons of Japanese descent . . . no reliable evidence is cited to show that such individuals were generally disloyal, or had generally so conducted themselves in this area as to constitute a special menace to defense installations or war industries, or had otherwise, by their behavior, furnished reasonable ground for their exclusion as a group."[40]

Murphy heaped contempt on the DeWitt report, relied upon in the majority decision in *Korematsu*, which made the "amazing" statement that, as of February 14, 1942, "The very fact that no sabotage has taken place to date is a disturbing and confirming indication that such action will be taken." Murphy continued, "Apparently, in the minds of the military leaders, there was no way that the Japanese Americans could escape the suspicion of sabotage."[41] To date, "not one person of Japanese ancestry was accused or convicted of espionage or sabotage after Pearl Harbor while they were still free, a fact which is some evidence of the loyalty of the vast majority of these individuals and of the effectiveness of the established methods of combatting these evils."[42]

To Murphy, the failure of the government to act expeditiously in expelling Japanese Americans was a sign that the crisis was a manufactured one: "[N]early four months elapsed after Pearl Harbor before the first exclusion order was issued; nearly eight months went by until the last order was issued, and the last of these 'subversive' persons was not actually removed until almost eleven months had elapsed. Leisure and deliberation seem to have been more of the essence than speed." And the president had not issued a declaration of martial law on the West Coast, thereby adding "strength to the belief that the factors of time and military necessity were not as urgent as they have been represented to be."[43]

Murphy acknowledged the need for deference to the executive branch in the context of national security. But he cautioned that "it is essential that there be definite limits to [the government's] discretion," as "[i]ndividuals must not be left impoverished of their constitutional rights on a plea of military necessity that has neither substance nor support."[44] In this regard, the judiciary was a check on presidential and congressional power. It needed to weigh in on a timely basis, and not years after the damage was done.[45]

Just two years before, in a speech before the Advertising Club of Boston, Murphy proclaimed that "a wise people will have faith in the ability of their responsible government officials and military leaders to deal with delicate questions of high policy and military strategy."[46] And just one year before in the *Hirabayashi* and *Yasui* curfew cases, he seemed to accept the government's rationale for the need to forcibly remove all Japanese Americans from the West Coast. As demonstrated by his savaging of the government's position, he no longer had that absolute faith.

Murphy indicated his limited tolerance to the assault on individual liberties represented by the internment laws. Even though he agreed to the curfews placed on Japanese Americans in *Hirabayashi*, he believed that this was a temporary measure, an aberration to the general rule: "When the [national] danger is past, the restrictions imposed on them should be promptly removed and their freedom of action fully restored."[47]

To the extent the government was worried about a fifth-column threat, it could have held individualized loyalty hearings, especially when a large segment of the Japanese-American population consisted of children and the elderly, and were obviously not threats: "No adequate reason is given for the failure to treat these Japanese Americans on an individual basis by holding investigations and hearings to separate the loyal from the disloyal, as was done in the case of persons of German and Italian ancestry."[48] Murphy further stated, "To infer that examples of individual disloyalty prove group disloyalty . . . is to deny that under our system of law . . . individual guilt is the sole basis for the deprivation of rights."

But what if the facts were different, and the government's position were proven instead of made up? That is, what if there were Japanese Americans committing sabotage or treason, and the government truly had no ability to sort through the "good" Japanese Americans from the "bad" ones? It appears this would not have made a difference, although he never addressed this point.

But he did say the inference of collective guilt "is at the very heart of the evacuation orders, [and it] has been used in support of the abhorrent treatment of minority groups by the dictatorial tyrannies which this nation is now pledged to destroy."[49] Murphy called out the president, Congress, the military, and his fellow justices: "Such exclusion goes over 'the very brink of constitutional power,' and falls into the ugly abyss of racism."[50]

In the most famous passage of his opinion, he penned that "all residents of this nation are kin in some way by blood or culture to a foreign land. They are primarily and necessarily a part of the new and distinct civilization of the United States."[51] It is perhaps the most concise and eloquent statement of a belief in America and its promise.

Although Murphy did not cite any sources for this statement, he was echoing the words of Theodore Roosevelt. It will be recalled that Murphy was a great admirer of the first President Roosevelt. Theodore Roosevelt proclaimed in a 1915 Knights of Columbus speech: "We of the United States need above all things to remember that, while we are by blood and culture kin to each of the nations of Europe, we are also separate from each of them. . . . We should freely take from every other nation whatever we can make of use, but we should adopt and develop to our own peculiar needs what we thus take, and never be content merely to copy."[52]

Theodore Roosevelt was a prime proponent of the idea that America was a melting pot of various ethnicities that would forge a mighty nation by picking and choosing from the best of the old world traditions. All ethnic and religious groups were firmly knitted together through common political values. Historians have called this adherence to liberal ideals, rather than nationalities, "civic nationalism."[53] In his dissent, Murphy drew upon Theodore Roosevelt's words in that 1915 speech, but without attribution. This is unfortunate not only because he passed off Roosevelt's thoughts as his own but also because he robbed his contemporaries and historians of a key insight into his deepest-held values. He was, essentially, channeling Teddy Roosevelt.

At the same time Murphy's views can be closely identified with Roosevelt's ideas; they were not identical. In addition to his more capacious definition of Americans to include non-Europeans, Murphy also did not completely adopt the "melting pot" metaphor. For Murphy, one's religion and ethnicity were points of pride and celebration in this new land. The only entry fee for groups desiring inclusion into the American way of life was to show a basic respect for the democratic institutions of the nation.

On the very day of Murphy's dissent in *Korematsu*, he used the word *racism* or a variant of it in two other cases. The second case relating to the Japanese-American internments was *Ex parte Endo*.[54] In contrast to the other three Japanese-American internment-era cases (*Hirabayashi, Yasui,* and *Korematsu*), the Supreme

Court sided with the Japanese-American plaintiff and found that Endo should be released immediately from the camps.

In distinguishing *Endo* from *Korematsu*, Murphy's brethren focused on the fact that Endo's continued detention was coordinated by a civilian organization, the War Relocation Authority, and not by the military.[55] In contrast, Fred Korematsu was convicted under a military order directing Korematsu's expulsion from the West Coast.[56] According to the majority opinion in *Endo*, this was an important distinction and warranted a different result.[57] Justice Black and Justice Douglas, the authors of *Korematsu* and *Endo* respectively, never explained why.

Murphy did not have to split hairs. He would not have allowed the implementation of these expulsion orders, whether by a civilian authority or the military. And his reasons for doing so were consistent with how he believed the country needed to treat its most vulnerable citizens. In *Endo*, he wrote a concurrence as follows:

> I join in the opinion of the Court, but I am of the view that detention in Relocation Centers of persons of Japanese ancestry regardless of loyalty is not only unauthorized by Congress or the Executive but is another example of the unconstitutional resort to racism inherent in the entire evacuation program. As stated more fully in [*Korematsu*], racial discrimination of this nature bears no reasonable relation to military necessity and is utterly foreign to the ideals and traditions of the American people.[58]

Murphy wanted to send a message to his colleagues and also to the country. His use of the words *racism* and *racial discrimination* in *Korematsu* and *Endo* was purposeful and not isolated. Murphy's Supreme Court decisions focused on his conception of American values, rather than on specific constitutional provisions or case-law precedent.

A belated obituary in the *New York Times* for Mitsuye Endo recounted the supreme sacrifices she made. The government had been prepared to let her leave the internment camp earlier if she had only dropped her appeal and agreed not to return to California. She refused the offer, choosing instead to stay in detention and allow the Supreme Court to decide her case. And once she was released, she was done with California. "My mom said no, she would never go back to California," her daughter recalled. Mitsuye settled in Chicago with her husband, whom she'd met in the camp in Utah.[59]

Before moving to the third case decided by the Supreme Court on that winter day in 1944 in which Murphy used the word *racism*, it should be noted that the conclusion of World War II did not end the difficulties for Japanese Americans.

To be clear, until the 1950s, there was no path to citizenship for Japanese Americans who were born in Japan, even if they had lived in the U.S. for 30 or 40 years, dating back to the 1922 Supreme Court decision of *Ozawa*. And the states, by tying certain rights to citizenship, could discriminate against Japanese Americans without being explicit. In *Oyama v. State of California* in 1948, Murphy in a concurrence criticized a California state law that prohibited "aliens ineligible for citizenship" from acquiring land. Because Japanese-born residents could still not become citizens under federal law at the time, the California law had the effect of discriminating against Japanese Americans without saying as much. Murphy wrote: "The California statute in question, as I view it, is nothing more than an outright racial discrimination. As such, it deserves constitutional condemnation. And since the very core of the statute is so defective, I consider it necessary to give voice to that fact even though I join in the opinion of the Court."[60]

In the post-war environment, the other justices were growing uncomfortable with laws that so obviously targeted Asian Americans. But most of the justices found ways to overturn these statutes without referencing their racial component. Justice Vinson, writing for the Supreme Court in this same case, found the California statute invalid, a victory for Oyama. He did not, however, reach the constitutional issue, instead stating that "this case presents a conflict between the State's right to formulate a policy of landholding within its bounds and the right of American citizens to own land anywhere in the United States. When these two rights clash, the rights of a citizen may not be subordinated merely because of his father's country of origin."[61]

Justice Black took a slightly different tack. He wrote, "I concur in the Court's judgment and its opinion. But I should prefer to reverse the judgment on the broader grounds that the basic provisions of the California Alien Land Law violate the equal protection clause of the Fourteenth Amendment and conflict with federal laws and treaties governing the immigration of aliens and their rights after arrival in this country."[62] Unlike Murphy, neither of these justices addressed the obvious racial component behind the law's enactment.

Next came *Takahashi v. Fish & Game Comm'n* in 1948.[63] The relevant California statute was signed into law by incoming governor Earl Warren, later of *Brown v. Board of Education* fame. The specific language prohibited the issuance of commercial fishing licenses to aliens who were ineligible for citizenship. As in *Oyama*, Americans born in Japan—and almost no other group—fit the four squares of the statute because they were "ineligible for citizenship." The Supreme Court overturned this law as well. But Murphy was again not satisfied and filed a concurrence. While not using the word *racism*, Murphy pointed out that the statute was a "direct outgrowth of antagonism toward persons of Japanese ancestry," disentitling it "to wear the cloak of constitutionality."[64]

The statutes that prevented Japanese "aliens" from becoming citizens remained stubbornly in place into the 1950s. Individuals born in Japan were not allowed to become naturalized United States citizens until 1952, and only over the veto of Truman.[65] President Truman, a decent man who otherwise promoted civil rights, had a hole in his heart when it came to Japanese Americans.

Even though *Korematsu* was overruled in 2018, other cases that used *Korematsu* as precedent have not been similarly overturned. *Korematsu* has been cited in other cases as precedent to solidify the idea that presidents are within their authority to restrict civil liberties when the nation is in a wartime setting.[66] This now-bedrock principle—that the Supreme Court does not generally overrule the executive and legislative branches on matters of national security—is not going away just because the Supreme Court overturned *Korematsu*. The case is like asbestos, built into the foundations of many old buildings to remain even though it was found to be toxic.

Endnotes

1. *Korematsu v. United States*, 323 U.S. 214, 216 (1944).

2. Erick Trickey, "Fred Korematsu Fought against Japanese Internment in the Supreme Court . . . and Lost," *Smithsonian Magazine*, Jan. 30, 2017, accessed Apr. 19, 2020, https://www.smithsonianmag.com/history/fred-korematsu-fought-against-japanese-internment-supreme-court-and-lost-180961967/ #hezp5fwhdpSHL7kj. 99.

3. "3 Japanese Defy Curbs: Army Says One Tried to Become 'Spaniard' by Plastic Surgery," *NYT,* June 12, 1942.

4. *Korematsu*, 323 U.S. at 242–243.

5. As recounted in a prior chapter, senators from certain agricultural states (including Colorado) had supported independence for the Philippines so that tariffs could be placed on its agricultural products, including beets. The point was to protect United States farmers from competition caused by lower Philippine wages. Now Japanese Americans, interned far from their homes, were released to work on the beet farms in Colorado.

6. Trickey, "Fred Korematsu," Jan. 30, 2017.

7. Ibid.

8. Paul R. Spickard, "The Nisei Assume Power: The Japanese Citizens League, 1941–1942," *Pacific Historical Review* 52, no. 2 (May 1983): 147, 154.

9. Ibid.

10. Ibid, 164.

11. Ibid, 162.

12. Ibid, 154.

13. Some of this information is taken from the Densho website, an "organization dedicated to preserving, educating, and sharing the story of World War II–era incarceration of Japanese Americans to deepen an understanding of American history and inspire action for equity." Densho website, accessed Apr. 19, 2020, densho.org/ Walter_Tsukamoto.

14. Article on Mitsuye Endo, Densho website, accessed Apr. 19, 2020, densho. org/mitsuye-endo. In subsequent years, she kept a low profile, rebuffing interview requests with the exception of a brief oral history that appeared in the anthology *And Justice for All* in 1984. Tateishi, *And Justice for All,* 60–61.

15. Tateishi, *And Justice for All,* 61.

16. "Japanese Ouster Under Advisement," *Oakland Tribune,* Feb. 21, 1943, A12.

17. *Korematsu*, 323 U.S. at 223.

18. U.S. Const. article I, § 8, cl. 11.

19. *Youngstown Sheet & Tube Co. v. Sawyer*, 1952, was one notable exception to a general deference of the Supreme Court to actions by the other two federal branches when they invoked "war powers" to justify an act to curb preexisting rights of citizens.

20. *Korematsu*, 323 U.S. at 219.

21. Ibid.

22. Ibid at 218.

23. Ibid (citing *Hirabayashi*, 320 U.S. at 90).

24. Eric L. Muller, "*Hirabayashi* and the Invasion Evasion," *North Carolina Law Review* 88 (2010): 1333, accessed Apr. 19, 2020, https://scholarship.law.unc.edu/cgi/viewcontent.cgi?referer=&httpsredir=1&article=4430&context=nclr.

25. "Medal of Honor Recipient Daniel Inouye Led a Life of Service to His Country," The National World War II Museum website, July 19, 2029, accessed Oct. 1, 2020, https://www.nationalww2museum.org/war/articles/medal-of-honor-recipient-daniel-inouye.

26. Tateishi, *And Justice for All*, 120–124.

27. Ganor, Solly, *Light One Candle: A Survivor's Tale from Lithuania to Jerusalem.* New York: Kodansha International, 1995. Kindle (describing encounter with the Japanese-American troops).

28. In one of the less publicized aspects of Japanese-American war service, 6,000 Japanese-American soldiers served in intelligence units in the Pacific theatre, interrogating prisoners and translating documents. "Military Intelligence Service (MIS): Using Their Words," The National WWII Museum Website, Sept. 30, 2020, accessed Oct. 9, 2020, https://www.nationalww2museum.org/war/articles/military-intelligence-service-translators-interpreters.

29. *Duncan v. Kahanamoku*, 327 U.S. 304, 325 (1946). Military rule applied to Caucasians as well as Japanese Americans in Hawaii. In a concurrence in this case, Murphy struck a familiar tone. Hawaii was under military rule mostly because it had a large Japanese-American population (nearly one half the population of the Islands), and not for any legitimate military reason. "Racism has no place whatever in our civilization," he said, taking on a familiar tone: "The Constitution as well as the conscience of mankind disclaims its use for any purpose, military or otherwise. It can only result, as it does in this instance, in striking down individual rights and in aggravating rather than solving the problems toward which it is directed. It renders impotent the ideal of the dignity of the human personality, destroying something of what is noble in our way of life. We must therefore reject it completely whenever it arises in the course of a legal proceeding." Ibid at 334.

30. *Korematsu*, 323 U.S. at 225.

31. Irons, *Justice at War*, 345. ("Second-hand evidence that Frankfurter leaked word of the timing of the *Endo* decision to McCloy comes from Roger Daniels, a historian who has written extensively about the internment.")

32. *Korematsu*, 323 U.S. at 226.

33. *Hirabayashi*, 320 U.S. at 96. The Roberts Report made an appearance in the *Hirabayashi* decision issued by the Supreme Court. It was not cited to show a lack of Japanese-American misconduct. Rather, it supported the following: "Espionage by persons in sympathy with the Japanese Government had been found to have been particularly effective in the surprise attack on Pearl Harbor." In the *Hirabayashi* decision, the Roberts Report was called the more bureaucratic "Report of the Commission Appointed by the President, dated January 23, 1942, S. Doc. No. 159, 77th Cong., 2d Sess., pp. 12–13."

34. *Korematsu*, 323 U.S. at 230.

35. Ibid at 240.

36. *Korematsu*, 323 U.S. at 247.

37. Ibid at 225. ("The respective spheres of action of military authorities and of judges are, of course, very different. But, within their sphere, military authorities are no more outside the bounds of obedience to the Constitution than are judges within theirs.")

38. Ibid at 248.

39. Fine, *Detroit Years*, 137.

40. *Korematsu*, 323 U.S. at 236.

41. Ibid at 243, ft. 15.

42. Ibid at 241.

43. Ibid.

44. Ibid at 234.

45. In *Trump v. Hawaii*, Justice Sotomayor in her own dissent made this point by citing to Murphy's opinion: "Although a majority of the Court in *Korematsu* was willing to uphold the Government's actions based on a barren invocation of national security, dissenting Justices warned of that decision's harm to our constitutional fabric. Justice Murphy recognized that there is a need for great deference to the Executive Branch in the context of national security, but cautioned that 'it is essential that there be definite limits to [the government's] discretion,' as '[i]ndividuals must not be left impoverished of their constitutional rights on a plea of military necessity that has neither substance nor support.' 323 U. S., at 234 (Murphy, J., dissenting)." *Trump v. Hawaii*, 138 S. Ct. at 2447–2448.

46. Associated Press, "Urges U.S. to Avoid Public Controversies," *The Daily Telegram* (Adrian, Michigan), Nov. 6, 1942, 7.

47. *Hirabayashi*, 320 U. S. at 113–114.

48. *Korematsu*, 323 U.S. at 241.

49. Westbrook Pegler, "Fair Enough," *The Index-Journal* (Greenwood, South Carolina), Feb. 26, 1945.

50. *Korematsu*, 323 U.S. at 233.

51. Ibid at 242.

52. Theodore Roosevelt, "Americanism," Speech at Carnegie Hall, Oct. 12, 1915, Philip Davis and Bertha Schwartz, eds., *Immigration and Americanization: Selected Readings* (Boston: Ginn and Co., 1920), 645.

53. Gerstle, "Civic Nationalism and Its Contradictions, 1890–1917," *American Crucible*, 44–80, accessed May 3, 2020. doi:10.2307/j.ctvc775dm.8.

54. *Ex Parte Endo*, 323 U.S. 283 (1944).

55. The word *War* in the title of this agency is misleading as this was a civilian organization, folded within the executive branch. It was not a branch of the military.

56. *Endo*, 323 U.S. at 289, ft. 2 (reciting that Civilian Exclusion Orders Nos. 1 to 99 were ratified by General De Witt's Public Proclamation No. 7 of June 8, 1942 [7 Fed. Reg. 4498] and Nos. 100 to 108 were ratified by Public Proclamation No. 11 of August 18, 1942 [7 Fed. Reg. 6703]).

57. *Endo*, 323 U. S. at 298.

58. Ibid at 307.

59. Stephanie Buck, "Overlooked No More: Mitsuye Endo, a Name Linked to Justice for Japanese-Americans," *NYT*, Oct. 9, 2019, accessed Apr. 19, 2020, https://www.nytimes.com/2019/10/09/obituaries/mitsuye-endo-overlooked.html.

60. *Oyama v. State of California*, 332 U.S. 633 (1948).

61. Ibid at 647.

62. Ibid.

63. *Takahashi v. Fish & Game Comm'n*, 334 U.S. 410, 413, 418, 423 (1948).

64. Ibid at 422.

65. In fairness to Truman, this law was otherwise a reactionary piece of national legislation, a product of the McCarthy era. It made deportation and revocation of naturalization much easier and imposed strict quotas on immigrants.

66. *Korematsu* and *Hirabayashi* have been used in questionable ways by the Supreme Court. In *Youngstown*, Justice Clark, in his concurrence, cited *Hirabayashi* as an example of the *appropriate* exercise of presidential power because Congress specifically authorized the president to establish the internment camps. *Youngstown Sheet & Tube Co. v. Sawyer*, 343 U.S. 579, 661 n.3 (1952). At least in *Youngstown*, the Supreme Court restrained a president's war powers, relying in part on the President's failure to obtain subsequent congressional approval for his actions.

CHAPTER 19

Last Years

Murphy maintained his vigorous lifestyle even as his health declined in the last five years of his life. He was a Supreme Court justice by day and attended parties and social events in the evening. He had done well for himself financially, even while spending nearly his entire career in public service. By 1945, Murphy had about $75,000 in his bank account, the equivalent of more than a million dollars today.[1] He enjoyed a Supreme Court annual salary of $25,000. Additionally, he collected fees for speaking engagements.[2]

During these last four years of his life, Murphy had a girlfriend, Joan Cuddihy. Prior biographies made scant reference to Joan. The letters she saved, however, reflect a deep but troubled relationship. They appear to be the only set of letters in Frank's amorous voice that survives.[3] Her files, donated to the Bentley Library, contained numerous photos of the two of them together with their arms entwined, and Murphy noticeably older.

In an enigmatic letter dated 1947, Supreme Court Justice Rutledge wrote to Joan on Supreme Court letterhead, telling her that Frank was trying to walk the "straight and narrow."[4] In a telegram from Justice Douglas to Murphy, he told Murphy, "HAPPY BIRTHDAY DONT RACE YOUR MOTOR TELL JOAN IM GLAD FOR HER YOURE ONLY 36 BILL."[5] Like everything else in Murphy's love life, these letters from the Supreme Court justices can be read in several ways.

Murphy lost some of his political influence in his later years. Although Murphy's name had come up as one of 12 possible vice presidential choices of FDR in 1944, the direct contacts between the two men by then largely ceased. Still, he mourned the death of FDR. Before an audience of 2,000 at Hunter College, upon the first year of FDR's death, Murphy paid Roosevelt what was for him the ultimate compliment, stating, "He had faith in the actual and potential goodness of the common folk and felt that glorification of the human personality was in the common people."[6]

After FDR's death, Murphy tried to establish a connection to President Truman. At one point, he requested a meeting to debrief the president after visiting the Pope and the Irish leader Éamon de Valera on a trip to Europe.[7] Truman's calendar reflects that he briefly met with Murphy.

The two men might have been much closer, as they shared some commonalities. They were both from the Midwest, and both came from humbler origins than many of their power-broker peers in Washington, DC. They were exceedingly proud of their Army service during World War I, and both used that service as a springboard to higher office. Each had a gift and passion for ferreting out wartime graft.

In searching for reasons for their apparent estrangement, one incident stands out as clouding their relationship. As the U.S. Attorney General for Roosevelt in 1939, Murphy was aggressively deploying the tax laws to pursue entrenched political bosses. One of Murphy's targets was Kansas City boss Tom Pendergast, who was very close to Truman. Pendergast had earlier given Truman his start in politics, installing him as a local Missouri judge at a time when Truman was no more than a failed haberdasher. Murphy and FBI Director Hoover ultimately caught Pendergast for failing to pay taxes on a bribe he had accepted.[8]

After Pendergast was indicted, Truman publicly vented against Roosevelt and his Justice Department for prosecuting the Missouri boss.[9] The outburst was not well received by the public. A humiliated Truman considered not running for his Senate seat in 1940. It is a testament to Truman's overall integrity that he soon after voted in favor of Murphy's appointment as a Supreme Court justice. But this incident may have been on his mind whenever he encountered Murphy.

Truman could not avoid Murphy completely. In 1948, Truman was locked in a contentious presidential campaign for reelection (this was the campaign where he later triumphantly held up the newspaper with the headline "Dewey Defeats Truman").

Truman needed the support of labor to win in 1948, so he appeared at the Annual Labor Day Banquet of the Detroit and Wayne County Federation of Labor. Murphy, by now a member of the Supreme Court, also attended the event. Murphy was likely invited by his old friend Frank X. Martel, who can be seen in photos of the event standing between Murphy and Truman. Murphy was well known and respected in union circles and was a welcome presence at union events like this one. His appearance was, in effect, a seal of good approval for Truman and probably had a favorable impact on the labor vote in that close presidential election.[10] Separately, Truman briefly considered, and then quickly rejected, the idea that Murphy could be his ambassador to France.[11]

Murphy never left the Democratic Party fold, but he chafed against efforts by the two major parties to cement their positions at the expense of other insurgent parties. While supporting Truman, Murphy struck perhaps his biggest blow against the two-party system in 1948, one year before his death, in the case of *MacDougal v. Green*.[12] That same year, two new formidable political parties were formed. One was the Progressive Party, calling for universal government health insurance, an end to the incipient Cold War, and the abolition of segregation. As its name implies, its goal was to shave off the progressives from the two major parties.

The Progressive Party candidate running for president in 1948 was none other than Henry Wallace, FDR's former secretary of agriculture and vice president. By this time, Wallace was finished with the Democratic Party and had joined forces with Elmer A. Benson, the former governor of Minnesota. Benson arose from the ranks of the Farm-Labor Party, whose platform was one of farmer and labor union protection, government ownership of certain industries, and enactment of social-security laws. The farmers in rural areas had a tradition of creating cooperatives whose lines of business included dry goods, groceries, fuel, agricultural goods, garages, and warehouses.[13] U.S. senators from Minnesota between 1920 and the 1940s came from the Republican Party or the Farmer-Labor Party but not the Democratic Party.

Wallace and Benson could have remained aligned with the Democratic Party but for one issue. Both major political parties accepted the premise that the Soviet Union was a dangerous ideological and military adversary. Truman was a Cold War advocate, but many others like Wallace and Benson were seeking a better relationship with the Soviets in a nuclear age.

The specific issue in 1948 before the Supreme Court was the denial of the right of the Progressive Party to appear on the ballot in several key states, most notably in Illinois. The Illinois statute in question required a certain number of signatures in all the different counties in that state. The effect of the statute was to require a political party to be organized in every county, no matter how small. Only the two major parties, the Democrats and the Republicans, had this organizational capability to obtain signatures throughout the state.

In 1948, in *MacDougal v. Green*[14] the U.S. Supreme Court upheld the Illinois statute that disenfranchised the Progressive Party. If Murphy were a Democratic Party hack, as many had complained, he would have found a reason to agree with the majority in this decision.

But Justice Murphy joined Justices Douglas and Black in dissent. They pointed out that Cook County had more than half of the state's registered voters and that it seemed unfair to require a new insurgent party to have an organization in even the smallest rural counties. Murphy signed on to the statement in the dissent that the "regulation thus discriminates against the residents of the populous counties of the state in favor of rural sections."[15] Perhaps Murphy was remembering his days as a Detroit mayor when he was stymied by the state legislature, controlled by rural districts, in the denial of crucial funds to Detroit when the city most needed it during the Great Depression.[16]

It should be noted that the same Illinois rule deployed against Wallace had not been used against FDR. Eight years before, a challenge to FDR's placement on the Illinois ballot when he ran for his third term was summarily dismissed by the certifying board controlled by Democrats, even though FDR had not, at the time, declared himself to be a candidate, let alone secured signatures in all the counties.[17] That is the way party organizers protect their own. Had Murphy's view prevailed, Illinois, a large state with many electoral delegates, might have been open to a third-party challenge. Today, we might have a system that is more welcoming of third parties.

While Murphy failed to charm Truman, his loyal circle of contacts remained largely intact. Eleanor Bumgardner was still with him. She had followed Murphy back from the Philippines to Michigan when he became the governor, and then she accompanied him to Washington, DC, when he became the Attorney General. After that, she became his secretary at the Supreme Court. In his later years, Murphy signed his letters to her "Love, Frank."[18] And there was Edward Kemp. The three of them often stayed together in the same hotel suite when traveling.

His lower-level staff also stayed in touch. Sanger Williams was Murphy's chauffeur from his Detroit days, and Murphy had convinced Williams to come with him to the Philippines and then to the nation's capital. Murphy must have sung the praises of Williams to the president because during his time in Washington, Williams was also the occasional driver and bodyguard of FDR. In a conversational letter to Murphy in 1947, two years before Murphy's death, Sanger inquired from his home in Indiana about various mutual acquaintances by now familiar: George and Marguerite Murphy, Bumgardner, and Kemp.[19]

Murphy also made new friends later in life. His law clerk on the Supreme Court, Eugene Gressman, served under him for five years, the longest such stint for any Supreme Court clerk. Gressman later became a Supreme Court scholar, writing the first version of a standard reference manual used by attorneys who appear before the High Court.[20] Murphy called Gressman "one of the most superb characters that I have met in my lifetime."[21] This was high praise from a man who only knew Gressman in the last years of his life and had met many illustrious people. Gressman lived until 2010, and throughout his life he kept up his defense of Murphy against other legal academics, who had low opinions generally about Murphy's legal scholarship.[22]

But Murphy was also losing friends and allies in addition to FDR. In 1946, Murphy suffered the severe blow of the death of his older brother Harold, who died of coronary thrombosis, the same heart malady that probably killed Murphy a few years later.[23] Harold had spent his career serving in various government functions, most recently as a clerk for a federal district court judge.[24] While Murphy did not rely on Harold for professional advice as he did for his brother George, the two men were close.[25]

In a letter to Joan Cuddihy in 1946, Frank described in tender terms how how he, George, and Marguerite, stayed with Harold in the hospital every night until their eldest brother fell asleep.[26]

In his later years on the court, Justice Murphy squarely confronted historical racial inequalities in the United States. The challenges to change were complex, as segregation operated not just under the law (de jure) but also was baked into the dominant culture and traditions, enforced with violence against Black people (de facto). The Supreme Court had already caused lasting damage to race relations with rulings that reinforced segregation in the country. Most notably, *Plessy v. Ferguson*, blessing the separation of the races on unequal terms, was decided in 1896 and remained the law of the land throughout Murphy's career on the High Court. In many places in the country, Black people had to go to separate schools and use separate entrances for public facilities of all types.

The NAACP's efforts focused on undermining the legal underpinnings of the Jim Crow system (we saw how the seeds for this legal strategy were planted with the Ossian Sweet case), and now cases were beginning to land before Murphy's Supreme Court. Specifically, in numerous states, the authorities kept Black students out of state-funded schools without bothering to create the "separate but equal" Black schools that were supposed to operate in tandem under the logic of *Plessy*. NAACP briefs suggested that states needed to provide these facilities for Black people (illogical, given the costs of maintaining two parallel, tiny programs) or, alternatively, integrate.

In 1946, the NAACP and its chief trial counsel, Thurgood Marshall, brought a test case before the High Tribunal. A young Black woman, Ada Lois Sipuel Fisher, applied for admission to the School of Law at the University of Oklahoma. The law school was the only institution for legal education supported and maintained by the taxpayers of the state of Oklahoma. The application for admission of Sipuel was denied, with the state stipulating that the sole reason was because of her color. Marshall now cannily exploited the fact that states such as Oklahoma had no alternative state-sponsored law schools for their African-American population.[27] The state could make no argument that Black students had a "separate but equal" public law school to attend.

The *Sipuel* case made its way twice to Murphy's United States Supreme Court. The first time, the Supreme Court heard arguments on January 7 and 8, 1948, and only four days later issued a unanimous three-paragraph opinion reversing the decisions of the Oklahoma courts to deny Sipuel access to the law school (*Sipuel I*).[28] Even though the decision was swift and positive for Ms. Sipuel, the state of Oklahoma had already delayed Sipuel's entry into the law school for two years. Many others in her shoes would have given up, and that was of course the point of the state's intransigence. Sipuel's brother did not wait and decided to enroll at Howard Law School (a historically Black college) rather than engage in the lengthy legal fight for a spot at the University of Oklahoma.

In a private conference held by the Supreme Court justices to discuss *Sipuel I* before the issuance of the decision, Murphy articulated his desire to end "separate but equal" as established law. Murphy was probably the first on the court to propose a *Brown v. Board of Education*–type solution to Jim Crow—that is, integration instead of segregation. In the end, the other justices convinced Murphy to join the majority decision. In *Sipuel I*, the court called for the University of Oklahoma regents to provide instruction for Black students equal to that of white students, required the admission of qualified Black students to previously all-white state law schools, and reversed the decision of Oklahoma's highest state court.

The decision had an immediate effect, but not in Oklahoma. After publication of the *Sipuel I* decision, Lewis W. Jones, the president of the University of Arkansas, announced that African Americans would be admitted to the university, thus becoming the first public, all-white university in the South to do so.[29]

In Oklahoma, though, the state courts reacted with defiance. Specifically, on January 22, 1948, the trial court in Oklahoma proposed a workaround. The local state court said Sipuel could in fact be barred from admission until a hastily proposed "separate school is established and ready to function."[30] The Oklahoma Senate, so desperate to create a segregated school, set aside several fourth-floor committee rooms in its legislative chambers to house the new Black-only school. The state law library on the first floor was designated as the law school's library.[31]

The NAACP promptly filed a writ of mandamus in the Supreme Court (in essence a pleading that the court direct the inferior court to abide by the law). Marshall alleged that the chief justice of Oklahoma improperly evaded the mandate of the Supreme Court when he did not order the immediate admission of Sipuel into the law school.

But the Supreme Court was not ready to act and denied the NAACP's writ (*Sipuel II*). History is filled with such "two steps forward, one step back" moments. *Sipuel II* was *per curium* (meaning the United States Supreme Court justices denying the writ did so anonymously).

Two justices dissented from this *per curium* result. One was Frank Murphy. In his dissent in *Sipuel II*, he wrote that Ms. Sipuel should have received a hearing before the High Court "in order to determine whether the action of the Oklahoma courts subsequent to the issuance of this Court's mandate constitutes an evasion of that mandate."[32] Murphy's friend Justice Rutledge provided more context, stating that "no separate law school could be established elsewhere overnight capable of giving petitioner a legal education equal to that afforded by the state's long-established and well-known state university law school. Nor could the necessary time be taken to create such facilities, while continuing to deny them to petitioner, without incurring the delay which would continue the discrimination our mandate required to end at once."[33]

Sipuel later attended, and graduated from, the School of Law at the University of Oklahoma, notwithstanding the rulings. The weight of public opinion to admit her proved overwhelming. Even so, she often had to attend class in a section separated from the white students. In one of the ironies of this case, her constitutional law professor was the same person who argued in the Supreme Court against her admittance. In her autobiography, *A Matter of Black and White*, Sipuel graciously stated that he treated her well in his classes.[34]

On April 22, 1992, Oklahoma governor David Walters symboli-cally addressed the wrongs of the past by appointing the now Dr. Ada Lois Sipuel Fisher to the Board of Regents of the University of Oklahoma, the same school that had once refused to admit her to its college of law. And the law school itself has a garden in Fisher's honor. The accompanying plaque does not, however, address the challenges she faced in attending the law school, including her separation from other students in classes and her need to leave Norman by nightfall. Norman was a "sundown town"—meaning people of color essentially had to leave town before sunset—and so Fisher lived in Oklahoma City while studying in Norman.

Murphy heard other discrimination cases later in his career. For example, the 1948 Supreme Court case of *Shelley v. Kraemer*[35] highlighted the pernicious effects of racial restrictive covenants.

The main case involved the Shelleys, a Black couple who had purchased a house in a white section of Saint Louis, Missouri. When they did so, they were unaware that a restrictive covenant had been in place on the property since 1911, which prevented "people of the Negro or Mongolian Race"[36] from occupying the property. Louis Kraemer, who lived a full 10 blocks away, sued under the restrictive covenant to prevent the Shelleys from gain-ing possession of the property. The Supreme Court of Missouri had previously held that the covenant was enforceable against the purchasers because it was a purely private agreement between its original parties with no state involvement whatsoever.

At the time Detroit land titles were laced with such restrictive covenants, and a companion case joined to the *Shelley* case involved a Black couple from Detroit, similarly restricted from buying prop-erty due to restrictive covenants. So this was not some abstract case for Murphy dealing with an issue arising in the segregated South.

The Supreme Court justices now reviewed the decision of the state court. As an initial matter, three of the nine justices recused (excused) themselves from the decision because they owned property with racial restrictive covenants.

Murphy joined the five other voting justices in a unanimous decision voiding the restrictive covenants in all the related cases, including the Detroit case. The court decided the imposition of racial covenants was not just a private contract between a buyer and seller, as the state court had concluded: "It is clear that, but for the active intervention of the state courts, supported by the full panoply of state power, petitioners would have been free to occupy the properties in question without restraint. . . . These are not cases, as has been suggested, in which the States have merely abstained from action, leaving private individuals free to impose such discriminations as they see fit."[37]

Rather, the full power of government denied the appellants, "on the grounds of race or color," the ability to own premises "which petitioners are willing and financially able to acquire and which the grantors are willing to sell." Further, the petitioners were "being denied rights of property available to other members of the community and being accorded full enjoyment of those rights on an equal footing."[38]

Murphy had been the judge in the Ossian Sweet trial more than 20 years before, and so he knew about the segregation in Detroit. He knew about the race riots in his home city during World War II, based in part on a lack of adequate housing for the African-American community. He had written to FDR about these riots, suggesting that the president send him back to his hometown to deal with the situation.[39] He had no taste for the de facto separation in his city, and now on the Supreme Court he had power to hinder the machinery in place to enforce it, which he exercised with his vote.

Following the *Shelley* ruling, restrictive covenants around the country fell almost immediately. In Chicago, on May 6, 1948, a judge dismissed an injunction to enforce a restrictive covenant against two Black couples. The judge left no doubt about the basis for his findings, stating that the Supreme Court decision "was very definite and left no room for argument. Restrictive covenants are at an end."[40]

If only it were that easy. States continued to devise creative ways to thwart residential integration. On July 19, 1949, the date of Frank Murphy's death, right below the story in the *New York Times* containing his obituary, was another article entitled "Stuyvesant Town Negro Ban Upheld by Court of Appeals." New York's highest state court, in a 4–3 decision, ruled that the Metropolitan Life Insurance Company had the right to bar African Americans, in this case three war veterans, from its massive Stuyvesant

Town housing project on the Lower East Side of Manhattan. Notwithstanding *Shelley*, rulings such as *Stuyvesant* had the effect of reinforcing continuing discrimination. Using the power of the state to remove residents in mixed neighborhoods, the federal, state, and local governments funneled resources to segregated housing on that same land.[41] In the New York City case, residences containing Black occupants were cleared to make way for Stuyvesant Town, which did not allow Black people, using insurance company funds. Therefore, federal funds were used to clear Black neighborhoods on valuable Manhattan real estate, replacing them with white-only housing.[42]

In the last three years of his life, Murphy was in and out of hospitals in both Washington, DC, and Detroit. In 1948, Murphy took a five-month "vacation" from the court because of a sciatica condition.[43] On December 7, 1948, the Associated Press reported that he was returning to the bench after a two-month absence after being treated for neuralgia. One doctor report revealed that he was being treated for hyperthyroidism, which could cause heart issues.

In an interview in 1965, Justice Douglas recounted some of his experiences with Murphy during those final years. Murphy often massaged his hands when sitting in conferences, Douglas recalled, "flexing his fingers and rubbing his hands because they were feeling numb. Frankfurter would make fun of him about this, mimicking him behind his back."[44] Most likely, Murphy was suffering from Buerger's disease, in which blood vessels become inflamed and can become blocked with blood clots (thrombi).

Sidney Fine emphasized Murphy's playful exchanges with the other Supreme Court justices while he was in a hospital in Detroit. The banter is jarring when read today, especially coming from men who reliably tried to extend rights and freedoms to the traditionally dispossessed. In one note, Rutledge wrote to Murphy about a woman they had all noticed in the gallery: "The raven-haired one continues to be absent." Justice Douglas added to the note, "And a damn good looking colored girl looks hungrily at the vacant chair on Wiley's left."[45] Rutledge urged Murphy not to forget "old and long attachments" and to return to the court even though surrounded by "beautiful nurses and basking in their adulation."[46] Responding in kind, Murphy wrote to the two justices while he was in the Ford Hospital during the fall of 1948 that the prospect of his departure created "pandemonium among the nurses. Why the line-up is all the way around the block to give me a rub I don't know."[47] These words are hard to read today, especially coming from a man largely viewed as being ahead of his times, both socially and politically. He *was* ahead of his time in identifying *racism* as the defining feature that sent Japanese Americans to internment camps and that kept discriminatory housing practices and Jim Crow laws in existence, when others of his time did not necessarily identify these acts as racist.

But as this exchange shows, Murphy was very much a product of his time, with his use or acceptance of the use of the word *girl* for woman—particularly a Black woman—and the comments about women generally. It will also be recalled that he referred to Japanese as "Japs" and considered all Germans to be "savages." Historians have often forgiven the private acts of powerful men, as long as their public actions were progressive.

Now in 1949, a few weeks from his own death, Murphy sounded confident about his prospects. He told a newspaper reporter, "They say I'm sick. But feel that muscle. They can't keep a man like me down."[48]

He was taking steps to hide his obvious decline. During his last hospital stay, he entered the hospital under the name "Francis Williams," a return to his birth name but one that might not be recognized by the press.[49]

Frank made his last public appearance at the Supper Club in Detroit early Monday evening, July 18, 1949. He was instantly recognized, and the owners, known as the four Dukes, escorted him and his nurse to a side booth. There, they quietly sang him songs. "I don't know when I've felt so relaxed," he said as he left a half hour later.[50]

Murphy died the next day. His brother George was at his side, the siblings linked to the end. George had been not only a friend but a trusted advisor. Frank had consulted George on many important matters, including the great sit-down strikes of 1937, when George had conveyed messages on Frank's behalf, and also accompanied him to Washington, DC, to discuss matters with administration officials such as Secretary of Labor Frances Perkins.[51]

And Frank in turn looked out for George, advancing his career. Frank was the instinctive politician who thrived on public attention and had dramatic methods of attracting it, while George avoided the limelight. When George first ran for a position on the Recorder's Court, he never publicized his candidacy. Frank stepped in to promote his brother's run, cabling from Manila to give journalists news about his brother. One journalist who observed George as a criminal court judge found that he dispensed justice "according to Hoyle" (i.e., per the rules) but went out of his way "in almost a saintly fashion" to give "every possible break to the down and out derelicts who appeared before him."[52] This echoed his brother's tenure on the criminal court, both eager to provide mercy when possible. George survived the longest of the Murphy siblings, dying in 1961.[53] Their sister Marguerite lived another nine years, passing away in 1958.[54]

In his last years, Murphy had large expenses. These included his own large medical bills and payments to family members dependent on his largesse. His brother George announced that Frank was "penniless" upon his death, and this was close to the truth.[55] In fact, he died with some money, about $2,000 in his bank account (of which $1,600 was owed to the hotel he was living in).[56]

Murphy received tributes from important people upon his death. President Truman sent a telegram of condolence to his brother George. The House of Representatives issued a proclamation and then stood adjourned thereafter as a sign of respect.[57]

Chief Justice Fred Vinson alluded to Murphy's prior health problems in his own statement, reflecting, "A courageous fight comes to an end. For months, Justice Murphy walked in the great shadow—unafraid. Even so his death is a great shock to me."[58]

Drew Pearson was a noted Washington, DC insider and news-paper columnist. He had met Murphy during the sit-down strikes in 1937 and became a frequent Murphy promoter through the years. He was crushed by Murphy's death. In a column memo-rializing Murphy, he fondly recalled Murphy's quirks and tre-mendous work ethic but was most taken by Murphy's efforts as champion of the "little people."[59]

Local Thumb newspapers, always complimentary about Murphy, now described him in hagiographic terms: "Frank Murphy has never loafed. Of him it has been said that no other man in American history has occupied as many important positions."[60]

Murphy's family saw no incongruity in asking Father Coughlin to speak at the funeral services. To them, a genuine friendship thrived, even as Coughlin moved away from Murphy's views and started to espouse anti-Semitic and anti-Roosevelt views to his millions of followers on his radio program. Murphy and Coughlin had met before either was famous. Coughlin was close enough to Murphy that he stayed with him in Murphy's hotel suite in New York during the Detroit banking crisis in 1933 when they learned together that Michigan's governor was closing all the banks in the state. In connection with the eulogy, however, Coughlin begged off, stating he had other commitments.

The funeral service itself was in the Catholic tradition. At the ceremony, the Reverend James Marvin applauded the "Christian spirit" in Murphy's Supreme Court opinions.[61] By all accounts, Murphy had been sincere in his religious beliefs. In a postcard to Joan from 1946, Murphy described a visit to Jerusalem and Bethlehem and the Christian religious sites in the Holy Land as "probably the greatest" day of his life. He "wished" she was with him.[62] His local priest recalled that Murphy would stay for more prayers after the other parishioners had gone their sepa-rate ways after mass.[63] "[T]he first thing friends usually men-tioned in describing the red haired, bachelor Murphy was his piety. He attended mass regularly and read daily the old Bible that his mother gave him when he graduated from high school in 1908."[64] That Bible had been falling apart, and he eventually tied it together with strings.[65]

Among those visiting Murphy's body was Joan Cuddihy. During her visit, George gave her the engagement ring that Frank had planned to give her that very week.[66] In a 1967 article, Bumgardner asserted that Murphy was secretly engaged to Cuddihy at the time of his death.[67]

President Franklin Roosevelt's desire to pack the court back in 1938 tainted all his subsequent appointees to the High Tribunal, and some words to this effect were published about Murphy. The perception was that FDR would stop at nothing to impose his views on the country, and his candidates were chosen for their fealty. Murphy often parted ways from Roosevelt, as exemplified in his *Korematsu* dissent. Nevertheless, upon Murphy's death in 1949, many would call for Truman to change course from past practice and now actually appoint a merit-based, independent justice.

What is clear is that Truman disappointed these good government types by choosing his Attorney General Tom C. Clark to be the successor justice to Murphy. Clark was a friend of Truman, but with few other qualifications.[68] And, although not a consideration at the time, it is an ironic fact that Murphy, a champion of the rights of Japanese Americans, was replaced on the Supreme Court by a man instrumental in carrying out the policies resulting in their expulsion.

In the final analysis, Murphy always spoke the truth, even to his most fervent admirers. During World War II, he advised workers to put the war effort first. The workers had significant leverage in extracting benefits from management and the federal government during this time of total war—they were producing the bombs and tanks necessary to support the troops. Further, based on their experiences during World War I, they had reason to believe the industrialists were getting rich while they were sacrificing.

Yet, Murphy urged cooperation between management and labor as a patriotic duty. "Labor," he said, "is not now fighting for the God-given right of collective bargaining but for the right to exist. If the Nazis win we will have an economy handed down from Berlin. All civil liberties will disappear—the legal system, the Constitution, Congress and the Supreme Court will perish."[69] The war against the fascist powers was a fight to the death, and labor had to wait to claim its gains until peace was restored.

Through it all, the workers knew Murphy was on their side. As noted at the beginning of the book, workers flocked to view his body and pay their respects. Laborers fashioned their own ad hoc tributes. At a Dodge plant in Michigan, workers stopped the assembly lines for five minutes on the day of Murphy's funeral. In retaliation, the company docked each man 15 cents' pay for the five-minute stoppage. Then, as a final tribute to Murphy, those workers went on strike to protest the docking of their pay. It was noted in contemporary newspapers that those same workers only gave FDR a two-minute tribute upon his death.[70]

Outside the Frank Murphy Hall of Justice, home to Detroit's criminal court, is Carl Milles's statue "The Hand of God," financed by the UAW. The UAW's commissioning of a statue was a recognition of Murphy's efforts to help unions. And the UAW had reason to be especially grateful. Murphy had chosen the UAW over others during the sit-down strikes of 1937, thereby virtually assuring it would be the union of choice for auto workers.[71]

Endnotes

1. This assumes an annual inflation rate of 3.64 percent between 1945 and 2019.

2. Thomas Brady to Eleanor Bumgardner, May 14, 1947, FMP, reel 87 (Brady was Murphy's publicist and he sent checks for speaking engagements). Supreme Court Justices today receive payments outside their jobs on book sales. Furthermore, their spouses may be involved in certain industries with business before the Supreme Court. In this regard, they are exempt from the rules that apply to all other members of the judiciary, https://www.uscourts.gov/rules-policies/judiciary-policies/code-conduct/outside-earned-income-honoraria-and-employment. The Editorial Board, "Justices' Junkets: Our View," *USA Today*, Mar. 7, 2016, accessed Apr. 19, 2020, https://publicintegrity.org/federal-politics/supreme-court-justices-earn-quarter-million-in-cash-on-the-side/.

3. FM to Joan Cuddihy, Apr. 15, 1946 (lamb reference); FM to Joan Cuddihy, March 21, 1946 (poem); St. Patrick's Dday card (probably 1946), JC, Correspondence from Frank Murphy.

4. Wiley Rutledge to Joan Cuddihy, July 6, 1947, JC, Correspondence from friends and Murphy family 1945–1972. The telegram was found in Joan's files and so it is likely Murphy gave it to her. The age reference was a joke. Murphy was in his late 50s at the time.

5. William Douglas to Frank Murphy, year unknown but on or around Murphy's birthday, JC, Correspondence from friends and Murphy family 1945–1972 (capitals and lack of punctuation in the original).

6. "Murphy Eulogizes Roosevelt Ideals," *NYT*, Apr. 13, 1946.

7. Harry S Truman daily calendar, Friday, Oct. 18, 1946 (allocating 15 minutes for Murphy to discuss his trip to visit the Pope and the Irish prime minister), Truman Library, Calendar, accessed Apr. 19, 2020, https://www.trumanlibrary.gov/library/appointment-calendar/1946-10-18t111500. Éamon de Valera had urged neutrality for the Irish Republic during World War II. Murphy was able to maintain a cordial relationship with de Valera, like Father Coughlin, despite this person's starkly different, and in certain cases abhorrent, political views. After Hitler's death, de Valera, accompanied by his secretary of external affairs, Joseph Walshe, called on Dr. Hempel, the German minister, to express his condolences. This move outraged many in the United States government.

8. Hartmann, *The Kansas City Investigation*, "Political Glamor Boys Dewey and Murphy Compete for Crime-Busting Honors," *Life Magazine*, July 31, 1939, 18.

9. David McCullough, *Truman* (New York: Simon & Schuster, 1992), 235–240.

10. Photograph, Frank Murphy with President Harry Truman, Sept. 6, 1948 (courtesy of Harry S Truman Presidential Library and Museum).

11. Eugene Gressman, Oct. 21, 1964, transcript of interview conducted by Sidney Fine and Robert M. Warner, Frank Murphy Oral History Project, FMP, pp. 15, 20.

12. *MacDougall v. Green*, 335 U.S. 281 (1948).

13. Nick Stewart-Bloch, "From Cooperative Commonwealth to Yardstick Capitalism," *Minnesota Historical Society Press*, Spring 2018, collections.mnhs.org/MNHistoryMagazine/articles/.../v66i01p6-19.pdf.

14. *MacDougal*, 335 U.S. at 281.

15. Ibid at 288.

16. "Justice Murphy of Supreme Court Dies," *NYT*, July 20, 1949.

17. "Roosevelt Is Put on the Illinois Ballot, Board Waives Oral Arguments and Acts despite Protest by Lieut. Gov. Stelle," *NYT*, Mar. 3, 1940, 1, 40.

18. Frank Murphy to Eleanor Bumgardner, undated but at 1:40 PM. (When writing of the death of Murphy's brother-in-law Raymond Byrne, Murphy related to her, "And since he and my sister are so very close to me, I am deeply shocked and terribly grieved." He signed off, "Love, Frank.") This author has been unable to identify Raymond Byrne's connection to Murphy. Murphy had only one sister, Marguerite, and she was married to William Teahan.

19. Sanger Williams to Frank Murphy, May 21, 1947, FMP, reel 87. The reference to Williams being the chauffeur was in the article previously cited, "A Confidential Secretary Recalls: My 16 Years with Frank Murphy," *DFP*, Sept. 10, 1967, 140.

20. Eugene Gressman et al., *Supreme Court Practice: For Practice in the Supreme Court of the United States*, 9th ed. His name came off the 10th and 11th editions.

21. Fine, *Washington Years*, 163.

22.   Eugene Gressman, "Mr. Justice Murphy—A Preliminary Appraisal," *Columbia Law Review* 50 (1950): 29. Gressman was a rousing apologist for Murphy. In the first paragraph of this *Columbia Law Review* article, he described the recently deceased Murphy as follows: "History has not yet had time to record her mature, detached judgment of his judicial career. Yet even a preliminary appraisal of his nine and a half years on the high bench reveals a significant and lasting legacy to our law. It is a legacy both pragmatic and idealistic, a legacy grounded on the proposition that the law need not and should not ignore the spiritual dignity of the individual."

23.   Coronary thrombosis is a type of heart disease, in which the blood flow to the heart is restricted and is often caused by a sedentary lifestyle or smoking. The term was also a bit of a catch-all diagnosis. Murphy had an active lifestyle and did not smoke. But Murphy had circulation issues and often rubbed his hands to increase the flow of blood.

24.   "Murphy Flies to Detroit for Brother's Rites," *DFP*, Oct. 22, 1946, 7; "Brother of Justice Frank Murphy Dies," *ESP*, Oct. 22, 1946, 14.

25.   "Kin of Frank Murphy Is Divorced by Wife," *LSJ*, June 11, 1936, 11.

26.   FM to Joan Cuddihy, Oct. 1, 1946, JC, Correspondence from Frank Murphy.

27.   Thurgood Marshall targeted segregated law schools throughout the South. United Press, "Negroes Seeking to Be Enrolled at Chapel Hill Unit," *Statesville Daily Record* (Statesville, North Carolina), Aug. 30, 1950, 1 (efforts to desegregate University of North Carolina Law School).

28.   *Sipuel v. Board of Regents of University of Oklahoma*, 332 U.S. 631 (1948).

29.   Fisher, *A Matter of Black and White*, 129–130.

30.   Dennis J. Hutchinson, "Unanimity and Desegregation: Decisionmaking in the Supreme Court, 1948–1958," *Georgia Law Journal* 68 (1980): 1–7.

31.   Fisher, *A Matter of Black and White*, 126.

32.   *Fisher v. Hurst*, 333 U.S. 147, 150 (1948) ("The only question before us on this petition for a writ of mandamus is whether or not our mandate has been followed. It is clear that the District Court of Cleveland County did not depart from our mandate.").

33.   Ibid at 151.

34.   Fisher, *A Matter of Black and White*, 145–146.

35.   *Shelley v. Kraemer*, 334 U.S. 1 (1948).

36.   Ibid 63 at 5.

37.   Ibid at 19.

38.   Ibid at 5.

39.   Frank Murphy to FDR, FDRL, Box 166, PSF, Supreme Court, 1938–1944 (referring to race riots in Detroit).

40.   Associated Press, "Restrictive Covenant Injunction Dismissed," *TNP*, May 6, 1948, 20.

41.   "Stuyvesant Town Ban on Negroes Upheld by State Court of Appeals," *NYT*, July 20, 1949.

42.   Richard Rothstein, in his book *The Color Of Law* detailed these kinds of "one-two" punches (clearing of Black neighbors and replacing them with white neighborhoods funded directly or indirectly by the Federal Housing Authority) were common in the 1940s and 1950s.

43.   Obituary, Frank Murphy, *NYT*, July 20, 1949.

44. William O. Douglas, Oct. 22, 1964, transcript of interview conducted by Sidney Fine and Robert M. Warner, Frank Murphy Oral History Project, FMP (describing the symptoms he observed).

45. Fine, *Washington Years,* 483-484.

46. Ibid.

47. Ibid.

48. Drew Pearson, "Merry-Go-Round," *Florence Morning News* (Florence, South Carolina), July 23, 1949, 4.

49. Article fragment, *Traverse City Record-Eagle,* July 19, 1949, 1.

50. Mark Beltaire, "Frank Murphy's Last Autograph," *DFP,* 28.

51. "Murphy to Consult Labor Secretary," *Baltimore Sun,* Jan. 19, 1937, 7 (photograph with the caption "Accompanied by his brother, the Chief Executive of Michigan leaves for Washington to conference with Miss Frances Perkins, Secretary of Labor, regarding the new deadlock in the General Motors-United Automobile Workers of America strike negotiations").

52. Jack Manning, "George Murphy, Quiet and Kindly Friend to Man," *DFP,* July 14, 1961, 6.

53. Ibid.

54. "Mrs. Teahan Dies in Windsor," *DFP,* Feb. 2, 1958, 23.

55. "Murphy 'Penniless' His Brother Reveals," *NYT,* July 27, 1949, 28.

56. Fine, *Washington Years,* 480.

57. The Proclamation of the House of Representatives, July 19, 1949, FMM.

58. "President Sends Tribute to Family; Truman Calls Murphy 'Great Civic Leader'—Colleagues in Capital Also Laud Him," *NYT,* July 19, 1949.

59. Drew Pearson, "Washington Merry-Go-Round," July 23, 1949 (reprinted in *Florence Morning News,* Florence, South Carolina).

60. Arthur Tholen, "Murphy Between Jobs," *TTH,* Sept. 21, 1942.

61. "Murphy is Buried at Scene of Youth," *NYT,* July 23, 1949, 11.

62. FM to Joan Cuddihy, Aug. 14, 1946, JC, Correspondence from Frank Murphy.

63. "Murphy Laid to Rest with Simple Rights," *DFP,* July 23, 1949, 10.

64. "Murphy Dies," *TNP,* July 19, 1949.

65. FDRL, Ernest Cuneo Papers, Box 105, Frank Murphy File.

66. United Press, "Report Murphy Planned to Wed Joan Cuddihy," *DN,* July 24, 1949.

67. "A Confidential Secretary Recalls: My 16 Years with Frank Murphy," *DFP,* Sept. 10, 1967, 140.

68. McCullough, *Truman,* 742 (describing Clark's appointment as Supreme Court justice without mentioning that he replaced Murphy).

69. "Murphy Sees Large U.S. Production Front," *The Herald Press* (St. Joseph, Michigan), Sept. 29, 1942.

70. "Frank Murphy Tribute Stirs Dodge Strike," *DFP,* Aug. 6, 1949, p. 1.

71. Walter Reuther and Murphy's friend Ira W. Jayne supervised the selection of the sculpture. It is the last work of the famous Swedish sculptor, Carl Milles who, for years, had been the sculptor in residence at the Cranbrook Institution in Bloomfield Hills. "Sites Studied for Murphy Statue," *DFP,* Jan. 16, 1959, 25.

CHAPTER 20

Conclusions

Murphy was born in 1890, on the cusp of the "American Century." The United States underwent dramatic changes during his life. The American brand of democracy had survived the shocks of the Great Depression and World War II and had emerged as a model for the world. And Detroit had grown from a backwater to a giant city of 1.6 million, a lively hub of great industry, wealth, and innovation.

The United States might have veered in directions that would have made the country a far different place for its citizens in the twenty-first century. It could have become more authoritarian; been less focused on universal education, science, and infrastructure; and had fewer safety nets for the poor, the unhealthy, and the dispossessed. Frank Murphy and others like him saved us from that fate, and we benefit to this day. His career as a politician was notable for his desire to uplift the truly destitute at a time when government was not yet seen as the protector and provider of those in need. He and others like him paved the way for FDR, who regularized a federal response for the poor, elderly, and those in need of assistance between jobs.

Murphy believed that an enlightened society was able to tolerate fringe views without the need to suppress them. As a Supreme Court justice, he seemed to go out of his way to defend unpopular groups from attack. In the case of *West Virginia State Board of Education v. Barnette*,[1] the High Court overturned a public school regulation making it mandatory to salute the flag. While agreeing with the result, Murphy wrote his own opinion:

> Any spark of love for country which may be generated in a child or his associates by forcing him to make what is to him an empty gesture and recite words wrung from him contrary to his religious beliefs is overshadowed by the desirability of preserving freedom of conscience to the full. It is in that freedom and the example of persuasion, not in force and compulsion, that the real unity of America lies.[2]

America, he was saying, could always survive dissent and different opinions. This was a defining strength of the United States and a reason why democracy could compete and prevail over other political systems. Each person can act with freedom, activating his or her potential, unlike in other countries. Through the clash and cacophony of this immigrant nation, and through persuasion and not coercion, the United States could fulfill its destiny as an entirely new society—dynamic, egalitarian, and with each person having value and adding value to the whole.

The American dream did not always meet reality. Throughout Murphy's life, the United States remained a place of great inequalities and unfairness. The country suffered from deep racial divisions. In addition, the country struggled with a growing economic gap between the rich and the poor. In a speech in 1937 before the Consumer League in New York City, Murphy identified "economic injustice and gross inequality" as the largest threat to American ideals, greater than the aggressive ideologies of foreign powers. "For where there is deprivation of the necessities of life—where there is exploitation of the downtrodden—there unmistakably lie the seeds of disruption and rebellion," Murphy said. "There are bred the forces which, if permitted to gain momentum, will steadily undermine democracy from within."[3] His words ring true today.

If Murphy had survived to the age of 79 instead of 59, he would have lived through the civil rights era as a member of the Supreme Court. Whenever *Brown v. Board of Education* is taught today, the reference is usually to the 1954 case (*Brown I*), with its high-minded language about ending "separate but equal" public education in the South.[4] But the ruling did not magically cure all ills. It became immediately clear after *Brown I* that many in the South had no intention of voluntarily desegregating. Within one year, the NAACP, whose lawyers had won *Brown I*, again placed the matter before the Supreme Court, arguing that school desegregation should begin right away. The states countered that doing so would be too difficult and too expensive, and that they needed more time to desegregate.

We know what happened without Murphy on the High Court. In *Brown II* in 1955, the Supreme Court, again in a unanimous ruling, directed the federal lower courts in the South "to take such proceedings and enter such orders and decrees consistent with this opinion as are necessary and proper to admit to public schools on a racially nondiscriminatory basis with all deliberate speed the parties to these cases."[5]

The language "all deliberate speed" is famous but open to interpretation and abuse. For example, based on the *Brown II* ruling, a federal district (trial level) court ruled that Prince Edward County, Virginia, did not have to desegregate its schools right away. In 1959, without much speed, a federal court of appeals acted and ordered the county to start desegregating its schools. Prince Edward County responded by refusing to fund the county's public schools. With no money, the public schools had to close. And they stayed closed for five years, from 1959 to 1964. The white students were funneled to white-only private schools. Black students generally could not go to school at all, unless they moved to a different county. Finally, in 1964, the United States Supreme Court ruled that what Prince Edward County was doing was unconstitutional, and ordered the schools to reopen—10 years after *Brown I*.

Justice Hugo Black, the former KKK member, penned the majority decision requiring the Prince Edward public schools to reopen.[6] He was now seen by many in the South as a traitor for opinions like this one. If Murphy had survived to weigh in, he—without question—would have lent his support to Black. But Justice Clark, Murphy's replacement on the High Court, proved less concerned. He and Justice John Harlan, an Eisenhower appointee, both "disagree[ed] with the holding that the federal courts are empowered to order the reopening of the public schools in Prince Edward County."[7]

If Murphy had lived into the 1950s, one can imagine that he would have signed on to *Brown I*. But one could also imagine his outrage when Thurgood Marshall appeared before the Court in *Brown II* one year later to report that nothing much had changed in the South. The word *racism*, noticeably absent in both *Brown I* and *Brown II*, with the evident intent of not antagonizing segregationists, might well have appeared in a Murphy dissent or concurrence when he realized that the South was engaging in a "slow roll" in implementing integration.

Murphy was unafraid to use language that seemed shocking to many when he felt it was necessary. On that day in 1944, Murphy used the word *racism* or its variant in three decisions. The first two related to the Japanese-American internments—*Korematsu* and *Endo*. But the third case was unrelated. In *Steele v. Louisville & N.R. Co.*,[8] the Supreme Court interpreted the Railway Labor Act (RLA), which allowed for the formation of unions in the railway industry. Before the court were the practices of a union local, which excluded Black people from its ranks. This local had been recognized as the official bargaining unit with its employer by the federal government under the RLA,[9] a problematic reality because of the racist exclusion of Black people. That particular issue, however, was not before the Supreme Court. Instead, before the High Tribunal was the issue of whether the white union leaders, recognized as the collective bargaining unit for all the workers, could legally agree to a contract that provided for the layoffs or demotions of Black employees before white employees.

The Supreme Court, to its credit, unanimously said no, condemning the practice. But Justice Stone, writing for the majority in *Steele*, did not ground his decision on the obvious racial dimension of the local union's exclusion of African Americans from its ranks. His use of the word *minority* in his opinion did not refer to Black people but more broadly to those who were excluded from the decision-making process of the union. A union that does not consider the point of view of all in the bargaining unit, whether

African American or members of a knitting club, is violating its duties to the entire group.

Stone's ruling did not specifically require the union local to change its rules to accept African Americans as members or to renegotiate its contract. Instead, "in collective bargaining and in making contracts with the carrier," the union needed to "represent nonunion or minority union members of the craft without hostile discrimination, fairly, impartially, and in good faith." If the union refused to act in this way, "the statute contemplates resort to the usual judicial remedies of injunction and award of damages when appropriate for breach of that duty."[10]

The court was unanimous in its decision that the union had acted improperly, and Murphy could have simply signed on. But he found the rationale of the majority to be lacking. This was all about discrimination against African Americans and not a more abstract definitional debate on "minority" rights. He wrote, "While such a union is essentially a private organization, its power to represent and bind all members of a class or craft is derived solely from Congress [through the RLA]." Therefore, the government had to act when the private organization did not follow the law. He acknowledged that the act contained no language directing the manner by which the union should perform its duties: "But it cannot be assumed that Congress meant to authorize the representative to act so as to ignore rights guaranteed by the Constitution. Otherwise the Act would bear the stigma of unconstitutionality under the Fifth Amendment in this respect."[11]

Murphy continued, "The utter disregard for the dignity and well-being of colored citizens shown by this record is so pronounced as to demand the invocation of constitutional condemnation."[12] Using a metaphor he would employ in two later decisions,[13] he referred to the "cloak of racism" that surrounded "the actions of the Brotherhood in refusing membership to Negroes and in entering into and enforcing agreements discriminating against them, all under the guise of Congressional authority, still remains."[14]

To Murphy, the union's actions were nothing less than an "ugly" example of "economic cruelty against colored citizens" of the United States: "Nothing can destroy the fact that the accident of birth has been used as the basis to abuse individual rights by an organization purporting to act in conformity with its Congressional mandate."[15] His separate opinions by now were marked by their fiery moral tone:

> The Constitution voices its disapproval whenever economic discrimination is applied under authority of law against any race, creed, or color. A sound democracy cannot allow such discrimination to go unchallenged. Racism is far too virulent today to permit the slightest refusal, in the light of a Constitution that abhors it, to expose and condemn it wherever it appears in the course of a statutory interpretation.[16]

Murphy prided himself on abiding by his principles. But as we have seen, his behavior was not always true in that regard. More often than not, he took positions that inflicted pain on allies and friends if he believed they were not meeting his expectations. He did not have to call a union "racist" in *Steele*.

The dictionary meaning in the American Heritage College Dictionary of *racism* is "the belief that race accounts for differences in human character or ability and that a particular race is superior to others" and "discrimination or prejudice based on race." As early as 1970, the U.S. Commission on Civil Rights defined racism as "any attitude, action, or institutional structure which subordinates a person or group because of his or their color."[17] In this way, Murphy's decision and words wore well, as his definition of racism aligned with the understanding of most Americans today regardless of political stripe.

It is not a coincidence that his words conform to our modern sense and is a powerful sign that Murphy was ahead of his time. More than this, Murphy helped to pave the road to the modern era by using these words that seemed so extreme to societal elites at the time. In doing so, he made them less extreme and more mainstream.

Murphy had higher ambitions than the Supreme Court. In spite of this, he never declared himself as a presidential candidate. This was partly because of his loyalty to FDR, who ran for president four times. There was never room for a serious Murphy run. But had FDR, in 1939, instead declared his intention to honor the two-term limitation dating back to the time of George Washington,[18] he would now have to consider his successor. Roosevelt would have wanted to protect his New Deal legacy, and few politicians at the time were more strongly associated to New Deal policies than Murphy. Murphy's reputation with FDR was at a high point in the late 1930s. Yes, Murphy had just lost his gubernatorial race, but he had secured a heroic status with labor unions for his work in defusing the strikes in Michigan. Murphy also retained the respect of other constituencies within the Democratic Party, most notably Catholics, women's groups, and African Americans. And his political career had been resurrected as Roosevelt's Attorney General.

Polls at the time placed Murphy in the mix of possible successors for FDR. An admitted partisan of Murphy, Eugene Gressman, claimed that Murphy was one of Roosevelt's three top choices to succeed him had he not run for a third term.[19] Gressman heard this third hand, stating that Murphy had heard this from Jim Farley. But Murphy did check numerous boxes for FDR, appealing as he did to various Democratic interest groups.

The "what ifs" can continue. How would Murphy have performed as president? Murphy had significant relevant executive experience. He was the mayor of Detroit, the top appointed United States official in the Philippines, and the governor of Michigan. He was lauded for his non-political, competent picks.

His creativity and energy in his executive roles have been downplayed. Many believed he was an indifferent administrator as an attorney general. As already discussed, these charges were in part political, based on Murphy's attacks on certain entrenched Democratic interests and his creation of a civil rights division. But Murphy was the mayor of a city that had a larger population than Florida at the time. He was the governor of a consequential state. Perhaps most impressively, he was at the helm as a governor general when the Philippines became a commonwealth. The turnover of power from the United States to local authorities was peaceful and celebrated in a joyous ceremony attended by hundreds of thousands. One only need look at the wrenching partitions and civil wars in most other areas of the world that followed colonial rule to know that events in the Philippines could have had a different ending.

As president of the United States, Murphy probably would have been an able administrator, delegating to highly qualified subordinates. But how would Murphy have performed as a "motivator in chief"? We know that Roosevelt masterfully steered the country, ensuring it was prepared not just in terms of manpower and material but also in maintaining morale. FDR recognized the fascist threat early on and did what he could to evade the Neutrality Act. In this regard, Murphy was also ahead of his time in identifying Nazi aggression. And he accurately assessed the immense military power of the Japanese Empire in the Pacific, disagreeing with General MacArthur that the United States could protect the Philippines in the event of a Japanese invasion.

In August 1941, the summer before the attack on Pearl Harbor, the country was divided on whether the United States should take sides in the conflicts raging in Europe and Asia. Murphy, now a Supreme Court justice, gave a speech to the Knights of Columbus in Atlantic City, New Jersey. He told the assemblage of 1,500 delegates of this Catholic group that they should affirmatively support the Soviet Union over Germany: "For men and women who cherish freedom of religion and other fundamentals of democratic rule, there is little to choose between the Communism of Russia and the Nazism of Germany. We want neither in our country." [20] He continued, "But we know that Nazism, with its superior competence and perverted intelligence . . . and its profound belief in racial superiority . . . is by far the greater menace to free nations and free institutions."[21]

This was *Realpolitik* at its core. In this regard, his views completely aligned with those of FDR, with his reluctant embrace of the USSR, itself a dictatorship, to defeat the greater evil. This ability to sacrifice the perfect for the good, to seek a moderate course, was a Murphy trait throughout his career. At all times, his goal was to protect the rule of law and the primacy of individual liberty in the United States—and he believed the Nazis were the more immediate threat.

With the success of the Normandy invasion, the Axis powers faced defeat, so FDR turned his attention to affairs after the war. In Roosevelt's State of the Union address on January 11, 1944—the last he delivered directly to Congress—he called for a "Second Bill of Rights." FDR argued that the "political rights" guaranteed by the Constitution and the Bill of Rights had "proved inadequate to assure us equality in the pursuit of happiness." His remedy was to declare an "economic bill of rights."[22] These included employment (right to work), food, clothing, and leisure—with enough income to support them; farmers' rights to a fair income; freedom from unfair competition and monopolies; housing; medical care; and social security.[23]

FDR was describing "positive" rights, or rights that the government would guarantee rather than promise not to impose upon. Murphy agreed with this approach. In a speech before an Irish-American group in 1937, Murphy decried the fact that, according to a Brookings Institution report, "Even during the prosperous boom year of 1929 . . . 21 percent of American families had incomes under $1,000, or about $84 a month. In the same year, 26,000 families at the top of the income scale had a total income equal to that of the 11,000,000 at the bottom of the scale." It was now the job of a "kindly, humane government" to provide "every family an annual wage on a fair, just basis."[24] For Murphy, as with FDR, the Constitution was the starting point, but not the end. To them, it was a living document, necessarily adapting to the realities of a country that was now an industrial giant with growing inequalities.

President Eisenhower famously feared the power of the "military-industrial complex" and its influence on the country's economic and political system. Murphy expressed similar sentiments years earlier. At the conclusion of World War II, Murphy proclaimed that the "supremacy of the civil over the military is one of our great heritages. It has made possible the attainment of a high degree of liberty regulated by law, rather than by caprice. Our duty is to give effect to that heritage at all times, that it may be handed down untarnished to future generations."[25] Eisenhower was focused on institutions, while Murphy was always more focused on individuals and their freedoms. Both were worried about the implications of a powerful military, which seems normal to us today but was a new phenomenon after World War II.

Intriguingly, as the wartime president, Murphy would have had to consider the evacuation of Japanese Americans from the West Coast. One can see him delaying the decision to act, hoping the growing hysteria against Japanese Americans might dissipate once people realized that this group was not a fifth column and had not engaged in sabotage. He had a flair for the dramatic and might have met with Japanese-American servicemen in the White House to influence public opinion and dampen the hysteria. Notwithstanding his choirboy image, he was willing to bend the rules to achieve his goals. When Murphy was governor during the sit-down strikes in Flint, he received a court order that was unambiguous in its direction to forcibly remove the strikers. He refused to enforce the order, fearing bloodshed. He gambled that he would reach a global labor resolution in the meantime, and his gamble paid off. In the same way, as president during World War II (or at least as the secretary of war, a position he coveted once the prospects of the presidency slipped his grasp),[26] Murphy might have delayed the implementation of legislation requiring him to remove Japanese Americans from the West Coast.

Was the country ready for a Catholic president, twenty years before Kennedy? If Murphy had the opportunity to run for president, he certainly would have faced anti-Catholic fervor, but he knew how to minimize fear. He followed Alfred Smith's run for president, with his clever deflection of the issue. Smith did lose badly against Hoover, but he also ran during a roaring economy, and before certain voting groups like Blacks and farmers had turned to the Democrats.

John F. Kennedy, the first Catholic president, famously proclaimed, "I am not the Catholic candidate for president. I am the Democratic party's candidate for president, who happens also to be a Catholic. I do not speak for my church on public matters, and the church does not speak for me."[27] Kennedy was theistic in his inaugural address, avoiding all mention of Jesus, and instead opting for a quote from Isaiah, the same biblical prophet that Murphy's mother had underlined in his Bible. Said President Kennedy, "Let both sides unite to heed in all corners of the earth the command of Isaiah—to 'undo the heavy burdens . . . and to let the oppressed go free.'"[28]

At least when not speaking to Catholic groups, Murphy generally avoided mentioning specific Catholic doctrines in speeches to the general public, and this may have made him seem less threatening. At a conference in 1937, while he was governor of Michigan, Murphy pointed to the Sermon on the Mount as being the most basic of Christian teachings. In paraphrasing Jesus, he said, "Christian essence is not to be found in beliefs about God . . . but in living as the disciples who in his name feed the hungry, heal the sick and create justice in the world." According to Murphy, the "imperishable splendor" of Christ's life is the fact that "[h]e lived solely to help others, not to help himself."[29] This statement could have been uttered in a church of any branch of Christianity. And, when Murphy was discussing Saint Patrick, he described his attributes in general terms, quoting an Irish poet, "Wrong and injustice to the poor he resented as an injury to God."[30]

Murphy remained a bachelor his entire life. His sexual orientation has been the subject of some fascination and speculation, particularly over the last 20 years. Edward Kemp is his most likely partner in any same-sex relationship. The two were lifetime companions from their college years until Murphy's death. At times, they were roommates. Sidney Fine, Murphy's great biographer, knew of the speculation that Murphy was gay. He wrote about the rumors in the third volume of his Frank Murphy trilogy. He certainly had the means to obtain the answer, with his encyclopedic knowledge of the man, and his countless interviews of people who knew Murphy. Yet, he publicly drew no conclusions.

Some avenues of inquiry in this regard do remain unexplored. Like Frank, his brother George was elected as a local criminal judge in Detroit. Both George and Frank would have heard crimi-nal cases involving gays or lesbians, arrested under a variety of laws, including loitering and lewd and indecent behavior. Did the brothers handle crimes associated with homosexuality harshly or leniently? Some review of how they treated these crimes is theo-retically possible by examining records at the Recorder's Office. But in the end, the utility of such a review is limited. Assuming it can be found that they treated men more harshly than other simi-lar criminal judges under these laws, this could mean they have a bias against those labeled homosexuals, or it could simply mean they were covering their tracks.

What is not emphasized enough in these debates about Murphy's sexual orientation is Murphy's long-term relationships with eligible women. Their letters back and forth are filled with innuendo about possible sexual encounters (including the letters with the three Anns). Joan Cuddihy was close to Murphy for the last four years of his life.[31] Although Beulah Young directed him to burn a letter that certainly would have caused a scandal had it became public, Murphy retained it for reasons that were known only to him. Perhaps we can say that he indeed had a forbid-den love, but that this romance was with the married African-American publisher Beulah Young.

Murphy had charisma. People wanted to be around him. In his prime, he was athletic and handsome. He used all the weapons at his disposal, including his sexuality, to capture the attention of those who could help him. He did not discourage women who believed he might commit to them. He probably did not discour-age men either. Although I wanted to provide a definitive answer about Frank Murphy's sexual orientation as part of this biogra-phy, I must concede defeat in this regard.

The idea of a strong national government was an alien concept for much of Murphy's life. Until the New Deal, the federal gov-ernment did not inject itself into such matters as protecting the population from starvation or putting people to work to build infrastructure. It was not seen as a protector of individual rights. The United States as a country was isolationist right up until 1941, with laws on the books restricting immigration and tying the hands of a president desperately seeking ways of getting aid to countries already being crushed by the Nazi menace as America sat on the sidelines. The United States had no army to speak of going into World War II.

As America was transformed into a world superpower in a few short years, Murphy accurately identified many of the ways that a strong federal government could abuse its power—such as when it incarcerated Japanese Americans. But Murphy also discerned the ways a strong federal government could promote civil rights, as when he formed the Civil Rights Division at the Department of Justice, and more generally when he interpreted the Constitution and Amendments in ways to stop states from enforcing Jim Crow and segregation.

Through the years, America has been rocked by various terrorist attacks caused by religious, nationalist, and ethnic extremist groups. When this happens, there are always those who attribute the acts of a few to an entire group and cry out for collective punishment. They take it for granted that the federal government has the power to take decisive action in this regard. Murphy would have required the federal government to leap over substantive and procedural hurdles in showing extreme steps are necessary. During World War II, he was brave enough to point out that Japanese Americans did not engage in acts of sabotage, even as United States service members were dying by the thousands in the Pacific theatre at the hands of the Japanese Empire. If he were alive today, he would ask the same question he presented to his fellow justices and the country in *Korematsu*: "Show me examples of disloyalty." He was confident that such examples would be few and far between. After all, he had faith in the United States to mold its immigrants into citizens.

This country continues to struggle with monumental problems in race relations and income inequality. Murphy would no doubt be surprised at the lack of progress but also quick to note the small victories. The hated "separate but equal" system has disappeared. As I have argued, not only would he have rejoiced in this, but he likely would have been the author of Supreme Court decisions on the subject in the 1950s. He would be happy and excited to hear that people generally have food security in this country, in stark contrast to his time as mayor of Detroit. These gains are fragile and incomplete, but real.

Murphy was generally confident about the sustainability of the American system, with its abilities to harness its resources as necessary while protecting freedoms and its ability to self-correct. He predicted an American victory in World War II at a time when Axis armies were sweeping through Europe and the Japanese Imperial Navy controlled much of the western Pacific.

The American system—as Murphy understood it—has in fact prevailed and spread through much of the world. Many countries now foster internal unity by stressing their own democratic systems and guarantees of freedom of religion, speech, and the press, with an emphasis on privacy and the rights of individuals. This is a tremendous change from 75 years ago, when many of these same countries limited the privileges of citizenship to natives or persons of a particular nationality. Many large (and small) cities in Europe and elsewhere are now dynamic, multicultural, and welcoming of those of different beliefs and faiths, completely different in their worldview from 70 years ago. To be sure, other systems compete as well against the United States model. Some have argued that the United States has forgotten its strengths. But in many ways, the defining virtues of the "new and distinct civilization of the United States" have survived and have now spread far and wide beyond the nation's borders.

Endnotes

1. 319 U.S. 624 (1943).
2. Ibid at 646.
3. Frank Murphy, "Speech before the Consumers League," May 14, 1937, New York, New York, *Murphy Collected Speeches, 1937–1938*.
4. *Brown v. Board of Education*, 347 U.S. 483 (1954). *Brown I* did not explicitly overturn *Plessy v. Ferguson*. The High Court said this: "Whatever may have been the extent of psychological knowledge at the time of *Plessy v. Ferguson*, this finding is amply supported by modern authority. Any language in *Plessy v. Ferguson* contrary to this finding is rejected. We conclude that in the field of public education the doctrine of 'separate but equal' has no place."
5. *Brown v. Board of Education*, 349 U.S. 294, 301 (1955) (what I referred to as *Brown II*).

Justice and Faith: The Frank Murphy Story

6. *Griffin v. County School Board of Prince Edward County*, 377 U.S. 218 (1964).

7. Ibid at 234.

8. *Steele v. Louisville & N.R. Co.*, 323 U.S. 192 (1944).

9. The RLA served as a model for the Wagner Act (otherwise known as the National Labor Relations Act or NLRA) of 1935, which applied more generally to private-sector employees. Both acts derived from the same source, a fear by government and industry that labor unrest might lead to shutdowns of major portions of the economy. Railways were seen as crucial to the nation's health, and so the federal government acted on that threat first—a Republican administration that was otherwise a champion of laissez faire supported the RLA's enactment in 1926. Unions were recognized by the federal government, giving labor legitimacy and a place at the negotiating table, in exchange for restrictions on permissible worker protests.

Section 2 of the RLA states its general purpose is "to avoid any interruption to commerce or to the operation of any carrier engaged therein." By contrast, the NLRA, by its own terms is not explicitly aimed at preserving the flow of commerce, but rather focuses on protecting the right of employees to organize and bargain collectively. Unlike the NLRA, recognitional picketing is not permitted under the RLA and is subject to court injunction.

10. *Steele*, 323 U.S. at 207.

11. Ibid at 208.

12. Ibid.

13. The *cloak* reference in his *Oyama* and *Takahashi* concurrences echoed his use of the word four years before in *Steele*, when he used the same word in condemning the racism displayed against Black union members. The fiery language he deployed in these three cases was distinctly his own style and so also partly answers the cry of later critics that Murphy was lazy and left the drafting of his opinions to others, including his clerks. It is true that Murphy delegated writing responsibility to his clerks and even other justices when he was sick and absent from the Supreme Court for long stretches at the end of his life. But his law clerks, even those who worked for him for years, would probably have not diverged without his guidance from the dry prose and adherence to precedence that landed them in their perches at the top court. They would not have used the word *racism* in a draft without clear guidance from Murphy. The key provisions in his most striking decisions, like his "cloak" references, are most likely Murphy's alone. Jeffrey Rosenthal and Albert Yoon had an interesting analysis of Supreme Court justices based on their use of common words in their opinions throughout their careers. The assumption of Rosenthal and Yoon was that if a particular justice was reliant on clerks, his writing style would change through the years as his clerks also changed. They listed Murphy in the middle of the pack in this regard, but not at the bottom. "Judicial Ghostwriting: Authorship on the Supreme Court," *Cornell Law Review* 96 (2011): 1307.

14. *Steele*, 323 U.S. at 209.

15. Ibid.

16. Ibid.

17. Anthony Downs, *Racism in America and How to Combat It*, (U.S. Commission on Civil Rights, 1970), 5–6.

18. If Theodore Roosevelt had been elected in 1912, he would have been president for more than eight years.

19. Eugene Gressman, "The Controversial Image of Mr. Justice Murphy," *Georgetown Law Journal* 47, no. 2 (1959): 631, 632. (noting James Farley's belief that Murphy was a top prospect).

20. Associated Press, "Back Reds vs. Nazis, Murphy Urges K. of C.," *DN*, Aug. 20, 1941, 10.

21. Ibid.

22. Franklin Delano Roosevelt, "State of the Union Message to Congress," Jan. 11, 1944, accessed Oct. 1, 2020, http://www.fdrlibrary.marist.edu/archives/address_text.html.

23. Ibid.

24. Frank Murphy, "Irish-Americans and the New Fight for Freedom, Address Delivered at the Annual Meeting of the Irish-American Association of Lackawanna County," Scranton, Pennsylvania, Mar. 17, 1938, *Murphy Collected Speeches, 1937–1938*, 77-82.

25. *Duncan v. Kahanamoku*, 327 U.S. 304, 324 (1946).

26. Frank Murphy to FDR, July 28, 1941, PSF, Box 166, Supreme Court, 1938–1944. (In this letter, Murphy was being discrete when he said, "While I find the work of the Court entirely congenial, and while such a move might be construed unfavorably in some quarters, in a time of crisis like the present primary consideration should be given to the nation's interests rather than one's personal interests.")

27. JFK's Speech on His Religion, Sept. 12, 1960, Houston, Texas, accessed Apr. 19, 2020, https://www.npr.org/templates/story/story.php?storyId=16920600.

28. Ibid.

29. Frank Murphy, "Commencement at the Detroit School of Law," June 8, 1937, *Murphy Collected Speeches, 1937–1938*, 41–46. ("It is difficult to look at the divinely inspired life without recognizing that its secret lies in an undying spirit of compassion for those in need of help.")

30. Frank Murphy, "Irish-Americans and the New Fight for Freedom, Address Delivered at the Annual Meeting of the Irish-American Association of Lackawanna County," Scranton, Pennsylvania, Mar. 17, 1938, *Murphy Collected Speeches 1937–1938*, 69–75.

31. And yet another question: Why would Ed Kemp write Joan a friendly letter in 1951, as he did, if she was a rival of Frank's attention during the last four years of his life? Edward Kemp to Joan Cuddihy without date, but referencing a memorial to Wiley Rutledge, who died a few months after Murphy. JC, Correspondence from friends and Murphy family 1945–1972.

BIBLIOGRAPHY

Alinsky, Saul. *John L. Lewis: An Unauthorized Biography*. New York: G.P. Putnam & Sons, 1949.

Angelou, Maya. *I Know Why the Caged Bird Sings*. New York: Chelsea House Publishers, 1996.

Bak, Richard. *A Place for Summer: A Narrative History of Tiger Stadium*. Detroit: Wayne State University Press, 1998.

Beschloss, Michael, *Kennedy and Roosevelt: The Uneasy Alliance*. New York: Open Road Media, 2016. Kindle.

Boyle, Kevin. *Arc of Justice: A Saga of Race, Civil Rights, and Murder in the Jazz Age*. New York: H. Holt, 2004.

Brinkley, Alan. *Voices of Protest*. New York: First Vintage Books Ed., 1983.

Buffa, Dudley W. *Union Power and American Democracy: The UAW and the Democratic Party, 1935–72*. Ann Arbor: University of Michigan Press, 1984.

Bundles, A'Lelia. *On Her Own Ground: The Life and Times of Madam C. J. Walker*. New York: Scribner, 2001.

Caro, Robert A. *The Power Broker: Robert Moses and the Fall of New York*. New York: Knopf, 1974.

Chauncey, George. *Gay New York: Gender, Urban Culture, and the Making of the Gay Male World, 1890–1940*. New York: Basic Books, 1994.

Crowther, Jane Morris. *The Political Activities of Detroit Clubwomen in the 1920s: A Challenge and a Promise*. Detroit: Wayne State University Press, 2013.

Daniels, Roger. *Concentration Camps USA: Japanese American and World War II*. New York: Holt, Rinehart and Winston, Inc., 1971.

Denis, Nelson. *War against All Puerto Ricans: Revolution and Terror in America's Colony*. New York: Bold Type Books, 2015. Kindle.

D'Este, Carlo. *Eisenhower: A Soldier's Life*. New York: Holt, 2002.

Dwyer, T. Ryle. *Irish Neutrality and the USA 1939–1947*. Dublin: Gill and MacMillan Limited, 1977.

Feldman, Noah. *Divided by God: America's Church-State Problem—and What We Should Do about It*. New York: Farrar, Straus and Giroux, 2005.

Fine, Sidney. *Frank Murphy: The Detroit Years.* Ann Arbor: University of Michigan Press, 1975.

Fine, Sidney. *Frank Murphy: The New Deal Years.* Chicago: University of Chicago Press, 1979.

Fine, Sidney. *Frank Murphy: The Washington Years.* Ann Arbor: University of Michigan Press, 1984.

Fisher, Ada Lois Sipuel. *A Matter of Black and White: The Autobiography of Ada Lois Sipuel Fisher.* With Danney Goble. Norman: University of Oklahoma Press, 1996.

Folsom, Robert G. *The Money Trail: How Elmer Irey and His T-Men Brought Down the Criminal Elite.* Washington, DC: Potomac Books, 2010.

Frank, John P. *Hugo Black: The Man and His Opinions.* New York: Alfred A. Knopf, 1949.

Friend, Theodore. *Between Two Empires: The Ordeal of the Philippines, 1929–1946.* New Haven: Yale University Press, 1965.

Ganor, Solly, *Light One Candle: A Survivor's Tale from Lithuania to Jerusalem.* New York: Kodansha International, 1995. Kindle.

Gerstle, Gary. *American Crucible: Race and Nation in the Twentieth Century.* Princeton: Princeton University Press, 2001.

Gordon, Rosalie M. *Nine Men against America: The Supreme Court and Its Attack on American Liberties.* Boston: Western Islands, 1958.

Haldeman-Julius, Marcet. *Clarence Darrow's Two Greatest Trials.* Girard, KS: Haldeman-Julius Co., 1927.

Hartmann, Rudolf H. *The Kansas City Investigation: Pendergast's Downfall, 1938–1939.* Columbia: University of Missouri Press, 1999.

Hayden, Joseph Ralston. *The Philippines, A Study in National Development.* New York: MacMillan Co., 1942, reprinted Arno Press Inc., 1972.

Healey, George William. *A Lifetime on Deadline: A Self-Portrait of a Southern Journalist.* Gretna, LA: Pelican Publishing Company, 1976.

Hiltzik, Michael. *The New Deal: A Modern History.* New York: Free Press, 2011.

Holli, Melvin G. *Reform in Detroit: Hazen S. Pingree and Urban Politics.* New York: Oxford University Press, 1969.

Howard, J. Woodward. *Mr. Justice Murphy, A Political Biography.* Princeton, NJ: Princeton University Press, 1968.

Ignatieff, Michael. *Blood and Belonging: Journeys into the New Nationalism.* New York: Farrar, Straus and Giroux, 1993.

Irons, Peter. *Justice at War.* New York: Oxford University Press, 1983.

Johnson, Christopher. *Maurice Sugar, Law, Labor, and the Left in Detroit, 1912–1950*. Detroit: Wayne State University Press, 2018.

Kamisar, Yale. *Police Interrogations and Confessions*. Ann Arbor: University of Michigan Press, 1980.

Kennedy, David M. *Freedom from Fear: The American People in Depression and War, 1929–1945*. New York: Oxford University Press, 1999.

Kraus, Henry. *Heroes of Unwritten Story: The UAW, 1934–1939*. Urbana: University of Illinois Press, 1993.

Lash, Joseph P. *The Diaries of Felix Frankfurter*. New York: W. W. Norton & Company, 1975.

Lipset, Seymour Martin, and Gary Wolf. *It Didn't Happen Here: Why Socialism Failed in the United States*. New York: Norton Paperback, 2001.

Long, Huey Pierce. *My First Days in the White House*. Harrisburg, PA: The Telegraph Press, 1935.

McRae, Donald. *The Great Trials of Clarence Darrow: The Landmark Cases of Leopold and Loeb, John T. Scopes, and Ossian Sweet*. New York: Harper Perennial, 2010.

Melville, Herman. *Moby-Dick; Or, The Whale*. New York: Harper & Brothers, 1851.

Murdoch, Joyce, and Deb Price. *Courting Justice: Gay Men and Lesbians v. The Supreme Court*. New York: Basic Books, 2001.

Newton, Jim. *Eisenhower: The White House Years*. New York: Doubleday, 2011.

Nishiura Weglyn, Michi. *Years of Infamy: The Untold Story of America's Concentration Camps*. Seattle: University of Washington Press, 1976.

O'Brien, Scott. *Ann Harding-Cinema's Gallant Lady*. Albany, GA: BearManor Media, 2010.

Plant, Rebecca Jo. *Mom: The Transformation of Motherhood in Modern America*. Chicago: University of Chicago Press, 2010.

Rogge, O. John. *Our Vanishing Civil Liberties*. New York: Gaer Associates, 1949.

Rothstein, Richard. *The Color of Law: A Forgotten History of How Our Government Segregated America*. New York: W.W. Norton, 2017.

See, Sarita Echavez. *The Filipino Primitive: Accumulation and Resistance in the American Museum*. New York: New York University Press, 2017.

Simon, James F. *FDR and Chief Justice Hughes: The President, the Supreme Court, and the Epic Battle Over the New Deal*. New York: Simon & Schuster, 2012.

Smith, Jean Edward. *FDR*. New York: Random House, 2007.

Tateishi, John. *And Justice for All: An Oral History of the Japanese American Detention Camps*. Seattle: University of Washington Press, 1999.

Tentler, Leslie Woodcock. *Catholics and Contraception: An American History*. Ithaca, NY: Cornell University Press, 2004.

Tentler, Leslie Woodcock. *Seasons of Grace: A History of the Catholic Archdiocese of Detroit*. Detroit: Wayne State University Press, 1990.

Vine, Phyllis. *One Man's Castle: Clarence Darrow in Defense of the American Dream*. New York: Amistad, 2005.

Welles, Benjamin. *Sumner Welles, FDR's Global Strategist*. New York: St. Martin's Press, 1997.

Williams, T. Harry. *Huey Long*. New York: First Vintage Books Edition, 1981.

Zinn, Howard. *A People's History of the United States*. New York: Harper & Row, 1990.

Law Review Articles and Other Secondary Sources

Berg, Thomas C., and William G. Ross. "Some Religiously Devout Justices: Historical Notes and Comments." *Marquette Law Review* 81, no. 2 (1998): 383.

Carr, Robert K. "Screws v. United States: The Georgia Police Brutality Case." *Cornell Law Review* 31, no. 1 (1945): 48.

Danelski, David J. "The Saboteurs' Case." *Journal of Supreme Court History* 21, no. 1 (1996): 61.

Dreisbach, Daniel L. "Micah 6:8 in the Literature of the American Founding Era: A Note on Religion and Rhetoric." *Rhetoric and Public Affairs* 12, no. 1 (Spring 2009): 91.

Flynn, George Quitman. "Franklin D. Roosevelt and American Catholicism, 1932–1936." PhD diss., Louisiana State University, 1966.

Frank, John P. "Justice Murphy: The Goals Attempted." *Yale Law Journal* 59 (1949): 1.

Goldfield, Michael, and Cody R. Melcher. "The Myth of Section 7(a): Worker Militancy, Progressive Labor Legislation, and the Coal Miners," *Labor* 16, no. 4 (2019): 49–65.

Gressman, Eugene. "*Korematsu*: A Mélange of Military Imperatives." *Law and Contemporary Problems* 68 (Spring 2005): 15–28.

Gudridge, Patrick O. "Essay: Remember Endo?" *Harvard Law Review* 116 (2003): 1933.

Hansen, Arthur A. "Oral History and the Japanese American Evacuation." *The Journal of American History* 82, no. 2 (1995). Accessed May 12, 2020. doi:10.2307/2082192.

Hutchinson, Dennis J. "Hugo Black among Friends." *Michigan Law Review* 93 (1995): 1885; "The Black-Jackson Feud." Sup. Ct. Rev., Vol. 1988 (1988); "Unanimity and Desegregation: Decisionmaking in the Supreme Court, 1948–1958." *Georgetown Law Journal* 68 (1980): 1.

Kalaw, Maximo. "The New Constitution of the Philippine Commonwealth." *Foreign Affairs* 13, no. 4 (July 1935).

Marshall, Thurgood. "Murphy and Civil Rights." *Michigan Law Review* 48, no. 6 (1950): 745.

Morgan, Alfred L. "The Significance of Pennsylvania's 1938 Gubernatorial Election." *The Pennsylvania Magazine of History and Biography* 102, no. 2 (1978).

Pickering, John H. "A Tribute to Justice Frank Murphy." *University of Detroit Mercy Law Review* 73 (1996): 703.

Rosenthal, Jeffrey, and Albert Yoon. "Judicial Ghostwriting: Authorship on the Supreme Court." *Cornell Law Review* 96 (2011): 1307.

Sharlow, Carrie. "Michigan Lawyers in History: Thomas F. Chawke." *Michigan Bar Journal* (November 2015).

Spickard, Paul R. "The Nisei Assume Power: The Japanese Citizens League, 1941–1942." *Pacific Historical Review* 52, no. 2 (May 1983).

Abbreviations in Endnotes

Primary Sources

FDRL   Franklin D. Roosevelt Library
         Hyde Park, New York
         PPF—President's Personal File
         PSF—President's Secretary's File
         If the reference is to the papers of someone else archived at this library, these are referred to by name: FDR, Ernest Cuneo Papers.

FMM   Frank Murphy home and Museum
         Harbor Beach, Michigan

FMP The Frank Murphy Collection at the University of Michigan
The Bentley Historical Library
Ann Arbor, Michigan
Roll—Microfilm Roll
JC The Joan Cuddihy Collection at the University of Michigan
The Bentley Historical Library
Ann Arbor, Michigan
WRL Walter P. Reuther Library
Wayne State University
Detroit, Michigan
UNC Wilson Special Collections Library
University of North Carolina
Chapel Hill, North Carolina

Others

BCE *Battle Creek Enquirer* (Battle Creek, Michigan)
CDS *Corsicana Daily Sun* (Corsicana, Texas)
DN *Daily News* (New York)
DFP *Detroit Free Press*
EMS *Escanaba Morning Press* (Escanaba, Michigan)
IDG *Ironwood Daily Globe* (Ironwood, Michigan)
LSJ *Lansing State Journal*
MMT *Medford Mail Tribune* (Medford, Oregon)
NYT *New York Times*
RG *Reno Gazette* (Reno, Nevada)
SFT *San Francisco Tribune*
TBES *The Bradford Evening Star* and *The Bradford Daily*
TEC *The Enquirer* (Cincinnati, Ohio)
TENS *The Evening News* (Sault Sainte Marie, Michigan)
THP *The Herald-Press* (Saint Joseph, Michigan)
TON *The Oshkosh Northwestern* (Oshkosh, Wisconsin)
TNP *The News-Palladium* (Benton Harbor, Michigan)
TSB *The South Bend Tribune* (South Bend, Indiana)
TTH *The Times Herald* (Port Huron, Michigan)

INDEX

academics, Murphy's, 6, 13–14
Adamson v. California, 217–218
Affordable Care Act (ACA), 141
Agricultural Adjustment Act
    (AAA), 119–120, 123n38
agricultural subsidies, 119–120,
    123n38
alcohol, 2, 29–31
Alien Enemy Control Program, 236
Alinsky, Saul, 156–157
All the King's Men (Warren), 142,
    186, 187
America First Party, 184
American Civil Liberties Union
    (ACLU) and Japanese-American
    expulsions, 252
American Federation of Labor
    (AFL), 52, 152, 154, 160, 182,
    196n3
American ideals, Supreme Court
    decisions based on, 218–219
Annenberg, Moses "Moe," 188–189
anti-Asian rhetoric, 244–245
anti-lynching laws, 191, 192
anti-Semitism, 40–41, 44n19,
    194–195
Arc of Justice (Boyle), 62
Article III courts, enforcement of
    military law by, 259
athleticism, Murphy's, 6

Baltimore Sun, 96
bank holidays, 112–113, 115
banks, 83–84, 112–114, 115
Battle of Belleau Wood, 21
Battle of the Overpass, 162
Battle of the Philippine Sea, 254

Bennett, Harry, 101, 162
The Birth of a Nation (1915 film), 40
Black, Edward D., 151
Black, Hugo: appointment to
    Supreme Court, 201; concurrence
    in *Oyama*, 265–266; decision
    upholding Japanese American
    internments, 252, 253–254,
    256, 264; dissent in *MacDougal
    v. Green*, 274; health issues,
    222; judicial experience of,
    205–206; KKK membership of,
    215; Murphy's involvement in
    appointment of, 145, 215; push
    for shorter workdays, 116, 145;
    In re Oliver decision, 103; in
    school desegregation case, 292;
    upholding of curfews, 240
Black community: and the Great
    Migration, 179; moving toward
    Democratic Party, 87; and
    Republican Party, 46; support
    for Murphy, 70, 71, 79, 85, 87; and
    unions, 293–295
Black Legion, 154
Black Panthers, 144
Black students and state-funded
    schools, 200, 214, 276–279,
    291–293
Black Tuesday, 75
Board of Water and Light building,
    118
Bontecou, Eleanor, 193
bootlegging, 30, 76
Bowles, Charles, 76–77, 78, 167
Brandeis, Louis D., 218–219
Breiner, Leon, 63, 65–66, 69, 70

Brennan, Mary (cousin), 6
Brown v. Board of Education, 214, 219, 291–293, 303n4
Bryan, William Jennings, 65
budget-balancing requirements, 89–90, 98
Bull Moose Party. *See* Progressive Party
Bumgardner, Eleanor, 128–129, 221, 275, 285
Bureau of Non-Christian Tribes, 131
Butler Act, 65

California Alien Land Law, 266
California State Personnel Board, 251
Camp, Lawrence, 169
capital punishment, 56–57, 131
Catholicism: and KKK, 40; and Murphy, 2, 3, 7, 58, 284–285; and the U.S. presidency, 299–300
Chauncey, George, 31, 32, 185, 207
Chawke, Thomas, 66–67
childhood, Murphy's, 1–6
Christian Front, 44n19
Chrysler, Walter, 41–42, 158
Chrysler Corporation, 41–42, 158
Chrysler strike, 158
Churchill, Winston, 135
cities, federal aid for, 90–91, 103–104
Citizens' Fact Finding Committee, 87
citizenship, denial to Japanese Americans, 109, 239, 265–266
city bosses, Murphy and, 119, 185–189
"civic nationalism," 262–263
civil liberties: ideal of, 104–105; Murphy's promotion of as attorney general, 189–193;

restriction of during wartime, 266; supremacy over military power, 298–299
Civil Liberties Section of Department of Justice, 189–191, 193
civil rights: grand juries as hindrance to, 193; and Murphy as attorney general, 185; promotion of through strong federal government, 302
civil rights movement and sit-down strikes, 160
Clark, Tom C., 236, 285, 292–293
Cleveland, Grover, 107
Cold War, 273
collective bargaining, 157–160, 165n44, 183, 294
collective guilt, evacuation of Japanese Americans and, 262
college, Murphy at, 10–12, 13–14, 22, 23
Committee on Public Information (CPI), 18
Communist Party, 33, 145, 160
communists: as a foil, 105, 175; influence on strikes, 155; Murphy as, 176; pro-labor politicians as, 172–175
concentration camps for Japanese Americans, 234–235, 245, 250, 252, 255
concurrences, Murphy's, 19; in *Bethlehem Steel,* 29; in *Endo,* 264; in *Hirabayashi,* 242–243; in *Oyama,* 265; in *Takahashi,* 266; in *WV State Board of Education v. Barnette,* 291. *See also* dissents, Murphy's
Congress of Industrial Organizations (CIO), 52, 152–153, 160. *See also* United Auto Workers (UAW)
conscription laws, 17, 18–19

constitution, Philippine, 130–132
Constitution, U.S., 90–91, 98,
    204–205, 259. *See also specific
    amendments*
corporate responsibility, 101
corporations, federal aid for, 90–91,
    97
corruption: of city bosses, 119,
    185–189; of governors general,
    127; in Louisiana, 186–187; of
    Michigan government, 162–163;
    of Philippine government, 133
Coughlin, Charles: from ally to
    critic of FDR, 130; anti-Semitic
    tone of, 40–41, 44n19; and food
    prices, 120; and Murphy's death,
    284; and the RFC, 113; satirized
    in *Pins and Needles*, 176; support
    of FDR, 124; support of Murphy,
    100; support of Murphy's rival,
    144; and the Union Party, 142
Court Diary, 216
*Courting Justice: Gay Men and
    Lesbians v. The Supreme Court*
    (Murdoch and Price), 206
court-packing of Supreme Court,
    121n10, 169, 201
court reforms: in Detroit, 45–46;
    and Murphy, 54–57; in the
    Philippines, 131; and societal
    prejudices, 57
Couzens, James, 33, 100, 112–113,
    129–130, 171
covenants, racial restrictive, 72,
    72n1
Creel, George, 18, 20
crime bosses, Murphy's pursuit of
    as attorney general, 189
Cuddihy, Joan, x, 227n43, 271, 276,
    285
cultural treasures, protection of,
    133–134
Cuneo, Ernest, 135, 178, 216
curfews, Japanese-American:
    and government's good faith,
    243–244; as initial step, 233–234;

Murphy's belief as temporary
    measure, 262; Murphy's
    upholding of, 242–243, 262; and
    the Supreme Court, 235, 237–245,
    258; and war powers, 237–238.
    See also *Hirabayashi v. United
    States; Yasui v. United States*
Curley, James, 100–101
Curtis, Charles, 101, 111

Darrow, Clarence, 31, 64–66, 67,
    98–99
death, Murphy's, 283–286
deflation, 115–116
Democratic National Convention:
    FDR at, 110; Murphy's input on
    platform, 144–145
Democratic Party: and Black
    voters, 87; in disarray, 139;
    and economic downturn, 171;
    FDR campaign for liberals
    within, 169; in flux, 46; Murphy
    as mayor, 76–77; Murphy's
    involvement with, 16; Murphy's
    nomination for Congress,
    20; and New Deal programs,
    141–142; progressives move to,
    111, 145; shift of energy to, 12–13;
    winning in Michigan, 111
Democratic Party bosses: Murphy's
    attack on as attorney general,
    119, 185–189, 272; Murphy's
    failure to reward, 128, 140, 142,
    168; and Murphy's nomination
    to Supreme Court, 188
Detroit, Michigan: banks in, 115;
    bootlegging in, 30; budget
    requirements of, 79, 89–90;
    debt obligations of, 83–84;
    growth of, 26; infrastructure
    funding, 82–83, 146n13; as
    leading industrial center,
    149–150; Murphy as mayor of, 71,
    76–77, 78–79, 86–87; newspapers,
    48–49; oversight board, 83–84;
    population of, 91; property taxes

in, 87–89; race riots in, 72, 280; restrictive covenants in, 279; as segregated city, 72; sit-down strikes in, 151; unemployment in, 77, 79, 80–82, 88, 90; WPA projects in, 117–118

Detroit Board of Commerce, 80

Detroit Bureau of Governmental Research, 90

Detroit City Charter, restructuring of criminal court by, 45–46

Detroit Federation of Labor (DFL), 51

Detroit Free Press, 53, 206

Detroit Independent, 79

Detroit Mirror, 85

Detroit News, 151

Detroit People's News, 85

Detroit Stereotypers' Union No. 9 v. Detroit Free Press and Detroit Times, 51–53

Detroit Times, 33, 48–49, 77

Detroit-Windsor Tunnel, 83

"dew-and-sunshine" candidate, Murphy as, 78

DeWitt, John, 235, 240, 258

Dewson, Mary W., 58–59

Dies Committee, 172–173, 175

Diggs, Charles C., Jr., 86, 94n57

Dingell, John, 221

discrimination through citizenship rights, 265–266

dissents, Murphy's: in *Adamson v. California*, 217–218; in *Korematsu*, 260–263; in *MacDougal v. Green*, 274; in *Screws v. United States*, 192–193; in *Sipuel II*, 278. *See also* concurrences, Murphy's

Dixiecrat Party, 273

Douglas, William O.: appointment to Supreme Court, 201; dissent in *MacDougal v. Green*, 274; on employers' speech as illegal, 214; *Endo* decision, 264; *Hirabayashi* concurrence, 243–244; on Murphy's health,

281–282; Murphy's involvement in appointment of, 215; *Screws* decision, 191–192

Douglass, Frederick, 46, 58n2

due process, 253

Duncan v. Kahanamoku, 19, 268n29

economic bill of rights, 298

economic inequality: as continuing problem, 302; in the Philippines, 133; as threat to American ideals, 291

economic plight in campaign emphasis, 78

Eighteenth Amendment (1920), 29–31

Eisenhower, Dwight D., 38, 126, 298–299

Eisenhower: A Soldier's Life (D'Este), 126

electoral systems, 131, 177

Emergency Relief and Construction Act, 103–104

employers' speech as illegal threat, 214

Employment of Homosexuals and Other Sex Perverts in Government (Senate committee publication), 206–211

Endo, Mitsuye, 249, 250–251, 264–265

ethnic groups: FDR's incorporation of, 109; support for Murphy from, 47

evacuation of Japanese Americans, 249–264; internment of Japanese Americans; inference of collective guilt in, 262; and racism, 262, 264; signing of Executive Order 9066, 232–233; and Supreme Court, 249. *See also* concentration camps for Japanese Americans; *Ex parte Endo*; *Korematsu v. United States*

Everand, Hester, 36–37, 206

executive experience, 205

Executive Order 9066, 233, 235,
241–242, 246n6, 250, 252
Ex parte Endo, 263–265

factories: Murphy's employment in,
5–6; as residential shelters for
unemployed, 82
Fair Labor Standards Act (FLSA,
1938), 175
Falbo v. United States, 40
Farley, James, 109–110, 196, 199n54,
221, 296
Farm-Labor Party, 273
fascism, 155, 174, 195, 234, 241, 286,
297
Federal Deposit Insurance
Corporation (FDIC), 115
federal government: aid for
unemployment, 96–98; aid to
cities, 90–91, 103–104; aid to
corporations, 91, 97; promotion
of civil rights through, 302
Federal Reserve, 114, 115
"Final Report: Japanese Evacuation
from the West Coast, 1942"
(DeWitt), 260–261
finances, Murphy's, 42–43, 163,
283
Fine, Sidney: and Irene Murphy,
127; on Murphy rewarding
newspapers, 85; on Murphy's
Hirabayashi concurrence, 243;
on Murphy's hospitalization,
281; on Murphy's masculinity,
17; on Murphy's sexual
orientation, 210–211, 300; on
Murphy's violation of public
trust, 41–42, on Murphy's WWI
experience, 21
First Amendment in *Thornhill*
decision, 212–213
Fisher, Ada Lois Sipuel, 276–279
Fisher Lodge, 82
Fisher Number One Plant, 150, 153

Fisher v. Hurst, 278
Fitzgerald, Frank D., 112, 139–140,
175, 176–177
Flint Alliance, 154
"Flint Strike." *See* General Motors
(GM) strike
food prices, 119–120, 123n38
Ford, Henry, 83, 112, 161
Ford Hunger March, 101–103, 133,
161, 184
Ford Motor Company, 77, 88, 101,
161–162
"forgotten man" rhetoric, 108–109
Four Freedoms Declaration, 135,
138n53
the Four Horsemen, 200–201, 214
442nd Regimental Combat Team,
255
Fourteenth Amendment, 189, 212,
213–214, 217–218, 266
Frankfurter, Felix: appointment to
Supreme Court, 182, 201; concern
of Murphy's use of "racism,"
243; criticism of incorporation,
217–218; decision upholding
Japanese-American internment,
256–257; dislike of Murphy, 216;
Korematsu concurrence, 259; and
Murphy's health, 281; respect for
Murphy, 219–220; upholding of
curfews, 240

Gaines v. Canada, 200
Garner, John Nance: and
Conference of Mayors, 100;
and Democratic National
Convention, 110; and Dies
Committee, 172; hostility toward
New Deal programs, 195; on
Murphy as attorney general,
183–184; as vice president, 111
Gay New York (Chauncey), 185, 207
General Motors (GM), Depression-
era finances of, 79, 83

General Motors (GM) strike,
149–159; and allegations of
Murphy's violation of public
trust, 42, 44n24; and collective
bargaining rights, 157–160;
Frankfurter's praise for Murphy
for, 219; Murphy as communist
because of, 173–174; Murphy's
challenge to legality of, 157;
and Murphy's confirmation as
attorney general, 184; Murphy's
preference toward UAW, 286;
settlement of, 157–158; Sugar's
respect for Murphy during, 39
German Americans, detention of,
234
Germany, 21, 174, 193–195, 297–298
gold standard, 114, 115
Gomon, Josephine, 82, 83, 93n39,
106n15
Gompers, Samuel, 152
"good government" approach, 32,
54, 128
Government Reorganization Act
(1939), 209
governor general, Murphy as,
124–132
governors general, corruption of,
127
governorship, Michigan: Murphy's
campaign for, 139–142; Murphy's
health issues during, 49–50;
Murphy's reelection campaign,
112, 158, 167, 171; Murphy's
reelection loss, 176–177;
Murphy's win, 148
grand juries, 102–103, 193
Great Migration, 177
*The Great Trials of Clarence Darrow:
The Landmark Cases of Leopold
and Loeb, John T. Scopes, and
Ossian Sweet* (McRae), 62
Gressman, Eugene, 210, 275, 296
Griffith, D. W., 40

Haldeman-Julius, Marcet, 64, 82
Hall, Robert "Bobby," 191–193
"Hand of God" (Milles statue), 153,
286,
Harbor Beach, Michigan, 1, 2, 4–5,
6, 7
Harding, Ann, 67–68
Hare-Hawes-Cutting (HHC) Bill,
130
Harlan, John, 293
Harrison, George, 114
Harvard Crimson, 194
Hawaii, Japanese Americans in,
234, 240, 256, 268n29
health insurance, government, 178,
273
health issues, Murphy's, 16, 49–50,
148–149, 215, 222, 271, 281–282
Heston, William, 38, 48
high commissioner, Murphy as,
132
Hirabayashi, Gordon Kiyoshi,
235–236, 243–244
Hirabayashi v. United States, 235–245,
253–254, 258, 262
Hitler, Adolf, 174
homosexuality, 32, 185, 207–209,
301. *See also* sexual orientation,
Murphy's
Hoover, Herbert, 75, 91, 101, 103, 111
Hoover, J. Edgar, 186, 208, 232, 272
Hope Diamond curse, 220–221
Hopkins, Harry A., 170–171, 184
horse riding, 6, 49, 60
House Committee on Un-American
Activities (HUAC), 172–173
House of the Masses, 33
Hughes, (Chief Justice) Charles
Evans, 117
Hull, Cordell, 194, 208, 209
humor, Murphy's sense of, 57–58,
118, 282
Hunger March. *See* Ford Hunger
March

Ickes, Harold, 195, 196
Illinois, Progressive Party on ballot
    in, 274
immigrant vote, support for
    Murphy as mayor, 86–87
Immigration Act (1924), 47, 109, 152,
    239
incarceration of Japanese American,
    231. See also concentration camps
    for Japanese Americans
income, guaranteed annual, 142,
    298
industrialists, prosecution of, 28
industrial might as key to winning
    wars, 224
infrastructure, funds for, 82–83,
    146n13
"Inhabitants of Quebec" letter,
    212–213
In Our Image: America's Empire in
    the Philippines (Karnow), 126,
    134–135
Inouye, Daniel Ken, 255
In re Oliver, 102–103
integration, residential, 280–281
integration of Japanese Americans,
    239, 243
internment of Japanese Americans,
    241, 256–257, 258. See also
    concentration camps for
    Japanese Americans; evacuation
    of Japanese Americans
Italian Americans, detention of,
    234

Jackson, Robert, 49, 60n18, 250,
    258–259
Japanese American Citizens League
    (JACL), 251
Japanese Americans: concentration
    camps for, 234–235, 245, 250,
    252, 255; curfews for, 233–245,
    258, 262; denial of citizenship

to, 239, 265–266; as disloyal, 233,
    240, 242, 260–261; evacuation
    of, 232–233, 241–242, 253, 299;
    failure to integrate, 238–240,
    243; in Hawaii, 234, 256, 268n29;
    incarceration of, 231; internment
    of, 241, 247n29, 256–257, 258;
    loyalty of, 302; propaganda effort
    against, 244; restrictions on
    property ownership, 239; special
    category of prejudice against,
    245; as state employees, 251;
    and Truman, 266; in U.S. armed
    forces, 254–256
Japanese Empire: capture of the
    Philippines, 132; declaration of
    war against, 231; growing threat
    of, 125–126; immigration from,
    239; industrial capacity of, 254;
    Murphy's assessment of military
    power of, 297
Jewish causes, Murphy's support
    for, 220
Jews, discrimination against, 40–41,
    44n19, 194–195
Jim Crow system, 72n1, 172, 177,
    191, 214, 276
Johnson, Lyndon B., 146n13
judicial experience, 205–206,
    226n20, 285
Judicial Procedures Reform Bill, 169
jury instructions in Sweet trial,
    68–70
jury selection, 70–71
justice, moral beliefs and
    administration of, 56–57
Justices at War (Irons), 257

Karnow, Stanley, 126, 134–135
Kemp, Edward G.: beginning of
    friendship with Murphy, 12;
    at the Bureau of the Budget,
    209–210; enlistment in WWI, 22;

lobbying for federal aid, 91; on the MUC, 81; in private practice, 181; relationship with Murphy, 206–211, 300, 305n31; travel with Murphy, 275
Kennedy, John F., 149, 299–300
Kennedy, Joseph, 41, 130, 149, 221
Knaggs, Daniel A., 153–154
Korematsu, Fred: constitutional rights of, 257; as free laborer, 125; legal representation of, 251–252; violation of evacuation laws, 249–250, 258, 264
Korematsu v. United States, 252–263; citation of *Hirabayashi* in, 253–254; Murphy's dissent in, 260–263; overruling of, 259, 266
Krock, Arthur, 203
Ku Klux Klan (KKK), 40, 59n6, 76, 87, 215

labor activism. *See* sit-down strikes; striking workers
Labor Board v. Virginia Power Co., 214
labor disputes, 50–53, 104, 158, 212–214
Labor Party, 145
LaGuardia, Fiorello, 103, 111, 177–178, 195
Landon, Alf, 148
law practice, Murphy's private, 16, 36, 38–39, 41–42, 183
law school, Murphy at, 13–14
law schools, segregation of, 200, 214, 276–279
League of Nations, 33
legislatures, unicameral, 131
Lend-Lease program, 194
leniency of the justice system, 27–28
Lewis, John L., 156
Lincoln, Abraham, 23

Long, Huey: assassination of, 144; channeled by FDR, 149; and corruption, 119, 186; courting of Murphy, 142–144; and the RFC, 113
Louisiana, political corruption in, 186–188
Louisiana State University, Murphy's honorary degree from, 186–187

MacArthur, Douglas, 125–126, 128, 134, 297
MacDougal v. Green, 273–274
Marshall, George C., 223–224, 225
Marshall, Thurgood: appreciation for Murphy, 190; and jury selections, 70–71; and McReynolds, 214; and *Sipuel,* 276
Martel, Frank X.: confirmation of Murphy as attorney general, 182; encouragement of Murphy running for state-wide office, 52, 140; Murphy's protection of disenfranchised, 131; support of Murphy, 52–53, 160, 273
Matsumura, Clarence, 255–256
A Matter of Black and White (Fisher), 278
Mayors, United States Conference of, 96–101, 104
mayorship of Detroit: Murphy's candidacy for, 71, 77–79; Murphy's reelection as, 86–87; Murphy's win, 78–79
Mayor's Unemployment Committee (MUC), 81–82
McLean, Evalyn Walsh, 220–221
McReynolds, James, 200, 214
men, Murphy's relationships with, 32, 206–211, 300–301
Metropolitan Life Insurance Company, 280–281

Michigan: bank holidays in, 112–113; FDR's win in, 148; government corruption in, 162–163; labor strikes in, 149–162; as Republican state, 26; votes for FDR, 111. *See also* governorship, Michigan
Michiganensian, 33
Michigan State Highway Commission, 140
Michigan Welfare Department, sit-down strikes and, 154
military force: must follow Constitution, 259; and strikes, 153–154, 156–157; supremacy of civil liberties over, 261–262, 298–299
"military-industrial complex," 298–299
military justice, 19–20
military orders, enforcement by Supreme Court, 259
military service, avoidance of, 39–40
Milles, Carl, 286, 289n71
Minidoka Relocation Camp, 237
moral beliefs, administration of justice and, 56–57
Morgenthau, Henry, Jr., 188
"Morning in America" speeches, 78
Mulcahy, Joseph, 48–49, 53
municipal ownership of utilities, 82–83
Murphy, George: as athlete, 6; closeness with Murphy, 3, 275–276, 283; elected to Recorder's Office, 183, 214–215, 283; financial support of, 43; health issues, 222; as judge, 300–301
Murphy, Harold, 4, 127, 276
Murphy, Irene, 127, 133, 227n43
Murphy, John, 1–2, 3, 10

Murphy, Marguerite: as confidant and hostess, 183, 221; death of, 283; as enamored with Murphy, 4; financial support of, 43; in the Philippines, 127, 129
Murphy, Mary, 2, 57
Mussolini, Benito, 174
My First Days in the White House (Long), 142–143

National Association for the Advancement of Colored People (NAACP), 64–65, 71, 72, 276, 278
National Conference for Clarifying the Constitution by Amendment, 204
National Guard, GM strike and, 156
National Industrial Recovery Act (NIRA, 1933), 116–117, 204
National Labor Relations Act (NLRA, 1935), 157, 159–160, 162, 172, 304n9
National Labor Relations Board (NLRB), 159, 160, 162
National Labor Relations Board (NLRB) v. Fansteel Metallurgical Corp., 165n44
National Negro Press Association, 85
Naturalization Act (1906), 239
Neutrality Act, 194, 297
New Deal Democrats, defeat of, 177
New Deal programs: and Democratic campaigns, 141–142; Garner's hostility toward, 195; loss of Southern Democratic support, 172; Supreme Court overturn of, 117, 121n10, 200–201. *See also specific programs*
newspapers: Black-owned, 70, 85; coverage of Murphy in Philippines, 129; and labor

disputes, 51–53; Murphy's
cultivation of, 84–85; portrayal
of striking workers, 155; support
for Murphy from, 48–49
Newton, Huey, 144
New York, FDR as governor of,
108
New York Daily News, 185
New York Times, 75, 86, 169, 186–187,
264, 280
Nineteenth Amendment, 48
Nixon, Richard, 172
Norris, George W., 111, 121n13, 131,
178
Northern California American
Civil Liberties Union (NC-
ACLU), 252
North Portland Livestock Pavilion,
236
NPL Party, 111

Obama, Barack, 141
Olmstead v. United States, 218–219
oratory skills, Murphy's, 10–11, 14,
27, 163
Order No. 34, 253
Osborn, Chase, 12, 13, 176
Oyama, Fred, 265
Oyama v. State of California, 265–266
Ozawa v. United States, 239

Palmer, A. Mitchell, 28, 32
Palmer Raids, 32–33
Parker, Ann, 37, 185
parole process, 56, 143
Pearson, Drew, 284
Pendergast, Tom, 119, 187–188, 272
Pendergast machine, 187–188
People v. Lewen, 38, 48
People v. Ossian Sweet, et al., 63–67
Perkins, Frances, 149, 150, 153, 161,
185
Pershing, John, 28

Philippines: corruption in, 133;
independence of, 124–125, 130–
132, 296–297; Japanese capture
of, 125–126, 132; Murphy in,
124–135; Murphy's lifestyle in,
126–127; protection of cultural
treasures in, 133–134; uprising
in, 133
Pingree, Hazen, 82–83
Plant, Rebecca Jo, 37–38
Pledge of Allegiance as mandatory,
290–291
Plessy v. Ferguson, 219, 276, 305n4
polio, 108
political corruption, Murphy as
attorney general and, 185–189
populists, courting of Murphy by,
142–143
Port Huron Times Herald, 131, 226
Potts, Frank, 2, 210–211, 221
president of the United States,
Murphy as (hypothetical),
296–299
Prince Edward County, Virginia,
school segregation in, 292–293
progressive movement: fissures
within, 46–47; let down by
FDR policies, 118–120; move to
Democratic Party, 145; and the
NPL, 111; rallying of support for
FDR, 177–178; and restructuring
of criminal courts, 45–46
Progressive Party, 12–13, 273–274
Prohibition, 29–32, 46, 76
pro-labor politicians as
communists, 172–173
propaganda, war, 18, 20, 244
property rights, denial of based on
race, 239, 279–280
prosecutors, political pressures on,
30–31
Psychopathic Institute (Chicago),
54–55

Public Law 503, 233, 235, 236, 241, 244, 250, 257, 258
public trust, allegations of Murphy's violation of, 41–42, 44n24
Purple Gang, 30

Quezon, Manuel, 129, 131, 132, 133

race relations: as continuing problem, 303; damage to through Supreme Court rulings, 276
race riots in Detroit, 72, 280
racial inequality: and denial of property rights, 239, 280; as threat to American ideals, 291. *See also* restrictive covenants; segregation
racism: and *Brown v. Board of Education*, 293; definition of, 295; evacuation orders as, 262; and *Hirabayashi* concurrence, 243; in Japanese-American evacuation program, 264; in Murphy opinions, 263–266, 268n29, 293–295, 304n13
racist terminology, Murphy's use of, 244–245
Railway Labor Act (RLA), 293–295, 304n9
Rankin, John E., 121n13
Reagan, Ronald, 78
recall elections, 76, 77
Reconstruction Finance Corporation (RFC) Act (1932), 91, 112–113
Recorder's Office, Detroit: George Murphy's campaign for, 283; George Murphy's election to, 182–183, 214–215; Murphy on the bench, 50–58; Murphy's election to, 47–49; Murphy's reelection to, 70, 76; Murphy's resignation from, 77–78; Murphy's run for, 45, 47

Red Scare, 32
religion debate during Conference of Mayors, 98–100
relocation camps. *See* concentration camps for Japanese Americans
Republican Party: and Black voters, 87; and Buckley murder, 77; as dominant in Michigan, 26; in flux, 46; progressives move out of, 111; schism in, 12–13; support of government programs, 171–172
reputation of Murphy as justice, 216–218
Reserve Officers' Training Camp, 17–18
restrictive covenants, 72n1, 279–280
Reuther, Walter, 161–162
rights, constitutional, under military necessity, 261–262
Roberts, (Chief Justice) John, 234
Roberts, (Chief Justice) Owen, 200–201, 239–240, 257–258
Roberts Commission, 239–240, 258
Roosevelt, Eleanor, 108
Roosevelt, Franklin D.: Coughlin from ally to critic of, 130; declaration of bank holiday, 115; defense of Murphy against communist rumors, 173–174; at the Democratic National Convention, 110; ending of gold standard, 115; ending of Japanese-American internment, 257; evacuation of Japanese Americans, 232; expansion of the Supreme Court, 118, 121n10; first election, 111–112; first presidential campaign, 110–111; incorporation of ethnic groups, 109; lessening of contact with Murphy, 222, 272; letting down progressives, 118–120; matchmaking for

Murphy, 221; and Murphy as
natural allies, 108–111, 118;
Murphy as possible successor
for, 296; Murphy's desire to
enter wartime Philippines, 225;
Murphy's first meeting with,
107; Murphy's loyalty to, 41, 120,
129, 140–141, 167, 296; Murphy's
progressivist recommendations
to, 178; and Murphy's run for
governor, 139–141; and Murphy's
settlement of GM strike, 158,
161; and Neutrality Act, 297;
opening of Blue Water Bridge,
170; placement on Illinois ballot,
274; political miscalculations,
168–169; refusal to campaign
trail, 168–169; reliance on party
bosses, 189; running for third
term, 145–146, 195–196; second
inaugural address, 149; State of
Union address, 298; toleration
of party bosses, 119; transfer of
Kemp to Bureau of the Budget,
209–210; and two-party system,
145; upbringing of, 107–108;
use of communists as foils,
175; views on homosexuality,
207–208; win in Michigan,
111–112, 148
Roosevelt, G. Hall, 81, 107, 124, 170
Roosevelt, Theodore, 12–13, 17, 263
Rutledge, Wiley Blount, 146, 205,
271, 278, 281, 282

*Schechter Poultry Corp. v. United
States,* 117, 204
schools, state-funded, segregation
of, 276–279, 291–293
Schuknecht, Norton, 63, 65–66
Scopes, John T., 65
Scopes "Monkey" Trial, 65
Screws, Claude, 191–192
Screws v. United States, 191–193
Section 20 (U.S. criminal code),
191

segregation: and Civil Rights
Division, 190; in Detroit, 72;
Plessy v. Ferguson, 276; and
Progressive Party, 273; of public
schools, 200, 214, 276–279,
291–293; use of Fourteenth
Amendment against, 218
sentencing reforms, 54–55, 143
"separate but equal," 276, 277,
291–293, 302
sexual orientation, Murphy's, 32,
206–211, 300–301
Shelley v. Kraemer, 279–280
*Sipuel v. Board of Regents of
University of Oklahoma,* 276–278
sit-down strikes: and civil right
movement, 160; and Supreme
Court, 159–160, 165n44; and
Woolworth employees, 155. *See
also* General Motors (GM) strike;
striking workers
Smith, Alfred, 58, 108, 299
Socialists, NLRA and, 160
social life, Murphy's, 17–18, 23, 31,
43, 220–221, 271
Social Security Act (1935), 141
Sotomayor, Sonia, 205, 269n45
Southern Democrats, 172, 185–189
Soviet Union, 155, 174, 274, 297–
298
starvation, 79, 119–120, 123n38,
303
state laws, Supreme Court and,
213–214, 218
Steele v. Louisville & N.R. Co.,
293–295
Stone, (Chief Justice) Harlan, 222,
237–239, 243, 245, 293–294
Stone, Ralph, 83, 105
Stone Committee, 83–84
striking workers: brute force to
quell, 161; foreign influence on,
155; as legal, 215; in Michigan,
149–162; and militias, 153–154;
portrayal in newspapers, 155; as
trespassing, 45, 46, 50, 151–152,

159, 160–161, 214; and violence, 151–152, 154–155, 159. *See also* General Motors (GM) strike; sit-down strikes

Stuyvesant, 280–281

Stuyvesant Town housing project, 280–281

Sugar, Maurice, 39, 51, 151–152, 157, 211

Supreme Court: Black's appointment to, 145; conceptions of American ideals in decisions, 218–219; in context of national security, 269; enforcement of military orders by, 259; expulsion of Japanese Americans, 249; *Hirabayashi*, 237–245; and Japanese-American curfews, 235, 237–245, 242–243; and Japanese-American interments, 256–257, 263–265; and Jim Crow system, 191; judicial experience of justices, 205–206; *Korematsu*, 252–263; misrepresentation of reports, 240–242; Murphy as FDR's choice to, 200; Murphy as first gay justice, 206; Murphy as restless on, 225; Murphy's appointment process to, 203–204; Murphy's decision in *Thornhill*, 212–213; Murphy's inability to cite precedent, 213, 216; Murphy's nomination to stop prosecution of party bosses, 188; Murphy's relationships with justices, 215–216; Murphy's resistance to being on, 202; New Deal programs as unconstitutional, 117, 121n10, 200–201, 204; and NLRA, 159–160; *Ozawa v. United States*, 239; packing of, 117, 121n10, 169, 201; powers during wartime, 243; race relations damaged through rulings, 276; and sit-

down strikes, 159–160, 165n44; and state laws, 213–214, 218; use of Fourteenth Amendment by, 213–214; *Yasui*, 237, 245

Sutherland, George, 200–201

Sweet, Gladys, 62–63, 64, 71

Sweet, Henry, 67, 72

Sweet, Ossian, 62–67, 68–70, 70–71

Taft, William, 13, 124

Takahashi v. Fish & Game Comm'n, 266

taxes, property, in Detroit, 87–89

tax evasion, 188–189

Teahan, Marguerite. *See* Murphy, Marguerite

term limits, 131, 199n54

Thornhill v. Alabama, 212–214

Till, Emmett, 193

Tolan Report, 241–242, 244, 247n30

trespassing, striking workers as, 45, 46, 50, 151, 159, 160–161, 214

Truman, Harry S, 21–22, 189, 197n28, 199n54, 266, 271–274, 275, 283, 285

Trump v. Hawaii, 259, 269n45

Tully, Grace, 225

Twenty-Second Amendment, 199n54

two-party system, 145, 273–274

unemployment: in Detroit, 77, 79, 80–82, 88, 90; federal aid for, 96–98, 178; in New York, 108

Union Guardian Trust, 112

unions: and Black workers, 293–295; and Ford Motor Co., 161–162; Murphy as friend of, 53; right to join, 158–159

United Auto Workers (UAW): boycott of strike conference, 154; collective bargaining instead of sit-down strikes, 158–159; commission of "Hand of God" statue, 153, 286; Murphy's preference toward in sit-down strikes, 52, 286; settling of GM strikes, 157–158; and sit-down strikes, 152; transformation to major organization, 160; unionization of Ford workers, 161–162

United States Army: Japanese Americans in, 254–256; Murphy's desire to join, 222–225; Murphy's enlistment in, 16–17, 19, 132, 232

United States Attorney, Murphy as assistant, 27–33

United States Attorney General: Democratic Party bosses and Murphy as, 185–189; Murphy's confirmation as, 183–184; Murphy's nomination for, 181–182; Murphy's promotion of civil liberties as, 189–193

United States Bureau of the Budget, 209–210

United States Commission on Civil Rights, 295

United States Conference of Mayors, 96–101, 104

United States Congress, Murphy's run for, 16, 20, 33

United States Steel Corporation, 75–76

United States v. Bethlehem Steel Corp., 28–29

University of Detroit Law School, Murphy teaching at, 77

University of Michigan: fundraising football game, 81; Murphy attendance at, 10–12, 13–14; Murphy's use of graduates as clerks, 216; support of Murphy, 33, 140

University of Oklahoma School of Law, 276–279

unpopular groups, Murphy's defense of, 131, 290–295

upward mobility, 46–47

urban areas, 97–99

USS *Arizona*, 108

utilities, municipal ownership of, 82–83

Van Devanter, Willis, 200, 202

vice squads, 32, 211

Vinson, (Chief Justice) Fred, 265, 283

violence, strikes and, 151, 153–154, 159, 161

wages, living, 52, 53, 178

wages, minimum, 53, 116, 145, 204

Wagner Act. *See* National Labor Relations Act (NLRA, 1935)

Wallace, Henry, 111, 123n38, 273

Walters, David, 279

war: industrial might as key to winning, 224; labor as patriotic duty, 285–286; moral toll of, 23; restriction of civil liberties during, 266; Supreme Court during, 243

war powers, 237–238, 247n17, 252, 253, 259, 269n45

war profiteering, 28–29, 113

War Relocation Authority, 264, 269n55

Warren, (Chief Justice) Earl, 205, 266

Warren, Robert Penn, 142, 186–187

Wartime Civilian Control Administration, 233

The Washington Years (Fine), 210–211

welfare department, Detroit, 80–82, 88

Welles, Benjamin, 208–209

Welles, Sumner, 208–209

West Virginia State Board of Education v. Barnette, 290–291

White, Walter, 70, 71, 79

Wilson, Woodrow, 12, 13, 18, 21

women, Murphy's relationships
with: with Bumgardner,
128–129; with Cuddihy, 285;
with Everand, 36–37, 206;
with Harding, 67–68; with
McLean, 220–221; with mothers,
37–38; with Parker, 37, 185; with
Perkins, 185; with Young, 85–86,
301
women's groups, support of
Murphy from, 38, 48, 59n12
women's suffrage, 12, 48, 131
Woolworth strikes, 155
workdays, shorter, 11, 162, 204
worker rights, Murphy's desire
for Constitutional amendment,
204–205
workers: concern about lives of,
11–12; Murphy as champion
of, 50–53, 212; supported by
Democratic Party platform,
144–145; supporting Murphy,
47, 175–176; tribute to Murphy
after death, 286; and war effort,
285–286

workman's compensation laws,
58–59
Works Progress Administration
(WPA), 117–118, 142
World War I: Armistice, 20, 21;
conscription laws during, 17,
18–19; long-term effects of, 23;
Murphy's enlistment in, 16–17,
19; profiteering during, 28–29
World War II: Japanese capture
of Philippines, 125–126, 132;
Murphy's enlistment during,
132, 232; United States entry into,
231
writing style, Murphy's, 29. *See
also* concurrences, Murphy's;
dissents, Murphy's

Yasui, Minoru, 231, 236–237, 245,
249
Yasui v. United States, 237, 245, 261,
263
Young, Beulah, 82, 85–86, 91, 301

Zinn, Howard, 195